Inside Windows NT

George Eckel

Forrest Houlette

John Stoddard

Richard Wagner

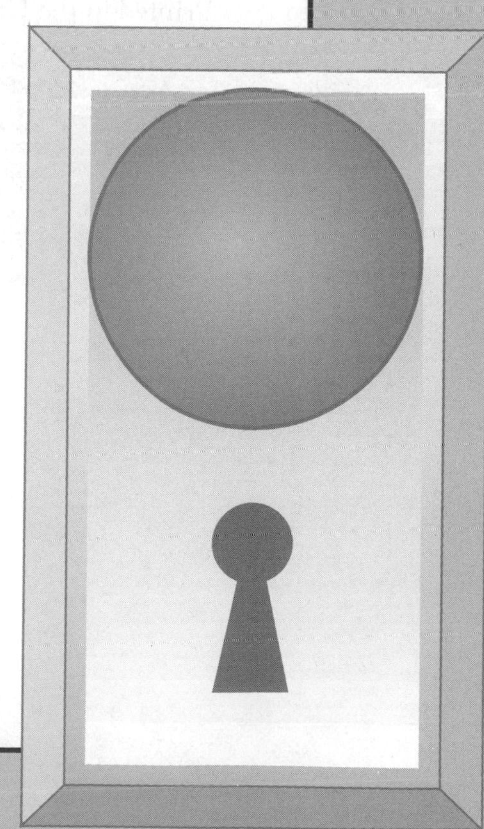

New Riders Publishing, Carmel, Indiana

Inside Windows NT

By George Eckel
Forrest Houlette
John Stoddard
Richard Wagner

Published by:
New Riders Publishing
11711 N. College Ave., Suite 140
Carmel, IN 46032 USA

Printed in the United States of America 1 2 3 4 5 6 7 8 9 0

Publisher
Lloyd J. Short

Associate Publisher
Tim Huddleston

Acquisitions Manager
Cheri Robinson

Acquisitions Editor
Rob Tidrow

Managing Editor
Matthew Morrill

Product Directors
Mike Groh
Richard Wagner

Senior Editor
Nancy Sixsmith

Editors
John Kane
Steve Weiss
Phil Worthington

Technical Editors
Eric Harper
Jon Reid

Acquisitions Coordinator
Stacey Beheler

Editorial Assistant
Karen Opal

Publishing Assistant
Melissa Lynch

Book Design and Production
Nick Anderson
Dennis Clay Hager
Carla Hall
Tim Montgomery
Roger Morgan
Juli Pavey
Angela Pozdol
Michelle M. Self
Dennis Sheehan
Susan VandeWalle
Barbara Webster
Mary Beth Wakefield
Alyssa Yesh

Proofreaders
Amanda Byus
Terri Edwards
Mitzi Foster Gianakos
Linda Koopman
Sean Medlock
Suzanne Tulley
Dennis Wesner
Donna Winter

Indexers
John Sleeva
Suzanne Snyder

Composed in *Stone Sans Serif Semi-bold* and *Palatino*

About the Authors

George Eckel has written manuals for a wide variety of audiences, including software engineers, end users, software-project managers, software instructors, and system administrators. Included are installation guides, programmer manuals, end-user manuals, tutorials, and computer language references.

Eckel has researched, designed, and created a graphical user interface design course for software engineers and project managers. He has revised courses on Windows and network management. Eckel is well-versed in a variety of computer languages, operating systems, software, and word processors.

Forrest Houlette began programming in 1977, when he took a FORTRAN class in graduate school. He entered the world of microcomputers when he began doing work on Apple II-series computers as a writing teacher. Houlette has since shifted to the IBM-compatible world, mastered Windows programming, and created a writing environment for the Windows operating system.

Houlette's work in artificial intelligence has won two academic awards: the Zenith Data Systems Award and the Ellen Nold Award, sponsored by Computers and Composition. He is the author of several books available from New Riders Publishing, including *Windows 3.1 on Command, Ultimate Windows 3.1,* and *7 Keys to Learning Windows NT.*

John Stoddard is a software developer for Micro Decisionware, Inc., of Boulder, Colorado. He has helped to develop two major distributed applications: MDI Database Gateway and Saros Mezzanine. Stoddard previously worked at Microsoft, and took part in the DOS, OS/2, and LAN Manager projects.

A dedicated mountain climber, Stoddard lives just outside of Rocky Mountain National Park with his wife (and climbing partner), Sally.

Richard Wagner is a specialist in Windows database management, applications integration, and applications development. He is the author of several books available from New Riders Publishing, including *Inside Microsoft Access*, *Integrating Windows Applications*, and *Ultimate Windows 3.1.*

Besides writing, Wagner performs consulting services and assists companies and nonprofit organizations in developing customized Windows solutions to their business problems. He also serves as a member of Team Borland, a group of volunteers who provide technical support on the Borland forums of CompuServe.

Wagner did his undergraduate work at Taylor University in Upland, Indiana, and finished graduate studies at The American University in Washington, D.C. He lives in the Indianapolis area with his wife and two sons.

Acknowledgments

New Riders Publishing expresses thanks to the following people:

Mike Groh and Rich Wagner, for developing the project.

Eric Harper and Jon Reid, for their thorough technical review of the manuscript.

Matthew Morrill and Tim Huddleston, for putting out many fires along the way.

Cheri Robinson and Rob Tidrow, for assembling and managing the excellent authoring team.

Nancy Sixsmith, for managing the project and steering it through the production process.

John Kane, Steve Weiss, and Phil Worthington, for their excellent editing (and smiles).

Stacey Beheler, Karen Opal, and Melissa Lynch, for assistance whenever needed (and for their Herculean labors on the appendix).

The Production Department of Prentice Hall Computer Publishing, for its expeditious handling and excellent layout of the book.

Trademark Acknowledgments

New Riders Publishing has made every attempt to supply trademark information about company names, products, and services mentioned in this book. Trademarks indicated below were derived from various sources. New Riders Publishing cannot attest to the accuracy of this information.

Apple and Macintosh are registered trademarks of Apple Computer, Incorporated.

CompuServe is a registered trademark of CompuServe Corp.

GEnie is a service mark of General Electric Company.

IBM and OS/2 are registered trademarks of International Business Machines Corporation.

Microsoft, Excel, Microsoft Works, MS-DOS, Windows, Windows for Workgroups, Windows NT, Word, and Word for Windows are registered trademarks of Microsoft Corporation.

Novell and NetWare are registered trademarks of Novell, Incorporated.

UNIX is a registered trademark of Unix System Laboratories, Inc.

WordPerfect and WordPerfect for Windows are registered trademarks of WordPerfect Corporation.

Trademarks of other products mentioned in this book are held by the companies producing them.

Warning and Disclaimer

This book is designed to provide information about the Windows NT computer program. Every effort has been made to make this book as complete and accurate as possible, but no warranty or fitness is implied.

The information is provided on an "as is" basis. The authors and New Riders Publishing shall have neither liability nor responsibility to any person or entity with respect to any loss or damages arising from the information contained in this book or from the use of the disks or programs that may accompany it.

Contents at a Glance

Contents

Introduction

It's finally here! After months of anticipation, thousands of reviews, hundreds of press releases, and endless speculation, Microsoft Windows NT is available for Intel-based computers.

When Microsoft released version 3.0 of the Windows operating system in 1990, PC users entered an entirely new world of computing. They were freed from the constraints imposed by the MS-DOS operating system and the underlying architecture of the original IBM PC (a computer originally conceived when no one thought that any computer user would need more than 64K of RAM).

In this new "Windows" world, PC users took advantage of all the memory their computers could access. Proportionally spaced fonts, a wide range of video and printer options, and updated screen graphics came to every desktop as a part of the operating system. Each user had a WYSIWYG (what-you-see-is-what-you-get) display, and could be reasonably assured that what was on the screen was what would print on paper. This was a brave and exciting new world.

With the introduction of version 3.1 of Windows, Microsoft updated these features and added a new font technology, more memory-management capabilities, integrated multimedia features, and advanced object-oriented data management. Shortly after Windows 3.1 appeared, Windows for Workgroups added peer-to-peer networking features to the Windows environment. The Windows world expanded greatly, becoming doubly exciting.

Since the introduction of Windows 3.1, Microsoft has been hard at work creating Windows NT, the "New Technology" that will lead Windows deeper into the nineties. This advanced operating system uses the Windows 3.1 interface, but adds significant capabilities underneath the interface.

For example, Windows NT introduces several security features: logon accounts; user privileges; and a new, optimized file system (known as the NT File System, or NTFS) that enables file-level security control and better data recovery.

In addition, this version of Windows is not intended just for the PC. Although the initial release of Windows NT runs on the Intel 80*x*86 hardware platform, versions also are available for RISC-based computers. Microsoft plans versions of Windows NT for an ever-expanding group of computer architectures. The enticing world of Windows becomes even larger!

Inside Windows NT prepares the experienced user of a command-line-based operating system—such as MS-DOS, OS/2, or UNIX—to productively enter the world of Windows NT. It helps you to make the shift from the command-line environment to the milieu of the graphical user interface quickly and easily.

Inside Windows NT teaches you the basics of the Windows graphical user interface, helping you to acquire the new working habits that such an interface demands of you. It also shortens your learning curve by introducing you to the advanced features that Windows NT offers a user of software written for Windows NT itself, Windows 3.1, MS-DOS, OS/2, and POSIX.

This book is also for the experienced Windows user making the transition to using Windows NT. It describes all the new features implemented by this new version of Windows, and it acquaints you with the differences you need to be aware of.

Most of all, *Inside Windows NT* is for real-world users of computer systems. It approaches the operating system from the point of view of the person who actually uses a computer to accomplish the tasks that make up the working day.

Many Windows NT books take a very high-level approach to explaining the complexities of the new Windows NT environment. *Inside Windows NT*, on the other hand, understands that you have a job to do and that you want to learn as much about Windows NT as you need to in order to get your work done.

With an operating system that offers the complexities that Windows NT offers, understanding the *Inside Windows NT* point of view is essential. Users easily can get lost by trying all the new features and capabilities, and easily can be intimidated by the sheer scale and power of Windows NT.

Inside Windows NT can serve as your guide to the part of the operating system that you use to accomplish work, placing all the new features and capabilities into your working perspective. *Inside Windows NT* not only shows you how to get up to speed quickly, but, more importantly, how to get your work done as efficiently as possible.

How This Book Is Different from Most Windows NT Books

Inside Windows NT is designed and written to accommodate the way you work. The authors and editors at New Riders Publishing know that you do not have a great deal of time to learn Windows NT, and that you are anxious to begin using

Windows NT to help you become more productive in your daily work.

This book, therefore, does not lead you through endless exercises in every Windows NT function, and it does not waste your time by repeating clearly obvious information. Each chapter introduces you to an important group of related Windows concepts and functions, and quickly shows you how these aspects of Windows NT relate to your computer system.

The chapters also lead you through the basic steps you must follow to incorporate each new concept and function into your own computing work. This book's tutorials are fast-paced; they help you to become productive in the shortest time possible after you understand the concepts and functions involved.

Later in this introduction, you will find descriptions of each of this book's sections and chapters. You also will find descriptions of other Windows and Windows NT books available from New Riders Publishing.

Who Should Read This Book?

Inside Windows NT is written for two types of readers: experienced users of a command-line operating system (DOS, OS/2, or UNIX), and experienced Windows users who want to upgrade to Windows NT.

Experienced MS-DOS, OS/2, and UNIX Users Who Are New to Windows NT

If you are a member of the first group of readers, you are comfortable using computer workstations (particularly with MS-DOS versions 3.3 and higher, OS/2 2.0 and higher, or

UNIX in one of its recent versions). This book assumes that you have experience using command-line applications and text-based user interfaces. This book also assumes that you are anxious to become productive with Windows NT. Specifically, this book makes the following assumptions about your skill level:

- You are an experienced workstation or PC user who knows the difference between a hard disk and a floppy disk.
- You have experience using a variety of operating system commands as you work at your workstation.
- You know that a file is the computer's basic information container and that files are hierarchically arranged in directories.
- You know that computers use different kinds of files: text, data (which may be text), executable, and so on. You are aware that file extensions typically are used to identify files of different types.
- You can type, and you know the location of the keys on the keyboard.
- You do not have the time to read long passages about computer and software basics; rather, you want to start working with Windows NT as soon as possible.

The Benefits of This Book for New Windows NT Users

If you are entirely new to the world of Windows NT and graphical computing, *Inside Windows NT* takes your needs seriously. Many Windows NT books are available, ranging from very basic books to advanced, specialized books for experienced users and software developers. Only a few Windows NT books, however, make a genuine effort to present information with comprehensive explanations, practical examples, and a minimum of hand-holding.

Because of the depth of the topic discussions and the breadth of the topic coverage in *Inside Windows NT*, you can use it both as a means of getting started and as a reference long after you have mastered the Windows NT interface.

Inside Windows NT contains all the information you need to make the transition from a command-line user interface to a graphical user interface. It highlights the things you need to understand as you make that transition in the early chapters. The later chapters, however, cover the advanced topics that help you become a real expert at using Windows NT.

This book's sections on DOS, OS/2, and POSIX applications are a valuable resource if you want to move existing command-line applications to the Windows NT environment. Windows NT provides a sound platform for most of your existing applications—even those that require exclusive use of the computer's resources (such as memory, serial ports, and graphics). In fact, your existing applications might run even better under Windows NT.

Experienced Windows Users Moving to Windows NT

If you fall into the second group of readers for whom *Inside Windows NT* is written, you are an experienced user of an earlier version of Windows. You have either upgraded to Windows NT, or you are considering making the upgrade. This book introduces you to the capabilities that are new to Windows NT. You can learn how to apply the latest enhancements to your own computing work without relearning the Windows concepts and functions you already know through your own experience. Specifically, this book makes the following assumptions about you:

- You are familiar with the mouse and mouse actions.
- You know how to use dialog boxes and list boxes.

- You understand the concept of windowed applications and you know how to use the maximize and minimize buttons.
- You are familiar with the Windows desktop, including Program Manager, program groups, and program icons.
- You know how to start and run applications under Windows 3.0 or 3.1.

The Benefits of This Book for Experienced Windows Users

In contrast to other books on Windows NT, *Inside Windows NT* does not overstate the obvious. For example, this book does not show you how to install applications. It emphasizes practical examples that demonstrate the subject material without belaboring the point. You should work through as many examples as you like, and feel free to experiment. As you already know, Windows keeps you from damaging anything in the process.

If you already are an experienced Windows user, you will want to skim many of the chapters, looking for the discussions of the differences between Windows NT and other versions of Windows. Checking chapter headings for unfamiliar information and figures for unfamiliar screens show you where the new material is. When you note unfamiliar information, slow down and read it carefully.

Although Windows NT is substantially like other versions of Windows, there are differences and new capabilities. You will want to focus your reading on what is new and different in Windows NT. Of course, you can keep this book as a handy reference to Windows NT features as you start work with Windows NT.

How This Book Is Organized

Inside Windows NT is organized into five logical parts. Each part dissects some aspect of Windows NT, and carefully documents what you need to know to get your work done.

Each part contains several chapters that discuss certain topics in sufficient depth to provide a solid foundation for your use of Windows NT. Skip over any chapters or parts of chapters that are obvious to you or irrelevant to your requirements.

Part One: Migrating to Windows NT: Concepts and Installation

This section provides the basis for users moving to Windows NT from other operating systems such as DOS or OS/2. These four chapters discuss everything from the overall design of Windows NT to installation and setup.

Chapter 1, "Exploring the Road to Windows NT," gives a brief history of Windows NT and discusses the long road that led to the initial release of Windows NT.

Chapter 2, "Revealing the Windows NT Operating System," explains the basic differences between Windows NT and other operating systems.

Chapter 3, "Migrating from Windows 3.1," provides a guide for the experienced Windows 3.1 or 3.0 user. Although Windows NT is superficially very similar to previous versions of Windows, important differences exist.

Chapter 4, "Installing Windows NT," is a guide to the job of installing Windows NT on the end-user workstation. The many installation options are described in detail to aid you as you perform this important task.

Part Two: Managing the Windows NT Desktop

This section, consisting of five chapters, takes a practical approach to learning everything you need to become productive with NT.

Chapter 5, "Learning the Windows NT Interface," is most useful to new Windows users. Even experienced Windows users, however, will be introduced to the many differences between Windows NT and earlier versions of Windows.

Chapter 6, "Mastering the Windows NT Desktop," provides insight into using the basic Windows utilities, navigating the Program Manager, and other basic Windows skills.

Chapter 7, "Configuring and Customizing the Windows NT Desktop," describes the steps necessary to customize Windows NT to suit your particular work style.

Chapter 8, "Using Windows NT Applets," describes the new Windows NT mini-applications that are not included in earlier versions of Windows.

Chapter 9, "Printing and Managing Fonts," tells you how to use the Windows NT Print Manager and TrueType fonts under Windows NT.

Part Three: Creating Solutions through Integration

This section explores one of the most exciting aspects of Windows NT. It offers unexcelled capabilities to run "foreign" applications from OS/2, DOS, and UNIX systems. No other operating systems offers such flexibility right out of the box. You will enjoy reading Microsoft's solution to the problem of porting your existing applications to Windows NT.

Chapter 10, "Running DOS, OS/2, and POSIX Applications," provides the background necessary to move your applications from your old operating system to Windows NT.

Chapter 11, "Exchanging Data between Windows Applications," explains the exciting capability to exchange data and information between applications.

Chapter 12, "Using Object Linking and Embedding," explains the Windows NT implementation of OLE. Experienced Windows users will recognize the value of OLE and be interested in seeing how to exploit this capability in Windows NT.

Part Four: Managing the Windows NT Network

This section explains the way that Windows NT implements peer-to-peer networking.

Chapter 13, "Exploring Networking with Windows NT," describes the Windows NT approach to networking.

Chapter 14, "Understanding the System Registry," explains how the NT System Registry works for system administrators.

Chapter 15, "Exploring the Windows NT Advanced Server," briefly examines Windows NT's fit as an enterprise computing platform. The advanced security and fault-tolerant features of Windows NT are important parts of Microsoft's strategy for moving Windows NT into more and more corporate environments.

Part Five: Windows NT Product Directory

This appendix provides a sampling of the wide variety of applications available for Windows NT. It is not intended to be a comprehensive list of all Windows NT; instead, it gives you an idea of the many types of applications that have been written for Windows NT.

Conventions Used in This Book

Throughout this book, certain conventions are used to help you distinguish the various elements of Windows, MS-DOS, OS/2, POSIX, their system files, and sample data. Before you look ahead, you should spend a moment examining these conventions:

- Shortcut keys normally are found in the text where appropriate. In most applications, for example, Shift+Ins is the shortcut key for the **P**aste command.
- Key combinations appear in the following format:

  Key1+Key2: When you see a plus sign (+) between key names, you should hold down the first key while pressing the second key. Then release both keys.
- On-screen, Windows NT underlines the letters of some menu names, file names, and options names. For example, the File menu is displayed on-screen as File. The underlined letter is the letter you can type to choose that command or option. In this book, however, such letters are displayed in bold, underlined type for emphasis: **F**ile.
- Information you type is in **boldface**. This applies to individual letters and numbers, as well as to text strings. This convention, however, does not apply to special keys, such as Enter, Esc, or Ctrl.
- New terms appear in *italics*.
- Text that is displayed on-screen but which is not part of Windows NT or a Windows application—such as command prompts and messages—appears in a `special typeface`.

Special Text Used in This Book

Throughout this book, you find examples of special text. These passages have been given special treatment so that you can instantly recognize their significance and easily find them for future reference.

Notes, Tips, and Warnings

Inside Windows NT features many special sidebars, which are set apart from the normal text by icons. This book includes three distinct types of sidebars: "Notes," "Tips," and "Warnings."

A Note *includes extra information that you should find useful, but which complements the discussion at hand instead of being a direct part of it. A note might describe special situations that can arise when you use Windows NT under certain circumstances and tell you what steps to take when such situations arise. Notes also tell you how to avoid problems with your software and hardware.*

A Tip *provides you with quick instructions for getting the most from your Windows NT system as you follow the steps outlined in the general discussion. A tip might show you how to speed up a procedure, how to perform one of many time-saving and system-enhancing techniques, or how to take advantage of an advanced feature of Windows NT.*

A Warning *tells you when a procedure may be dangerous—that is, when you run the risk of losing data, locking your system, or even damaging your hardware. Warnings generally tell you how to avoid such losses, or describe the steps you can take to remedy them.*

Another Windows NT Title from New Riders Publishing

New Riders Publishing offers another book on Windows NT, *7 Keys to Learning Windows NT*, for those who need a task-oriented command reference. This book covers Windows NT from the same perspective as *Inside Windows NT*, but it does not serve as a tutorial. Instead, each task that you need to perform is broken out as a separate section, with clear directions about when to use the task and which steps to follow.

7 Keys to Learning Windows NT is an excellent companion book for *Inside Windows NT*, especially for intermediate and advanced users who need a quick reference to tasks and procedures within Windows NT.

Further Reading

Because Windows NT uses the Windows 3.1 interface, several other New Riders titles may help you, as a user of Windows NT, as you interact with other users who use other versions of Windows.

Maximizing Windows 3.1, now entering a special edition, is a guide to Windows 3.1 for advanced users.

Windows 3.1 on Command provides a task-oriented command reference that is similar to *7 Keys to Learning Windows NT*. If you must switch among versions of Windows frequently, you will probably want to own both *Windows 3.1 on Command* and *7 Keys to Learning Windows NT*.

Ultimate Windows 3.1 is a comprehensive reference to the Windows 3.1 operating system, including systems integration and troubleshooting.

Inside Windows for Workgroups introduces users to Windows for Workgroups and peer-to-peer networking concepts.

Windows for Non-Nerds acquaints new users of computer systems to Windows and Windows concepts, avoiding all the jargon typically associated with books for and by "technonerds" and "technogeeks."

New Riders Publishing

The staff of New Riders Publishing is committed to bringing you the very best in computer reference material. Each New Riders book is the result of months of work by authors and staff, who research and refine the information contained within its covers.

As part of this commitment to you, the NRP reader, New Riders invites your input. Please let us know if you enjoy this book, if you have trouble with the information and examples presented, or if you have a suggestion for the next edition.

Please note, however, that the New Riders staff cannot serve as a technical resource for Windows NT or Windows application-related questions, including hardware- or software-related problems. Refer to the documentation that accompanies your Windows NT, Windows, or Windows application package for help with specific problems.

If you have a question or comment about any New Riders book, please write to NRP at the following address. We will respond to as many readers as we can. Your name, address, and phone number will never become part of a mailing list or be used for any other purpose than to help us continue to bring you the best books possible.

New Riders Publishing
Prentice Hall Computer Publishing
Attn: Managing Editor
11711 N. College Avenue
Carmel, IN 46032

If you prefer, you can FAX New Riders Publishing at the following number:

(317) 571-3484

or call the New Riders Reader Support Line at

(317) 571-3248

Thank you for selecting *Inside Windows NT*!

Migrating to Windows NT: Concepts and Installation

Exploring the Road to Windows NT

Revealing the Windows NT Operating System

Migrating from Windows 3.1

Installing Windows NT

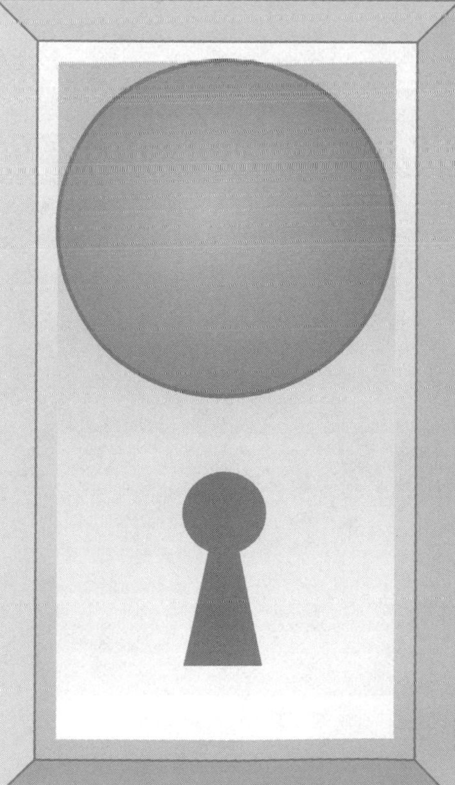

PART 1

Exploring the Road to Windows NT

Windows NT's conceptual roots stretch back to the beginnings of UNIX in 1969. Windows NT developers have tried to incorporate into Windows NT all the major innovations in user interfaces and operating systems that have transpired since then. This chapter provides you with an understanding of the ways in which Windows NT has been shaped, including the following:

- Understanding OS/2's lack of success
- Developing Windows NT
- Reviewing the evolution of Windows NT

Understanding OS/2's Lack of Success

In the mid-1980s, Microsoft and IBM developed an operating system so superior to DOS that it was to become the dominant operating system of the 1980s and 1990s. They called it *Operating System 2*, or *OS/2*.

Incorporated into OS/2 were many of the features that make UNIX so powerful, including multitasking, multiprocessing, multithreading, and 32-bit addressing. An operating system with such prowess easily should have overshadowed the offerings of DOS and Windows. At least, that's what Microsoft and IBM thought.

History had a different ending to the story, however. OS/2 sales were meager, at best. The third version of Windows took off like fireworks and banished OS/2 to obscurity. Why?

The developers of OS/2 made a fundamental miscalculation when they created their product. The microprocessor at the leading edge of technology for the 1980s desktop was the 80286—not a speed demon by today's standards. The desktop operating system had to be large—much larger than DOS or Windows—to realize the power of UNIX. So, in their effort to make a large operating system run as fast as possible on a slow platform, Microsoft and IBM developers chose to write OS/2 in assembly language.

Assembly language—unlike C, Pascal, and other higher-level languages—manipulates data in the CPU and memory.

The problem with assembly language, however, is that it is not portable; that is, it must be written for specific processors—the 80286, in this case. As technological innovations sped by and microprocessors came and went, the 80286 was left behind (and with it, OS/2). Developers never took to OS/2.

With a new version of software necessary for each new microprocessor, OS/2 applications required a lot of work to maintain. For that reason, OS/2 never enjoyed the number of applications that were written for DOS or Windows.

Although Microsoft enjoyed moderate success with Windows 2.0, they knew that with more powerful processors, more powerful applications, and higher user expectations on the horizon, Windows needed to be replaced. People were turning to UNIX to fulfill their needs for a complex networking, multitasking, multiprocessing, and secure operating system.

Microsoft developers knew they had to create an operating system for the future that offered the power of UNIX. The sales figures told them that OS/2 would not be that system. So in 1988, Microsoft hired David Cutler to create a new operating system, the operating system for the nineties.

Developing Windows NT with David Cutler

David Cutler was project director at DEC in the 1980s for a variety of products, including the very successful VMS operating system. In 1985, DEC assigned him the task of developing a super operating system, called Prism, that was to supersede VMS and Ultrix, DEC's flavor of UNIX. After three years of work, however, DEC decided to cancel Prism because it was incompatible with the company's proprietary products.

DEC's cancellation of Prism hit Cutler like a bomb. He immediately gave his 180-person staff a one-month furlough. During that month he weighed his options. Although entrepreneurs offered him money to begin his own company, he refused their offers because he didn't aspire to running a company. He wanted, instead, to create a great operating system.

OS/2 was released in 1987, and by 1988 it was clear to Microsoft that it was floundering. Bill Gates, cofounder of Microsoft, learned of Cutler's situation at DEC and began to court him for Microsoft.

Microsoft released Windows 2.0 in 1988. It was better than the first version—for example, it enabled windows to overlap rather than tile—but it in no way approximated the sophistication of the Macintosh graphical user interface (GUI) to offset the weakness of Windows 2.0.

Microsoft aggressively enlisted the services of developers to create applications for Windows. It also leaked word about what would be included in version 3.0. The rumors about version 3.0 excited developers; it sounded as if Windows would finally catch up to the Macintosh interface.

Attracted by the marketing might of Microsoft and the promise of Windows 3.0, Cutler left DEC for Microsoft. Although Cutler began work on Windows NT in 1988, Windows NT reflects his three years of work on Prism. Also, many of DEC's contract software engineers and programmers followed Cutler to Microsoft. So not only did Microsoft get three years of research paid for by DEC, Microsoft also got an entire core of programmers who, during those three years, had grown expert at designing operating systems.

Determining Primary Marketing Requirements

From the fall of 1988 until early in 1989, David Cutler and his core group of engineers defined the primary marketing requirements for Windows NT. These requirements were as follows:

- **Portability.** Everyone had learned from OS/2's downfall about the danger of making an operating system that wasn't portable across a variety of processors. Windows NT had to move easily between many processor architectures.

- **Multiprocessing.** Computers that use more than one processor were becoming more common in the marketplace. Because few operating systems at the time took advantage of multiple processors, developers decided that Windows NT had to offer multiprocessing.

  Windows NT wasn't just for high-end computers, however. Not only did Windows NT have to take advantage of multiprocessing, the same applications had to work on single-processor computers.

- **Networking.** The number of desktop computers skyrocketed in the eighties. Gone forever was the dominance of the single mainframe computer that served an entire company. Because sharing files between isolated desktop computers was a problem, companies began using networks to tie together computers so that users could share information and system resources.

  With networking, users also could take advantage of distributed computing. Instead of making networking a third-party, add-on facility, Windows NT developers decided to make it part of the operating system.

- **POSIX compatibility.** *POSIX* is an acronym for *Portable Operating System Interface based on UNIX*. The Institute of Electrical and Electronics Engineers (IEEE) created the POSIX standard (1003.1) in 1988 to encourage vendors to standardize the UNIX-type interface so that applications could be portable across systems.

  POSIX is one of the U.S. government's procurement requirements. Because the government represents the single largest potential buyer for Windows NT, developers decided to provide a POSIX environment.

- **Security.** If Microsoft considered the government an important potential buyer of Windows NT, a government-approved security system had to be part of Windows NT. The first release of Windows NT qualifies for a class C2 security rating.

The government has seven classes of security; class A is the highest. The C2 rating allows for ownership of objects, restricted read/write/execution of those objects, and restricted system access. Plans for later versions of Windows NT include satisfying class B2 security requirements.

Class B2 security requires Windows NT to recognize user and process security levels (such as Secret and Top Secret), and to support compartments *(groups of users that are entirely isolated from other users).*

Originally, the new technology (Windows NT) operating system was to look and work like OS/2. That was understandable, considering the investment Microsoft had already made in OS/2. By the late 1980s, however, it was not hard to figure out that Windows NT should look more like Windows than OS/2.

Instead of making one Windows operating system obsolete in favor of another, Microsoft decided to develop a family of Windows operating systems, each with its unique user profile. Windows 3.*x* is for individual users, Windows for Workgroups is for small businesses, and Windows NT is for power users and large organizations (see fig. 1.1).

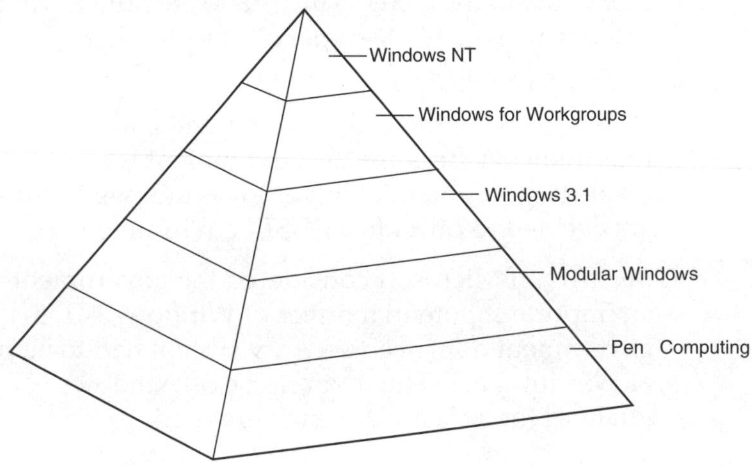

Figure 1.1: *The Windows family.*

Other new members of the Windows family include Windows for Pen Computing, which is used for pen-input devices; and Modular Windows, which is designed for consumer hardware interfaces. All members of the Windows family have the same look; all provide different features.

Understanding Software Design Goals

With a product as complex as Windows NT, planning was an absolute necessity before beginning to code. Developers resolved many design conflicts and answered many questions by defining software design goals. The goals were as follows:

- **Flexibility.** Windows NT had to be easily modifiable to accommodate changing hardware and software requirements.
- **Portability.** Windows NT had to satisfy the marketing goal of being applicable to a wide variety of system architectures.
- **Stability.** In a networking environment, it is crucial that applications not crash the operating system. Windows NT had to isolate the kernel from user applications and, at the same time, monitor any attempts, inadvertent or otherwise, to compromise the security and normal functioning of the system.
- **Compatibility.** Microsoft's trump card in catapulting Windows NT past UNIX and OS/2 in sales was the number of Windows applications already sold. By enabling Windows 3.*x* applications to run on Windows NT, Windows NT automatically would be supported by programs already in the marketplace and in the office. Thus, users and businesses did not have to buy all new software, or learn new systems and applications.

Although the 16-bit Windows applications do not run as fast as Win32 applications, companies can get most of the power of Windows NT and be up and running with it for only the cost of the operating system.

- **Speed.** Given all the other goals, Windows NT had to run as quickly as possible on all platforms.

The rest of this section examines the way developers sought to accomplish these goals.

Flexibility

With the continuous introduction of new hardware devices, such as scanners and CD-ROM drives, Windows NT developers wanted to make the job of modifying Windows NT to accommodate these changes as easy as possible. Their solution to the problem was to develop a unique operating system design that put some of the operating system in user mode.

Windows NT consists of two basic parts, the privileged Executive and the nonprivileged protected subsystems. The concept of privilege derives from processors themselves, which have two modes of operation: *privileged*, called kernel mode, and *nonprivileged*, called user mode.

In an operating system, the kernel *is the core portion that performs the most essential tasks.*

In *user mode*, certain commands and memory addresses are inaccessible; in *kernel mode*, all machine commands and memory addresses are accessible (see fig. 1.2).

Windows NT's *Executive*, which runs in kernel mode, provides elemental services. It relies on the protected subsystems—running in user mode—to provide additional capabilities, including operating system APIs.

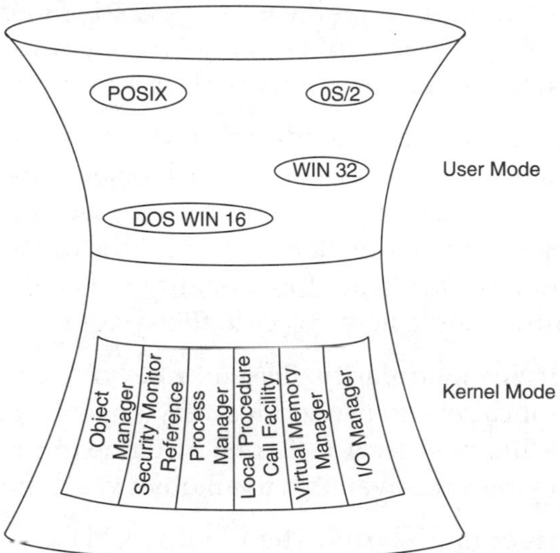

Figure 1.2: *User and kernel mode modularity.*

By dividing the operating system in this way, Microsoft can leave Windows NT's Executive alone and simply add or replace an entire protected subsystem as a unit. This modular approach to revising the software clearly limits the lines of code that need revision, and isolates the changes from the rest of the system so that the rest of the system can remain up and running and free of bugs.

An application programming interface (API) *is a library of routines and services, each built from low-level operating system commands, which accomplish common tasks.*

In addition to splitting up Windows NT into both kernel and user modes, Windows NT developers included the following additional features to make it flexible:

- **Executive modularity.** Developers used a modular approach when designing the Executive (see fig. 1.2). Each of these modules, such as the virtual memory manager and the object manager, interact with one another only through kernel interfaces.

This design makes it easy to upgrade or add new functionality. Instead of working on the entire kernel, a programmer can simply replace a module.

- **System resource modularity.** Windows NT treats all system resources as objects. All objects are manipulated by the same set of object services. Adding or subtracting objects, therefore, does not affect the other objects. To add new hardware functionality to Windows NT, you simply add a new object to the system.
- **Service modularity.** *Remote procedure calls (RPCs)* enable applications to use services anywhere in the network. By adding new services to one machine in the network, they become available to all other machines.
- **Driver modularity.** The Windows NT I/O consists, in part, of a number of drivers. To add new file systems, hardware devices, and networks, you simply add to the I/O new file system drivers, device drivers, or transport drivers, respectively.

Portability

Although an operating system can be rewritten for any processor or configuration, a system is considered *portable* only if it is easy to do so. Developers used the following guidelines to make Windows NT portable:

- **Use high-level languages.** To make a system portable across many processors, you must write the code in a language that all the processors understand. High-level languages, such as C, are standardized without regard to the processors on which they run.

  Microsoft chose to write Windows NT in C. (A small portion, including the graphical user interface and portions of the networking interface, is written in C++.) Only those very few operations that needed maximum speed, such as precision-integer arithmetic, were written in assembly language. Developers isolated the assembly language code in well-defined modules so they could easily change them.

- **Minimize hardware-dependent code.** Code that directly manipulates hardware, such as registers, is inevitably dependent on the machinery. By eliminating or minimizing as much of this code as possible, you can make the system more portable.
- **Isolate hardware-dependent code.** Some of the code in an operating system must be hardware-dependent. By placing this code in well-defined modules, revising the code for different processors is easy, and bugs do not spread throughout the system.

Not only did Windows NT developers isolate hardware-dependent code, they also isolated platform-dependent code in a dynamic link library called the hardware abstraction layer (HAL). *Vendors sometimes build different platforms around the same processor, such as the MIPS R4000. The low-level code in HAL makes the differences between platforms invisible to the higher-level operating system code.*

Stability

Windows NT developers considered two facets of stability. First, Windows NT had to anticipate, prevent (if possible), and respond effectively to errors, both in software and hardware. Second, the operating system had to be impervious to user applications that, intentionally or not, might damage or crash the system. Microsoft developers made Windows NT stable in the following ways:

- **Error handling.** Windows NT uses a method known as *structured-exception handling* for detecting and dealing with errors. When the operating system or the hardware detects errors, the kernel switches control to the exception handler, which responds to the error and prevents user programs from running amok or from damaging the operating system.

- **Windows NTFS.** Developers created a new file system, called *new technology file system (NTFS)*, which enables Windows NT to recover from virtually any kind of disk crash. It works by storing information in more than one place.
- **Security.** The security system, discussed in Chapter 2, helps eliminate or limit damage caused by users.
- **Isolated APIs.** By making each API a separated protected subsystem, a crash in one cannot affect the others.
- **Virtual memory manager.** The Executive's virtual memory manager swaps programs between disk and RAM. It assures that one application's memory addresses don't overlap another's.

Compatibility

Compatibility refers to an operating system's capability to run applications that were designed for earlier versions of the operating system (or for other operating systems). Compatibility is one of Windows NT's most unique features and greatest strengths.

When you purchase an operating system, you usually must use only those applications written for it. With Windows NT, however, you can run most DOS, Windows, character-based POSIX, and OS/2 applications (as well as Windows NT applications).

There are two levels of compatibility: binary and source-level. The difference between the two is determined by whether or not an application must be recompiled before it runs on a different operating system.

If the machine language in the executable file of the application works on the different operating system, the operating system is considered *binary compatible* because the machine code, which is binary, is the same in different operating systems. If the application must be recompiled before it can work on the new operating system, the system is considered *source-level compatible,* because it is the source code, not the executable code, that is the same.

Because recompiling inevitably introduces bugs in the application, binary compatibility is highly preferable to source-level compatibility.

The processor on which an operating system runs determines whether or not an operating system is binary compatible. Different processors generally use different machine-language command sets. Processors within a family, such as Intel's *x*86 processors, often can achieve binary compatibility with applications. Processors from different makers can achieve binary compatibility only if the makers provide an emulation program that translates the machine language code of the executable application from one processor to another. Without that translation software, developers must recompile, relink, and debug the application for the new processor.

On Intel processors, Windows NT provides binary compatibility with existing Microsoft applications, including MS-DOS, 16-bit Windows, OS/2, and LAN Manager. On MIPS RISC processors, Windows NT provides binary compatibility with MS-DOS, 16-bit Windows, and LAN Manager (with emulation). Windows NT provides source-level compatibility for POSIX applications.

Windows NT also is compatible with a number of different file systems, including FAT (MS-DOS), HPFS (OS/2), CDFS (CD-ROM), and Windows NTFS (Windows NT).

Speed

The speed of an application is both hardware- and software-dependent. The faster a microprocessor is, the faster the application executes. The better the operating system is, the more it can take advantage of the faster microprocessor. For example, the 80486 is a 32-bit chip. Sixteen-bit applications, however, generally move information only 16 bits at a time, even on 32-bit processors. The 32-bit applications move twice that amount in the same time. Thus, Win32 applications run roughly twice as fast as 16-bit Windows applications.

The developers of Windows NT maximized its execution speed in the following ways:

- **Performance testing.** Developers carefully optimized each part of the system that influenced the execution speed of Windows NT, including system calls and page faults.
- **Local procedure call.** The protected subsystems that provide the operating system APIs communicate frequently with one another and with their client applications. To make these communications move as quickly as possible, Microsoft incorporated a *local procedure call* (a fast message-passing facility) in the operating system.
- **System services.** When Microsoft engineers created the protected subsystems that provide the operating system APIs, they determined which system service calls were used most often, and then maximized their execution speed.
- **Networking.** Networking is a central feature of Windows NT. To make Windows NT run quickly, components of the networking software were included in Windows NT's Executive.

Reviewing the Evolution of Windows NT

It is difficult to say exactly where Windows NT began. Here are some of the milestones in the generation of the ideas that went into Windows NT:

- **1969.** Ken Thompson at Bell Labs writes UNIX, which is a time-sharing, multitasking operating system that enables his DEC PDP-7 to support several users at once. UNIX sets the standards by which people judge all other high-end operating systems for the next 25 years. Microsoft incorporates UNIX's multitasking, multiprocessing, networking, platform-independent, and security features into Windows NT.
- **1973.** Xerox's Palo Alto Research Center (PARC) designs a radically different kind of operating system for a computer: the Alto (and its successor, the Bravo). Neither are commercially produced.

Instead of using an arcane command-language interface, like those of UNIX and DOS, PARC uses high-resolution monitors to show a desktop with pictures of file folders, mail, and in-and-out baskets. They name these graphical elements icons, *and use a mouse to manipulate them. They create a laser printer called Dover, which enables them to print* WYSIWYG (what-you-see-is-what-you-get) *documents.*

The graphical user interface of Windows NT derives directly from the applications started at PARC.

During the same time period at PARC, researchers create a way to share system resources, such as laser printers, among users. They use coaxial cable to support data throughput of 10 megabits per second, which is 10,000 times faster than current phone lines can support

(1200 bits per second). They call the linkage between computers a *local area network*, and name their version *Ethernet*.

Today, Microsoft considers networking so integral to the design of Windows NT that developers decide to put part of the network programming into Windows NT's Executive.

- **1975.** Bill Gates and Paul Allen, undergraduates at Harvard, enter a contest to write a BASIC programming language for the first personal computer, the Altair. It uses an 8088 chip with 4K of RAM. Allen writes an emulator that simulates the 8088 chip on Harvard's PDP-10 mainframe. Gates writes the BASIC language for the Altair. Together they win the contest.

Today, Microsoft uses an emulator, called the virtual DOS machine (VDM), *to enable DOS and 16-bit Windows applications to run in Windows NT.*

- **1979.** Steve Jobs sees the Alto computer and decides that Apple's next computer, the Lisa, will use a graphical user interface. Only a few months later, Bill Gates visits PARC, and makes a commitment to a graphical user interface that he calls Windows.
- **1983.** Microsoft and IBM start work on an operating system to replace DOS. They incorporate into the new operating system many ideas borrowed from UNIX, such as multitasking, multiprocessing, multithreading, and 32-bit addressing. Bill Gates expects this to be the next super operating system. Microsoft calls it OS/2.
- **1985.** David Cutler begins work on a super operating system for DEC called Prism. After three years of work, DEC cancels Prism.

- **1987.** Microsoft releases OS/2. It flops. Gates realizes that Microsoft must create a new super operating system, called Windows NT, which will capitalize on the research done for OS/2.
- **1988.** Bill Gates succeeds in bringing Cutler and a core group of engineers to Microsoft. Cutler uses his three years of research at DEC to devise Windows NT.

  Microsoft releases Windows 2.0. Sales go well, and Microsoft leaks rumors about version 3.0. IBM and Gates announce a renewed effort to support OS/2.

  Microsoft changes direction, abandons OS/2, and pours its energy into developing Windows 3.1 and Windows NT. Microsoft managers decide that Windows NT should look like Windows, not OS/2.
- **1990.** Microsoft spends $18 million to market Windows 3.0. Sales exceed wildest expectations. Finally, Windows approaches the graphical user interface started by PARC and successfully implemented on the Macintosh.

The stage is set for the introduction of Windows NT. Although it was designed for high-end systems, the market penetration of Windows 3.*x* leads the average user to wonder if Windows NT is also for him.

Will Windows NT hit the market like the skyrocket Windows was or like the dud that OS/2 was? Will Windows NT remain a system for high-end users only, or will the average user pine for the added performance that 32-bit applications provide? Will Windows NT be the super operating system of the nineties or a high-tech novelty? We all will watch together.

Summary

Like many great creations, Windows NT stands on the shoulders of its predecessors. Microsoft engineers, benefiting from 25 years of operating-system evolution, bundled the best parts of UNIX, Prism, OS/2, Windows, and object-oriented programming into one single package: Windows NT.

The power of Windows NT rivals that of UNIX, and its ease of use matches that of Windows. The well-defined, interchangeable parts of the protected subsystems in user mode (and of the Executive kernel mode) make Windows NT easy to upgrade.

Revealing the Windows NT Operating System

Windows NT has the potential of being the best of two worlds: a popular graphical environment for end users and a full-fledged 32-bit operating system every bit as powerful as UNIX is. Although the heart of this book is devoted to the end-user aspects of Windows NT, this chapter looks under the hood to examine the core architecture of the Windows NT operating system.

This chapter is technical in nature, but it offers something for everyone. Operating system "neophytes" should not be scared away. Most of the discussion is intended as an introduction to such concepts as 32-bit processing, preemptive multitasking, and peer-to-peer networking. In reading this, you can get a better grasp of what Windows NT is really all about.

For those well-versed in operating systems, you will find the discussion substantive in its examination of Windows NT's underlying architecture. Moreover, if you have experience with OS/2 or UNIX, the last part of this chapter will be particularly interesting to you as it compares Windows NT with these two operating systems.

The major subjects this chapter focuses on include the following:

- Windows NT's 32-bit architecture
- Multitasking
- Multithreading
- Multiprocessing
- Windows NT subsystems
- Windows NT networking
- System security
- The way Windows NT works with your existing applications
- Windows NT versus other 32-bit operating Systems

Understanding Windows NT's 32-Bit Architecture

If you read about Windows NT in any computer magazine, the term *32-bit operating system* usually surfaces somewhere. What exactly is a 32-bit operating system? To answer that question, this section looks at Windows NT's 32-bit addressing and 32-bit processing capabilities.

32-Bit Addressing

Before looking at Windows NT's 32-bit addressing, take a look back at the world of DOS and Windows 3.1. DOS was developed in the early 1980s for 8088 and 8086 chips. These 16-bit chips had a limited number of memory addresses that they could access.

A memory address *is like your home address—it defines a specific location. In computer memory, this address defines the location of a byte of information.*

When computers were sold with 128K, 256K, and 512K of random-access memory (RAM), an address space of 1M seemed like an ocean of memory. To accommodate the memory requirements of hardware such as video boards and network cards, developers agreed to segment the 1M of memory in the following way: the first 640K were reserved for the operating system and its applications, and the remaining 360K were divided into 64K sections, called *pages*, each having a different purpose. A system with this address structure is known as a *segment-addressing system*.

An address space of 640K seemed more than ample for applications. That was true until personal computers found their way into business applications, such as spreadsheets and database management systems. Because only a limited amount of data can fit into 640K of memory, spreadsheets and databases were limited in size. This created a problem for all but the smallest of companies. In a short time, 640K changed from an ocean of memory to a barrier with which programmers and users alike have had to deal.

The 80386 chip was the first to implement a *linear* (non-segmented) 32-bit address space. In theory, applications did not have to be crammed into the first 640K of RAM. The reality, however, was that the 32-bit address space was incompatible with applications written for the older processors. Therefore, to remain compatible with these applications, the 386 chip ran in real mode, which enabled the 386 to function like a fast 8086.

Developers also enabled the 386 chip to run in another mode, called *protected mode*, in which memory was accessed in a linear address space. Protected mode also prevented one application's data from occupying the address space of another application's data. Although this was an advance, the DOS 640K barrier still proved a big impediment to the development of more sophisticated applications.

Although other modes have also been created, DOS and Windows 3.1 programmers still labor to circumvent the 640K barrier.

Windows 3.1 is an environment, not an operating system. It rides on top of DOS. Many functions that Windows performs take place through DOS.

Windows NT, like other 32-bit operating systems (such as OS/2 and UNIX), leaves these artificially imposed barriers far behind. Because it is a true linear-addressing system, it takes better advantage of 386, 486, and Pentium processing power.

Windows NT benefits in many ways from abandoning the segmented addressing system. First, the amount of available space for Windows NT applications is huge—two gigabytes (G)—and another 2G are reserved for the Windows NT operating system. There are not many applications that require even a significant fraction of that memory space. Second, Windows NT programmers do not have to battle with the 640K barrier. Making life easier for programmers means quicker software-development time.

Although Windows NT supports a linear address space of 4G, chances are your computer does not have 4G of RAM. So what is the advantage of having an address space greater than the amount of RAM in your computer?

> *Your computer can work only with data in RAM. When you initiate an action that requires more RAM than your computer has (such as starting a second application), Windows NT's virtual memory manager moves data out of real (RAM) memory into* virtual memory *(memory on the hard drive). Moving data between the hard drive and RAM is called* swapping.
>
> *The less RAM your computer has, the more swapping to disk your computer must perform, and the slower the performance of the application. That is because executing data already in RAM is dramatically faster than accessing data from a disk. (Virtual memory is discussed later in this chapter.)*

Windows NT supports a 4G virtual address space. During setup, Windows NT suggests that you create a permanent area on your hard disk for a swap file that is at least the size of your RAM. So, if you have 8M of RAM, Windows wants at least an 8M swap file. (In practice, Windows NT prefers more space than that.)

The swap file in Windows 3.1 is limited to about 30M. Although most casual users find this adequate, it poses a significant barrier for larger applications and servers. Windows NT has no such barrier on the size of the swap file, enabling it to run applications that are too big for Windows 3.1.

The third benefit of using a linear address space is that programs run more quickly as the convolutions in memory management that programmers employ to overcome the 640K barrier are gone.

Finally, eliminating the 640K barrier means that memory managers are not needed. Memory managers, such as QEMM 386 and 386MAX, are powerful and clever, but they often cause hardware conflicts, and they do not carry over from one version of DOS to another. To use a memory manager, you have to buy a new version of it with each new version of DOS. Windows NT eliminates the bother of memory management.

Memory managers take device drivers, memory-resident applications, and operating systems out of conventional memory (the first 640K of RAM) and stuff them in upper memory (between 640K and 1024K).

32-Bit Processing

The 80386 chip is a *32-bit processor*, which means that the processor can move 32 bits (four bytes) of data at a time. Because DOS was designed for 16-bit operating systems, Windows 3.1 is limited to this processing speed. Applications written for DOS and Windows 3.1 are thus called *16-bit applications*.

In contrast, Windows NT is a 32-bit operating system. For that reason, it can use 32-bit processors to greater advantage. Application execution is a product of processor speed and the operating system; thus, if both can process data at 32-bits, the amount of time to perform a task is greatly diminished. In fact, 32-bit applications can run roughly twice as fast as their 16-bit counterparts.

Windows NT still offers a 16-bit environment for DOS and Windows 3.*x* applications known as the Virtual DOS Machine (VDM) API. For this reason, 16-bit applications running on Windows NT do not magically turn into 32-bit applications—they run at the slower 16-bit rate. They still run properly, but to take advantage of Windows NT, you need to purchase a 32-bit version of your applications as they become available.

With Windows NT, Microsoft wanted to escape the limitations of DOS—namely, segmented memory. Yet Microsoft wanted to remain backward compatible to DOS and Windows 3.x applications. To do this, Windows NT provides a DOS emulator, *which is an environment that makes applications believe they are in a DOS operating system. This emulator is called the* Virtual DOS Machine (VDM).

Understanding Multitasking

A second demonstration of Windows NT's power is its support for multitasking. A typical computer multitasks by switching between two (or more) active programs, running each for a short period of time before turning to another. If this switching is rapid and efficient enough, the programs appear to the human operator to be running simultaneously. Although multitasking is a nearly universal feature of larger computers such as UNIX-based workstations, minicomputers, and mainframes, it only recently has become common on PC platforms.

For the end user, multitasking can mean the capability to print a document while still running a word processor, or to read one's electronic mail (e-mail) while a spreadsheet program does a recalculation. For a networked server machine, multitasking can mean the capability to support multiple user connections and services.

To fully understand multitasking, you should understand the concepts of tasks, memory management, privilege, and timeslicing. These features are discussed in the following sections.

Tasks

When a program is put into memory and run, it is known as a *task*, or *process*. The familiar DOS facility for accomplishing this is to type the name of the executable file, without the EXE extension, at the command prompt. A sequence of instructions is read from disk (where it is stored as the EXE file), loaded into memory, and started at a predefined point.

The task consists of the sequence of machine instructions executed by the processor, the memory occupied by those instructions and any associated data, and other system resources such as stack space, opened files, or display windows. An operating system is said to support multitasking, then, when it can run more than one task at a time.

One of the basic jobs of a multitasking operating system is to ensure that tasks do not interfere with each other. Tasks must not overwrite each other's memory or data, or conflict with each other's use of the file system or peripherals. If a user is going to run his e-mail while a spreadsheet is active, it is unacceptable for the e-mail program to cause the spreadsheet to miscalculate or stop running. In addition, there is always the chance that some task will terminate abnormally, or *crash*. (Even crashing should not affect the operating system or any of the other running tasks.)

The operating system itself, when active, also is a task or collection of tasks. If a program were able to access and corrupt the operating system's resources, the computer's entire operation would be affected, and the machine might cease to operate at all until re-initialized. Users of DOS and early generations of Windows are all too familiar with this situation of a "hung" computer requiring a reboot.

Memory Management

In a multitasking environment, it is critical that memory be closely managed by the operating system. The goal of memory management is to enable each task to run in its own section of memory to which no other tasks have access. The capability to strongly enforce this separation determines to a large extent the fault tolerance of the operating system toward unruly tasks.

Protected Mode

As stated earlier in the chapter, most modern microprocessors have a protected mode of operation, in which hardware features built into the processor itself enforce this separation.

Attempts by a task to write to memory that it does not own—perhaps because of programming errors or invalid data—cause an *exception* or *trap*, and the offending task then can be terminated by the operating system without affecting other active tasks or the operating system itself.

Virtual Memory

A second aspect of memory management is virtual memory. The physical memory available to the system is utilized more efficiently by enabling idle sections of memory to be written, or paged, out to disk (so termed because a standard-sized piece of memory known as a *page* is the unit by which this process occurs, at a size characteristic to the processor type).

Programs running on older PC operating systems, such as MS-DOS, could use only the memory physically present in the PC. Often the hardware used two separate 16-bit numbers or addresses to refer to a particular location in memory, and the program had to be written in a special way to reflect this two-part, or segmented, *physical address. Windows NT, on the other hand, enables all programs to use a single 32-bit address to refer to a memory location, whether or not the hardware actually has a physical memory address corresponding to the one the program uses.*

Program-memory addresses are mapped into hardware memory-addresses automatically by the system. This is called virtual memory. *A single physical memory address can be used for more than one virtual memory address. Data at virtual memory addresses currently not being used by a program can be saved temporarily on the disk, and another program or task can use the same physical memory for data at a different virtual address.*

Privilege

Another memory-management tool is the capability to run tasks at higher or lower *privilege* levels. Tasks at higher privilege levels are capable of accessing the data and resources of tasks that run at lower privilege levels, but not vice versa.

This feature typically is used, along with memory protection, to run the operating system itself at a higher kernel privilege level, and all other tasks at a lower user privilege level. Thus, although the operating system can manipulate the execution of running user tasks, a user task cannot affect the operating system or other user tasks.

Kernel *tasks have higher priority than* user *mode tasks. User tasks, for example, cannot infringe on kernel-mode memory. Kernel operations, on the other hand, can interrupt user tasks. User tasks include all the applications that run on the computer, such as word processors and spreadsheet programs. These operations also include subsystems, discussed later, that enable those applications to run in Windows NT.*

Kernel tasks include more elemental services. They communicate either directly or through the hardware abstraction layer (HAL) with the hardware of the computer. Some of those operations include the virtual memory manager, *which controls how and when data in RAM is swapped to disk; and the* input/output manager, *which controls the operation of device drivers, network drivers, cache managers, and file systems. The kernel operations also are referred to as the Windows NT* Executive. *Except for a user interface, it is a complete operating system.*

In some cases, user tasks may want to legitimately access data owned by other user tasks. Various methods can enable such access of data, but it is always necessary that both tasks cooperate. A common example is shared memory, in which two or more programs attach to a section of memory and then can read from and write to it. The burden is on the cooperating programs to manage access to this memory because the operating system is no longer involved in its management.

UNIX, OS/2, and Windows NT all use some variation of privilege. As with memory protection, support for privilege levels typically is built into the hardware of modern microprocessors.

Timeslice

A multitasking operating system needs some method for allocating processor time between the various tasks it is running. This can be done in a number of ways, most of which share the idea that tasks wait in a list, or queue, to get execution time. This time is allocated by a part of the operating system known as the *scheduler*.

The period of time during which a program runs is referred to as its *timeslice*. The process of switching from one program to another, saving information about the current state of the first, and loading saved state information about the second, is known as *context switching*.

In some operating systems, such as Windows 3.1 (real mode) and Novell NetWare 386, the tasks themselves must decide when to release the processor so that another task can be scheduled. This is known as *cooperative*, or *nonpreemptive*, multitasking.

Most such systems are programmed to cause a task to yield control of the processor on operations such as disk or console I/O, but an ill-behaved task can monopolize the processor and cause other tasks to wait interminably for processor time. Because such systems do not require the operating system to be capable of accessing user tasks directly, they can be implemented on processors that do not support privilege or memory protection. Cooperative multitasking implementations are inherently less stable, however; failure of a user program can more easily cause scheduling or memory-management problems.

In *preemptive multitasking*, the operating system is able to interrupt, or preempt, the execution of a user task without the cooperation of that task. This allows for a more stable system, but it is more difficult to implement, and requires the processor to support privilege levels and protected memory.

UNIX, OS/2, and Windows NT are examples of preemptive multitasking operating systems, as are nearly all operating systems used on larger computers. Under such a system it is much more difficult for a user program to corrupt the operating system.

Although it is frequently said that "under normal circumstances this cannot happen," system corruption still occasionally does occur, usually when a user-installed device driver crashes, fatally affecting the system.

A device driver *is a special process that runs in kernel mode and controls the operation of a physical device such as a disk, CD-ROM driver, network card, or parallel (printer) port. Because device drivers run at the same kernel-privilege level as the operating system, and are closely linked with it, a malfunctioning device driver can corrupt the operating system and cause the computer to hang.*

Device drivers are commonly packaged with hardware peripherals by the manufacturer and must be considered a likely suspect in system failures under OS/2 and Windows NT.

Most multitasking operating systems also support the concept of priority. Tasks can be assigned high or low priority, with higher-priority tasks scheduled ahead of lower-priority tasks. Task priority may be user controlled, dynamically controlled by the operating system, or both. An e-mail task, for example, might run at a lower priority than a spreadsheet task, checking for new mail only when the spreadsheet is idle and waiting for user input.

Windows NT supports three priority classes—High, Normal, and Idle—as well as five priority levels per class. These classes and levels are set by the program at process start-up, but may be adjusted dynamically by Windows NT during operation.

Understanding Multithreading

A third example of the power of Windows NT is its support of multithreading. If an operating system is able to execute more than one sequence of instructions within the same task, it is said to support *multithreading*.

Each thread is scheduled for execution (like the tasks in the above discussion), but threads within the same task are not separated from each other for purposes of resource ownership. They can access each other's data, and a file opened by one thread can be written to by another.

Threads *are the unit of scheduler dispatch;* processes *are the unit of resource ownership, each of which consists in part of one or more threads. The threads must cooperate in their use of resources because the operating system enforces no separation or protection.*

The programmer determines the number of threads in a process. Many processes contain only a single thread. A programmer may use multiple threads if a process initiates more than one action.

When a user schedules a meeting for a group of people in a scheduling program, for example, a number of things can happen (the personal schedule for each person is updated, an agenda is printed, and the person in charge of reserving rooms is notified). Each of these actions can be a thread in a process, or a programmer can make the entire process one thread. In this case, each action executes sequentially. (A multithreaded process, however, executes more quickly.)

Windows NT, OS/2, and NetWare 386 are examples of multithreading PC operating systems. UNIX, in contrast, does not support multithreading, although this useful feature is now finding its way into some variants of UNIX.

Multithreading enables the programmer to produce programs with interacting parts more easily. Threads can be started or stopped quickly because a new task and its attendant operating system structures and protections do not have to be created or destroyed. For example, a common scheme for server-based processes is to create a new thread to service each new client connection; this is less practical if an entirely new process has to be created and shared memory areas set up.

Most multithreaded applications also can be written (albeit with somewhat more effort) under multitasking systems that do not support multithreading. For a server-based process, a pool of tasks might be created during initialization to service client requests. The capability to multithread is more a matter of increased efficiency and ease of programming than of extended functionality.

Microsoft is encouraging programmers to take advantage of multithreaded processing. In fact, Windows NT itself is multithreaded.

Understanding Multiprocessing

The two preceding sections discussed multitasking and multithreading on single-processor computers (that is, those with one central processing unit (CPU), such as a 486 or Pentium). If a computer has more than one processor, however, it truly can run more than one task at the same time without switching between them. By implementing multitasking (and perhaps multithreading) on such a computer, there is more timeslice available for each task in the system. A system that is able to exploit more than one processor is said to support *multiprocessing*.

The creation of a newer, more powerful microprocessor is a huge undertaking, beyond the resources and expertise of all but a very few computer manufacturers. On the other hand, creating a computer with multiple processors, although certainly not a trivial task, is much simpler. Multiprocessing thus offers a means of producing higher-powered computers using existing processor technology—if an operating system is available to take advantage of its power.

Multiprocessing operating systems fall into two categories: asymmetric and symmetric. These systems are described in the following sections.

Asymmetric Multiprocessing

An *asymmetric multiprocessing* operating system has dedicated uses for some or all of its processors. For example, one processor might be dedicated to running the operating system itself, another to running a network operating system, and a third to running user programs.

Asymmetric multiprocessing is somewhat easier for the operating system designer to implement because the operating system itself can be based on one processor, which controls the operations of the other processors in the system. The operating system need not even be designed explicitly for multiprocessing.

An example of an asymmetric multiprocessing operating system is an adaptation of OS/2 that ran on a dual-processor Compaq SystemPro in the late 1980s.

There are certain drawbacks to this design, including the fact that the processing load is not evenly distributed among the processors. A bottleneck can occur when one processor is overloaded, causing all other processors to wait for tasks on that one processor to complete.

Symmetric Multiprocessing

A *symmetric multiprocessing* system can run any task or thread on any available processor. This sort of system is more difficult for the operating-system designer to produce because synchronization of operating-system tasks on different processors must be handled. The reward is the fuller utilization of the processor power available on the computer.

Symmetric multiprocessing makes you less vulnerable to problems associated with CPU failure. In asymmetric multiprocessing, if the CPU dedicated to the operating system fails, the system crashes. In symmetric multiprocessing, the operating system can use other CPUs. Symmetric multiprocessing also is more portable across platforms because the operating system is not dedicated to a specific CPU type.

Windows NT supports full symmetric multiprocessing. Although some adaptations of operating systems to multiprocessing systems have been produced, such as the OS/2 variant mentioned earlier, no other mainstream PC operating system has been designed from the beginning to support symmetric multiprocessing. This feature enables Windows NT to run on increasingly powerful computers without waiting for new generations of microprocessors to become available.

Understanding Windows NT Subsystems

You were introduced to kernel and user tasks earlier in the chapter. As you look further into the Windows NT architecture, you can see that there are protected subsystems within user mode operations.

One subsystem controls system security, and most of the others relate to the diverse operating systems that Windows NT accommodates, such as OS/2, POSIX, and DOS; 16-bit Windows applications (the VDM); and 32-bit (Win32) Windows applications. All these subsystems, except for the security subsystem, work with the Win32 subsystem to translate their system requests into a language that Windows NT (the kernel) can understand.

Each subsystem acts like a server for client applications. In other words, OS/2 applications (clients) work with the OS/2 protected subsystem (server). The OS/2 subsystem, in turn, works with the Windows NT Executive to provide the services requested by the applications.

Microsoft chose this system architecture for several reasons. First, because each protected subsystem acts like a separate server, errors in one do not affect the others. Second, it is easy to add other subsystems to such an architecture. Third, each server can run on a separate processor, either locally or remotely. Finally, this architecture eliminates the duplication of kernel-mode operations.

Each subsystem makes similar requests of the Windows NT Executive. You can either create a system in which each subsystem has its own Executive functions, or share a single Executive among all the subsystems. Writing an operating system that provides a kernel for each subsystem is difficult and prone to errors. Microsoft chose instead to use the model of a network to share the Executive among subsystems.

The kernel mode is divided into discreet units, including the virtual memory manager, object manager, security-reference monitor, process manager, local procedure call facility, I/O manager, kernel, and hardware abstraction layer (see fig. 2.1).

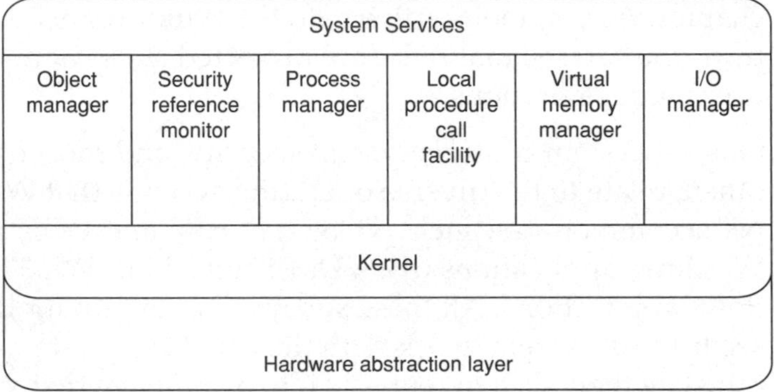

Figure 2.1: *The kernel mode is comprised of many discreet units.*

The following list describes the function of each object in the Executive.

- **Virtual memory manager.** The virtual memory manager governs the movement of data in and out of virtual memory. When the user initiates an action that requires the computer to load data from disk into RAM, there sometimes is not enough RAM. The virtual memory manager selects the data to transfer from RAM to the TEMP file (called the paging or swap file) on the hard disk. The data that is stored in the TEMP file is known as virtual memory.

  When the virtual memory manager loads the data, it makes sure that every running application has an exclusive subset of memory addresses so that the data from one application does not spill into the data of another.

- **Object manager.** Windows NT uses *objects*—abstract data types—to represent system resources. The object manager creates, terminates, and manages these objects in the Executive.

- **Security reference monitor.** The security reference monitor implements Windows NT's security functions on the local computer.
- **Local procedure call facility.** Modeled on the remote procedure call (RPC) facility that acts between computers, the local procedure call (LPC) facility optimizes communications between protected subsystem APIs and their client applications.

Microsoft developers chose to create LPC because they feared that an application acting through a protected subsystem such as OS/2, which in turn acts through the Win32 protected subsystem to access the kernel, would be too slow.

- **Kernel.** The *kernel* gives to all the other Executive managers elemental objects to implement higher-level requests. It schedules threads, coordinates the execution of multiple processes aimed at accomplishing a specific task, and responds to exceptions and interrupts.
- **I/O system.** The *I/O system* manages input/output devices, such as disk drives. A number of subprocessors comprise the I/O manager, including the following:
    - **Network drivers.** *Network drivers* receive and transmit I/O requests to remote machines across a network.
    - **Cache manager.** The *cache manager* is responsible for holding in RAM a certain amount of data that was the last data read from the disk drive. Instead of reaccessing the disk drive to retrieve the same information, the data is read directly from the cache in RAM. This process is dramatically faster than accessing the hard drive.
    - **Windows NT Executive device drivers.** *Executive device drivers* directly manipulate devices to receive or retrieve data.

  - **File systems.** *File systems* translate file-oriented I/O requests into I/O commands for specific devices.
  - **I/O manager.** The *I/O manager* manages device-independent I/O requests.

- **Hardware abstraction layer (HAL).** The *hardware abstraction layer (HAL)* translates Executive requests into actions in the computer's hardware. To move to a different processor, only this layer needs to be changed because all hardware-dependent features, such as interrupt controllers and I/O interfaces, are hidden by HAL from the Executive. HAL makes Windows NT very portable across computer platforms.

Understanding Windows NT Networking

Windows NT provides support for two types of networking: peer-to-peer networking and client/server networking.

In *peer-to-peer networks*, every computer in the network can access every other. Computers can, for example, share files on their hard drives and share printers. Windows for Workgroups 3.1 offers peer-to-peer networking. Windows NT also includes this functionality.

One of the problems with peer-to-peer networks is that when several users access many computers, computer performance lessens. When someone else is accessing your hard drive, for example, it takes longer for you to open and save files on your system. In small office environments, peer-to-peer networking works fine; when there are more than 15 computers, another (more hardware-intensive) networking scheme is necessary.

For more information on networking with Windows NT, see Chapter 13.

In *client/server networks*, a dedicated computer with massive hard drives serves as the central repository for shared files. Instead of accessing files on other people's computers, the user looks for shared files on the dedicated computer, called the server. Windows NT supports client/server networking through the Windows NT Advanced Server edition (discussed in detail in Chapter 15).

The term client/server *derives from the idea that your computer, the client, makes requests of the server; the server (like a butler) carries out the request.*

Understanding System Security

Windows NT is a secure system. The security system operates on the following three levels:

- Protects against people who are not authorized to log on to the system
- Protects against unauthorized access to files and system resources
- Protects the operating system and application processes from destructive applications and viruses

Windows NT also monitors attempts to breach the security system.

Windows NT, in its initial release, conforms to the U.S. government's Class C2 level of security. To qualify, it must contain the following features:

- A secure logon system, in which users identify themselves by a unique logon name and password
- Discretionary access control, in which the owner of a resource determines who has access to it

- Auditing, in which the system can detect and record events related to the security of the system and its components
- Memory protection, in which files are read- and write-protected from others in a network

In future releases, Windows NT will satisfy the criteria for a Class B2 level of security (second to the top of seven levels).

The following sections discuss the security measures used by Windows NT.

Crash Prevention

System crashes on personal computers are frustrating. If more than one application is running during the crash, unsaved data may be lost. The magnitude of the consequences grows dramatically, however, if the computer is on a network. It is possible for one workstation to hang an entire system. A system crash in which dozens or even hundreds of accounts are open truly can be catastrophic. For this reason, the system must have adequate safeguards against such intentional or unintentional crashes.

Windows NT protects the system in four ways:

- Each application runs in a separate address space in virtual memory. One application cannot access another's virtual memory addresses.
- User mode is separated from kernel mode. If an application or a subgroup crashes in user mode, it cannot harm the operating system in kernel mode.
- Protected subgroups, such as OS/2 and POSIX, run separately from one another. Even if one protected subgroup crashes, the other subgroups are unaffected.

- Each page of virtual memory has indicators that describe whether (and how) they can be accessed in user or kernel mode.

Logon and Access Security

One of the protected subsystems in Windows NT's user mode is the security subsystem—the gateway through which all users must travel. When you log on, the security subsystem looks at your user name and password to determine whether you have access to the computer system. If you do, it looks at your user profile, which specifies the files and system resources you can and cannot access, and what you can and cannot do with those files and resources. The system administrator may allow you to view a file but not change it, for example, or to print a document but not change the printer's setup.

With the user profile, the security subsystem creates an *access token*, which is the key that gets passed with whatever action you perform. It contains the specifics of what you can and cannot do on the system.

The sophisticated security that Windows NT provides is overkill for users who work at home on their own computers. Security is absolutely necessary, however, when computers are linked to a network. Not only does a security system prevent criminals from stealing information and planting viruses, it also prevents inadvertent corruption of files by fellow workers.

Windows NT provides the following user groups:

- **Administrators.** *Administrators* have access to all system resources and rights and built-in capabilities in Windows NT. Administrators can create users and groups, shut down the system, force the shutdown of a remote system, and assign user rights.

Administrators do not, however, have automatic access to all files on the system. The person who creates a file in the system is its owner, unless she declares otherwise. The owner of a file also determines its access rights. The administrator, however, can take ownership of the file.

- **Power Users.** *Power users* have many administrative rights: managing printers, creating and modifying user accounts and groups, and creating common programming groups. Power users do not have the same number of rights as administrators; for example, they cannot take ownership of files, manage security logs, back up files and directories, or override the lock on a workstation.
- **Users.** *Users* are the most common type. Common group permissions include opening and closing files, and accessing system resources (such as printers). The administrator can select the permissions for each user, create subgroups of users (for example, secretary, accountant, and stockroom person), and assign permissions pertinent to the job description of each group.
- **Guests.** *Guests* use the system only occasionally. Often, their access to files and system resources is severely restricted. The administrator can choose, for example, to limit their access to only the files they create.
- **Backup operators.** *Backup operators* back up to and restore the files and directories on the system from a storage media, such as a tape drive.

These built-in groups have default rights and built-in capabilities. Permissions can be modified, but capabilities are an innate characteristic of the user type. To change capabilities, a user must change to a different user type. Table 2.1 shows the rights and capabilities of the various user groups.

Table 2.1
User Groups' Rights and Capabilities

	Administrators	*Power Users*	*Guests*	*All*	*Backup Users*	*Operators*
Rights						
Log on	Yes	Yes	Yes	Yes	Yes	Yes
Access computer from network	Yes	Yes	No	No	Yes	No
Assume ownership of files	Yes	No	No	No	No	No
Manage security and auditing log	Yes	No	No	No	No	No
Modify system time	Yes	Yes	No	No	No	No
Shut down system	Yes	Yes	Yes	No	Yes	Yes
Remotely shut down system	Yes	No	No	No	No	No
Back up directories and files	Yes	No	No	No	No	Yes
Restore directories and files	Yes	No	No	No	No	Yes
Capabilities						
Manage and create user accounts	Yes	Yes	No	No	No	No
Manage and create user groups	Yes	Yes	No	No	No	No
Define user rights	Yes	No	No	No	No	No
Lock workstation	Yes	Yes	Yes	No	No	No
Override workstation lock	Yes	No	No	No	No	No
Format hard disk of workstation	Yes	No	No	No	No	No
Keep local user profile	Yes	Yes	Yes	No	No	Yes
Share (or stop sharing) directories	Yes	Yes	No	No	No	No
Share (or stop sharing) printers	Yes	Yes	No	No	No	No

User Privileges

As described earlier, access tokens describe what a user can and cannot access. An *access token* is a small repository of information that accompanies a process, such as a request to open a file (see fig. 2.2).

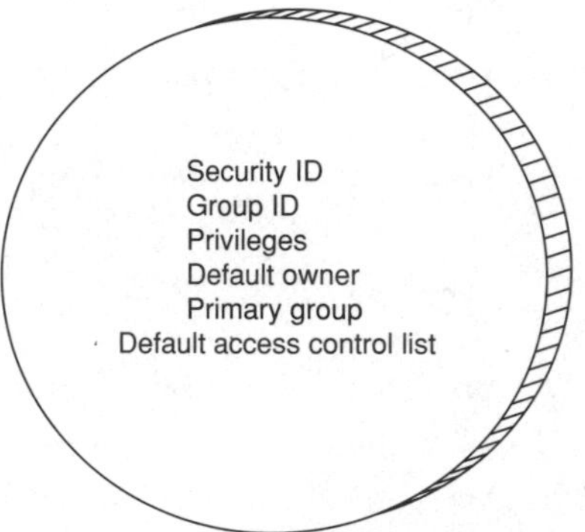

Figure 2.2:
Access token.

The access token contains the following information:

- **Security ID.** The user's logon name.
- **Group IDs.** The groups to which the user belongs.
- **Privileges.** The special services the user can use, usually none.
- **Default owner.** The default owner of the object the user creates, usually the user.
- **Primary group.** The group of security IDs that can use the object.
- **Default access control list (ACL).** The default list of groups and individual users and their read/write/execute privileges for user-owned objects.

The access token also includes the following services the user can perform: create token, open token, query token information, set token information, duplicate token, adjust token privileges, and adjust token groups.

Token *is a term taken from networking jargon. Just as a bus or subway token buys you a bus or subway ride, an access token enables your process to travel in the system.*

When a process tries to access an object, such as a file, Windows NT's Object Manager (in the Executive) examines the access token to determine whether the process can open a handle to the object.

Access Control Lists

Windows NT attaches security descriptors to all objects—including files, threads, events, and access tokens—when they are created. The *security descriptor* is an ACL that specifies who can use the objects created by the user and how they can use them. To assign security to an object, the creator of the object does one of three things:

- Explicitly states, in the ACL, which users and groups can use the object and which access rights (read/write/execute) they have.
- Names the object, but does not explicitly state the ACL. The security system looks in the object directory for the name of the object. In the directory, some elements of the ACL list might be marked "inherit." The security system applies those elements to the object.
- Does not name the object or explicitly state the ACL. In this case, the security system applies the default ACL listed in the creator's access token.

Security descriptors also contain an audit field, which enables the security system to set off alarms and send messages when it detects users trying to access objects restricted from them. For example, the security system records the security ID (the user's logon name) of a user who tries to modify a system-owned file in the security log.

ACLs actually are composed of a number of smaller lists, called *access control entries (ACEs)*. Each ACE contains the name of one user or group and their read/write/execute permissions (see fig. 2.3).

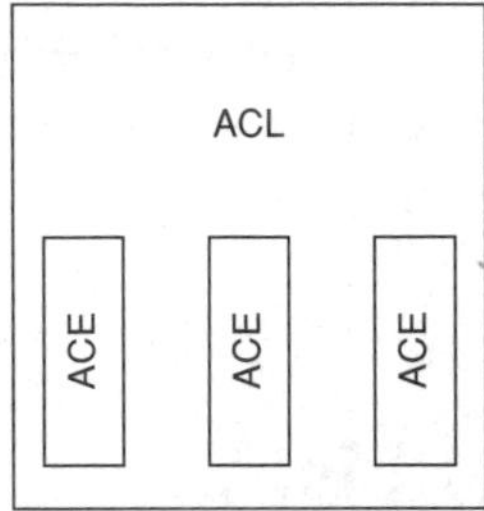

Figure 2.3:
Every ACL contains a number of access-control entries (ACEs).

The security system reads through the ACEs sequentially, and stops reading at the first ACE that either grants or denies the process access to the object. If the security system reads all of the ACEs and does not find the security or group ID of the user, the security system denies access to the object.

The security system reads through the ACEs only when a handle to the object is first opened, not each time the handle is used. It is possible to change an object's ACL while it is in use. Even if the new setting disqualifies current users from accessing the object, once a handle is opened to an object, the object remains accessible until the process completes.

Some interesting inconsistencies can elude Windows NT's detection. Suppose, for example, that the security ID is JDoe, and he belongs to the Stockclerks group. If the first ACE grants permission to JDoe, the security system stops reading the ACEs, and opens a handle to the object—even if the second ACE denies access to everyone in the Stockclerks group.

Understanding How Windows NT Works with Your Existing Applications

One of the most appealing aspects of Windows NT is its capability to run applications written for a variety of operating systems, including OS/2, DOS, 16-bit Windows, and POSIX. The price Windows NT pays for this versatility is slower performance. Some of the applications in these operating systems are not compatible with Windows NT, and the ones that are compatible might run faster on systems that run only 16-bit Windows, OS/2, or UNIX.

Win32 provides the graphical interface for Windows NT, and handles inputs from other devices, such as your keyboard, scanner, mouse, and other pointing devices. Win32 also is the gateway into the Windows NT kernel for all operating systems that Windows NT supports.

When you double-click on an application, Win32 determines whether it is a Win32 application—that is, a 32-bit Windows application. If it is, Win32 controls the execution of the application. If not, Win32 passes control to the appropriate operating subsystem, called a *protected subsystem* (the VDM, for example).

DOS and 16-Bit Windows Compatibility

Using the Virtual DOS Machine, Windows NT is 100-percent compatible with DOS and Windows 3.1 software, except for those programs that access the hardware directly or rely on their own device drivers—either for printers, disk drives, scanners, or video cards. Because, for security reasons, Windows NT only permits access to the hardware through the Win32 API or the Windows NT Executive, this type of software will fail.

There are a variety of applications that might be incompatible, including those that are display-intensive, such as paint programs; those that directly access FAX, scanner, or terminal-emulation cards; those that access disk drives, such as disk-maintenance applications; and disk-doubling applications that have their own disk device drivers.

You might be able to use some of these applications by upgrading their device drivers. Others need an application upgrade.

DOS applications appear in windows, just as they do in Windows 3.1. The only difference is that you can launch 32-bit Windows and 16-bit DOS programs from the DOS window. These programs are routed to the appropriate protected subsystem—Win32 or the VDM.

16-bit Windows applications open the VDM that, in turn, opens the Windows on Win32 (WOW) environment. WOW contains an emulation of Windows 3.1, DOS, and the Windows application. Each additional Windows application becomes another thread within WOW, not part of a new VDM.

In this way, WOW controls the multitasking of 16-bit Windows applications. This points out the only difference between the simulated (WOW) version of Windows 3.1 and Windows 3.1 itself: WOW controls multitasking, not the 16-bit Windows environment.

Most Windows 3.1 applications run in Windows NT. Although the 32- and 16-bit versions probably look identical, the 32-bit applications run directly through the Win32 API, and the 16-bit versions run in the VDM.

A number of applications written for Windows 3.0, particularly graphics-intensive applications such as paint programs, skipped the Windows API altogether and accessed the window manager directly for better display performance.

Windows NT uses its own window manager and *graphical device interface (GDI)*, which controls display elements, in place of those in the 16-bit version of Windows. Applications that try to access the 16-bit version of the Window Manager or the GDI find them missing, with the Windows NT Window Manager and GDI in their place. For this reason, these applications do not run on Windows NT.

On the whole, you will find that 16-bit Windows applications run more slowly in Windows NT than in Windows 3.1. This is because of the massive overhead of Windows NT, the extra steps required to funnel system calls through the Win32 API, and the inability of 16-bit applications to take advantage of multitasking threads. As revisions of 16-bit software become available, the new 32-bit applications will run faster on Windows NT.

OS/2 Compatibility

Current support for OS/2 applications is limited. Windows NT supports only 16-bit, character-based OS/2 applications (and only on *x*86 computers). As a result, most OS/2 2.*x* applications do not run under Windows NT.

In contrast to DOS and 16-bit Windows applications, OS/2 applications do not need an emulator because they were written for a multitasking, 32-bit environment. Instead, they work as clients to the OS/2 protected subsystem API.

POSIX Compatibility

Windows NT also provides support for POSIX applications. *POSIX* is a UNIX variant, designed for the U.S. government, that supports application portability across computing platforms. Like OS/2, POSIX-compliant applications run as clients through the POSIX API protected subsystem. Also like OS/2, Windows NT's first version supports only character-based applications in POSIX. This is not a significant restriction for POSIX applications because, like UNIX, its applications generally are character-based.

Comparing Windows NT with Other 32-Bit Operating Systems

Windows NT takes its place in the marketplace beside several other major operating systems, most notably OS/2 and UNIX. This section compares and contrasts Windows NT with each of these competitors.

Windows NT and OS/2: A Comparison

Windows NT and OS/2 have common origins. The two operating systems, consequently, share many features. Microsoft and IBM worked together in the 1980s to produce OS/2 1.0. The relationship was rocky at times. When OS/2 commercially failed in 1987, Microsoft began to withdraw support from OS/2. When Windows 3.0 exceeded all sales expectations, Microsoft turned away from upgrading OS/2. Instead, Microsoft used its OS/2 research as the basis of Windows NT. To this day, IBM remains the sole supporter of OS/2. This section looks at the similarities and differences between OS/2 and Windows NT, including:

- Graphical user interface
- Operating-system architecture
- Virtual memory space
- Application compatibility
- Application-memory protection

- File systems
- Networks
- Script language
- Symmetric multiprocessing
- Cross-platform compatibility
- Security

Graphical User Interface

Both OS/2 and Windows NT use *graphical user interfaces (GUIs)*. The center point for the OS/2 interface is called the Workplace Shell. The typical center point in Windows NT is the Program Manager, although other third-party shells will soon be ported to the Windows NT platform.

In the Workplace Shell, all desktop objects, such as files, printers, and utilities, are treated the same. You can manipulate a file the same way you can a printer (within reason). You might, for example, copy a file from one directory to another as you copy the printer icon from one folder to another. This provides a uniform and easy-to-learn interface.

The Workplace Shell provides a desktop for direct access to all objects. OS/2 includes a folder icon for organizing desktop objects. Users can put anything on the desktop into a folder, such as a spreadsheet icon, a printer icon, and a fax icon. You easily can move icons from one group to another.

Windows NT's Program Manager as the shell is far less sophisticated than OS/2's Workplace Shell. Although the icon groupings provide structure, they require the user to traverse several layers of the interface before reaching the window in which the desired task appears.

Microsoft recognizes the inefficiency of the interface, and pledges to create a more integrated, object-oriented interface in later versions of Windows 3.1 and Windows NT. Fortunately, there are a multitude of third-party shells in Windows 3.1 that will be ported to the Windows NT platform.

Operating-System Architecture

Both OS/2 and Windows NT are 32-bit operating systems. There are some differences between them, however. OS/2 2.1 completes many, but not all, of its tasks using 32-bit processing; Windows NT performs all tasks with 32-bit processing.

Both operating systems provide 16-bit processing in protected subsystem APIs for DOS and 16-bit Windows applications.

Both operating systems use message passing between applications and the operating system to facilitate multitasking. OS/2 implements message passing differently from Windows NT, however. In OS/2, messages and interrupts enter a single queue. Once there, they wait until the application they are bound for is ready to accept them. Each message is processed in the order in which it arrives. Problems occur when a message cannot be processed. It sits at the top of the queue, blocking all other messages from being processed—thus hanging the entire system (see fig. 2.4).

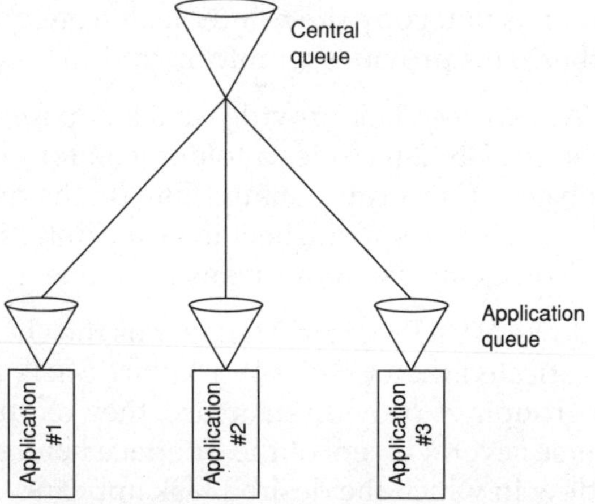

Figure 2.4:
OS/2's single message queue.

Windows NT also uses message passing to implement multitasking. Windows NT, however, does not use a central distributing queue as OS/2 does. Instead, messages are passed directly to the queue of each application (see fig. 2.5).

If one of the messages cannot be processed, the operating system passes processing time to the next application. This feature makes Windows NT more difficult to crash.

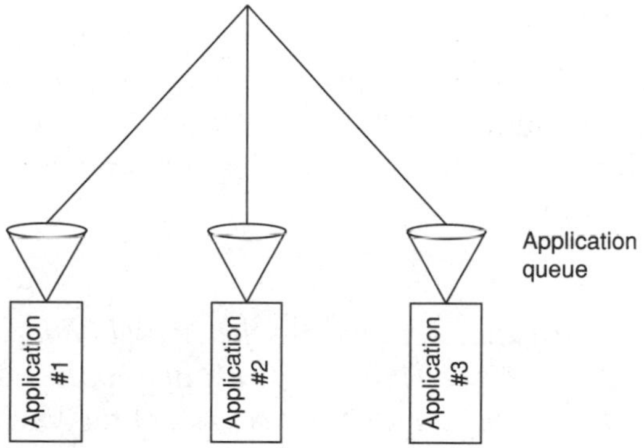

Figure 2.5: *Windows NT's decentralized messaging queues.*

Virtual Memory Space

Both OS/2 and Windows NT use a 4G virtual-memory address space. Although Windows NT reserves 2G for the operating system and 2G for applications, OS/2 limits each application to 512M. For most users, these numbers far exceed even the smallest percentage of virtual memory that their applications will ever use.

A more realistic limit on virtual memory space for either Windows NT or OS/2 is the sum of RAM memory and free disk space. In other words, if you have 8M of RAM and 50M free on your hard disk, the maximum amount of virtual memory available on your system is 58M, not 2G. In this respect, only users with very large disk drives can fully utilize the virtual memory potential of either operating system.

Application Memory Protection

Both OS/2 and Windows NT offer applications protection from other running applications by utilizing the built-in features of Intel microprocessors, called *virtual 86 mode.* Both OS/2 and Windows NT refer to this mode as the virtual DOS machine (VDM), as described earlier in the chapter.

Using VDM, if an application tries to use memory reserved for another application, OS/2 displays an error message, called the Hard Error Popup, and enables you to either terminate the errant application or display the contents of the debug registers.

These options leave the operating system and other running applications intact. DOS or Windows 3.1, in comparison, might display a system error message and the entire system might crash.

In addition to using the virtual 86 mode built into 80386, 80486, and Pentium processors, Windows NT provides a software version of the VDM. The simulated environment makes DOS run more slowly than it would on a PC running DOS. This is a result of the processing overhead of simulating the hardware VDM with a software program. The software VDM enables Windows NT to run DOS and 16-bit Windows applications on non-Intel processors.

OS/2 provides more flexibility than Windows NT when running Windows applications. In OS/2, you have the option of running all your Windows applications in the same VDM or in separate VDMs.

Running all Windows applications in the same VDM is faster than in separate VDMs because they share the same Windows operating system.

Because all the applications are running in the same VDM, there is the potential danger of one application crashing all the other running applications in that VDM. The damage is limited to that VDM; other VDMs, other running applications, and the operating system are impervious to the corruption in one errant VDM. As a user, you have to decide what best fits your needs: security or speed.

Application Hardware Protection

Hardware devices also are protected from errant applications in OS/2 and Windows NT. To enforce security (in Windows NT) and to exercise control over system resources, applications must access hardware devices, such as printers and disk drives, through a *virtual device driver (VDD)*. The VDD prevents more than one application at a time from accessing a hardware device.

Both Windows NT and OS/2 can tell when applications try to illegally access hardware devices. This situation is particularly important for Windows NT, whose security system must protect system resources, like disk drives, from illegal access. You are given the option of terminating the offending application.

Some DOS and Windows applications were written to access hardware directly to speed program execution. These applications are incompatible with OS/2 and Windows NT.

File Systems

The file system that DOS uses is called the *File Allocation Table (FAT)*. All DOS and Windows 3.1 applications use this format; Windows NT and OS/2 also support it. In addition to FAT, OS/2 also can use another file system, called the *High Performance File System (HPFS)*. HPFS was designed to access files more quickly on large disk drives (over 200M). Access time is equal to that of using FAT for smaller disk drives.

HPFS uses multithreaded write-caching to disk, in which files are dumped into RAM and written to disk when there is time. This enables you to (almost) immediately proceed to another task without waiting for the file to save to disk.

HPFS also provides support for very large files and file names, up to 254 characters long. It enables you to use a variety of characters—such as spaces and multiple periods—in file names (unlike FAT file names).

Although it is handy to have long, descriptive file names, there is a limitation to their usefulness. Because DOS and Windows 3.1 can run in OS/2, OS/2 applications that are saved with file names longer than eight characters are inaccessible by DOS and Windows 3.1. Windows NT, on the other hand, automatically reduces large file names to the eight-character maximum allowed by DOS and Windows 3.1.

Although you might find it confusing to refer to the same file by using two different names, at least Windows NT enables you to take full advantage of longer names while maintaining compatibility with older operating systems.

HPFS offers another major advantage over FAT: *extended attribute files*, which describe the file to which they are attached. You can put almost any kind of information into the file, such as keywords you use to search for the file, the name of the owner of the file, or historical information about the file (such as when and who modified the file). You can use the Workplace Shell to record most information (by using the File section of the system settings notebook). Applications are free to use the extended attributes file any way they please.

Extended attribute files can help you speed up tasks by searching for keywords in extended attribute files instead of in long data files; record information that cannot be part of a file, such as historical information; or perform tasks you might otherwise not be able to perform, such as when the file is write- or read-protected.

Windows NT can use three filing systems: FAT, HPFS, and its own file system, called *New Technology File System (NTFS)*. Like HPFS, NTFS can access files on large disks more quickly than FAT. Unlike HPFS, however, NTFS can enforce the U.S.

government's level C2 security; that is, system administrators can restrict users or user groups from accessing files, directories, and subdirectories.

Networking

Both OS/2 and Windows NT work with a variety of transport protocols, such as TCP/IP and IPX. OS/2 also uses IBM's protocol, SNA. Both operating systems can function as clients on Novell's NetWare systems. Only OS/2 can function as a server for NetWare, however.

Although both operating systems support server/client local area networks (LANs), only Windows NT supports peer-to-peer networking, which is less hardware-intensive and suited to small office installations. Instead of a dedicated computer (server) that serves as a storage facility, peer-to-peer networking enables users to access each others' hard disks.

Script Language

IBM created a new script language for OS/2, called *REXX*, to replace IBM's older, more difficult batch language. REXX is an easy-to-use, powerful language that you can use for a variety of tasks. For example, you can modify desktop objects, run automated tasks (such as downloading data about stocks at midnight every day), and run programs to change downloaded stock data into written and graphical reports.

You also can create macros for OS/2's Enhanced Editor with REXX. REXX runs on many platforms, from mainframe to microcomputer, from Amiga to UNIX to Macintosh. Many consider REXX to be one of OS/2's most valuable features.

Windows NT does not offer a script or macro langauge such as REXX. It does not even have the oft-maligned Windows Recorder applet found in Windows 3.1! In the future, however, Windows NT will be very strong in this area. Look for an object-oriented script language—often referred to as *Object Basic*—to be built into the next versions of Windows 3.1 and Windows NT.

Multiprocessing

As discussed earlier in the chapter, Windows NT fully supports symmetric multiprocessing. OS/2, in contrast, does not. Although multiprocessing computers are not on a typical desktop now, Intel has announced plans to sell multiprocessor chips within a matter of years. Multiprocessing provides orders-of-magnitude faster computing. When multiprocessors become common, the symmetric multiprocessing capability of Windows NT will be invaluable.

Cross-Platform Compatibility

Wouldn't it be great to take your favorite applications and run them on faster computers? For years, there have been CPUs that run faster than Intel processors—for example, DEC's Alpha series and MIPS processors. Although system administrators pine for faster processors because their favorite applications can't run on non-Intel processors, changing to a new platform is daunting.

Windows NT was designed to run on a variety of processors. The hardware abstraction layer (HAL) acts as the interface between function calls and the computer's hardware. When software developers want to port Windows NT to new processors, they need only to revise the HAL. Windows NT already is compatible with RISC processors.

In contrast, OS/2 2.*x* is tied to Intel-based processors. IBM promises that future versions will be portable.

Software developers have a vested interest in the portability of an operating system. If they can port applications that they create for one platform easily to another, they save valuable developmental hours.

Application Compatibility

Both OS/2 and Windows NT can run DOS and 16-bit Windows applications. Windows NT, however, can run only character-mode OS/2 1.*x* applications. These applications represent only a small minority of the OS/2 applications available, however.

OS/2 2.1 supports Windows 3.1 applications, in part, as a result of an agreement reached between IBM and Microsoft. In the process of disentangling who owned what of OS/2, Microsoft and IBM agreed to share with each other the source code of Windows 3.x and OS/2.

That agreement expires in September 1993. Without access to source code, it is much more difficult to support new versions of operating systems. Because there are far more Windows than OS/2 applications in the marketplace, it is essential to the success of OS/2 to remain compatible with future versions of Windows.

The reverse is not true. Windows NT would not be crippled by deciding not to support OS/2 applications. It took IBM a year to support Windows 3.1 in OS/2, and that was with the benefit of seeing the Windows source code. OS/2 faces the real problem of losing compatibility with Windows applications.

In addition, Windows NT supports POSIX (character-based only) and 32-bit Windows NT applications; OS/2 does not. Because most POSIX (UNIX) applications are character-based, this restriction does not significantly reduce the number of POSIX applications that can run in Windows NT.

Portability *ensures an application's compatibility across processors;* extensibility *ensures an application's compatibility across operating systems.*

continues

Extensibility enables you to run a greater variety of software on your system. In that way, you can convert to an extensible system, such as Windows NT, more easily and cheaply because you do not need to give up your old applications. Also, because subsystems are relatively easy to add to Windows NT, it does not become outdated.

Each operating system in Windows NT is implemented in its own protected subsystem. This component architecture enables system administrators to update individual subsystems while Windows NT is running, without affecting the other subsystems. Adding new operating systems simply entails adding subsystems, not intertwining new code into current code. As a result, Windows NT is less vulnerable to bugs that come with operating-system updates (or additions).

Security

Windows NT's security system is much more comprehensive than that of OS/2. As described in this chapter, virtually every object in Windows NT—such as files, memory, threads, directories, and hardware—has security measures built in. Each process has a descriptor, defined by the capabilities of the user or user group, that system resources review before performing tasks.

Additionally, Windows NT monitors a series of security parameters, and keeps a security log that notes events such as attempts to gain illegal access to the system or system resources, system shutdowns, and user logons.

OS/2 provides watered-down versions of some of Windows NT's security features. OS/2 relies on other systems for security. For example, IBM's LAN Server records security-related events in a log, and provides some system-resource security. None of these security features, however, matches the sophistication of Windows NT.

Windows NT and UNIX: A Comparison

UNIX, written in 1969, is the benchmark against which all other powerful operating systems are measured. Just about every operating system, including DOS, borrows UNIX concepts and terminology. (For example, the command to change directories is the same in DOS and UNIX.) The enormous system requirements of UNIX, however, both in memory and computational needs, and its arcane command language have largely prevented it from moving to the PC desktop.

Some companies have tried to bring UNIX to the PC platform. Microsoft, for example, created Xenix, a variant of UNIX, to run on a normal PC. Xenix was a commercial flop, causing Microsoft to license Xenix to Santa Cruz Operations (SCO) in return for a piece of the company.

In recent years, UNIX variants have sprung up after UNIX source code was released. Examples include: NeXTStep, SCO UNIX, Solaris from SunSoft, and UnixWare from Univel/Novell. To include a discussion of each of these operating systems is beyond the scope of this book.

The UNIX that is discussed in this section is generic, such as that supported by UNIX System Laboratories (now owned by Novell). At its most basic level, UNIX is a 32-bit, multiuser, multiprocessing, and multitasking operating system that supports linear memory addressing, virtual memory, networking, and sophisticated security.

The following section looks at the similarities and differences between Windows NT and UNIX, focusing on the following areas:

- Process execution
- Multiprocessing

- Objects
- Interprocess communications
- Flat memory
- Modes
- Security
- Networks
- Cross-platform compatibility
- Multiusing
- Parallel processing
- Distributed file systems
- Applications
- Variants
- Size
- Market penetration

Process Execution

Both Windows NT and UNIX have managers in the kernel that govern processes. In UNIX, that manager is called the Process Scheduler. In Windows NT, the Process Manager and Object Manager in the NT Executive fulfill the same functions.

These managers determine which processes get executed, their priorities for execution, and when they get executed. They detect the length of time since the processes last received a CPU timeslice, and monitor the access permissions of the process's owner. These managers also make sure that processes and subprocesses are executed in the correct order so that tasks are accomplished correctly.

Multiprocessing

Most variants of UNIX support either symmetrical or asymmetrical multiprocessing; Windows NT supports symmetrical multiprocessing. Both operating systems also support remote procedure calls (RPCs), which enable one computer to spawn a process or thread, send it to another computer, communicate with it, and terminate it. In this way, one computer gets the benefit of two processors. To the user, however, everything appears to happen locally.

Objects

Windows NT treats everything—files, system resources, memory, and processes—as objects. UNIX treats everything as if it were a file. For example, you generally find hardware device drivers in the `/dev` subdirectory. Windows NT's I/O Manager, likewise, makes device and network drivers appear as file systems to user-mode processes and higher-level executive processes.

The advantage of making everything look the same is that you then can manipulate everything in a similar way. Access to all objects (or files), for example, can be governed by the same security procedures. This makes adding and subtracting objects from the system easy because all objects respond to the same operations.

Device drivers used to be integrated into the operating code. Adding or revising a driver required the system administrator to shut down the entire computer system and then reinstall or rebuild the operating system. This process caused a variety of problems, especially the loss of computer time. By making device drivers independent entities—objects—they can be added while the computer is running without the threat of introducing bugs to other parts of the system.

Flat Memory

Both UNIX and Windows NT use 32-bit addresses in flat (non-segmented) virtual memory. Gone is the segmented memory of DOS and Windows 3.1, in which physical and virtual memory is broken into conventional, upper, expanded, high, and extended memory. UNIX uses a 2G virtual-memory space; Windows NT uses a 4G virtual-memory space (2G for the application and 2G for the operating system). Both operating systems support 64K or more of physical memory.

Modes

Both UNIX and Windows NT separate user and kernel modes (called *spaces* in UNIX). Kernel processes have higher priority over user processes. Kernel processes, for example, can suspend user processes. Also, user processes are protected in memory from one another by kernel processes. Except for interprocess communications, user-mode processes do not interact with one another. Kernel processes, in contrast, interact both with other kernel and user processes.

In UNIX, the *system call interface (SCI)* can change user processes into kernel processes to execute system-level functions, and then change them back to user processes. The SCI is the communication tool that goes between user and kernel mode. Because applications can cross the line between user and kernel modes, the operating system is vulnerable to errant applications.

In Windows NT, applications and protected subsystems, including different operating systems, such as DOS and Windows 3.*x*, occupy user mode. Kernel processes execute user processes, but (unlike UNIX) neither applications or subsystems can penetrate kernel mode. When a user process wants the kernel to perform a task, it issues a system service call that starts one or more kernel-mode processes. Separating user and kernel modes so completely makes Windows NT less vulnerable to errant applications that try to invade kernel-mode processes.

Security

Windows NT satisfies the government's C2 security requirements. Although UNIX, by itself, satisfies C1 security requirements (which are slightly less stringent), many UNIX variants satisfy C2 security requirements. For this reason, UNIX and Windows NT provide similar security features, including object ownership, user and group access rights, and object-level security.

Both operating systems maintain detailed security logs that record security-related events, such as attempts to illegally access system resources. Both systems offer robust recovery systems after hardware, software, and power failures.

Networking

Both Windows NT and UNIX offer powerful networking features that are based on the *open systems interconnect (OSI)* model. For example, both UNIX and Windows NT support RPCs.

UNIX can access a variety of UNIX and non-UNIX operating systems by using Sun's Network File System (NFS). UNIX uses USL's remote file system (RFS) to share peripherals. Unlike NFS, however, RFS requires all computers to run UNIX file systems.

NFS rides on top of the file system of the remote computer. For that reason, NFS supports a variety of file systems, including FAT (DOS), HPFS (OS/2), UNIX, BSD, VMS (DEC), and—in the near future—NTFS (Windows NT).

Both UNIX and Windows NT support client/server and peer-to-peer networking.

Cross-Platform Compatibility

UNIX runs on far more platforms than does Windows NT (from mainframes to microcomputers). Windows NT runs only on Intel, MIPS, and DEC Alpha processors. This list of platforms will grow as the product matures.

Multiusing

UNIX was written specifically to enable more than one user to share a computer. UNIX enables many users to use dumb terminals to access the same computer. Windows NT, on the other hand, is a single-user operating system. Although many computers can be networked together to a Windows NT server, the computers cannot be dumb terminals.

Parallel Processing

UNIX offers full parallel-processing capabilities, including vectorized compilers. Windows NT offers a more limited form of parallel processing with synchronized multi-threading.

Distributed File Systems

UNIX fully supports distributed file systems. In UNIX, files appear local, even though they can be anywhere in the network. Windows NT does not offer distributed file systems.

Microsoft will offer distributed file systems in its next-generation operating system (code-named "Cairo").

Applications

UNIX applications already take full advantage of multitasking, multiprocessing, and multiuser functions. Windows NT applications only now are being rewritten to take advantage of 32-bit processing.

Variants

Because the source code of UNIX was made available, many people hacked on UNIX, creating many variants. Most of the variants now comply with set standards at the system level. There remains enough difference between the variants of UNIX, however, that applications must be adjusted for each. Since there is no standard GUI for UNIX, developers must write for Motif, Open Look, and others.

In contrast, do not expect Microsoft to release the source code of Windows NT. As a result, software developers do not need to worry about writing more than one version of their application for Windows NT.

Size

UNIX is huge. It requires 60–95M of disk space and at least 8M of RAM for a single user. Although Windows NT is not small, a large part of the 75M that it requires is a swap file that you can adjust.

Market Penetration

There is no comparison between the number of UNIX versus Windows operating systems, or the number of applications available for each. UNIX has a great following in the scientific and engineering community. An entire generation of users and programmers has grown accustomed to the power of UNIX.

The number of UNIX users is small compared to the number of Windows 3.*x* users, however. If a significant number of those users decide to migrate to Windows NT, Microsoft could sell more NT operating systems in one year than UNIX has sold in its 25-year history.

The number of applications that will run on Windows NT might even make UNIX users envious and create converts. Third-party support might make the difference between the usability of UNIX versus Windows NT and thus determine the predominant high-end operating system for the next 10 years. Although UNIX applications have the advantage of being 32-bit applications, Windows NT applications will take only a short time to also become 32-bit applications.

The following table summarizes many of the functions of these systems that were discussed in this chapter.

Table 2.2
Functions of Windows NT, UNIX, and OS/2

Function	*Windows NT*	*UNIX*	*OS/2 2.1*
Multitasking	Yes	Yes	Yes
Multiuser	No	Yes	No
Multithreaded	Yes	Yes	Yes
Symmetric multiprocessing	Yes	Most variants	No
Virtual memory	Yes	Yes	Yes
Protected mode	Yes	Yes	Yes
C2-level security	Yes	Optional (some variants)	No
Object-oriented user interface	No	No	Yes

Function	Windows NT	UNIX	OS/2 2.1
Portable	Yes	Yes	No
Networking	Yes	Yes	Yes
Client or server	Both	Both (most variants)	Both
Runs DOS applications	Yes	Some variants	Yes
Runs 16-bit Windows applications	Yes	Some variants	Yes
Runs 32-bit Windows applications	Yes	No	No
Runs OS/2 16-bit applications	Character mode only	No	Yes
Runs OS/2 32-bit applications	No	No	Yes
Runs POSIX applications	Character mode only	Most variants	No

Summary

Although the long-term success of Windows NT certainly is open to question, the underlying technology behind the 32-bit operating system surely has few equals. This chapter examined the architecture of Windows NT and looked at its many strengths and occasional weaknesses.

The chapter covered such topics as Windows NT's 32-bit architecture, multitasking, multithreading, multiprocessing, networking, and security. It also chronicled the similarities and differences that exist between two alternative operating systems, UNIX and OS/2.

The next chapter continues in this comparison mode, looking at the new features that a Windows 3.1 user will see as he begins to work with Windows NT.

3

CHAPTER

Migrating from Windows 3.1

If you are a Windows 3.1 user, one of the great benefits you will discover as you migrate to Windows NT is that Windows NT looks and feels almost exactly like the Windows you already know. With only a few additions, the Windows 3.1 interface is duplicated in Windows NT. Beneath the surface, however, a lot has changed. This chapter introduces you to many of the new features of Windows NT, including the following:

- Booting Windows NT
- Quitting Windows NT
- Using Program Manager's new features
- Using Control Panel's new features
- Using Print Manager's new features

Most of the sections in this chapter do not provide detailed instructions about ways to complete tasks. Instead, they are meant to introduce you to many of the new and revised functions of Windows NT. Later chapters in the book describe in more detail many of the new features mentioned here.

Booting Windows NT

As you start your computer, you immediately notice the absence of the familiar DOS command line. Instead, you automatically boot up the graphical interface of Windows NT. Instead of seeing the traditional Program Manager used in Windows 3.1, an initial dialog box appears, as shown in figure 3.1.

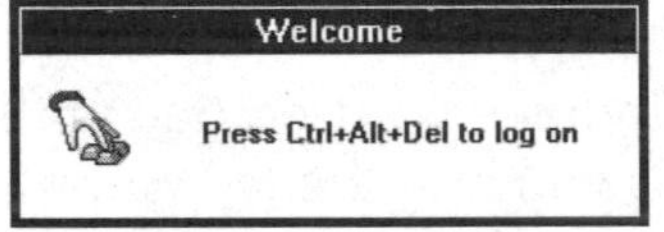

Figure 3.1: *Windows NT's secure attention sequence dialog box.*

This securing dialog box forces you to press Ctrl+Alt+Del before proceeding into Windows NT. This key combination is normally used to reboot your computer or, in Windows 3.1, to close a "hung" application. Windows NT uses Ctrl+Alt+Del to ensure that no *trojan horse*—a program loading before Windows NT—violates the security of your computer or network.

The Ctrl+Alt+Del procedure is but one example of why some people will migrate to Windows NT and some will not. Most of the security measures are entirely unnecessary for the individual user. For large companies managing confidential mission-critical information, however, Windows NT can be the perfect secure fit.

After the Ctrl+Alt+Del key sequence, a second Welcome dialog box appears for logging on to the Windows NT system (see fig. 3.2).

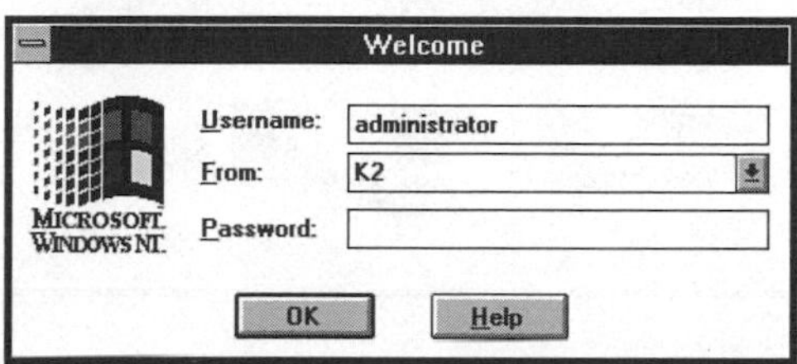

Figure 3.2: *Windows NT's Logon window.*

Windows NT is a secure system that can restrict your rights as a user. If you are not on a network, you are the superuser, which means that you can view and change all the files and use all the system resources. You enter your superuser password during Windows NT's Setup program.

If you are on a network, the system administrator creates a user profile for you. The *user profile* is a small database that specifies which files you can see and access, edit, and execute; and which system resources, such as printers, you can use.

Notice that Windows NT fills the Username field with the user name of the previous user. If you logged on last, this feature saves you some typing.

After you supply your user name, the name of your computer (or the server your computer belongs to), and your password, the security subsystem makes sure the entries are correct. If they are, the security subsystem creates an access token, which is your personalized key that allows you to view, edit, and execute files, or use system resources in Windows NT. The access token is derived from your user profile, which lists your privileges in the system.

The security subsystem sends the access token to the Win32 subsystem. Win32 displays Program Manager (see fig. 3.3).

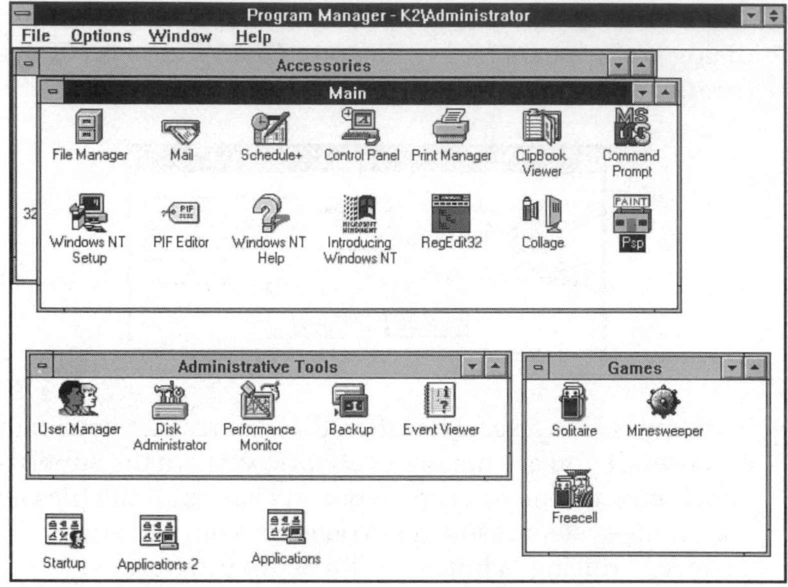

Figure 3.3:
The Windows NT Program Manager.

The only difference between Program Manager in Windows NT and in Windows 3.1 is the File menu. In addition to the Windows 3.1 options, the Windows NT File menu includes Logoff and Shutdown, described next.

Quitting Windows NT

To quit Windows NT, you need to take a few more steps than when you quit Windows 3.1. Choose Logoff in the File menu of the Program Manager, or press Ctrl+Alt+Del. Windows NT responds by displaying the Windows NT Security dialog box, as shown in figure 3.4.

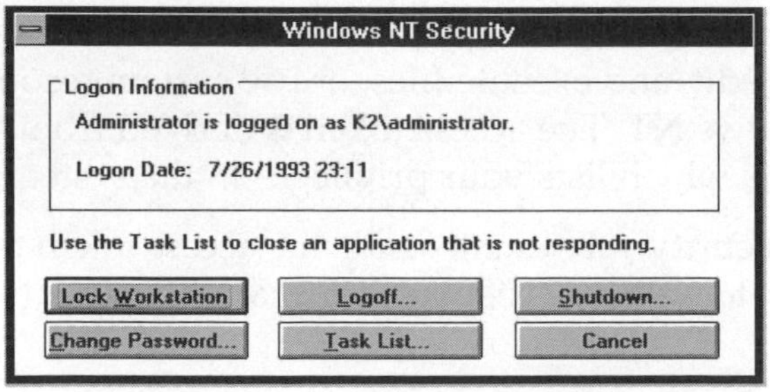

Figure 3.4:
Windows NT Security dialog box.

Windows NT Security

Logon Information

Administrator is logged on as K2\administrator.

Logon Date: 7/26/1993 23:11

Use the Task List to close an application that is not responding.

Lock Workstation | Logoff... | Shutdown...

Change Password... | Task List... | Cancel

To end a Windows NT session, do not just turn off the computer! You might lose data.

To log off only, click on the Logoff button in the Security window. To turn off the computer, click on the Shutdown button. Shutdown saves all changes in active files, then closes applications and services correctly.

Surveying New Windows NT Applets

Most of the familiar Windows 3.1 applets remain unchanged in Windows NT. A few new applets also are included, as described in table 3.1.

Table 3.1
New Windows NT Applets

New Application	*Use*
Mail	Sends and receives electronic mail. (This applet is included in Windows for Workgroups.)
Schedule+	Schedules meetings with fellow employees, creates a personal calendar, and sets alarms. (This applet is included in Windows for Workgroups.)
ClipBook Viewer	Shares excerpts of files across a network. (This applet is included in Windows for Workgroups.)
Introducing Windows NT	Shows a demonstration of the many features new to Windows NT.

continues

Table 3.1
Continued

New Application	*Use*
User Manager	Creates user profiles and user groups, and defines access rights.
Backup	Backs up the hard drive onto another storage medium, such as a tape drive. (This application is included in DOS 6.)
Event Viewer	Displays a list of events performed on a computer, such as warning messages, error messages, and information messages. Time, date, user, and source are included with the event description.
Disk Administrator	Partitions a disk, creates or deletes Administrator volume sets, extends volumes and volume sets, creates and deletes stripe sets, changes drive labels, and displays general information about a disk, such as partition information and free space.
Performance Monitor	Displays performance characteristics (by using Monitor charts and reports) of processors, memory, cache, threads, and processes; either on your computer or in the network.

Using Control Panel's New Features

Most of the icons in Control Panel are familiar, and the configuration utilities they start are identical to those found in Windows 3.1. Figure 3.5 shows the Control Panel icons.

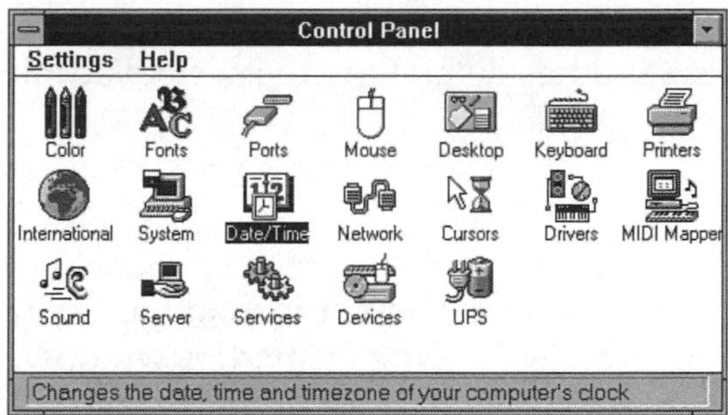

Figure 3.5:
Control Panel.

There are, however, several new ones, as shown in table 3.2.

Table 3.2
New Control Panel Icons

Application	*Use*
Cursors	Changes the appearance of the cursor.
Devices	Configures, starts, or stops device drivers
Server	Starts and manages print, file, and communication services on the local computer.
Services	Starts, stops, pauses, or continues services, such as the printer; and defines setup options.
System	Specifies the default operating icon system. This is valuable only if you have more than one operating system installed on your computer.
UPS	Configures the uninterruptible power supply that saves open files during power failures.

Control Panel Features for the System Administrator

Windows NT provides the system administrator with the tools to assign users to groups, to define the users' access to files and system resources, and to field system errors. The following utilities detail how the system administrator can accomplish those tasks.

Server

When you click on the Server icon in the Control Panel, Windows NT displays the Properties window. This window shows you the number of users connected remotely (Sessions), the number of file locks (File Locks), the number of resources open (Open Files), and the number of open pipes (Open Named Pipes).

Viewing Sessions

You can view the list of users working on the system and the resources they use by clicking on the Server icon and choosing the Users button in the Properties window.

This dialog box shows the name of the user, the computer on which he is working, the number of resources being used, how long the present session has lasted, and how long the computer has been idle. When you select a user, the dialog box displays the resources he has used, how many times the user has used the resources, and times of use. From this dialog box, the system administrator can terminate one or all user sessions by clicking on the Disconnect or Disconnect All buttons, respectively.

Viewing Resources

You can view the list of resources in use on the system and the names of the users connected to them by clicking on the Server icon and choosing the Shares button in the Properties window. Windows NT displays the Shared Resources dialog box.

From this window, the system administrator can eliminate from the system one or all resources by clicking on the Disconnect or Disconnect All buttons, respectively.

Replicating Directories

You can copy directories from a server to computers in the network by using the Directory Replication option. When you click on the Server icon and choose the Replication button in the Properties window, Windows NT displays the Directory Replication dialog box.

In this dialog box, you specify the parameters, such as the computer and path, into which you are importing directories.

To prevent directories from being replicated, click on the Manage button in the Directory Replication window. Windows NT displays the Manage Imported Directories dialog box.

This dialog box enables you to lock or unlock directories and view information pertinent to locking directories.

Alerting Users

Alert messages signal problems with resource use, such as a full disk. They also show problems with the server, such as printer errors, access problems, user-session problems, and power losses. The Alerts dialog box enables the system administrator to list users who should receive alert messages.

Display the Alerts dialog box by clicking on the Server icon in the Control Panel and choosing Alerts from the Properties dialog box.

Services

When you click on the Services icon in the Control Panel, the Services dialog box appears (see fig. 3.6).

The Services dialog box enables you to start, stop, pause, and continue system services. You also can specify parameters for services when Windows NT starts, including which services should start automatically. Services include servers, schedule, logon, and the uninterruptible power supply. The Services dialog box displays the status of each service on the computer. Many of these services are new to Windows users; the new services are listed in table 3.3.

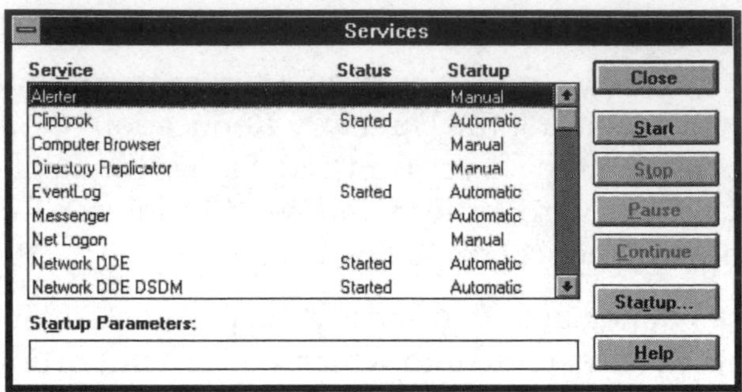

Figure 3.6:
Services dialog box.

Table 3.3
Services Available in the Services Window

Service	*Description*
Alerter	Sends alert messages to selected users. This service enables users other than the system administrator to receive alert messages.
Computer Browser	Records and updates a list of all the computers in the network.
Directory Replicator	Copies directories from one computer to another.
Event Log	Maintains the event log that lists system, security, and application events.
Messenger	Sends and receives system administrator or Alerter messages.
Net Logon	Verifies user logon requests.
Schedule	Runs programs and commands at a defined time and date.
Server	Provides file, printer, and pipe sharing through remote procedure call (RPC) support.
UPS	Monitors the uninterruptible power supply.
Workstation	Establishes network communications and connections.

Devices

The Devices dialog box enables you to start and stop device drivers, and to specify which devices should begin automatically when the computer starts or when the system starts. Devices include network cards, disk drives, and printers.

Clicking on the Devices icon in the Control Panel displays the Devices dialog box, as shown in figure 3.7.

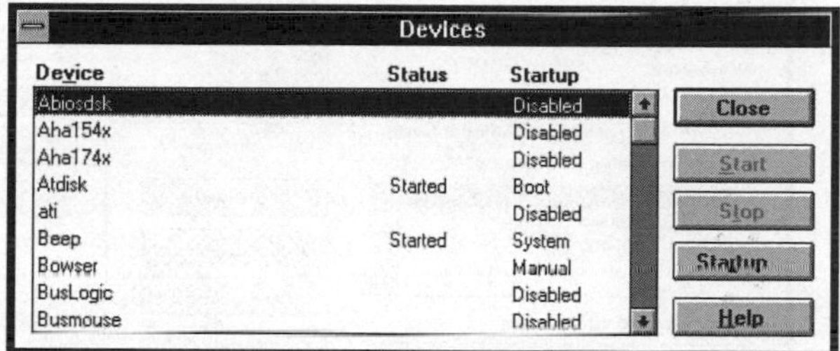

Figure 3.7:
Devices dialog box.

Revised Control Panel Features

In addition to the brand-new features in the Control Panel, Windows NT offers enhanced versions of previously existing utilities.

Date/Time

New to the Date/Time dialog box is the option to set your time zone and to denote when you switch to daylight savings time. Among other reasons, this feature eliminates the need to reset your clock whenever you switch from daylight savings to standard time, and vice versa. The Date/Time dialog box is shown in figure 3.8.

Network

The features in the Network Settings dialog box are greatly enhanced. Clicking on the Network icon displays the Network Settings dialog box (see fig. 3.9).

Figure 3.8: *Date/Time dialog box.*

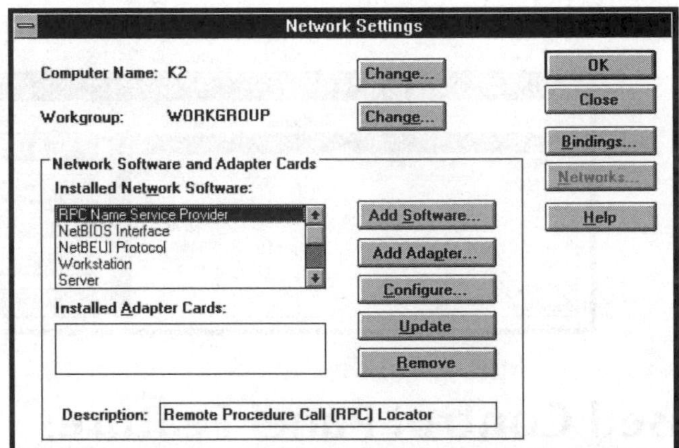

Figure 3.9: *Network Settings dialog box.*

This new version of the Network utility bears little resemblance to that found in Windows 3.1. The Network Settings dialog box displays the software installed on the network and the network adapter cards installed in your computer. You can add, update, configure, and remove network software and adapter cards through this dialog box.

Joining Workgroups and Domains

You also use the Network Settings dialog box to join a workgroup or domain. By clicking on the Change button next to the Workgroup field, Windows NT displays the Domain/Workgroup Settings dialog box, as shown in figure 3.10.

A workgroup *is a set of computers with names that appear together when you browse the network for resources. Anyone can join any workgroup.*

A domain *is a set of computers assembled by the network administrator. This set of computers also appears together when browsing the network for centralized user and group accounts. The network administrator assigns computers to domains, which provide you access to the network. If you change the name of the domain, you cannot log on to the network without asking for the network administrator's assistance. You can, however, still log on to your computer.*

Domain/Workgroup Settings
Computer Name: K2
Member of:
Workgroup: WORKGROUP
Domain:
Create Computer Account in Domain
Domain Administrator User Name:
Domain Administrator Password:
This option will create a computer account on the domain for this computer. It is for use by domain administrators only.
OK
Cancel
Help

Figure 3.10: *Domain/ Workgroup Settings dialog box.*

Renaming Your Computer

You also can rename a computer by clicking on the Change button next to the Computer Name field in the Network Settings dialog box. Windows NT displays the Computer Name dialog box (see fig. 3.11).

Figure 3.11: *Computer Name dialog box.*

If you are connected to an NT Advanced Server domain, the new computer name must have an account on the active domain; otherwise, you cannot access files on the network.

Binding Network Cards

When you click on the **B**indings button in the Network Settings dialog box, Windows NT displays the Network Bindings dialog box. The Network Bindings dialog box enables you to unbind (disconnect) a network adapter card from all network components. You might do this if you rarely use one of the cards in your computer and want to eliminate from memory the software drivers associated with the card.

Changing the Default Network Order

If you click on the Networks button in the Network Settings dialog box, Windows NT displays the Network Provider Search Order dialog box. If your computer is connected to more than one network, use this dialog box to set the order of networks through which your computer searches to complete various operations.

MIDI Mapper

The MIDI Mapper dialog box has a different look. In addition to choosing the driver to match your sound board, for example, the MIDI Mapper dialog box enables you to display the setup configuration, patch maps, and key maps.

System

You might have noticed the absence of the 386 Enhanced icon. In its place, the System dialog box (accessed by double-clicking on the System icon in the Control Panel) enables you to define, among other options, the size of the paging files to use for virtual memory. The System dialog box is shown in figure 3.12.

When an application requires more RAM than is available, Windows NT moves some memory from RAM into the paging file. As with Windows 3.1, Windows NT suggests an appropriate size for the paging files. Unlike Windows 3.1, however, you can spread the paging files across several drives.

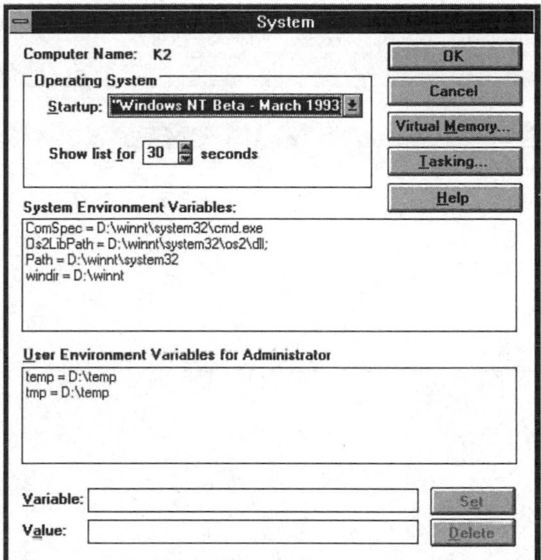

Figure 3.12:
System dialog box.

The System dialog box also enables you to view (not edit) system environmental variables, such as those used with Path; and to view and change user environmental variables, such as the drive on which you want to put the paging file.

Using Print Manager's New Features

The Print Manager in Windows NT is far more powerful than that of Windows 3.1. The Windows NT Print Manager is shown in figure 3.13.

Windows NT's Print Manager is actually three windows in one:

- **Print Manager window.** Provides the tools to work in the other two windows. It also displays the printers installed on your computer as icons, and displays the server to which your computer is connected.

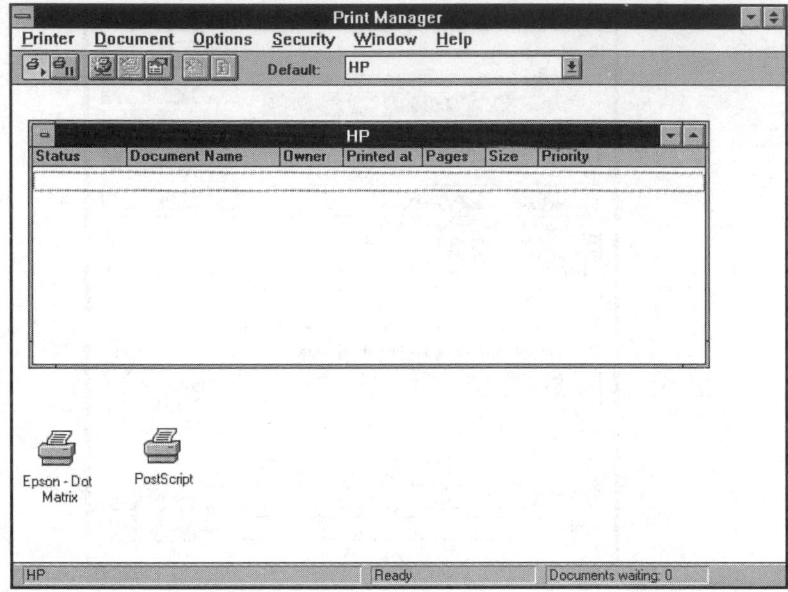

Figure 3.13: *Print Manager.*

- **Printer window.** Displays information about one of the printers to which your computer is connected on the network (the name of the printer appears in the title bar). It shows the printer queue with a variety of values associated with each print job, including the number of pages, the owner of the print job, and the name of the document printing.
- **Server dialog box.** (Accessed by choosing the Server Viewer option from the Printer menu.) Displays information about all the printers connected to your computer through the network.

Summary

As you have seen in this chapter, Windows NT has a similar "look and feel" of Windows 3.1, but also has capabilities far more extensive than its 16-bit cousin. This chapter highlights a sampling of these differences.

Because Windows NT is a secured operating system, not just an operating environment like Windows 3.1, its start-up and shutdown procedures are much more structured and controlled. Consequently, you have to log on to Windows NT—even if you are running it on a stand-alone PC on which security is never an issue.

On the surface, Windows NT's Program Manager, Control Panel, and other applets look identical to their Windows 3.1 counterparts. As you look more closely, however, you can see many key enhancements. Control Panel, for example, has several new or revamped configuration utilities designed for the system administrator. Additionally, the Print Manager is completely overhauled and now provides extensive control over printers and print jobs.

As you work through the next chapter on installing Windows NT, and actually set up Windows NT on your machine or network, you have much to learn about the new 32-bit operating system. Windows 3.1 users should take comfort in the similarity of the two interfaces. Thus, although you may not understand all the new features on your Windows desktop, the resemblance of Windows 3.1 and Windows NT will make your transition to a new operating system much easier and smoother than you may have thought possible.

Installing Windows NT

Before you install Windows NT, make sure your computer meets minimum hardware requirements. If your computer barely qualifies, Windows NT runs very slowly. Instead of increasing your computer's performance, the 45M operating system drags out the simplest commands.

The installation process is simple, much like the installation of Windows 3.1. If you choose a custom installation, you need to know a number of things about your system.

This chapter tells you what you need to know to complete a Windows NT installation, including the following:

- Understanding hardware requirements
- Preparing to install Windows NT
- Understanding Windows NT setup
- Configuring Windows NT for users
- Solving installation problems

Understanding Hardware Requirements

The hardware requirements for Windows NT are more stringent than those to which the casual user is accustomed. The following list summarizes Microsoft's recommended minimum hardware configuration:

- A 32-bit processor, 386 (25 MHz) or higher. Actually, Windows NT runs like molasses on anything less than a 486.
- Alternatively, Windows NT runs on RISC-based microprocessors, such as the MIPS R4000 and DEC Alpha.

If you are a PC user, skip the discussions concerning RISC-based computers.

- A high-resolution video display, VGA or better.
- A minimum of 65M of free hard disk space (45M for the operating system; 20M minimum for the swap file).
- A high-density floppy drive for *x*86 processors. If you have only a low-density drive (one that holds only 1.2M of information), you need to buy a higher-density drive that holds either 1.44M or 2.88M of memory.

Make sure your computer's BIOS supports a 2.88M drive before you buy one.

- For RISC processors, an SCSI CD-ROM drive. Windows NT doesn't support all CD-ROM drives or SCSI controller cards. Check with manufacturers for Windows NT compatibility.

Access CompuServe (WINNT forum) to find out whether a drive or card is supported.

- A minimum of 8M of RAM (12M is recommended).

Remember that minimum requirements mean minimum performance. You can put premium gas in a Model T, but it doesn't run any faster than on regular gas. Likewise, you can use Windows NT on a relatively slow computer, but program execution may be slower than with Windows 3.1. Exceed the minimum hardware requirements by as much as you can afford.

Optional hardware includes the following:

- A mouse or other pointing device.
- An SCSI CD-ROM drive for *x*86-based processors (required for RISC processors).
- A network card if you want to run Windows NT on a network.

The CD-ROM drive for *x*86-based computers is used simply to install Windows NT and future Windows NT applications. You can install Windows NT instead from 21 high-density floppies.

Windows NT can run on individual computers, but many of its features are geared for network environments such as sophisticated security, mail, and scheduling systems. Thus, if your computer is not on a network, you should consider whether Windows NT will benefit you.

Preparing To Install Windows NT

The Windows NT Setup program requires the following information:

- If your computer is on a network, you must know the computer's name and the name of the workgroup or domain to which your computer belongs.

A workgroup *is a group of servers and computers that can easily share information in a peer-to-peer manner (similar in functionality to Windows for Workgroups).*

A domain *is a group of computers and servers, but a single security system governs access to the individual components of the group.*

- If a printer is connected directly to your computer, you must know the port (LPT1, for example), and the brand and model number of the printer.
- If your computer is on a network, you must know the following features about the network adapter card in your computer:

    The name of the adapter card

    The Interrupt Request Number (IRQ)

    The base I/O address

- You must know the partitions on your hard drive using disk-compression products. You cannot place Windows NT on a compressed partition.
- You must know the amount of free space on the hard drive. Eliminate files and applications from your hard disk until it has 75M or more of free memory. (You should know this information before you install Windows NT.)

- Decide whether you want to keep Windows NT as an upgrade to Windows 3.1 or as a separate operating system.

Consult your network card manual or your system administrator for information.

Understanding Setup

You can install Windows NT in the following three ways:

- From a CD-ROM or floppy disks
- Over a network
- By using the Computer Profile Setup

If your computer has a CD-ROM or floppy drive, install Windows NT directly from those drives. Windows NT takes more hard disk space when you install over a network.

The Computer Profile Setup enables system administrators in large corporations with many identical computer platforms to install Windows NT easily.

Installing Windows NT from a CD-ROM or Floppy Disks

Windows NT comes with a boot disk and a CD-ROM (or a set of 21 floppy disks). It has the information necessary to initiate Setup, including the Setup application, mechanisms to identify SCSI adapters on the computer, a list of the most popular SCSI device drivers—located in the *.SYS file—and the Setup instruction routine (called TXTSETUP.INF).

Windows NT does not support all CD-ROM drives and SCSI controllers. If you have problems, consult the manufacturer of your SCSI controller, and ask if there is an updated device driver that is compatible with Windows NT. If there is not, consider buying a compatible controller card.

If your SCSI driver is Windows NT-compatible but is not contained on the boot disk, copy the driver to the boot disk. Then you should be able to proceed with Setup by using your CD-ROM drive.

An SCSI connector *is a 25- or 50-pin (SCSI-2) cable that enables fast throughput of data.*

When you are ready to begin installation, put the boot disk in drive A (and the CD-ROM disk in its drive, if you have one) and reboot the computer. The Setup program begins in text mode. During the setup process, Setup reboots your PC again; at that time, the installation continues. Later, after you reboot the computer again, the program continues in graphical mode. The following discussions explain both of these modes.

A nice feature of the Setup program is that it creates an emergency disk. You use this disk to recover your system if you inadvertently erase a system file or the Boot Loader. To create the emergency disk, you need a blank floppy for drive A.

Text-Mode Setup

The *text-mode* portion of Setup works like a traditional DOS display: no windows, few graphics, mostly text.

After you reboot the computer with the boot disk, the Setup Loader file (SETUPLDR) loads a file (Windows NTDETECT) that detects the hardware in your system. Setup then gives you the opportunity to choose Custom Setup or Express Setup.

Express Setup uses the hardware configuration detected with Windows NTDETECT, and assumes what you might like Windows NT to install.

Custom Setup enables you to control other important features, such as the size and location of the paging file. If you have more than one hard disk, or your hard disk has more than one partition, you might want Windows NT to put the paging file on the least-fragmented hard disk for optimum speed. Setup might otherwise automatically choose the drive with the most free space.

After you choose Express Setup or Custom Setup, Setup looks in your computer for one of the SCSI drivers listed on the boot disk. If it finds one of the drivers, it accesses the CD-ROM drive. If it doesn't, it continues to check hardware features such as the display adapter type, mouse, machine type, and keyboard.

Setup then asks you to confirm the disk drive, partition, and directory name where Windows NT is to be copied. Here, you can create or delete partitions on the disk. You might want to put Windows NT on its own partition if the rest of the disk is compressed. You also can change from the present disk file system, such as FAT (the file system used with DOS and Windows 3.*x*), to the Windows NTFS format.

If you change the format of a disk, you can reformat or convert from one disk filing system to another. Be careful! If you choose to reformat the partition, all files in the partition are destroyed. Converting the format, on the other hand, preserves the files on the partition.

The Windows NT File System (Windows NTFS) offers a number of advantages over FAT, including the following:

- Enables Windows NT's security system to enforce various access rights to files and directories
- Keeps an event log that you can use to restore the system if a power failure or other problem happens
- Accepts file names of up to 256 characters
- Enables DOS, Windows, OS/2, and POSIX programs, running through Windows NT, to access Windows NTFS files

Only Windows NT has access to partitions formatted in Windows NTFS. If you want to run DOS or OS/2 sometimes, instead of Windows NT, use the FAT format. DOS and OS/2 do not have access to files on Windows NTFS partitions.

If you format your entire hard disk with Windows NTFS, you can't even run DOS from your hard disk (although you can still run DOS-based applications through Windows NT).

You can change the file systems on any partition after you complete Setup. To change from Windows NTFS to FAT or HPFS (OS/2's high-performance file system), you must reformat the partition, which destroys the information on it. You need to back up all files on the partition before you reformat.

After you specify the destination for Windows NT, Setup uses CHKDSK to check the partition to confirm that it is in good shape. If so, Setup then looks on your hard disk to see whether Windows 3.*x* or Windows for Workgroups is installed.

If it is, Setup recommends that you upgrade to Windows NT, which means that Windows NT will go in the same directory as Windows 3.*x*. You can choose, instead, to create a new path for the installation (such as \WINNT), and leave Windows 3.*x* as is.

If you choose the default setting, it installs on top of Windows 3.1, and it is removed from your system.

At start-up, you can run DOS, Windows 3.x, or Windows NT. If Windows NT is in a different directory from Windows 3.x, the two do not readily share information.

After you decide whether to upgrade Windows 3.*x* or provide a separate directory for Windows NT, Setup copies the core files of Windows NT to the hard disk, including the files that enable you to boot and operate in graphical mode. After you remove the boot disk in drive A, reboot your computer. The computer screen turns blue, which is your confirmation that Windows NT is loading. Windows NT then displays the device drivers it is loading into the system.

Graphical-Mode Setup

After rebooting, Setup continues in *graphical mode*, which looks like a traditional Windows display. It has windows, rich graphics, buttons, and task-completion indicators.

The first window that appears in graphical mode prompts you for your name and the name of your company. The second window asks for the name of your computer. Ask your system administrator if a name is already chosen for your computer or if the computer name is determined by applying a certain pattern or logic, such as DepartmentName02.

Do not name your computer with the domain's name or workgroup's name. Windows NT will reject your choice.

If you chose Express Setup, Setup continues the installation process automatically. If you chose Custom Setup, however, you can install printer drivers, install network drivers, and create groups of applications already on your drive. If you install these features, Setup asks for the following information:

- **Virtual Memory.** Setup asks for the location and size of the paging file (PAGEFILE.SYS). The *paging file* is where Windows NT swaps data from RAM to disk when too much data must be loaded into RAM. Because the data is on disk, not RAM, it is called *virtual memory*.

Setup puts the paging file at the root directory of the hard disk because it operates faster that way. Setup displays the minimum size of the paging file (usually 20M) and a larger, recommended size.

If you chose Express Setup, Windows NT automatically makes your paging file the recommended size. In Custom Setup, however, you have the opportunity to change the size of the paging file, as long as it equals or exceeds minimum requirements.

- **Printer Setup.** You have full configuration control over your printers. You can specify a default printer, the port to connect it to, the size of its memory, the paper size and tray, and a variety of other variables.

  Setup enables you to install printer drivers for printers shared by non-Windows NT computers. If, however, you need access to a printer shared by a Windows NT computer, you only need to put the printer drivers on the computer that is sharing the printer.

- **Network Setup.** Setup automatically detects and displays information about your network card, including the I/O port address, the memory address setting for the card, and the IRQ setting. You can check and correct these settings with Custom Setup.

  After you approve the settings, Setup constructs the default client/server relationship and installs the appropriate network services and support files.

  Setup displays the Network Control Panel so that you can confirm the software and hardware configuration of your network. After you approve the settings, Setup binds the network card to the system.

- **Workgroup and Domain Setup.** Setup enables you to join a workgroup, a domain, or both.

  If you join a workgroup, Setup asks for your user name and password. If you join a domain, Setup asks for the domain to which you want to belong. If the name of your computer is not listed in the domain, you must supply the name of an administrator and a password. Otherwise, you cannot join the domain.

If you work on an isolated computer, it makes no sense to join a workgroup or a domain.

- **Application Setup.** Setup creates the application groups in Program Manager that are familiar to Windows 3.*x* users, including Main, Accessories, Startup, Games, and Administrative Tools.

The Administrative Tools group, new in Windows NT, is accessible only to members of the administrative group. Administrators use these tools to manage Windows NT. For example, administrators create users and user groups on the system, and define their access rights and permission sets (such as read-only permissions).

Setup detects all the applications on the hard disk and places them as icons into the Program Manager groups, as long as Windows NT and Windows 3.*x* are in the same directory. In Custom Setup, you can create the groups manually.

Now that you have completed the major installation steps, Setup is ready to make an emergency disk for you. Setup makes sure that the disk in drive A is not the boot disk before it copies the configuration information onto the disk.

Because you specified the name of the computer and the name of the workgroup and domain to which it belongs, the emergency disk applies only to your computer. You can't use someone else's emergency disk on your computer in the case of a disaster. Be sure to keep the emergency disk with the computer at all times.

To complete Setup, you are prompted to enter your time zone. Choose it from the drop-down list. Remove the emergency disk, reboot your computer, and begin to enjoy Windows NT.

When you reboot your computer, Windows NT starts. If you have other operating systems on the hard disk, the Windows NT Boot Loader asks you to choose the operating system you want to boot. (It starts Windows NT by default if you do not select another system within 25 seconds.)

Installing Windows NT over a Network

If a corporation has a large number of computers, the WINNT Setup utility makes it easier to install Windows NT on every computer. Windows NT Setup records all the Setup files found on the CD-ROM and floppy disks into a server directory, the *WINNT sharepoint*. (Setup /n, in Windows 3.1, performs a similar action.) All other computers on the network then install Windows NT from the sharepoint.

WINNT Setup is just like Windows NT Setup, except that it sits on a file server in its own directory, and it creates the boot disk on client computers.

The command to install the WINNT sharepoint is:

```
SETUP -n -i initial.inf -s <source_path> -d
<destination_path>
```

You can install a WINNT sharepoint on a non-Windows NT-supported network. The command that creates the WINNT sharepoint must run Windows NT, however. You must, therefore, install Windows NT on at least one computer in the network to perform this action.

Although you can install Windows NT over a non-Windows NT-supported network, your computer no longer sees that network after you install and run Windows NT.

If you use WINNT Setup to set up Windows NT on a computer, WINNT Setup first creates the boot disk that comes with the CD-ROM disk (and is the first disk in the set of installation floppy disks). WINNT Setup then downloads all files necessary to complete the installation into a directory called WIN_NT.~LS on the local computer.

WINNT Setup instructs you to reboot your computer with the boot disk in drive A. The rest of the setup procedure is identical to that described for the CD-ROM and floppy-disk installation.

Besides the obvious convenience of using WINNT Setup to install Windows NT on a large number of computers, WINNT Setup has some other advantages:

- Because the installation files reside on the local hard disk, the installation procedure goes more quickly because accessing a hard disk is faster than accessing a CD-ROM or floppy disk.
- More than one computer can use WINNT Setup simultaneously.
- If the system administrator customizes the Windows NT installation, that customization carries through to all computers on the network.

Installing Windows NT by Using Computer Profile Setup

The Computer Profile Setup is appropriate for businesses in which all the computers on the network have identical configurations.

You complete the Computer Profile Setup in two steps. In the first step, Create Profile, you create an installation template. In the second step, Install Profile, you apply the template to all the computers.

You run the *Create Profile* utility on a computer that is configured exactly the same as all others in the network. This utility detects a wide variety of information about the computer's setup, including device drivers, Program Manager groups, and user databases. It then puts that information into a file (which has a CPS extension) with all other installation files.

The *Install Profile* utility takes the information in the CPS file and uses it as an installation template for all similar computers in the corporation. The user is prompted to supply only the name of the computer and the domain to which it belongs, if any.

Installing Windows NT on a RISC-Based Computer

Installing Windows NT on a RISC-based computer is the same as installing it on an *x*86 (Intel-based) computer. Only the task of starting the Setup program (from the CD-ROM disk) is different.

You can install Windows NT only from a CD-ROM disk on RISC-based computers. Consult the manufacturer of your system to find out the correct way to boot your system from a CD-ROM disk.

Although different computers start in different ways, once the Setup program starts, it is identical to the *x*86 installation, described previously.

You must create a FAT partition, called the *system partition*, on your hard disk. The hard disk must contain at least 2M of memory to hold the files that load Windows NT, including OSLOADER.EXE and HAL.DLL (in the \OS\NT directory).

You can make the partition large enough to include all the Windows NT files. If your hard disk doesn't have a system partition, consult the manufacturer's instructions for creating one.

An installation procedure that works for some RISC-based computers is as follows:

1. After restarting your computer with the CD-ROM disk in its drive, select Run A Program from the menu on the ARC screen.
2. Type **cd:\mips\setupldr** at the prompt and press Enter.

   If Setup doesn't begin, try substituting the full device name in place of cd:.

Configuring the Operating Systems

After Windows NT is installed, the system administrator has duties to perform for each of Windows NT's operating systems. The following sections discuss these responsibilities.

Configuring the Windows NT Environment

The system administrator can perform the following tasks to configure Windows NT for users:

- Set up accounts for users in workgroups and domains by using User Manager.

The User Manager, *an application in the Administrative Tools group in Program Manager, enables system administrators to create users and user groups.*

- Specify the applications in the Program Manager groups. Program Manager groups come in two types: common and personal. Applications in the *common* groups are available to all users of the computer.

  Applications in the *personal* group appear to (and are accessible by) specific users only. Even when many people use the same computer, the Program Manager can individualize the applications that are available to each user.

- Set up access privileges for users by using the User Profile Editor. You can, for example, restrict the user from accessing games, specific Program Manager groups, or the File Run menu.

- Define various user variables; for example, the local group to which the user belongs, the home directory, and the automatic expiration date of the account.

Configuring the Windows 3.1 Environment

As in the past, all environmental information for Windows 3.1 is in the WIN.INI and SYSTEM.INI files. If Windows 3.1 and Windows NT are in the same directory, Windows NT can use and update these files to configure the Windows environment. Windows NT, however, stores environmental information in a database called the Registry, not in these files.

If the operating systems are in the same directory, Windows NT can coordinate the two Window environments in the following ways:

- Windows NT records the information in WIN.INI and SYSTEM.INI files into the Registry each time you start Windows NT. The changes you make to the Windows 3.1 environment transfer to the Windows NT environment.

- Changes made to the Windows NT environment also transfer to the Windows 3.1 environment. Windows NT updates the WIN.INI and SYSTEM.INI files when you shut down Windows NT.

If you erase Windows 3.1 from your disk, Windows NT provides empty WIN.INI and SYSTEM.INI files for Windows 3.1-based applications to record configuration data.

Configuring the DOS Environment

To create the DOS environment, Windows NT reads the AUTOEXEC.BAT file when you log on; it reads the AUTOEXEC.NT and CONFIG.NT files when you start DOS applications.

The AUTOEXEC.NT and CONFIG.NT files are the equivalents of Windows' AUTOEXEC.BAT and CONFIG.SYS files.

The AUTOEXEC.BAT and CONFIG.SYS files define a variety of variables that your operating system uses every time it runs. Some examples of these variables include the kind of keyboard you use, the mouse type, the applications you can start from any prompt, and the language (such as French) that your system uses to communicate with you.

The CONFIG.NT file supports, with few exceptions, the same configuration variables found in Windows 3.1, including `country`, `device`, `dos`, `echoconfig`, `fcbs`, `files`, `install`, `loadhigh`, `rem`, `shell`, and `stacks`. The new variable, `echoconfig`, if selected, displays messages from CONFIG.NT and AUTOEXEC.NT when you begin applications.

The AUTOEXEC.NT file supports, with few exceptions, the commands found in MS-DOS 5.0 and 6.0.

PIF Files

The AUTOEXEC.NT and CONFIG.NT files create the general environment for DOS applications. As in Windows 3.1, however, you can use *program information files (PIFs)* to customize the environment for individual applications.

In PIF files, you specify environmental variables for DOS applications running in Windows, such as the amount of expanded and extended memory to reserve for the application, the name of the file displayed in the application's icon, and the name of the file that initiates the application, such as Word.

The PIF files in Windows NT are somewhat different from those in Windows 3.1 because Windows NT is a preemptive multitasking operating system.

As in Windows 3.1, you can use the PIF editor (an application in the Main group) to create the PIF file, use the default PIF (_DEFAULT.PIF), give the PIF file the same name as the DOS application to which it pertains, and create more than one PIF file for an application.

You can create more than one PIF file if you want Windows to reserve two different amounts of expanded memory for a DOS application, depending on the size of the data file processed by the application.

You can even continue to use old PIF files in Windows NT. However, Windows NT precludes the use of many PIF variables, and simply ignores them if they are set (for example, the priority settings or when the application runs exclusively in the foreground). Windows NT manages the timeslices that applications get, not the applications themselves.

Windows NT adds one new feature to PIF files. You can create start-up files to configure the environment for each application you run.

Configuring the OS/2 Environment

Launching an OS/2 application starts the OS/2 protected subsystem in Windows NT.

The OS/2 protected subsystem *is the OS/2 operating system. You do not see OS/2's GUI (graphical user interface), however. Instead, you see Windows NT's GUI.*

Remember that the OS/2 subsystem runs only character-based OS/2 applications.

The first time the subsystem starts, Windows NT uses the information in the Registry to configure the OS/2 environment. If no information is found, Windows NT uses the data in the original CONFIG.SYS file. If Windows NT doesn't find a CONFIG.SYS file, the following default information is added to the Registry:

```
PROTSHELL=c:\os2\pmshell.exe c:\os2\os2.ini
c:\os2\os2sys.ini   %SystemRoot%\system32\cmd.exe
SET COMSPEC=%SystemRoot%\system32\cmd.exe
```

Windows NT supports a subset of the configuration variables found in the OS/2 CONFIG.SYS files, including `protshell`, `devicename`, `libpath`, `set`, `country`, `codepage`, and `devinfo=KBD`.

The `libpath` variable adds path information in the Windows NT environment to the OS/2 library path. The `devicename` variable names device drivers for OS/2 applications (that are compatible with Windows NT).

Some of the OS/2 commands that are not supported in Windows NT include `set path`, `set compspec`, `set video_devices`, `set vio_ibmvga`, `set vio_vga`, *and* `set prompt`.

Solving Installation Problems

You can run up against a number of common installation problems. The following list describes some solutions to those problems.

Solving SCSI Problems

If Setup can't find your CD-ROM drive, try the following:

- Make sure that the last and first devices in an SCSI chain are terminated properly.
- Make sure that all terminations are removed from devices in the middle of an SCSI chain.
- Make sure that the last devices internally and externally are terminated properly if you have both internal and external devices in an SCSI chain.
- Make sure that your SCSI controller card is not terminated.
- Make sure that the drivers for your SCSI controller are compatible with Windows NT. If not, ask the manufacturer for an upgraded version of the driver.
- Make sure that the CD-ROM drive does not have 0 or 1 as an ID. 0 and 1 are often reserved for hard disk IDs.

Solving Boot Problems

If, after completing Setup, Windows NT doesn't start after rebooting the computer, check the following:

- Make sure that your hard disk has enough space for the paging file (20M minimum).
- Make sure that BOOT.INI values use the correct Windows NT path.
- If you see the message `BOOT: Couldn't find NTLDR`, insert another disk. (You have inadvertently erased the NTLDR file, and you need to copy it back to your systems file.)
- If you see a similar message about NTDETECT, copy NTDETECT.COM into your systems directory.
- You may see the following message:

  ```
  Couldn't open boot sector file.
  multi(0)disk(0)rdisk(0)partitions(1)\bootsec.dos
  ```

  This message means that the file BOOTSEC.DOS, which enables you to load alternate operating systems, is not at the root directory. This is trouble, and it is best to reinstall Windows NT.

  If you have a second computer with exactly the same disk tracks, heads, cylinders, and sections, you can copy its BOOTSEC.DOS file to your computer.

If this procedure fails, your entire hard drive may become unreadable. Try this rescue only if you are familiar with binary-editing tools and low-level disk structures.

- Most other boot problems can be solved by recopying BOOT.INI to your systems file and making sure that BOOT.INI and NTLDR are both in the system root directory.

Solving Networking Problems

If Setup cannot install on the network your computer is on, check the following:

- Make sure that the IRQ setting for the network card doesn't conflict with another device's IRQ setting.
- Make sure that the computer's name is unique and is not the same name as a domain or workgroup.
- Review Windows NT's error log by using the Windows NT's Event Viewer. It might identify the problem.

A variety of incompatibility problems can occur with specific pieces of hardware. If problems persist, call the dealer or manufacturer for technical help.

Summary

This chapter examined the three different ways of installing Windows NT, and explained Custom and Express setup procedures. You learned how to configure different operating systems in Windows NT. The chapter ended with suggestions for solutions to common installation problems.

Once you get the Setup program running, installing Windows NT is no more difficult than installing Windows 3.1. As long as your computer equipment exceeds the minimum hardware requirement for Windows NT, and you are armed with the appropriate knowledge of your hardware before you begin the installation, Setup should proceed smoothly.

Configuring the operating system environments requires a bit more expertise, however. It is usually a good idea to let the system administrator set the operating system environments.

Managing the Windows NT Desktop

Learning the Windows NT Interface

Mastering the Windows NT Desktop

Configuring and Customizing the Windows NT Desktop

Using Windows NT Applets

Printing and Managing Fonts

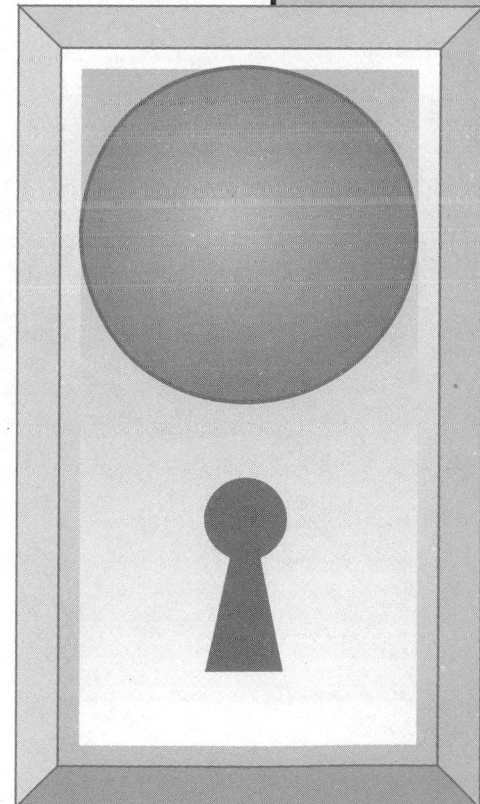

PART 2

Learning the Windows NT Interface

Paradoxically, as operating systems have become much more powerful and architecturally complex, they also have become easier to use. Today's state-of-the-art operating systems (particularly Windows NT and OS/2) are graphical environments, in which you use a pointing device to perform many actions instead of typing archaic instructions at a command prompt. New Windows NT users should take comfort in the fact that the graphical nature of Windows NT makes it easy to navigate and use.

This chapter begins a discussion of the Windows NT interface. An *interface* is what an operating system uses to interact with the user. Windows NT uses the familiar Windows interface found in Windows 3.1.

Additionally, the chapter talks about the concept of Common User Access (CUA), by which basic commands (such as opening or printing a file) are done similarly across different applications. The following topics are covered:

- Examining the Windows NT interface
- Using the mouse
- Working with windows and icons
- Performing common Windows tasks
- Introducing WYSIWYG and MDI

Historically, the interface used in most operating system environments has been the *command-line interface* (CLI), and the operating system is represented by the *command prompt* (`C:>` on most MS-DOS systems, `$` on most UNIX systems).

You enter commands at the command prompt by typing at the keyboard. The prompt tells you that the computer is ready to receive information. To start a program, type the program's name and press Enter.

In most operating systems, simple file-manipulation commands consist of two words—a verb followed by a noun, as in the MS-DOS command DELETE MYFILE.TST. Commands can be complex (involving other nouns and options), and the command-line interface can be intimidating to the novice user. Although MS-DOS and OS/2 commands are based on the English language, they can appear cryptic (for example, RD stands for Remove Directory in DOS). UNIX commands are famous for being cryptic because each consists of such a two-letter abbreviation.

In Windows NT, this verb-noun process is reversed. First, you select the item to be manipulated; you then indicate the action to be performed. The action can involve moving the mouse and clicking the mouse button, selecting an item from a menu, or entering text from the keyboard. In many cases, especially within applications in which the same item is manipulated a number of times, the item already is selected by Windows NT, and you need to specify only the action.

Examining the Windows NT Desktop

As you have learned, Windows NT is a graphical user interface (GUI) that dramatically changes the way in which users interact with the computer. To become comfortable with the Windows NT environment, you must get used to a different way of doing things. Instead of entering commands at a prompt, you use the keyboard or mouse to manipulate symbols on the screen. This collection of symbols is the heart of the Windows NT environment.

As you enter Windows NT after logging on, you see the Windows NT desktop, as shown in figure 5.1. The term *desktop* often is used to refer to the entire Windows NT environment. Technically, the desktop is the screen background for Windows NT, but the term is used to signify all the things you see when you look at the Windows NT screen (like the items on an office desktop). Each new task is run within individual display areas called *windows*.

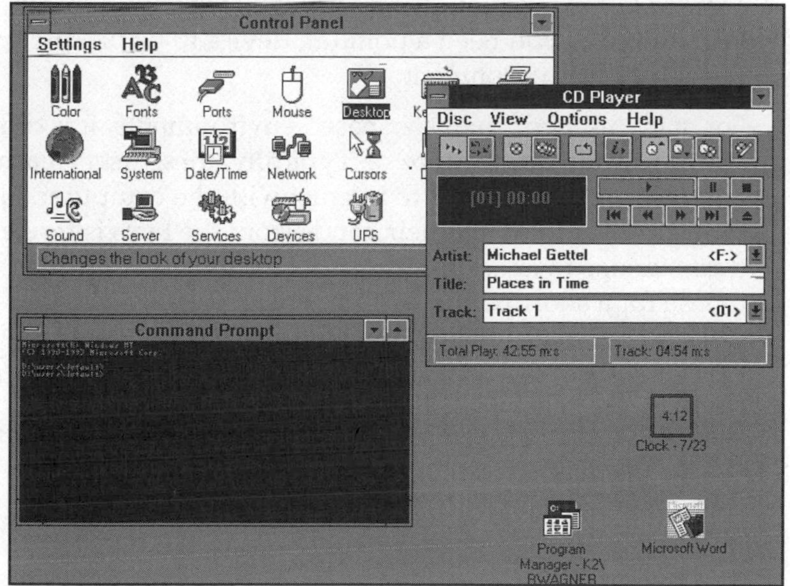

Figure 5.1: *Windows NT desktop.*

Many users who are used to DOS and UNIX find multiple windows a curiosity because few DOS or UNIX programs have exotic options that give you new ways to look at your documents.

If you use a spreadsheet, for example, you can use one window for the data-input area; another window can show the grand totals for the worksheet. As you enter new numbers, you see the effect in terms of total expenditures on the bottom line, even hundreds of rows below. You even can compare two versions of a letter you are writing, or you can keep an outline in one window while writing the body of your text in another.

Using the Mouse

While in Windows NT, most actions are performed by using a mouse or other pointing device. Although there are keyboard equivalents for most mouse actions, they are cumbersome to use. Even though a mouse is not required to run Windows NT, you need a pointing device to be productive in the graphical environment.

For many users of character-based environments, it is difficult to learn to use the mouse. Typically, these users learned how to use the keyboard to interact with the computer. Now, the action of removing their hands from the keys is foreign to their standard way of working. Once they work with a mouse for a short period of time, however, the actions become second nature.

A single mouse action can replace several commands that you must type and execute individually at the command prompt.

The location of the mouse is represented on-screen by the *pointer* (sometimes described as the *mouse cursor*). The standard pointer is the arrow, as shown in figure 5.2.

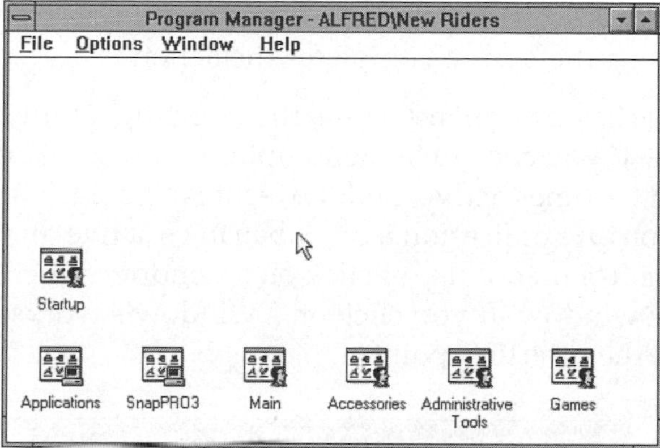

Figure 5.2:
The location of the mouse, represented by the arrow pointer.

The pointer and the mouse move together. By sliding the mouse away from you, you move the pointer up on the display. By pulling the mouse toward you, you move the pointer down on the display. Side-to-side motions move the pointer to the left and right on the display. This activity of changing the location of the mouse pointer is often called *pointing* in Windows NT.

Windows NT enables you to choose a custom mouse cursor. Chapter 7 describes ways to customize your mouse cursor.

Besides pointing, there are four other mouse actions; each one has an action associated with it that application programs exploit. These mouse actions are described in the following sections.

Clicking with the Mouse

Mouse actions are performed by using the mouse buttons. In a standard Windows NT environment, the left mouse button is the select button. Depressing and releasing the mouse button is referred to as *clicking* the button. In most situations, clicking the mouse button while the pointer is over an object selects that object, causing it to become active. The item actually is selected when the mouse button is first pressed; releasing the button completes the action.

If you click on a menu name, the menu opens and becomes active. If you click on a menu option, the associated command becomes active, and it executes (see fig. 5.3). If you click on an application icon, it becomes active and displays its Control menu. If you click on a window, it becomes the active window. If you click on a window's workspace, you move the insertion point.

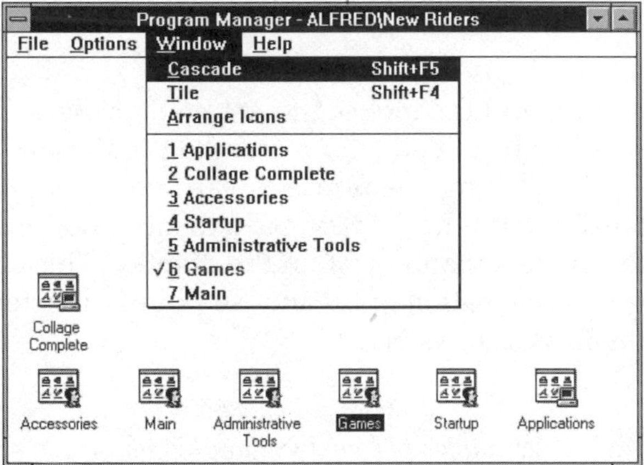

Figure 5.3:
The result of clicking on a menu.

In addition to activating objects on screen, you also can use the click to execute an action. For example, dialog boxes often have OK and Cancel buttons. By clicking the OK button on the Open dialog box, you open the specified file. If you click the Cancel button instead, the dialog box closes without taking any additional action (that is, opening a file).

Because a click action is not performed until you release the mouse button, you can cancel a click action in progress by moving the mouse pointer away from the object before releasing the mouse button.

One mouse click saves you multiple keystrokes when you have to cycle through a list of objects on the screen or move the cursor from the lower right corner to the upper left corner. The mouse enables you to be more efficient.

By default, the left mouse button is used to select an object. However, you can change your mouse configuration to enable the right button to act as the select button. Instructions are given in Chapter 7.

As Windows 3.1 and Windows NT become more object-oriented, a trend gaining increasing popularity is the *right click*—clicking the right mouse button over an object. The right click is used to inspect and/or change the properties of a given object. Right-clicking on a cell in Quattro Pro for Windows, for example, brings up a dialog box in which you can change a host of cell properties, such as the font, color, and so on.

Right-clicking is much easier and faster than moving the mouse to the menu at the top of the window to perform an identical action.

Paradox for Windows, Excel, and Quattro Pro for Windows are three examples of Windows applications that use the right click. Expect this feature to be added in future versions of other applications as well. In fact, it is likely that the right click will be integrated into future versions of Windows 3.*x* and Windows NT.

Double-Clicking with the Mouse

Double-clicking is pressing the mouse button twice in rapid succession (usually within one-half of a second). Double-clicking has a rhythm to it, so do not be disappointed if it takes some time to get the hang of it. Double-clicking activates an object and causes it to take a predefined action.

If the two clicks are not done within the time limit, the action is seen as two separate clicks rather than as one double-click. The double-click action typically is used to start applications and open new windows.

Double-clicking on an icon, for example, activates the icon and causes it to open and display the associated window (see fig. 5.4). Each type of icon opens and displays its window differently. It might launch a new application, for instance, or display information present in memory.

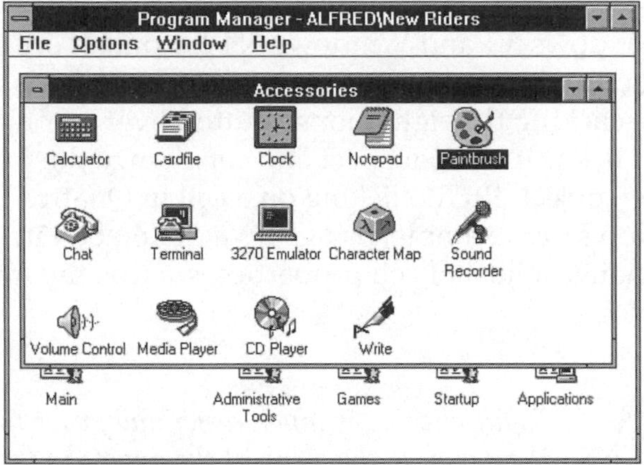

Figure 5.4:
The result of double-clicking on the Accessories program item icon.

Double-clicking on the Control menu box activates the Control menu and selects the Close option. You can exit any window that has a Control menu box in this manner.

Dragging an Object

Many actions within the Windows NT environment involve changing the position of an item on-screen by *dragging* the item to a new location. To drag an item, position the pointer over the item, press the mouse button, move the mouse to the new location (while still holding down the mouse button), and then release the mouse button. Each of these steps serves a specific function.

The item first is selected by positioning the pointer over the item and pressing the mouse button. Because the action is not yet completed, the mouse button is not yet released. Moving the mouse moves the items, and when the item is in its new location, the action is completed by releasing the mouse button. Although this combination of actions might seem awkward at first, it quickly becomes a simple task.

Dragging can dramatically affect objects. If you drag the title bar of a window, the entire window moves about on the screen. Dragging a window border changes the window's size. Dragging an icon moves it about on the screen. Dragging the insertion point selects an area of the workspace.

Dragging is like using the arrow-control key combinations in DOS programs. Screen items change position, and you can mark screen blocks for block operations. Using the mouse to perform such actions is faster than using the keyboard, and boosts efficiency. Figure 5.5 shows a result of dragging.

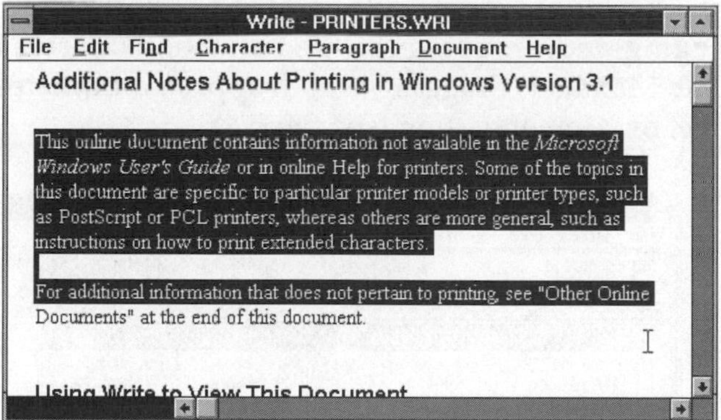

Figure 5.5:
The result of dragging on the workspace.

Dragging in Windows NT is like using the keyboard to mark screen blocks in programs that run under other, nongraphical operating systems.

Dragging and Dropping

The final mouse action is called *dragging-and-dropping*. In this action, you drag an object with the mouse as previously described. The goal of dragging the object is not to change its location on the screen, but to take an action on the object. You drag the object over another object—one that is capable of taking action on the object you are dragging. Then you release the mouse button, dropping the dragged object on its destination. The destination object opens and takes a default action on the dropped object.

File Manager is one application in which you can put drag-and-drop to good use. You can, for example, select a text file from the file list and drag-and-drop it on an open Notepad window; this action causes Notepad to open the text file automatically.

You also can drag-and-drop a file name onto a directory icon to move the file from its current path into the chosen directory. Or you can copy a selected file to another drive by dragging-and-dropping the file name onto a drive icon. Thus, in File Manager, dragging and dropping automates an open, move, or copy operation (see fig. 5.6).

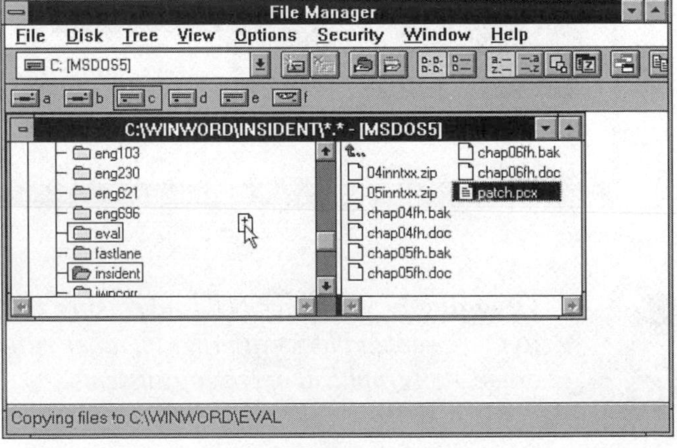

Figure 5.6:

A drag-and-drop in process in File Manager.

Dragging-and-dropping enables you to perform very complex processes with a fraction of the effort of typing commands at a command prompt. As a result, you gain in productivity.

Use the following exercise to become familiar with basic mouse actions:

1. Click on the Program Manager window to make the Program Manager the active application. (If you do not see the Program Manager on the desktop, check to see if it has been reduced to an icon at the bottom of the screen. If it has, double-click on the icon to activate the Program Manager.)
2. Open the Accessories program group by double-clicking on the icon labeled Accessories.
3. Select the Notepad icon by moving the mouse, placing the pointer over the icon labeled Notepad, and pressing the select button once. This process is known as *clicking on the item.*
4. Select the Write icon by placing the mouse on the icon and clicking it.
5. Double-click on the Notepad icon. This process opens the Notepad program.
6. Place the pointer at the bottom right corner of Notepad's window so that the pointer changes to a double diagonal arrow.
7. To resize the Notepad window, drag the window by pressing and holding the select button, moving the mouse to make Notepad's window smaller, and then releasing the select button.
8. Double-click on Notepad's title bar, which is located at the top of the program. It shows the name of the application or document.
9. Select Notepad's minimize button, which is the down-arrow button in the upper right corner of the Notepad window.

10. In the Program Manager, drag any icon from within the Accessories window and drop it on any group icon that appears along the bottom edge of the window. You have moved the program represented by the dropped icon into the group you dropped it on. (You can undo this move by opening the group, dragging the icon back where it was, and dropping it in place.)

You can see that manipulating items in the Windows NT environment is an easy task when you use the mouse.

Windows NT often uses a three-dimensional appearance for buttons and other screen objects. Usually, these 3-D objects "move" when you click on them with the mouse—indicating that the mouse click is seen by Windows NT.

Using the Mouse Pointer

Within the Windows NT environment, the pointer often changes to indicate the type of action being performed. Figure 5.7 shows several common Windows NT pointers. These pointers inform the user that Windows NT is ready to perform a special type of task.

When resizing an object, the pointer changes to a multi-headed arrow. The directions of the arrows indicate the directions that the object can be moved. When moving an object, the pointer changes to a ghost of the object. A *ghost*, within Windows NT, is an object that is represented with a light gray outline or a special picture.

One of the most common (and least-loved) pointers is the hourglass, which appears when Windows NT is performing a task that requires you to wait. Although it is annoying to have to wait, the hourglass lets you know that the system still is functioning.

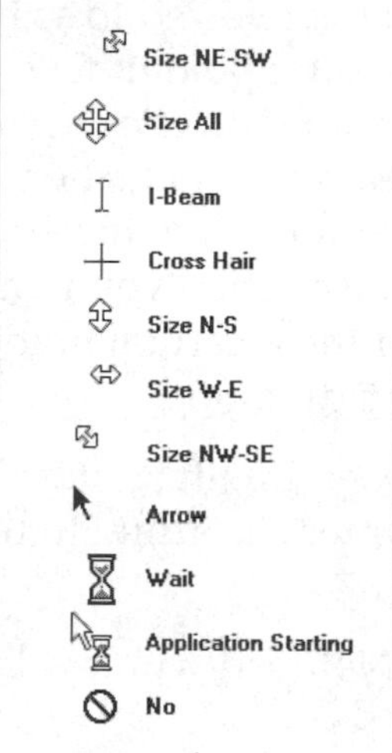

Figure 5.7:

Pointer appearance indicates Windows NT's current function.

Because Windows NT is a multithreaded and multitasking operating system, a new mouse cursor that combines the arrow and the hourglass has been added. It shows you that the system is busy with one application, but that you are free to continue work with others.

Users familiar with Windows 3.1 also know that the hourglass rarely appears over the background layer of the desktop in Windows NT. Usually it appears only while the cursor is over a busy application. One of the advantages of multithreading and multitasking strategies employed in Windows NT is that you can work with other applications even though one application is busy.

When working with text in Windows NT, the standard pointer is replaced with a steadily flashing dark vertical bar called the *insertion point*. This bar indicates the location at which new text is inserted when you start typing. This mouse pointer looks like a capital I.

A related pointer is referred to as the *I-beam pointer* because of its shape. This mouse pointer tells you where you will move the insertion point if you click at the current location of the mouse. The I-beam appears when you move the mouse pointer over a window in which you can insert text, and tells you that the mouse action you would perform by clicking is the relocation of the insertion point. It also tells you that you can select text by dragging.

The following exercise illustrates the way Windows NT changes the pointer according to the current action. Follow these steps:

1. Select the Notepad window by clicking inside it with the mouse.
2. Place the pointer inside the Notepad window and notice the shape of the pointer. It changes to the I-beam pointer.
3. Move the pointer into the title bar. The pointer changes back to the arrow pointer.
4. Place the pointer on the top window border. The pointer changes to an up/down arrow to indicate window resizing.
5. Select the Program Manager window, and choose the Accessories group.
6. Drag the Clock icon outside of the Accessories group window (not inside another group window). The pointer changes to a prevent pointer to indicate that the icon cannot exist outside of the group window.

You see from this exercise that Windows NT gives you visual clues about the function of the pointer as the task changes. Windows NT also uses the shape of the pointer to give you information about your actions, as is the case with the prevent pointer.

Working with Windows and Icons

As its name suggests, the basic element of the Windows NT interface is a *window*, which is a rectangular area on the screen that displays information from a program. A window can be expanded to cover the entire screen. In this state, the window is said to be *maximized*.

If you no longer need to view the information in the window, but you want to keep it active, you can reduce the window to an *icon* (a small graphical representation of an application). This process is referred to as *minimizing* a window. To restore the icon to a window, double-click on it. Figure 5.8 shows several common Windows applications as windows (Clock and Notepad) and as icons (Program Manager and File Manager).

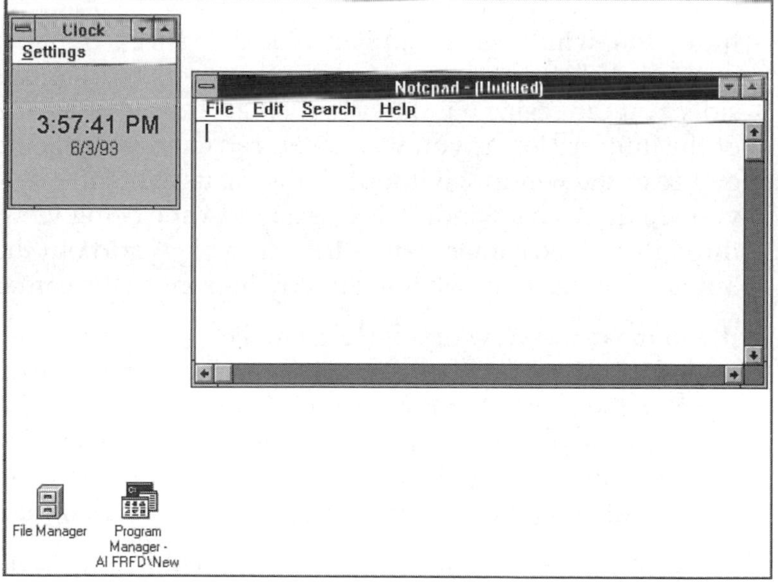

Figure 5.8: *Program windows and icons on the desktop.*

Each Windows NT application has its own window, referred to as a *parent window* or *application window*. The coordination of the parent windows is managed by the Windows NT environment.

Each application may in turn contain windows of its own. These windows, called *child windows* or *document windows*, are managed by the application. A child window always is contained within its parent window, but all the child windows are not necessarily displayed. The terms child window and parent window are used when discussing the window's relationships; the terms application window and document window are used when discussing the window's contents.

If an application supports child windows, it is said to have a multiple document interface *(MDI). For more information on working with an MDI application, see the discussion later in this chapter.*

Individual windows are similar to flexible sheets of paper: you can stack them on top of each other or place them side by side. You can resize windows to display as little or as much of the information as you want. You can change the position or size of the window without changing its content. The view you see through a window is like a landscape being viewed through a video camera lens—there is a big world out there, but you can see only what is directly in front of the camera.

If you make the view or aperture smaller, you see less of the same view. To see an item that is not in the current view, increase the amount of information in the view (make the view larger). If that does not work, move the camera. If you want to maintain your first view and see another item, get a second camera (open a new window), as shown in figure 5.9.

Not all of the spreadsheet can be shown within a document window. To view the remainder of the spreadsheet, you must change the view in one of the document windows by using the scroll bars.

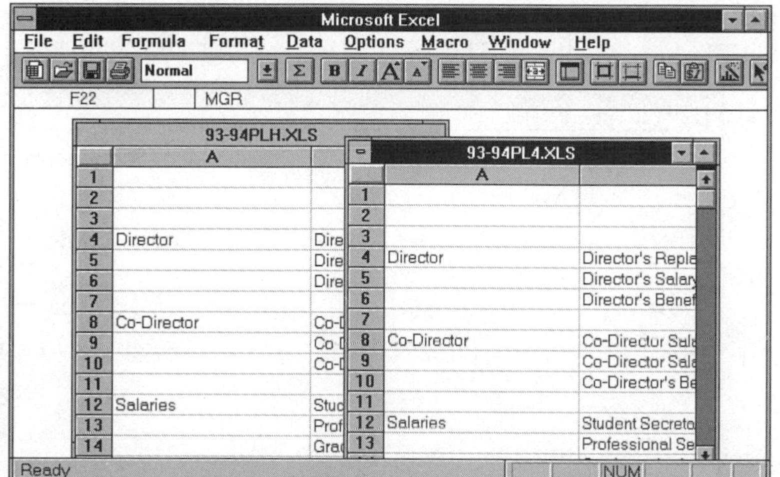

Figure 5.9: *Two spreadsheet windows in Excel.*

Basic Window Elements

All windows within the Windows NT environment have the same basic set of elements. These elements enable you to manipulate the window's view and its position. Each component is used to perform a specific windows-management task. As with all actions within Windows NT, each of the tasks associated with managing windows can be accomplished a number of distinct ways. Figure 5.10 shows these window elements.

The Windows components are discussed in the following sections.

The Title Bar

Every window has a *title bar* across the top that contains the name of the application (Notepad or Microsoft Excel, for example). If the application window contains a document window that is maximized, the document name also appears in the title bar. Document windows that are not maximized display a document name in the title bar of the document window.

Figure 5.10:

An empty Notepad document, showing the basic window elements.

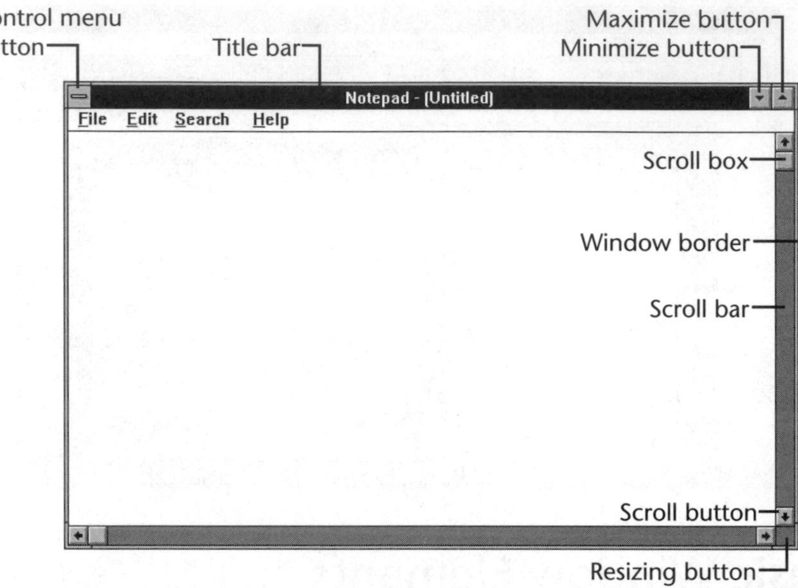

The title bar also is used to indicate the active window. If your desktop is cluttered with many open windows, you easily can tell which window currently is active: the active window's title bar looks different. In Windows NT's default colors, the active title bar is a medium blue; other title bars are gray.

You easily can change the colors of most Windows NT components by using the Color application in the Control Panel. Chapter 7 shows you how to change the color of interface components, such as title bars and background.

Aside from providing information about the program and current document, the title bar can be used to move and change the size of the window. To move a window that is not maximized (or full-screen), select the title bar by clicking on it with the mouse and holding down the mouse button, and then drag the window to the desired location.

To manipulate the Notepad window by using the title bar, follow these steps:

1. Select the Notepad window.
2. Select Notepad's title bar and drag it with the mouse. To do this, press and hold the select button, then move the mouse.
3. Relocate the window by dragging it, as described in step 2. Release the select button to position the window.
4. Select File, and choose Open.
5. Type **BOOTLEG**, and press Enter (or click on OK). Notepad's title bar now includes the name of the file you just loaded.
6. Double-click on Notepad's title bar.

As you discovered in the previous exercise, the title bar has a second function. When you double-click on the title bar, the size of the window toggles between the maximized and windowed states. The same control can be obtained by clicking on the maximize button on the far right of the title bar, as the next section explains.

Maximize and Minimize Buttons

Application windows have two buttons in the upper right corner. These buttons are used to control the way that the application is displayed—as an icon, a window, or maximized. Some document windows contain only the button on the far right, called the *maximize button*. The second button on application windows (the leftmost of the two) is called the *minimize button*. By clicking on the minimize button, you reduce the application to an icon.

The maximize button is a toggle switch—it switches between two functions. When a window is not maximized, the symbol on the button is a single up arrow. By clicking on the button, you can fill the entire screen with the window. When a window is maximized, the symbol changes to up and down arrows, and clicking on it makes the window return to its previous size and position. This button sometimes is referred to as the *restore button*.

Window Border

The *border* around each window can be used to change the size and shape of the window. If you grab the side of the window, you can change only the position of that side. By grabbing a corner, you change the dimensions of both neighboring sides. When you place the mouse on the border or corner, the mouse pointer changes into a double-headed arrow, enabling you to drag the window border to enlarge or shrink the window.

The shape of the pointer when it is over a window border indicates the way in which the window can be resized. The pointer changes to a pair of vertical arrows (resize vertically), a pair of horizontal arrows (resize horizontally), or a pair of diagonal arrows (resize diagonally).

The lower right corner of most windows is an empty square. This square, often called the *resizing button*, also can be used to change the size of the window. Because it is larger than the window border, the resizing button is much easier to grab. You can move the bottom and right sides of the window by dragging the resizing button. When you try to position a window accurately, position the upper left corner of the window by dragging on the title bar, and then use the resizing button to position the remaining two sides.

Not all Windows NT programs provide a resizing button. The Windows NT applets Write and Notepad, for example, do not; Excel and Word for Windows resize in this manner.

Scroll Bars

If a program contains more information than can fit in a window, vertical and horizontal *scroll bars* appear along the right and bottom sides of the window. If all information is displayed within the current window, scroll bars are not needed (many applications thus do not display them). As shown in figure 5.11, Clock does not have scroll bars. Because you can see only one thing inside the window—a clock—you have no need to scroll its window. Notice, however, that the Clock window has all the other window components.

Figure 5.11:
Clock's display does not require scroll bars.

The scroll bar along the bottom shifts the view across the document; the scroll bar along the right side moves up and down through the document. If the document is too large in one direction, only one set of scroll bars appears. A word processing document, for example, may be too long to be displayed in a single view, so the scroll bars on the right side appear. If the document is narrow enough to fit in the window, however, the bottom scroll bars may not appear. Figure 5.12 shows a long list within a Notepad window.

The *scroll buttons* are used to move the document view in the indicated direction. By clicking on the scroll button at the bottom of the scroll bar, you move the view down through the document. You can make the view scroll down (or up) the document by pointing to the scroll button and holding down the mouse button.

To move quickly through the document, you also can drag the *scroll box* along the scroll bar. If you know that the text you are looking for is two-thirds of the way down your document, for example, you can drag the scroll box to a position two-thirds down the scroll bar. When you release the mouse button, the view jumps to the new location.

Figure 5.12:

Notepad always displays scroll bars.

Notepad - WINPERMS.TXT

File Edit Search Help

```
.\ 2,13,4,17
.\system32 2,13,4,17
.\system32\config 2,4,14,17
.\system32\drivers 15,4,2,17
.\system32\drivers\etc 15,4,2,17
.\system32\os2 2,13,4,17
.\system32\os2\dll 2,13,4,17
.\system32\spool 15,4,2,17,18
.\system32\spool\prtprocs 15,4,2,17,18
.\system32\spool\prtprocs\w32x86 15,4,2,17,18
.\system32\spool\prtprocs\w32x86\winprint 15,4,2,17,18
.\system32\spool\printers 15,4,2,17,18
.\system32\spool\drivers 15,4,2,17,18
.\system32\spool\drivers\w32x86 15,4,2,17,18
.\system32\repl 15,4,2,17
.\system32\repl\import 15,2,5,7,4,17
.\system32\repl\import\scripts 15,2,5,7,4,17
.\system32\repl\export 2,8,4,17
.\system32\repl\export\scripts 2,8,4,17
*\ 2,13,4,17
*\boot.ini 2,15,17
```

Besides the scroll bars, most applications allow you to scroll document windows by using the Page Up and Page Down keys.

You can move the view down the document to display the next full window of information by clicking in the scrolling region below the scroll box. Or, by clicking above the scroll box, you move the view up one full window. This technique is recommended for reading through a document. Most programs move slightly less than a full window to enable you to recognize the transition between images.

The Control Menu

On the far left of the menu bar is a button that activates the Control menu, which is a special menu that is a part of both icons and windows. You can click on the Control menu button of a Windows NT application to display the Control menu, as shown in figure 5.13.

Notepad - WINPERMS.TXT
Restore
Move
Size
Minimize
Maximize
Close Alt+F4
Switch To... Ctrl+Esc

Figure 5.13:
All Windows NT applications have the same items on the Control menu.

The same Control menu is displayed by clicking on a program icon on the Windows NT desktop. The Control menu is available even when an application is running full-screen. To display the Control menu for a maximized window, press Alt+space bar.

The Windows NT environment enables you to continue using your MS-DOS and POSIX-compliant UNIX application programs. A DOS or POSIX application that runs under the Windows NT environment is said to run within a DOS or POSIX window.

Windows NT enables DOS programs to use graphics mode and text mode when running in a window. Most DOS and POSIX windows have the Control menu, as shown in figure 5.14.

PWB
Restore
Move
Size
Minimize
Maximize
Close
Switch To... Ctrl+Esc
Edit
Settings...
Fonts...
Screen Size And Position...
Screen Colors...
Hide Mouse Pointer

Figure 5.14:
The Control menu for DOS applications has additional commands.

Document windows also have Control menu buttons. The main difference between a Control menu button for an application and that for a document is that the icon and the keyboard command to activate the menu are slightly different.

The Control menu of a program looks like a long hyphen; the document menu's hyphen is very short, as shown in figure 5.15. This is because each picture (or icon) represents a different key that is required to access the menu from the keyboard.

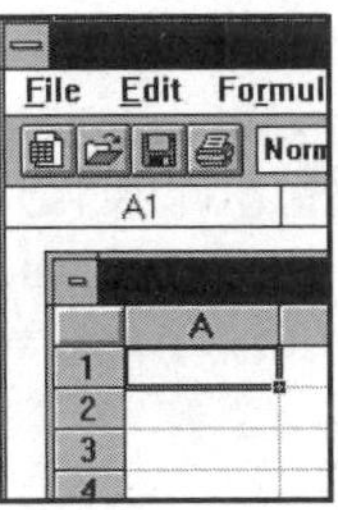

Figure 5.15: *Application and document Control menu buttons are slightly different.*

As mentioned previously, an application's Control menu can be accessed by pressing Alt+space bar. The Control menu for a document window is activated by pressing Alt+hyphen.

Most of the commands on the Control menu are for tasks that can be performed by manipulating the window with the mouse. One of the requirements of the Windows NT user interface is that all tasks also can be performed by using the keyboard. The Control menu provides a way of moving, resizing, and controlling windows by using the keyboard. These commands appear on all Control menus (whether from an application, document, DOS, or POSIX window).

- The **Restore** command is available in Control menus when an application is maximized or minimized. This command is used to return a window to the position and size it was before it was maximized to full-screen or minimized to an icon. (The same action can be done by clicking on the restore button on the far right of the menu bar.)
- The **Move** command is active only when a window is not full-screen. When you choose it, the mouse pointer changes to a four-arrow pointer. By pressing an arrow

key, you can move the current window. You can continue to use the keyboard arrow keys to move the window in small increments, or you can move the mouse. The window moves with the mouse without you having to press the mouse button; clicking (or pressing Esc) stops the window's movement and deselects the command. A window also can be moved by dragging the title bar to the new location. Press Enter to end the procedure.

Some actions are quicker to perform by using the keyboard. When you use a DOS program in a window and you want to switch to full-screen mode, for example, press Alt+Enter. To perform the same action by using the mouse, you must select the program's control button and choose the Maximize command.

- The **Size** option is available only when a window is not full-screen. When you choose Size, the pointer changes to a four-arrow mouse pointer (as with the Move command). You can press any arrow key to select a border, and you then can extend or shrink that dimension of the window. If you press the right arrow once, for example, the right border is selected; if you press the right arrow again, the right border expands to enlarge the window. If you press the left arrow, however, the right border shrinks to reduce the window's size.

You also can select a corner by first selecting one side and then using the arrow to select one of the adjacent sides. You now can expand the window in two directions. Press Enter to end the procedure.

- The Minimize option shrinks the current program to an icon; it is not available when a program already is minimized to an icon.

- The Maximize command is available for both icons and windows, enlarging the current window to fill the screen. (These commands perform the same tasks as the minimize and maximize buttons on the right side of the menu bar.)
- The Close option is used to close a document window or to quit a program. If the Control menu is for an application, Close quits the program. The same task can be performed by double-clicking on the Control menu button. If you forget to save the contents of a document window before you choose Close, Windows NT asks whether you want to save the document before closing.
- The Switch To menu command is found only on an application's Control menu; it is used to activate the Task List. You use the Task List to move from the current program to any other running program.
- The Edit command appears only on the application's Control menu for DOS windows.
- The Settings command appears only on the application's Control menu for DOS windows.
- The Fonts option is available only for DOS windows. It selects the font to be used when displaying the DOS program in a window.

The following exercise takes you through some of the options in a Control menu:

1. Select the Notepad window, then choose the Control menu.
2. Choose **M**ove. The pointer changes to a four-way arrow.
3. Press the right-arrow key on the keyboard a few times.
4. Press Esc.
5. Press Alt+space bar to open the Control menu again.
6. Choose Minimize. Notepad minimizes to an icon.

7. Select the Notepad icon with a single click. The Control menu appears.
8. Choose **R**estore. Notepad restores to a window.

To help you understand the way other commands work in the Control menu, experiment with them. When you are ready to go on, the next section shows you the other types of menus available in a Windows NT program.

Menus

Every Windows NT program, even a simple application program such as Clock, has a menu bar. The *menu bar*, which always is located directly below the title bar, has a collection of the most commonly used commands. The menus within the Windows NT environment are drop-down menus. By selecting a menu name from the menu bar, you can view a list of menu items that drop down from the menu bar. The menu bars of Word for Windows and Excel are shown in figure 5.16.

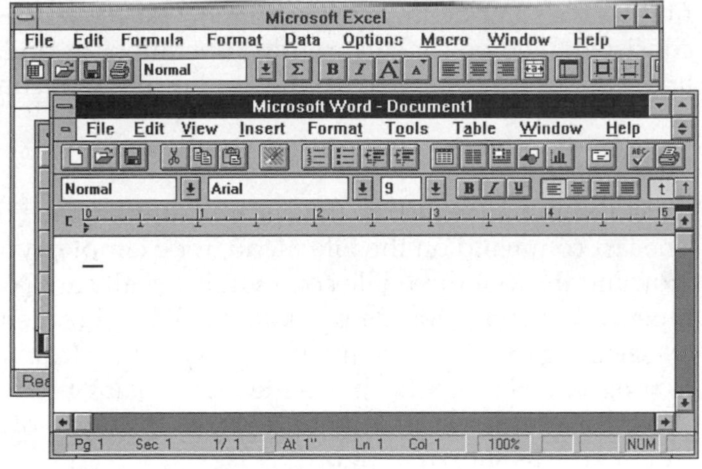

Figure 5.16:
Menu bars for Excel and Word for Windows.

The menu system in Windows NT is very different from that of older DOS and UNIX programs. Windows NT's menus and dialog boxes (discussed later) have streamlined the way you interact with programs. A Windows NT menu is designed to tell you which options are available at any level of the Windows NT menu system.

All menus in a Windows NT application appear as names on the menu bar. Whenever possible, the commands and their locations on the menu bar are consistent from program to program. File, for example, always is the first menu choice, and Help always is the last. The Open command always is on the File menu, and it is used by most programs to open their data files. These common menus are described in the next section.

Common Menus

The File, Edit, and Help menus typically are consistent from one program to another. This consistency is a powerful timesaver for you when you learn a new Windows NT program. After you learn to exit one Windows NT application, for instance, you know how to do it in every other Windows NT program. If you have ever opened a new MS-DOS or UNIX program and not known how to quit the program (without finding the computer's on/off switch), you can appreciate a consistent method for such routine operations as quitting applications and opening, saving, and printing documents.

The File Menu

Several commands nearly always are found on the File menu. The last command on the File menu, for example, typically is Exit, and the first three File commands usually are New, Open, and Close. More important, the dialog box generated by selecting the Open command also is similar from program to program. Figure 5.17 shows the Open dialog box from Word for Windows 2.0. Compare this to the Open dialog box from Excel, as shown in figure 5.18.

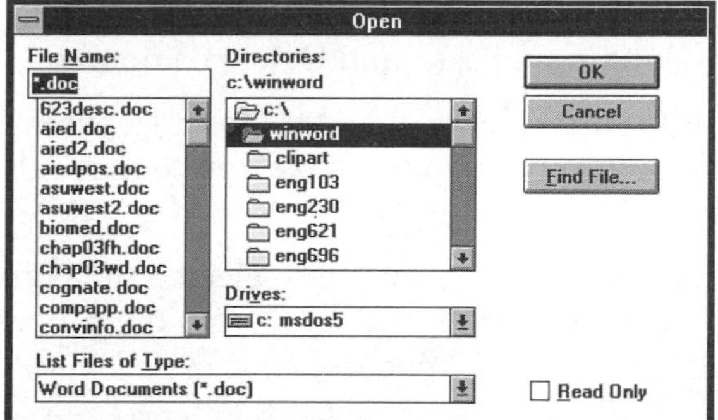

Figure 5.17:

Open dialog box from Word for Windows.

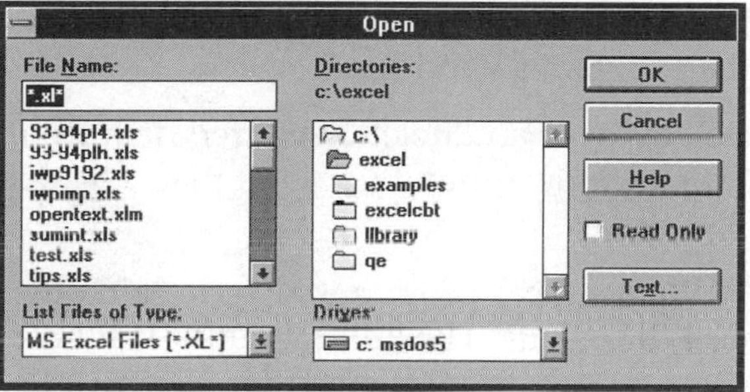

Figure 5.18:

Open dialog box from Excel.

The next pair of commands found on most File menus are those used to save a file—Save and Save As. Not only are the commands the same, but the accelerator keys and shortcut keys (if any) are the same between programs.

The other command commonly found on the menu is the Print command. Depending on the program, a single Print command or a collection of printing menu items (such as Print, Printer Setup, and Print Preview) can be found here.

The Edit Menu

The Edit menu contains commands for moving data between a program and the Windows NT Clipboard, which is a common storage area for data. Data is copied to the Clipboard, and then it is pasted from the Clipboard into the same program or a different program.

The Edit menu for most Windows NT programs contains the Undo, Cut, Copy, Paste, and Delete commands.

The Undo command enables you to cancel your last action; the remaining commands enable you to move data in and out of the Clipboard.

The Cut command removes the selected data (you must select the data prior to cutting it) from the program's window and places it in the Clipboard.

The Copy command copies selected data from the program to the Clipboard.

The Paste command pastes (copies) data from the Clipboard into the program's window.

The Delete command deletes selected data from the program's window, but it does not place the deleted data in the Clipboard.

Many Windows NT programs also contain other commands in their Edit menus. The Edit menu for WinGIF, for example, contains a variety of commands for editing a graphics image (see fig. 5.19).

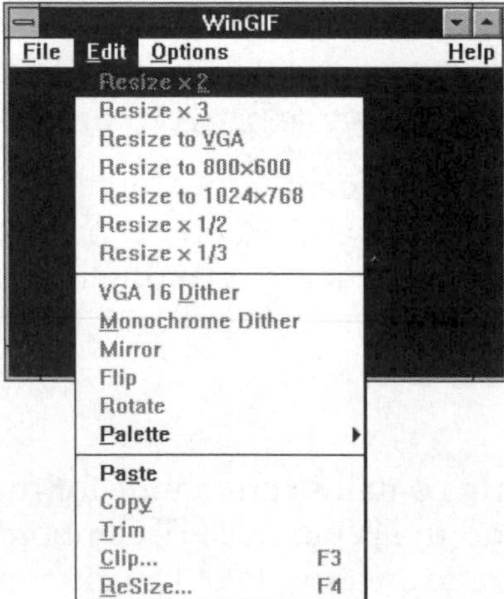

Figure 5.19:
WinGIF's Edit menu.

The Help Menu

Although the Windows NT manuals are helpful, it can often be inconvenient to stop work to look up something. You can get on-line help whenever you need it by selecting the Help command from the menu bar of the program in which you are working.

A Windows NT Help file consists of individual pages of information displayed within a standard window. Only one page can be displayed at a time, but the Help utility provides a variety of methods for moving between pages. The file becomes available through the standard Help menu, as shown in figure 5.20.

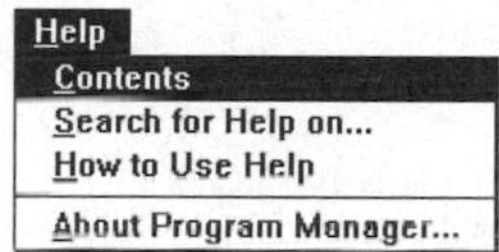

Figure 5.20: *Program Manager Help menu.*

The Contents command on a Help menu opens the Help program and displays a table of contents for the program. Some Windows NT programs include keyboard commands on their help menus that display a list of topics related to keyboard combinations and equivalents for the program's commands. This information can be found within most Help files by searching for the keyword key.

Help menus between programs are not standard because the program, not Windows NT, determines the commands that appear in the help menu. A program's help menu may include a tutorial command, for example, that starts a tutorial program to help you learn to use the program. Most Windows NT programs also include a How to Use Help command on their help menus. By selecting this command, you start Help, and Windows NT then displays a topic page explaining how to use the Help program.

By choosing an item from the Help menu (or by pressing F1), you automatically start the Help utility. After you choose a command from the Help menu (or press F1), the program starts and displays the appropriate topic page of the Help file. Figure 5.21 shows the help information that appears when you choose the How to Use Help command from Program Manager's Help menu.

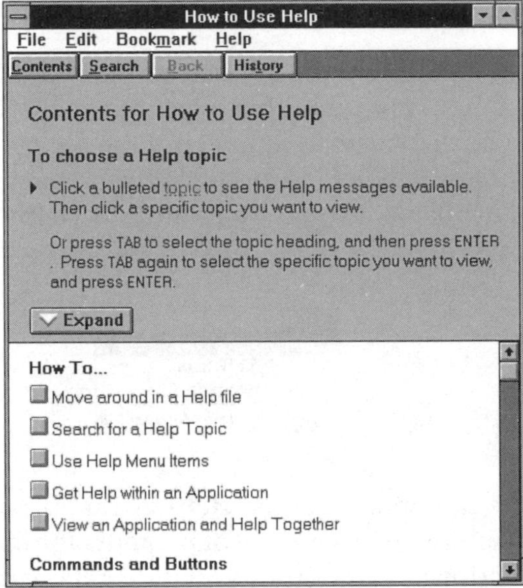

Figure 5.21:

Help even contains information about the Help utility.

The same information is displayed if you press F1 from within a Help file. If you have not taken the time to explore the help system, this is an excellent way to become familiar with it.

In most Windows NT programs, you can click on the Help menu and choose the About option. As shown in figure 5.22, the program displays a dialog box with an OK button, informing you of its manufacturer, version, and other related information.

Many Windows NT programs also display information in the dialog box about available physical memory. This feature is a function of the individual program, not of Windows NT, so the software manufacturer decides what type of information you see when you choose the About option.

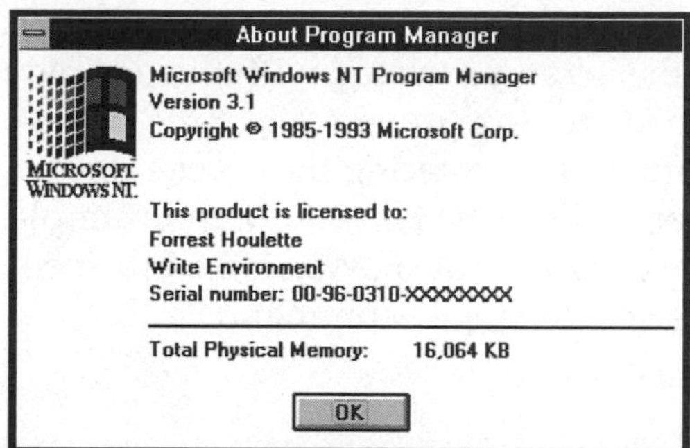

Figure 5.22: *The About Program Manager dialog box, accessed through the Help menu.*

Common Menu Actions

As you work with menus, you will find that there are common actions you can perform on menus. These actions are discussed in the following sections.

Selection Methods

The menu system of Windows NT is powerful because of the number of methods it provides to select menu items. The most obvious selection method is to use the mouse. By clicking on a menu name on the menu bar, you display that menu. By clicking on an item in the menu, you activate that item (usually a command). By clicking on another part of the display, you cancel that menu selection. You can close the menu, but leave the menu bar selected, by pressing Esc when a menu appears.

Another way to choose a menu option is to point to the menu name, press the mouse button to display the menu, drag the pointer down the menu until the desired menu item is highlighted, and then release the mouse button. (This method is more familiar for Macintosh users, because this is the way menus work on the Macintosh. In Windows NT, however, you do not have to hold the mouse button down to keep the menu displayed.)

Windows NT menu names on the menu bar contain one underlined character that can be used to select that menu. These characters are referred to as *accelerator keys*. Press Alt (or, in some applications, F10) to activate the menu bar, and then press the letter associated with the desired menu to cause the menu to drop down. When the menu appears, select a command by entering the accelerator key associated with that command. The File menu, for example, can be activated by pressing Alt+F. When the File menu appears, press **O** to select the Open command.

The menu bar is activated when the Alt key is pressed, not when it is released. Note that you do not have to wait to see the menu before you choose the next letter.

The arrow keys also can be used to select menus and menu items. The menu bar first must be activated by pressing Alt or F10. Use the left- and right-arrow keys to move between menus; use the down-arrow key to display the contents of a menu. After a menu appears, press the up- and down-arrow keys to highlight the menu item you want, and then press Enter to select the highlighted item. Press Esc to close an open menu or to cancel the activation of the menu bar if no menu is displayed.

In the menu shown in figure 5.23, notice that some items have keystroke combinations written after the command name. These key combinations are called *shortcut keys* and are a very efficient way to use Windows NT menus. A major advantage of the standard Windows NT interface is that the same shortcut keys work in most Windows NT programs.

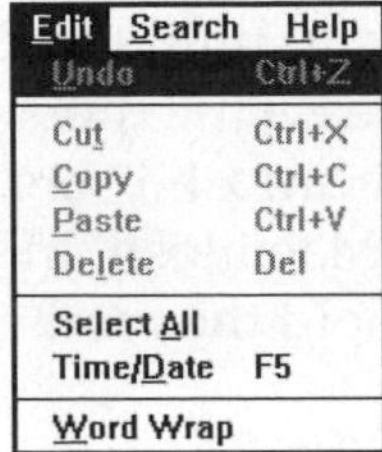

Figure 5.23: *Many commands on the Edit menu are universal to Windows NT programs.*

Because programs share a common interface, learning the shortcuts of the environment can save time. The command to copy information to the Clipboard is always the Copy command in the Edit menu (select the Edit menu, and choose the Copy command). You also can press Alt, **E**, and **C** at the same time. Or you can press Alt, and then press **C** after you press **E**.

An even faster way to invoke Copy is with the keyboard shortcut Ctrl+C (or Ctrl+Ins). These methods all work, regardless of your current program—the same process is followed in Excel and Word for Windows, for example.

Windows NT features two styles of keyboard shortcuts for cut, copy, and paste the older Windows standard (Windows 3.0 and earlier) and the new standard for Windows NT/Windows 3.1. These are shown in the following table:

Function	Win 3.0	Win 3.1/NT
Cut	Shift+Del	Ctrl+X
Copy	Ctrl+Ins	Ctrl+C
Paste	Shift+Ins	Ctrl+V

Menu items within Windows NT are more than a series of commands. Information on the menus changes to provide information about whether commands are available, which options currently are set, and which commands require multiple steps.

Dimmed Options

Windows NT is a "smart" operating environment: it knows, for example, that a maximized window simply cannot be made larger. One of the big advantages of Windows NT over MS-DOS and UNIX programs is that you cannot select an option that is inappropriate or unavailable. Thus, if a menu item is unavailable, Windows NT automatically changes the color of the menu item to gray (by default). If you then try to choose the unavailable menu item, the program ignores your request.

Dimmed menu items sometimes are referred to as being grayed out.

Menu commands often are unavailable because you still need to select some object or because a previous action is required. The Undo command in the Edit menu, for example, is dimmed in all Windows NT programs until you do something that can be undone, such as deleting some text. You cannot cut or copy information from a document until data is selected; these options are dimmed until you make a selection. Likewise, because you cannot paste anything until something has been cut or copied, the Paste option is dimmed until information has been placed in the Clipboard.

The following exercise illustrates dimmed menus:

1. Select the Notepad window. Make sure that the README.TXT file is loaded on-screen.
2. Select Edit. Note that the Undo, Cut, Copy, and Delete commands are dimmed.
3. Select Edit, and choose Select All. The entire document is highlighted.
4. Select Edit again. Note that the Cut, Copy, and Delete commands are no longer dimmed.
5. Choose the Copy command.
6. Select Edit. Note that the Paste command is no longer dimmed.
7. Press Esc to cancel the menu.

Throughout Windows NT programs, menu items are dimmed (and sometimes removed) if the command does not make sense for the worksheet or document being displayed.

Items with a Solid Arrow

Some applications have an additional level of menus. A solid arrow to the right of a menu item indicates that a second menu appears after you choose that item (see fig. 5.24). This type of menu is called a *cascading menu.*

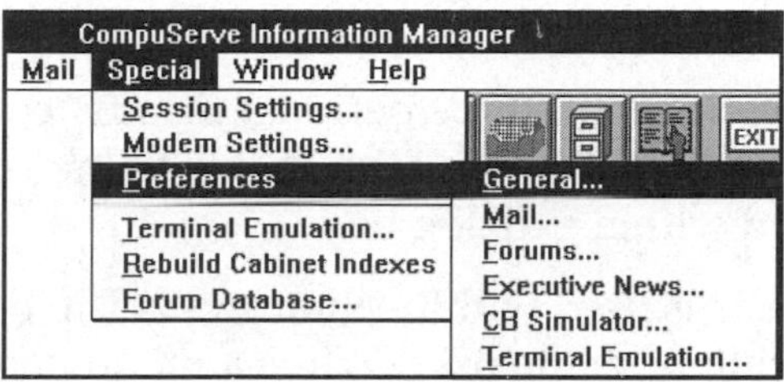

Figure 5.24:
An example of a cascading menu.

Cascading menus present a series of options or offer a new level of menu choices. If the menu presents a series of options, selecting the value sets the menu item equal to that value. If the cascading menu presents a series of menu items, choosing one of those items is the same as choosing an item from a first-level menu (a drop-down menu from the menu bar).

Items with Check Marks

In some programs, a menu-bar selection actually is a list of options that can be either on or off. If an option is turned on, it has a check mark beside it; if it is turned off, it is not checked. Figure 5.25 shows five checked options on the File Manager menu.

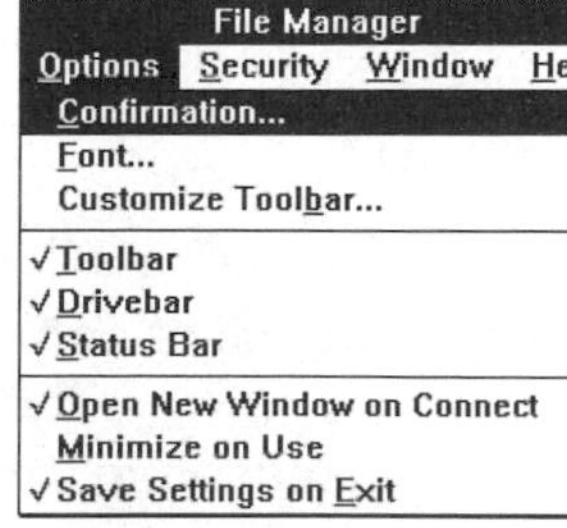

Figure 5.25:
Active options within File Manager.

This type of menu item is referred to as a *toggle switch*. Just like a light switch, it can move between two settings. Some programs change the name of the item rather than display a check mark, but this method of handling a toggle switch has grown increasingly uncommon among applications.

Items with an Ellipsis (...)

The *ellipsis* symbol (three periods) means "continued." An item on a Windows NT menu that is followed by an ellipsis is continued within a dialog box.

A *dialog box* is used within Windows NT to obtain additional information from the user. When a menu item is followed by an ellipsis, additional information is needed to complete the command. When you choose Find from the Search menu in Notepad, for example, Windows NT produces a dialog box similar to the one in figure 5.26. This dialog box asks what you want to search for and how you want to search for it.

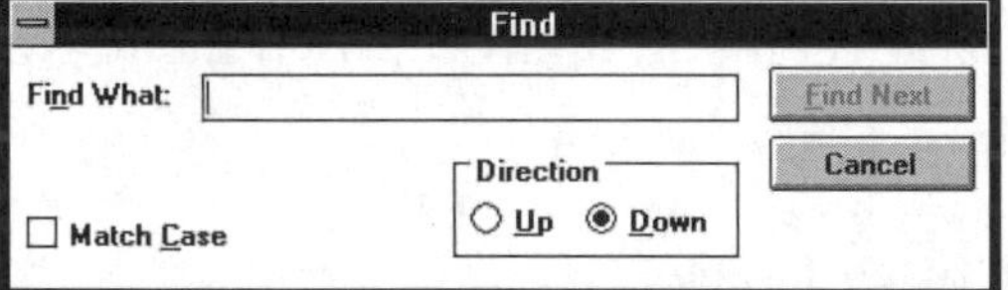

Figure 5.26: *Notepad's Find dialog box.*

The ellipsis provides guidance when you explore a new program and are not sure what is safe to click on. If the menu option has an ellipsis, you can safely click on it and review the box that pops up on-screen without activating any commands. You can press Esc to cancel the dialog box without making any changes.

Dialog Boxes

Dialog boxes come in many sizes and flavors, but they all have one thing in common: they gather and contain information that relates to the current action. Although each dialog box is different, they all are composed of a combination of specific items. Figure 5.27 shows a dialog box that contains a number of standard controls. The controls used in a dialog box are described individually in the following sections.

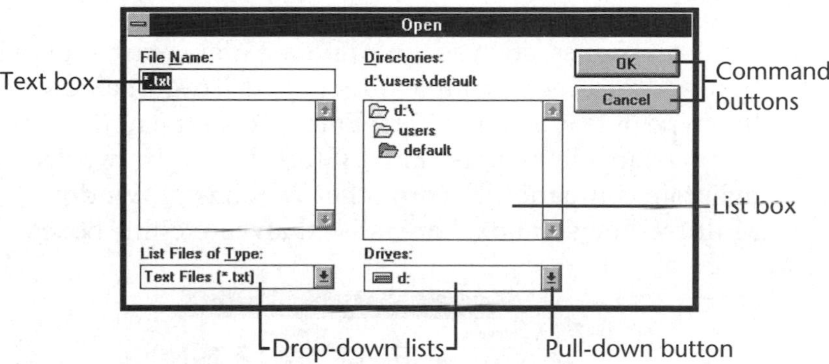

Figure 5.27: *A typical dialog box, showing its controls.*

The information can be entered into the dialog box by using a combination of the mouse and keyboard. You can use the mouse to select an item on the dialog box, including the location in which text is to be entered. Although the mouse can be used to directly select any item, Tab is used to move from one item to another, in a pattern similar to the standard Western reading style (left to right on the first line, and then moving to the next line). Shift+Tab moves you in the opposite direction.

Most items within a dialog box have an accelerator key (underlined letter). To select the item, press the Alt key and the accelerator key.

Text Boxes

A *text box* (sometimes referred to as an *edit box*) is a rectangular box that accepts input from the keyboard. The simplest way to use a text box is to start typing. In most text boxes, any existing text is highlighted automatically and is deleted when you begin typing.

You also can use the mouse (or the arrow keys) to move to a specific point within the text and insert new text. Backspace and Del can remove single characters or blocks of characters when highlighted with the mouse.

To highlight with the keyboard, move to the starting location, hold down Shift, and use the arrow keys to move to the ending location.

Some text boxes, such as the Annotate dialog box shown in figure 5.28, accept multiple lines of text. To start a new line in this type of text box, use Ctrl+Enter. To start a new paragraph (skip a line), press Enter (Shift+Enter also works to maintain compatibility with other versions of Windows). Multiple-line text boxes are taller than single-line boxes.

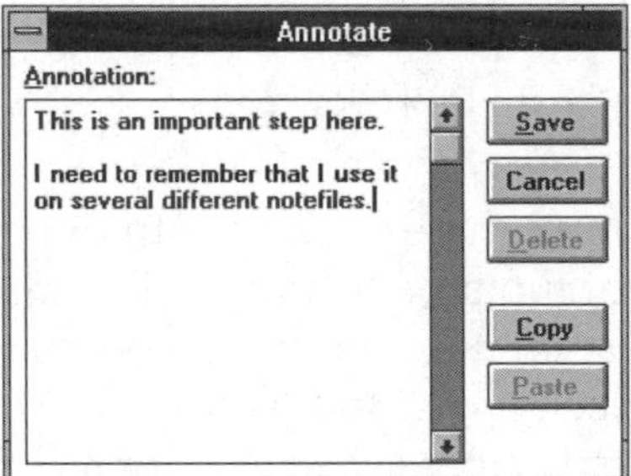

Figure 5.28: *The Annotate dialog box.*

You can use the cut, copy, and paste shortcut keys in a text box.

List Boxes

A *list box* shows choices, often sorted alphabetically. You can scroll up and down the list by using vertical scroll bars such as those used to navigate a window's screen display. When the desired item is displayed anywhere in the list box, you can select it with the mouse by clicking on it. If you double-click on an item in the list, the program selects the item and closes the dialog box.

If you do not use a mouse, you can move to the list box (either by using Alt and the accelerator key, or by pressing

Tab), and then press the up- and down-arrow keys to make your selection. When the selection has the gray outline, press the space bar to highlight it, or press Enter to select the item and close the dialog box in a single step. You also can use Page Up and Page Down to move through the list more quickly.

Although most list boxes enable you to select only a single item, some enable you to select multiple items from a single list. To select multiple items with the mouse, hold down Shift while you click on additional items. If you use the keyboard, hold down Ctrl, move the focus with the arrow keys, and press the space bar for each item you want to add. This type of list box is common in programs that manipulate groups of files, such as the File Manager.

Most list boxes that are sorted also support a technique known as *First Character Goto*. In Excel's Function's list under the Paste Function command on the Formula menu, hundreds of items are available. If you want to select the WEEKDAY function, for example, you must scan more than 100 choices before WEEKDAY scrolls into view. With the First Character Goto technique, press **W**; you are taken to the first entry that begins with the letter W in the list.

Some list boxes and text boxes are linked to form a unit known as a *combination box*, such as the File Name text box and the list box in the File Open dialog box (see fig. 5.29).

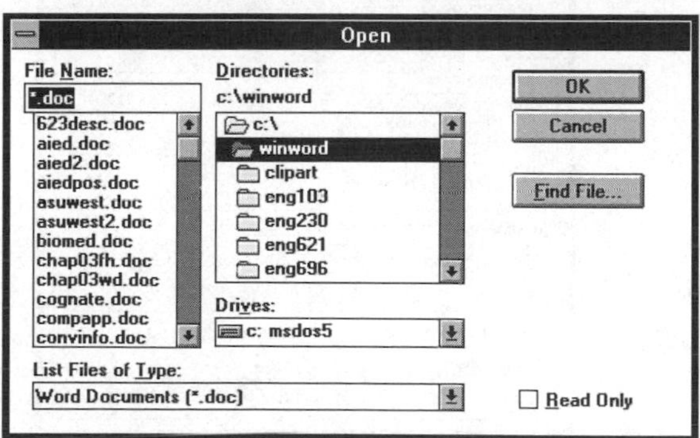

Figure 5.29:
The Open dialog box.

You can access a file by typing its name directly in the text box or by scrolling through the File Name list box until you find the file you want. The information displayed in the files list box is based on the value shown in the Directories list box (it displays the files contained in the directory specified in the Directories list box). After you choose a file name from the File Name list box, that file name instantly appears in the text box.

When a list box is connected to a text box like this, selecting an item from the list is the same as having Windows NT do your typing for you with no chance of error. You can elect to do your own typing, however, and enter the same information into the text box directly from the keyboard.

Drop-Down Lists

A normal list box takes up a large amount of space inside a dialog box. In the Files list box in the Open dialog box in the File menu, for example, room for eight file names exists. A drop-down list is a space-efficient way of combining a text box and a list box, enabling several lists to be included in a single dialog box, as shown in figure 5.30.

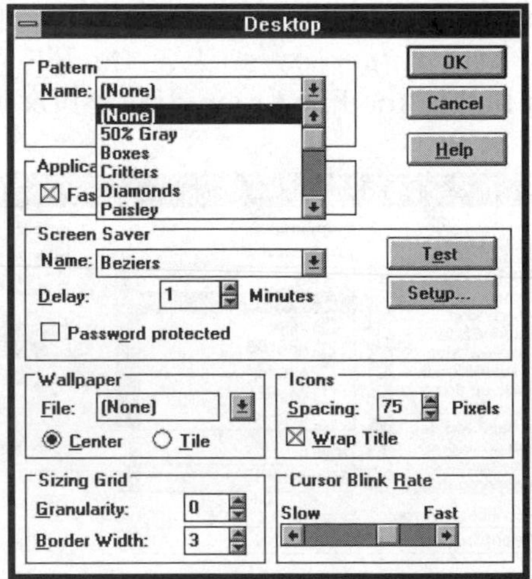

Figure 5.30:

Drop-down lists in the Desktop dialog box.

To display the drop-down list in figure 5.30, open the Control Panel (double-click on the Control Panel icon). Select Desktop by double-clicking on it. The Name text box in the Pattern box is a drop-down list.

The text box displays the most current selection from the list (or the top item, if no item was selected previously), and it has a pull-down button on the right side. (The *pull-down button* looks like other buttons, but it contains a down arrow.) You can click on the pull-down button to display the other choices available for that item. You then can make your selection as you would in any list box.

For keyboard use, move to the drop-down list by pressing Tab or pressing Alt, followed by the character associated with the drop-down list box. The icon on the drop-down list is an underlined down arrow. The items on the list can be displayed by pressing Alt and the down arrow.

When the list appears, you can press a letter to take you to that portion of the list. If you type **C**, for instance, the highlight bar instantly moves to Critters in the selection list. This is another example of the First Character Goto feature, discussed as part of the standard list box. Finally, if you highlight the text in the top portion of the drop-down list, you can enter text directly as though it were a standard text box.

Option Buttons

Option buttons (known in early versions of Windows as *radio buttons*) in a dialog box always are grouped so that only one button in each group can be selected at a time. (When you select a button in a group, any other button that was selected is turned off.) Option buttons are referred to as radio buttons because they resemble the tuning knobs of an old-fashioned radio.

Select an option button by clicking on it with the mouse, or by changing the focus to that group and using the arrow keys on the keyboard to select a particular button. Option buttons sometimes have underlined shortcut keys in their description labels; they can be selected by holding down Alt and pressing the underlined letter key.

The paper Orientation group on the Document Properties dialog box, shown in figure 5.31, is an example of a group of option buttons. It contains two choices: Portrait and Landscape orientation. The printer's paper can be in only one of these two conditions, so if you choose Landscape, the dialog box automatically turns off the Portrait button.

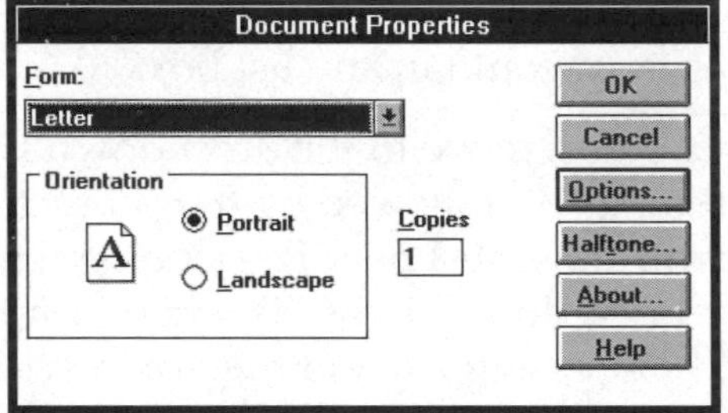

Figure 5.31: *Only one choice in the Orientation group can be selected.*

Option buttons are grouped within a named border, called a *group window*. (The option buttons discussed in the Printer Setup dialog box are in the Orientation group.) Option buttons within a group are mutually exclusive: if you select one, all others are deselected.

Check Boxes

A *check box* enables you to specify a preference in the same way you check a box on an order form. When the box is checked, it is considered on or true; when it is empty, it is considered off or false. The Word for Windows Print Options dialog box, shown in figure 5.32, for example, has several check box items, including Draft Output, Reverse Print Order, and Update Fields. You also can include Summary Info, Field Codes, Annotations, and Hidden Text.

A check box acts like a toggle switch: clicking on an empty box checks it, and clicking on a checked box clears it. Most check boxes can be accessed by using an accelerator key.

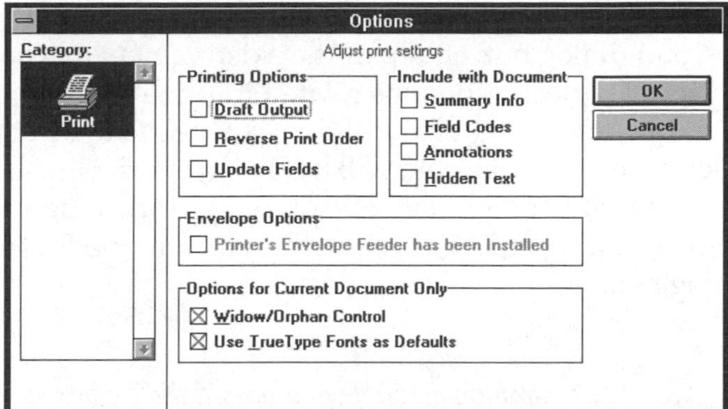

Figure 5.32:

Any combination of check boxes can be selected.

If you use the keyboard, press the space bar to change the status of a check box from checked to cleared (or from cleared to checked). Check boxes are grouped by the type of action they control, but, unlike option buttons, the grouping is not restrictive: each check box is independent of the other check boxes within the group. You can select one, none, all, or any combination of check boxes within any dialog box.

Command Buttons

The command buttons on a dialog box are used after you complete all necessary information. Two command buttons included on almost every dialog box are OK and Cancel. By clicking on OK, you tell Windows NT to proceed with your selections; clicking on Cancel tells Windows NT that you want to exit without selecting.

The keyboard equivalent of Cancel is always Esc. Enter is a key equivalent for the default command button. (The *default* is the item selected before you make any changes.) In most dialog boxes, the OK button is the default; pressing Enter accepts the changes.

When you use the keyboard and move to a command button, the outer edge of the button becomes darker, meaning that the button is selected. You will notice that the OK button in figure 5.32 is selected, while the Cancel button is not. You can activate the current button by pressing Enter.

Besides OK and Cancel buttons, another type of button opens a second dialog box on top of the existing one; this *nested dialog box* typically contains related information that cannot fit on the first dialog box or that rarely needs to be changed. (Such a button invariably will be labeled with ellipsis dots to indicate that another dialog box will appear.) When you close a nested dialog box, you generally return to the first-level dialog box.

A common example of a nested dialog box is in the Print dialog box of most applications, such as Word for Windows. Select Print from the File menu to open the Print dialog box. When you click on the Setup button, a second dialog box opens, enabling you to specify which printer to use. When you close the Print Setup dialog box by clicking on OK or Cancel, you return to the original Print dialog box.

Icons

Windows NT uses *icons* on the desktop and in the Program Manager to represent application programs, common and personal application groups, and program items. Each icon conveys information about the program or group it represents. If an icon represents an application or document window, the associated window is said to be minimized.

An icon is a representation of an object or concept. Within Windows NT, an icon is a small picture (usually 32×32 screen dots) that represents an application, a file, or an action. Icons can be manipulated by the mouse by clicking (to select the icon), double-clicking (to activate the associated program), dragging (to move the icon), and dragging-and-dropping (to cause another application to take action on the icon).

An icon is not a program—the icon merely represents a program. If you delete an icon from a group, for example, you delete only the reference to the program, not the program itself.

Application Icons

Application icons represent programs that have been minimized by clicking on the Windows NT minimize buttons. These icons are arranged along the bottom edge of the desktop. Application programs that are minimized to icons still run, and they can perform complex actions. They do not occupy as much memory, however, because they do not need to display their application window. (They often run in the background.) An application shrunk to an icon also presents less clutter on the desktop than if it is left as an application window.

Application icons access application programs the same way hot keys access terminate-and-stay-resident (TSR) programs. By double-clicking on the application icon (the same as pressing a TSR's hot key), you activate the application.

Group Icons

Group icons appear in the Program Manager and represent application groups. They are arranged along the bottom edge of the Program Manager window. If you double-click on a group icon, Windows NT opens the application group and displays it as a document window filled with program item icons. Application groups shrink to a group icon to prevent clutter in the Program Manager window. Windows NT includes separate icons for common and personal program groups.

See Chapter 6 for more information on working with Program Manager groups.

Program Item Icons

Program item icons represent application programs that are not currently running. They appear in application group windows. You run an application by double-clicking on the program item icon.

Program item icons are equivalent to the operating system command you type to run an application. You might, for example, type the following command to launch Microsoft Word in MS-DOS:

```
C:\WORD\WORD
```

To launch the same application in Windows NT, however, you merely double-click on its program item icon.

Performing Common Windows Tasks

As mentioned earlier in the chapter, Windows NT applications and Windows NT itself follow strict guidelines regarding the design of the interface of an application.

The reason for these guidelines is obvious. In the DOS world, time spent learning the command structure of one application, such as WordPerfect, does not help you when you learn another application, such as Lotus 1-2-3. Most DOS applications have unique command

structures, so the steps required to open a file in WordPerfect are entirely different than those required by Lotus 1-2-3.

In contrast, Windows applications adhere to stricter command structure guidelines known as the *Common User Access* (CUA) standard. The benefit for the user is that after you learn a single Windows application, learning future applications becomes much easier because the basic commands are identical across applications. Therefore, you do not have to worry about whether to use Alt+F or Ctrl+F to open a file because all applications use a single menu action or key sequence. Additionally, you do not need to wonder where the print commands are hidden on the menu, because CUA helps ensure that the Print command is always in the same place.

Windows NT's implementation of the CUA standard makes working with your PC and your programs easier. You can focus on the work at hand and not on figuring out how to use the software.

Basic File Operations

If a Windows NT application works with files, it presents a File menu as the first menu on the left side of the menu bar. All File menus in Windows NT applications are the same—they enable you to work with files by using the same command structure, no matter what the files contain. Every File menu enables you to perform at least four different file operations.

Creating a New File

In any Windows NT application, you can create a new, empty file by selecting the File menu and then choosing the New option (see fig. 5.33). The application opens a new, empty file and displays it in the workspace.

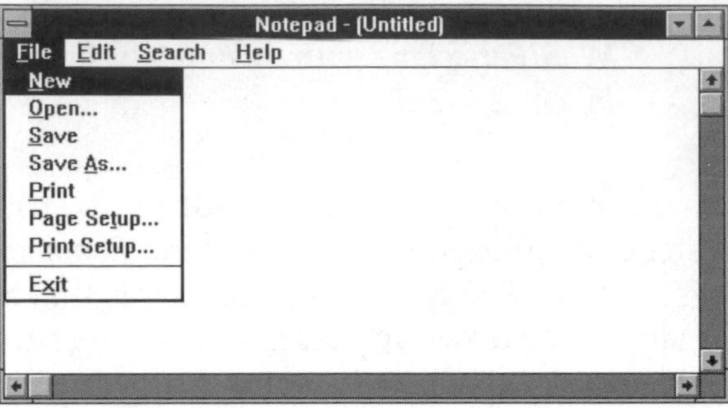

Figure 5.33: *The File menu.*

The Write, Cardfile, and Paintbrush applications provide examples of ways to use this action to create a variety of files in different applications. In Windows NT Write, the file you create has a format that keeps track of information about fonts, pictures, embedded objects, and text. Select the **F**ile menu and choose the **N**ew option to bring up a workspace that is ready to accept all information and display properly formatted text (see fig. 5.34).

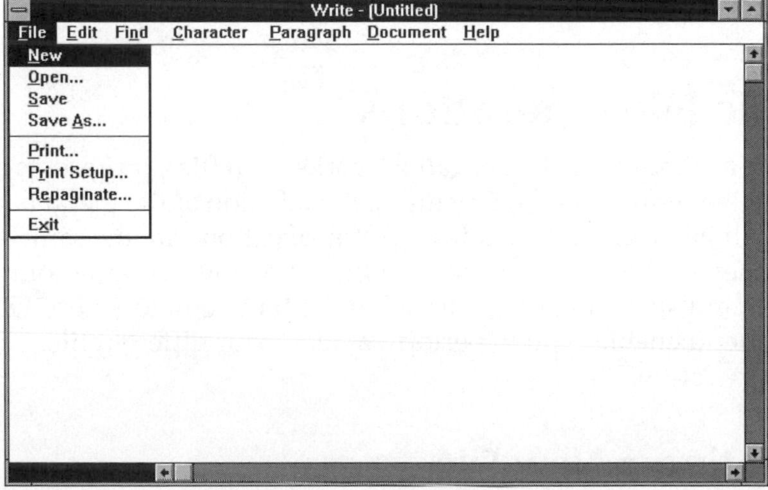

Figure 5.34: *The New command in Write.*

In Windows NT Cardfile, however, you choose the **N**ew command in the **F**ile menu to create a file that can contain graphical index cards, text, and pictures (see fig. 5.35). The new file is presented as a single blank card in the workspace.

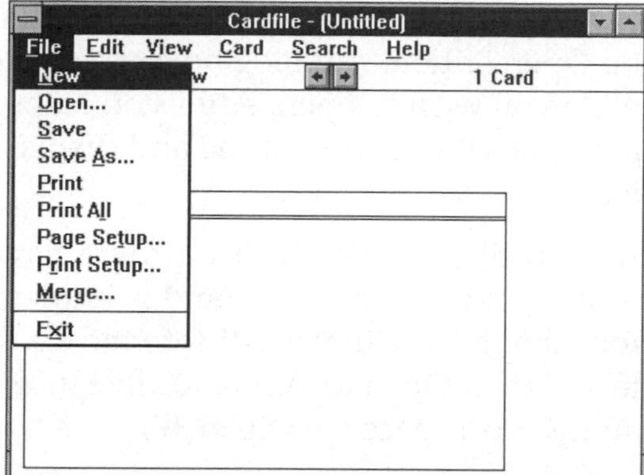

Figure 5.35:

*The **New** command in Cardfile.*

Windows NT Paintbrush presents a file in which you can turn individual pixels on or off. In addition, the file holds information about the color of each pixel. Select File, and then choose New in Paintbrush to create a file that is ready to hold information (see fig. 5.36).

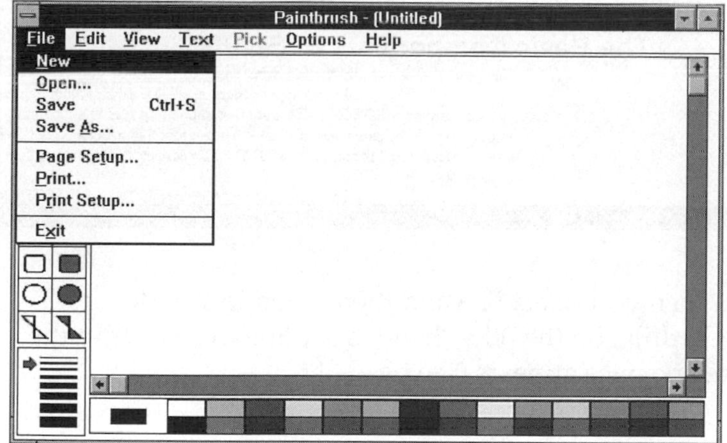

Figure 5.36:

*The **New** command in Paintbrush.*

Opening an Existing File

Just as you can create new, empty files in different applications with the same command, you can open existing files in different applications by using the same command sequence.

In Windows NT applications, select the **F**ile menu and then choose the **O**pen option. A dialog box appears for you to select the file you wish to open. After you respond, the application opens the requested file and displays it in the workspace.

The Write, Cardfile, and Paintbrush programs provide examples of ways the same command is implemented across applications that deal with very different data. When you select **F**ile and then **O**pen in Write, for instance, a document appears in the workspace (see fig. 5.37).

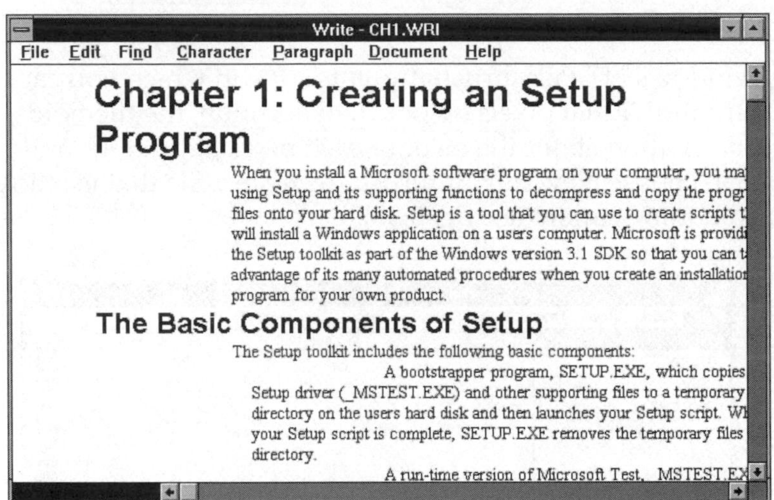

Figure 5.37:
*The result of the **O**pen command in Write's **F**ile menu.*

When you select **F**ile and then **O**pen in Windows NT Cardfile, on the other hand, a set of index cards in the workspace appears (see fig. 5.38).

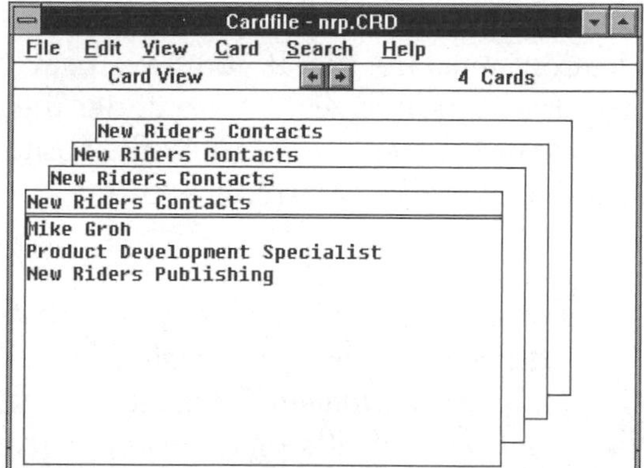

Figure 5.38: *The result of the Open command in Cardfile's File menu.*

Selecting File and then Open in Windows NT Paintbrush (see fig. 5.39) makes a picture appear in the workspace.

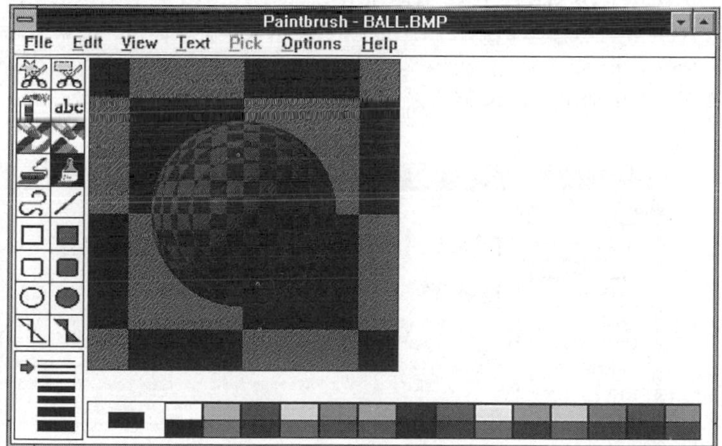

Figure 5.39: *The result of the Open command in Paintbrush's File menu.*

Saving a File

Windows NT has the same command structure for saving files in different applications. To save a file, click on the File menu, and then choose Save in any application. If you have not yet saved the file, a dialog box appears and asks you to type a file name into a text box. After you enter a file name, the application saves the file. If you have previously saved the file, the application saves the file under the same name. If you wish to save the file under a new file name, use the Save As command (covered later in this section).

When saving a file, you usually do not need to type the extension, because most applications add their default file extension to your file name automatically (unless you have explicitly typed an alternative extension). Some applications, however, such as Quattro Pro for Windows, do not add an extension.

The Write, Cardfile, and Paintbrush applications provide examples of ways that the same command is implemented across applications dealing with different data. In Write, select File and then choose Save to save a file in Windows NT Write file format (see fig. 5.40).

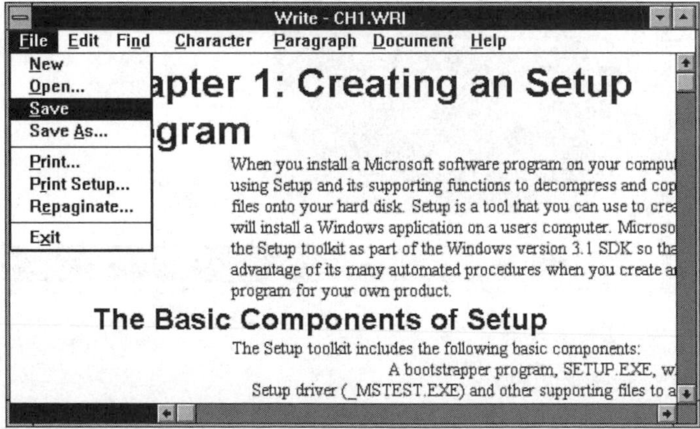

Figure 5.40:
The Save command in Write.

In Cardfile, select File and then choose Save to save a set of index cards in Cardfile's file format (see fig. 5.41).

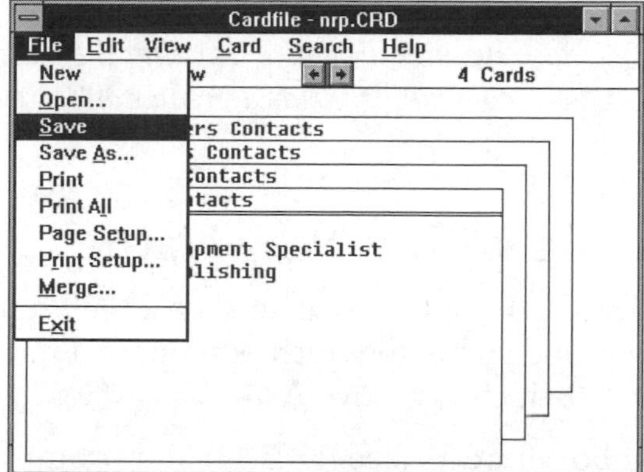

Figure 5.41:

The Save command in Cardfile.

In Paintbrush, select **F**ile and then choose **S**ave to save a picture in Paintbrush's file format (see fig. 5.42).

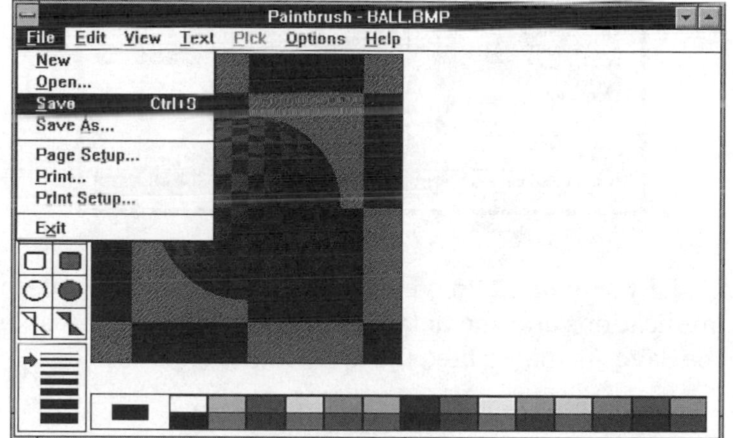

Figure 5.42:

The Save command in Paintbrush.

Paintbrush can accommodate three different file formats—the Save and Open dialog boxes enable you to choose the format you prefer.

*More programs are beginning to standardize shortcut key combinations to make life easier for Windows NT users. Shift+F12, for example, automatically invokes the **S**ave command in the **F**ile menu, whether you are*

continues

in Word for Windows or Excel. As this trend continues, the investment of learning the standard Windows NT commands yields a greater and greater reward.

Saving a File with a New Name

In Windows NT applications, to save a file under a different name from the one with which you opened it, select the File menu and then choose Save As.

A dialog box appears (see fig. 5.43) and prompts you to type the new file name into a text box.

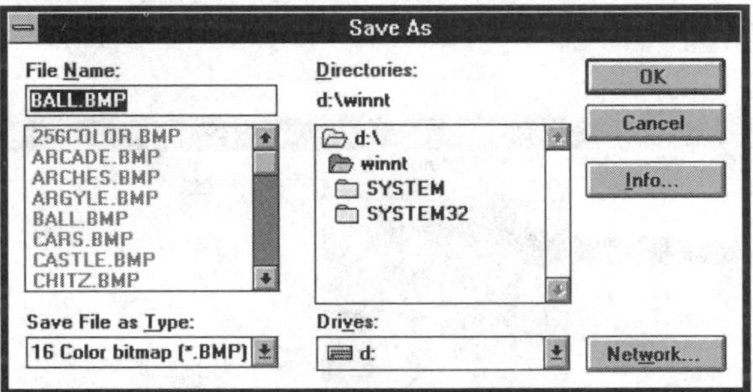

Figure 5.43:
The Save As dialog box.

Usually you do not have to type the extension because most applications add the default extension. After you respond to the Save As dialog box, the application saves the file.

Windows Printing

All applications in Windows NT have the same set of commands for printing files. If an application allows you to print, the print commands appear on the File menu.

Printing a File

To print a file in most Windows NT applications, select the File menu and then choose Print (see fig. 5.44).

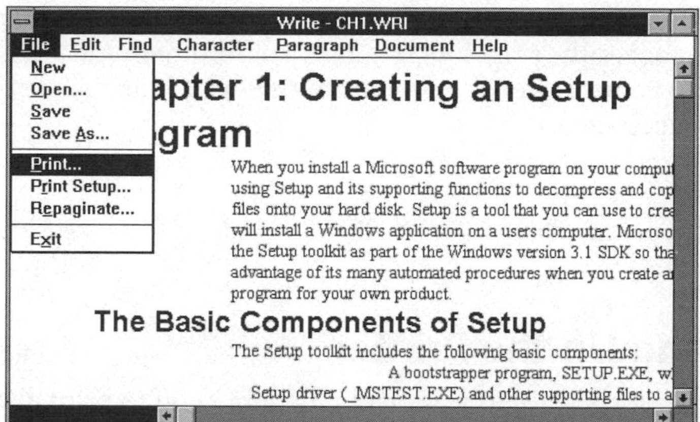

Figure 5.44: *The **Print** command in Write's **File** menu.*

A dialog box appears and prompts you to enter the number of copies or to print only a selected portion of the file (some applications do not offer this option). After you determine the characteristics of your print job by setting the controls in this dialog box, click on the OK button to begin the printing operation.

After the print job begins, a dialog box appears to inform you that the file is printing (see fig. 5.45).

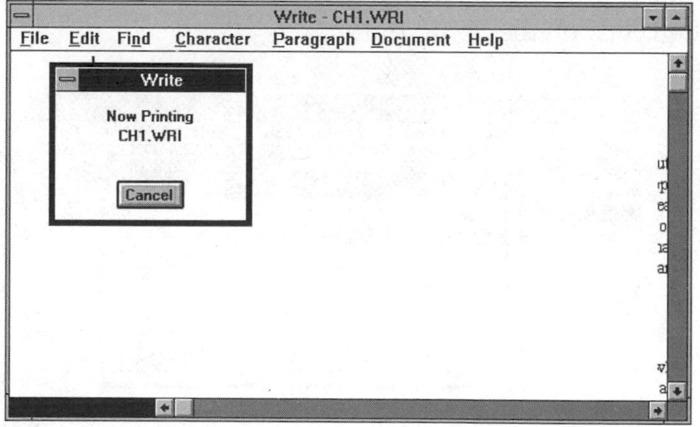

Figure 5.45: *The Print Cancel dialog box in Write.*

Halt the printing operation by clicking on Cancel in the dialog box or by pressing Esc.

After the Print Cancel dialog box disappears, Windows NT manages the print job, freeing you for other work. You still can control your print job from the Print Manager application if necessary.

See Chapter 9 for more information on printing.

Setting Up the Printer

Windows NT applications that enable you to print also enable you to control the printer setup. The actual management of the print job and communication with the printer is performed, not by individual applications, but by Windows NT itself. As part of this management, Windows NT gives application programs access to the installed printers.

You can access a Printer Setup dialog box and specify printer settings in each application. To access the printer setup, select the File menu and then choose the Print Setup option.

As figure 5.46 illustrates, the Printer Selection dialog box appears, which contains a list of the printers attached to the system. Click on the name of the printer you want to use, and then click on the Setup button.

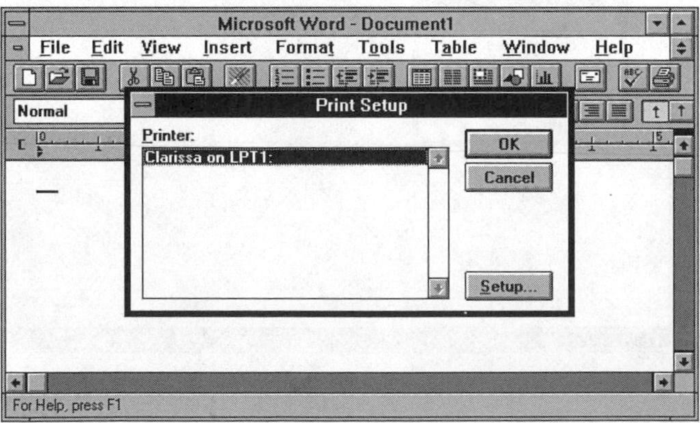

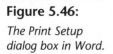

Figure 5.46:
The Print Setup dialog box in Word.

Another dialog box then appears, which enables you to adjust the printer settings (see fig. 5.47). After you adjust the settings, click on the OK button. You return to the Printer Selection dialog box. Click on OK; your printer is set up.

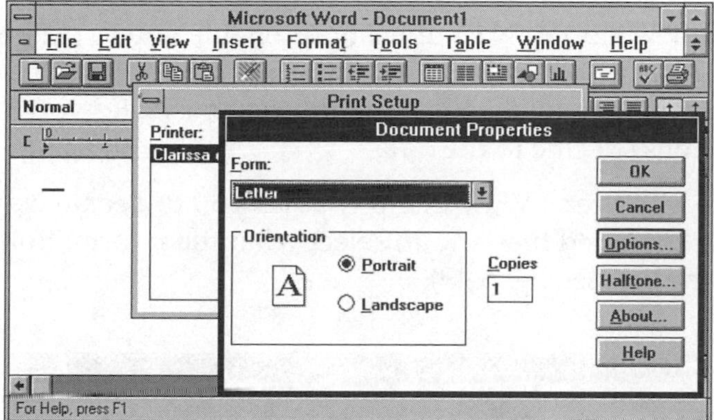

Figure 5.47: *Document Properties dialog box.*

Workspace Searches

Many Windows NT applications (particularly word processors and editors) enable you to search for information in their workspaces (see fig. 5.48).

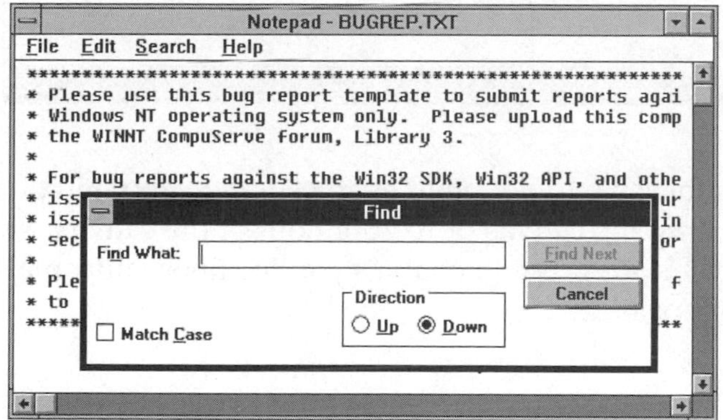

Figure 5.48: *The Find dialog box in Notepad enables you to search for information.*

Select the appropriate menu name to search for information in the application. A Search dialog box appears and asks you to enter the string to search for (you often are offered the opportunity to enter a replace string as well). Click on the Find button to begin the search.

Views of Your Workspace

Many Windows NT applications enable you to decide how you want to view the data. If the application has this capability, you may find a View menu, which enables you to display options specific to the data.

File Manager's View menu enables you to decide ways to sort the listed files and to select what file information appears in the list (see fig. 5.49).

Figure 5.49:

*File Manager's **V**iew menu.*

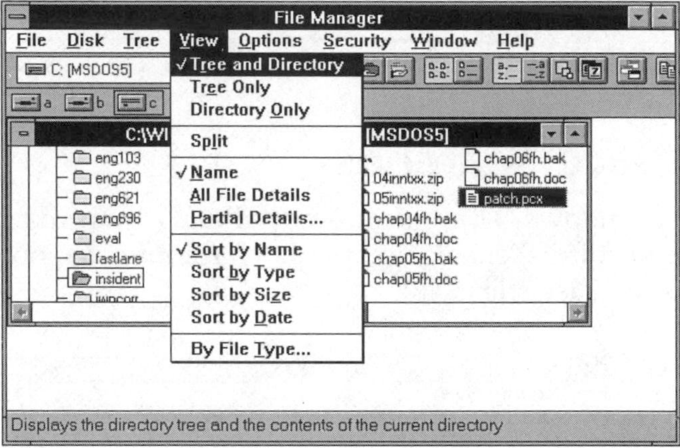

Paintbrush's View menu enables you to zoom in on a part of the drawing canvas or to zoom out of the canvas. The CD Player's View menu enables you to choose information about the current CD.

The View menu is less standardized across different Windows applications. Some applications do not provide the capability to change the view of your document or workspace; others place the command

elsewhere. For example, Paradox for Windows enables you to change the view of a form or report through the Zoom option on the Properties menu.

Option Selection

Many Windows NT applications have special settings that you can use to customize appearance or behavior. An Options menu on the menu bar typically indicates this capability (see fig. 5.50).

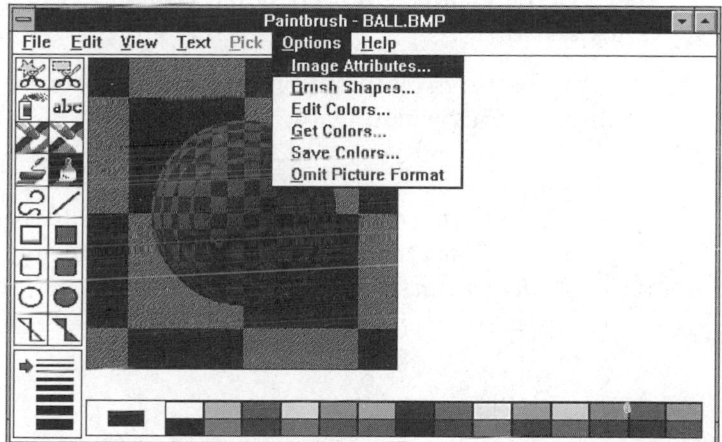

Figure 5.50:
The Options menu in Paintbrush.

The Options menu is another case in which different application vendors have chosen different paths. Although many Microsoft products (such as Word for Windows and Excel) have an Options menu, Borland's Paradox for Windows provides a Properties menu to do essentially the same task.

Various applications enable different degrees of customization. Paintbrush, for instance, enables extensive control of its appearance and features.

Program Manager, on the other hand, enables you to control only four aspects, which are found in the Options and Window menus. These are described as follows:

- If you select Auto Arrange, icons in a program group rearrange themselves after the program group is resized. The icons move into rows and columns that most efficiently use the available space.
- If you select Minimize on Use, icons shrink when you launch an application, clearing the screen of clutter and making all desktop space available to the application.
- The Save Settings on Exit option saves the position and status of the group windows when you end your Windows session.
- The Save Settings Now option enables you to save settings whenever you want.

Options under the Window menu specify the arrangement of the program groups within Program Manager's desktop. The Cascade and Tile options are discussed later in this chapter.

Font Selection

Windows NT provides a pool of fonts that are available for each application for printing and displaying on screen. You typically select a font within a given application by choosing a Font option from a menu.

For more information on fonts, see Chapter 9.

Depending on the application, a dialog box might appear with a list of available fonts. Select the font you want by clicking on a font name. This font is used to write to the screen until you select another one. When you save the file, you save the current font. TrueType font files contain an unlimited number of font sizes because the fonts automatically are scaled to fit the screen.

Although TrueType renders virtually any point size for a given font, most applications display only those fonts with point sizes between 4–127 points.

You use different menus and commands to select fonts in different applications. The following four figures show different ways to select fonts in various applications.

Paintbrush presents a Text menu on which Fonts is an option (see fig. 5.51).

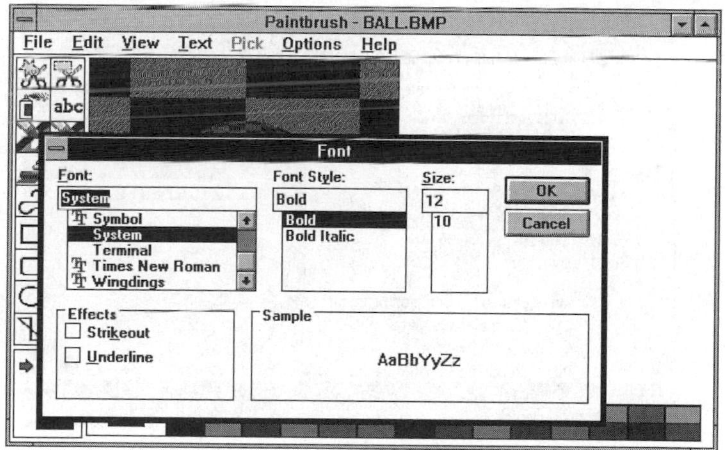

Figure 5.51: *Font selection in Paintbrush.*

Write presents a Character menu on which Fonts is an option (see fig. 5.52).

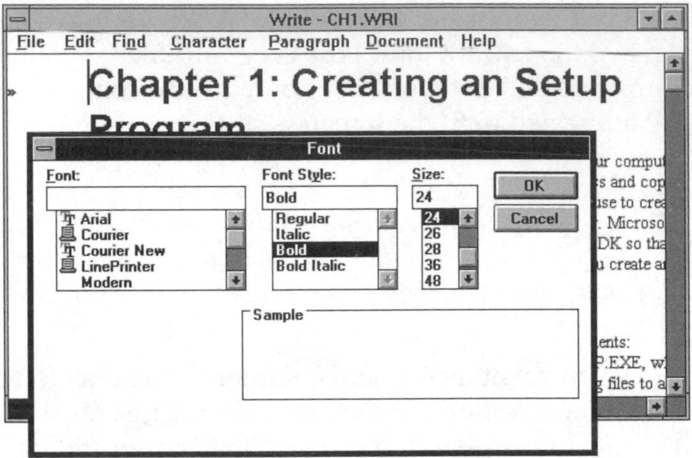

Figure 5.52: *Font selection in Write.*

Word for Windows uses two drop-down list boxes that enable you to select the font and its size (see fig. 5.53).

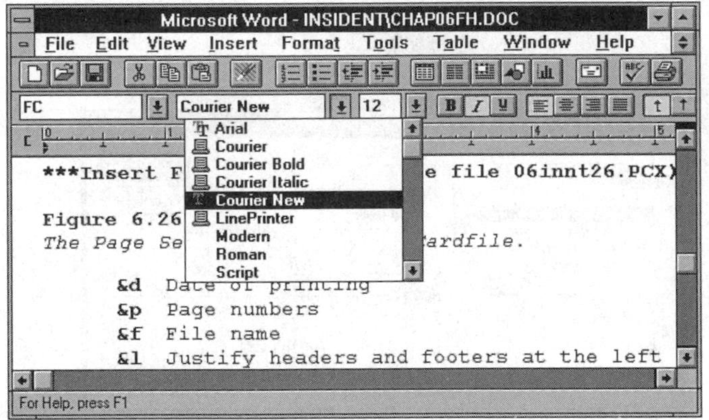

Figure 5.53: *Font selection in Word for Windows.*

Microsoft Excel places the Font option on the Format menu (see fig. 5.54).

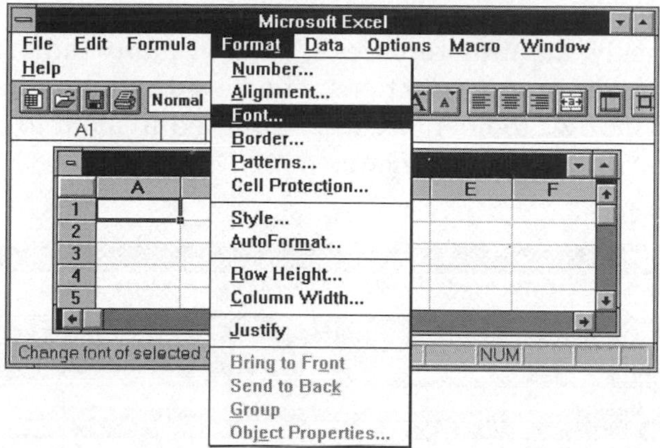

Figure 5.54:
Font selection in Excel.

Although applications use different ways to select fonts, Windows NT provides sophisticated fonts and font management for your applications. Because you do not have to install fonts for each separate application, you gain disk space and execution speed.

Toolbars

Windows NT applications often offer you the chance to work with a *toolbar,* which is a strip of buttons that typically appears just under the menu bar of an application. You can initiate an action by clicking on a button on the toolbar.

The actual name of the toolbar depends on the software vendor. For example, Microsoft Word for Windows and Excel have Toolbars, Borland Paradox for Windows and Quattro Pro for Windows have Speedbars, and Lotus 1-2-3 and Ami Pro have Smart Icons. Although the names are different, they are designed to do essentially the same thing—speed up your work.

Every toolbar button has a picture that indicates its function. Normally, a button replaces several or many individual keystrokes or mouse actions. The **S**ave button on the Word for Windows toolbar (see fig. 5.55) is equivalent to the **S**ave option under the **F**ile menu.

Figure 5.55:
The Word for Windows toolbar.

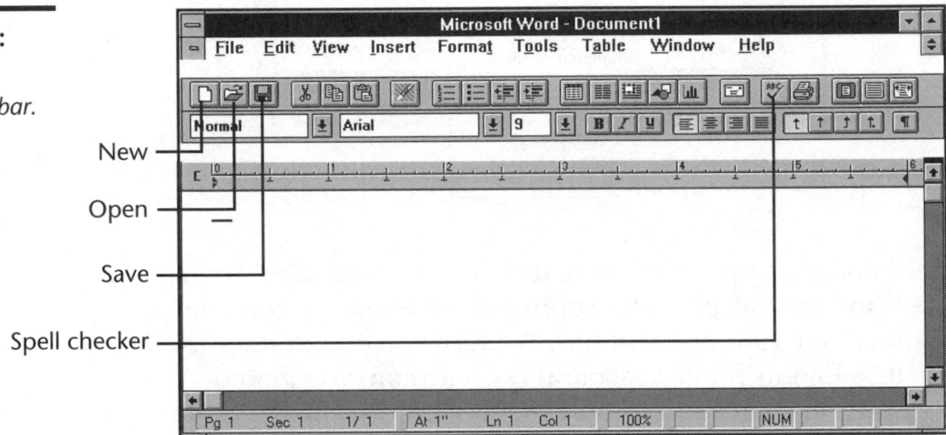

Word for Windows uses a toolbar to provide immediate visual access to 22 common actions in the Word for Windows menu system, as you can see in figure 5.55. By clicking on the first button on the left, for example, you can create a new document. The next button opens an existing file.

Toolbars are gaining in popularity as the Windows interface becomes more complex. When Apple first introduced a menuing system in the Lisa and early Macs, the actual size of the screen was very small. As a result, using the mouse to select a menu option did not take too much hand movement.

With today's large 1024×768 super-VGA screens and complex menuing systems, selecting a toolbar option requires much less hand movement than the equivalent command found on the menu.

If you want to print, click on the Printer button. If you want to check spelling, click on the Spell checker button. You do not have to remember where the options are on the menus, so you are more efficient and less distracted by the Word for Windows command system.

A *toolbox* (see fig. 5.56) is similar to a toolbar. It presents a grid of tools represented by icons. Usually the grid has two columns. To select a tool, click on the corresponding icon in the toolbox. You then can use the tool to take an action in the workspace, such as spray painting in Paintbrush.

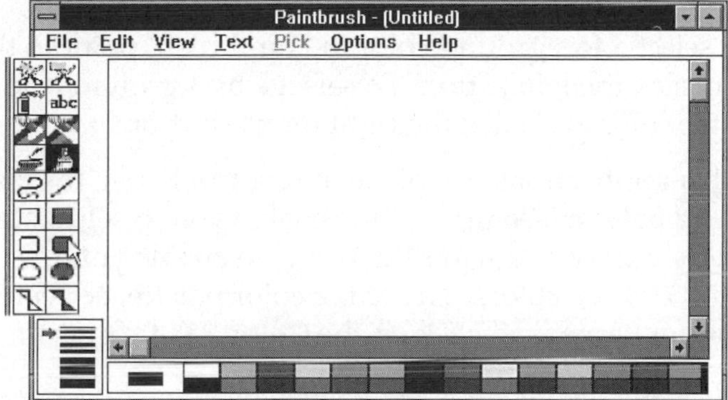

Figure 5.56: *The Paintbrush toolbox.*

The primary difference between a toolbar and a toolbox is the presence of command buttons with actions attached to them. Toolbars use buttons; toolboxes do not. Toolbar buttons initiate actions; toolbox icons select tools to use later. You find both kinds of tool-selection controls in Windows NT applications.

Palettes

A *palette* is similar to a toolbox, but it enables you to select colors. Paintbrush, for example, uses a color palette (see fig. 5.57) to enable you to select the foreground and background colors as you draw.

Figure 5.57:
The Paintbrush color palette.

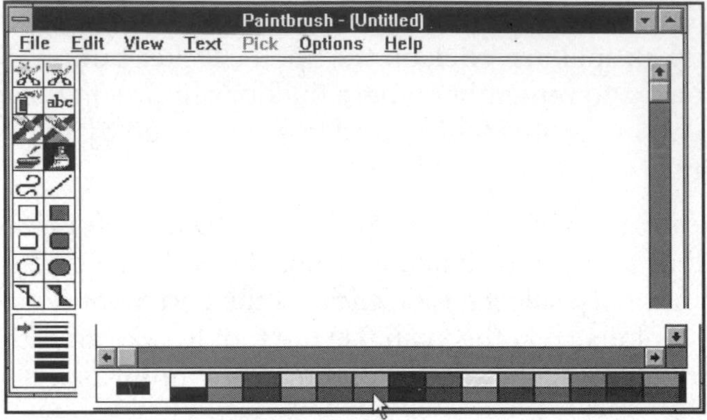

To select a foreground color in Paintbrush, point to the color and click the left button. To select a background color, point to the color and click the right mouse button.

Other applications use palettes. Control Panel, for instance, uses a palette (see fig. 5.58) to enable you to select standard colors, and uses a separate palette to enable you to create and select custom colors. To see the color palette, activate the Control Panel, and click on the Color Palette button.

Figure 5.58:
The Control Panel color palette.

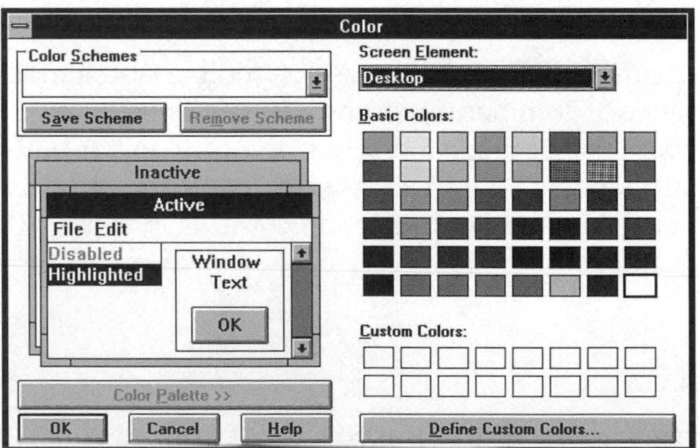

Character Map uses a palette to help you find special characters to use in other applications.

On-Line Help

Windows NT provides a consistent way for help in any application. A function key, F1, is reserved as the help key for any application. Pressing F1 always brings up the Help index.

Almost every Windows NT application has a **H**elp menu option at the far right on the menu bar (see fig. 5.59). The options on the **H**elp menu can vary from application to application, but the first option always takes you to the index or table of contents for the application's **H**elp menu.

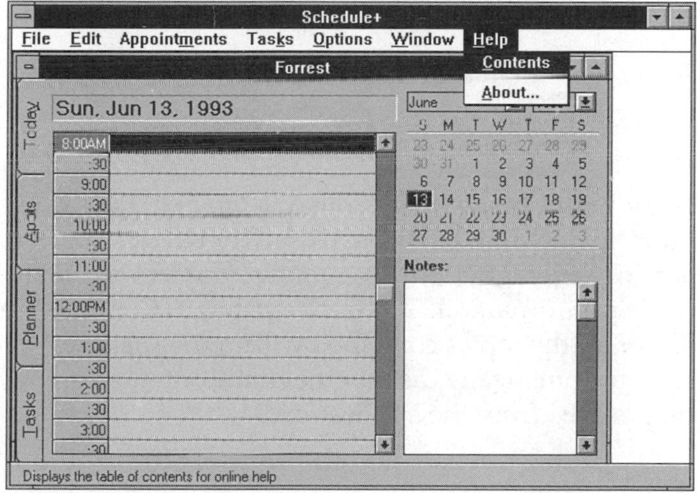

Figure 5.59:
*The Schedule+ **H**elp menu.*

Windows NT has a consistent interface for Help files in all applications, and different topics are linked to each other as hypertext. A *hypertext system* enables you to retrieve information in a nonsequential manner through the use of links between associated topics. Any topic in (typically) green underlined text has more information elsewhere in the Help file. Click on the topic to see that information. Figure 5.60 shows the Schedule+ Help window.

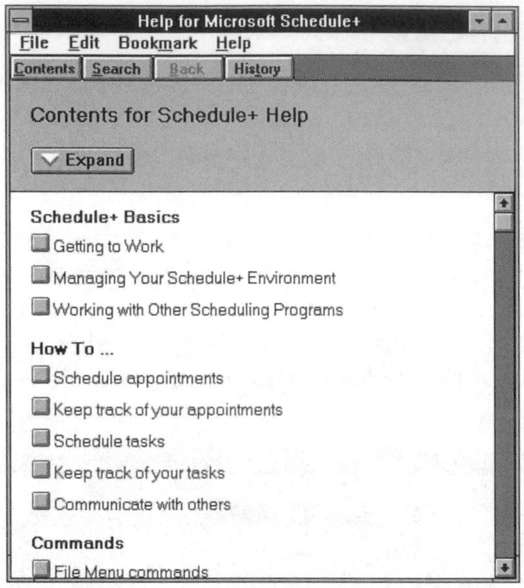

Figure 5.60: *The Schedule+ Help window.*

The Help utility menu bar contains the File, Edit, Bookmark, and Help commands. Below the menu bar is a toolbar, which contains several buttons that control ways to move through the Help information. The Contents page (Contents) provides a list of all the topics contained within the file. Most programs automatically display the first Contents page when you press F1 from the application.

You can press F1 within Help to produce an index of helpful information about the Help utility.

The Windows NT Help application provides four ways to keep you from getting lost in hypertext Help:

- The Back button returns you to the previous Help topic. Repeatedly pressing the Back button cycles you through the series of Help topics you viewed.
- The History button displays a list of the topics you viewed. Return to any previously viewed topic by double-clicking on it.

- The Contents button immediately takes you to the Help index or table of contents for the Help file you select.
- The Search button presents a dialog box that enables you to search for concepts and topics.

In addition, two browse buttons may be visible; if they are, they can be used to flip forward (>>) and backward (<<) through the Help pages as if they were bound in a book.

A Windows NT application controls the buttons that appear when the Help program window opens. Therefore, the browse buttons are not visible if the program does not activate them. Program Manager, for example, does not enable the browse buttons.

The text displayed within the Help utility has special notations to indicate references to additional information. These special references usually are indicated in green type in the standard Windows NT environment.

If the mouse is pointing to one of the references, the pointer turns into a pointing hand. The first reference on the page is selected when the page is displayed. Tab is used to move from one reference to the next.

A typical Help file usually has two types of references. A solid underline indicates a cross-reference to another topic; this type of reference is a *JumpTo* reference. You can click on a topic to jump to a new topic page.

A dotted underline indicates a definition; this type of reference is called a *PopUp* reference. You can click on a definition to view a text window with additional information.

Many applications offer *context-sensitive help*, which works in two ways. One approach provides different Help information, based on the most recent action you have performed. This type of Help still is activated by using the F1 key, but the Help page displays changes, based on your recent action.

The second type of context-sensitive help enables you to interact with the program and the Help utility. In these systems, you can press Shift+F1 within a document to change the pointer to a question mark. By selecting an on-screen item, you can view Help information about that item.

Alternatively, you can first select (but not activate) a menu item by using the keyboard, and then press Shift+F1.

Not all Windows NT programs have context-sensitive help; each program must be specifically written to have that capability. When in doubt, press Shift+F1. If you get the question mark pointer, context-sensitive help is available.

Some programs also provide an on-line tutorial, as described previously. The Tutorial option usually is located on the pull-down **H**elp menu. If the program provides this feature, Tutorial activates instruction on the use of the program.

Tutorials are not part of the Windows NT Help system; they are part of the program itself. Thus, not all tutorials work in exactly the same way. In general, the tutorial consists of a number of lessons, each started from a central screen. The tutorial prompts you to complete certain actions and to display the results as you work through each exercise.

Introducing WYSIWYG

Because of Windows NT's graphical environment and the use of TrueType and related technologies, Windows NT supports the principle of WYSIWYG. *WYSIWYG (What-You-See-Is-What-You-Get)* signifies that what you see on-screen in your application can be printed and look identical on the final output.

Most Windows NT applications can implement a WYSIWYG display because all their display elements are controlled by Windows NT rather than by the application itself. Windows NT renders all graphics and TrueType (and other scalable) fonts you use on-screen exactly as they will print on your printer. Figure 5.61 shows a WYSIWYG display.

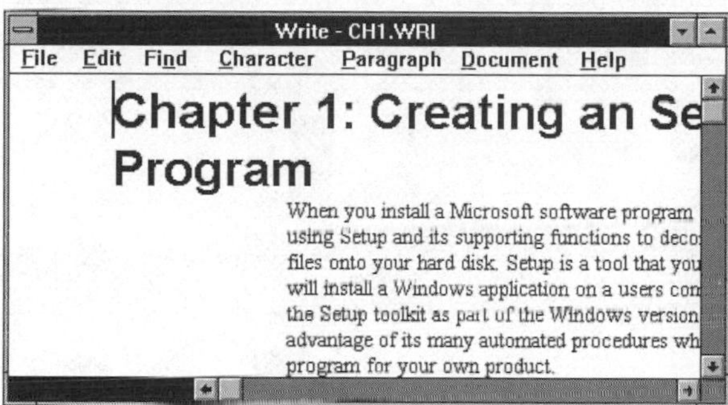

Figure 5.61:
A WYSIWYG display in Write.

WYSIWYG depends on the types of fonts you are using. Bit map fonts (such as MS Sans Serif and MS Serif) do not print exactly as they are viewed on screen. In contrast, TrueType and ATM (Adobe Type Manager) fonts are WYSIWYG.

Managing the Multiple Document Interface

The Multiple Document Interface (MDI) is another standard to which Windows NT adheres. MDI enables you to open multiple files with a single application window, displaying each in a separate window called a *document window*. Because Windows NT document windows belong to the application window, they appear only in the workspace. Parts of a document window that slide past the workspace border are hidden from view.

MDI enables you to open multiple word processing documents and exchange data among them. You can open several Excel spreadsheets at once, for example, and link cells among them (see fig. 5.62).

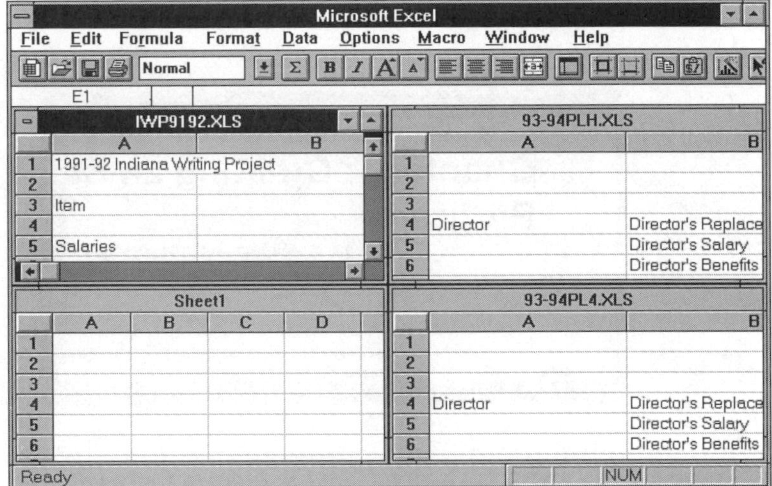

Figure 5.62: *Multiple documents in Excel.*

MDI offers simultaneous views of different drives or directory structures in File Manager.

MDI applications have a special menu, the **W**indow menu, for managing the multiple document Windows NT. The **W**indow menu appears to the left of the **H**elp menu.

The **N**ew option on the **F**ile menu (see fig. 5.63) enables you to open a new document window.

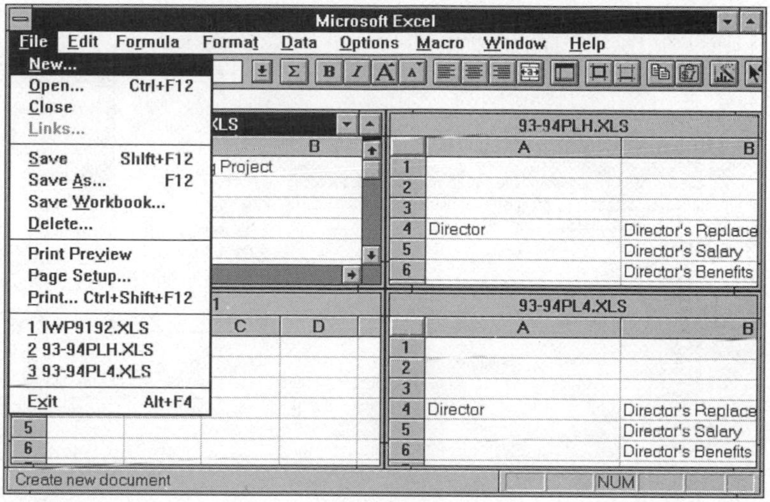

Figure 5.63:

The ***N****ew command under the* ***F****ile menu in Excel.*

You can enter data and save it in a file from this window. The type of file created by **N**ew depends on the application. Excel, for instance, opens an XLS (Excel spreadsheet) file; Word for Windows opens a DOC (document) file.

The **O**pen option on the **F**ile menu opens an existing document and displays it in an additional window. Any other document window already open remains undisturbed. Normally, you do not have to specify the file extension when you open a file. The application accesses only appropriate file types.

The **N**ew Window option on the **W**indow menu (see fig. 5.64) opens another window that displays the same file as the document on-screen. This option enables you to open multiple windows of the same document.

Figure 5.64:
Using the New Window option to display multiple views of the same document.

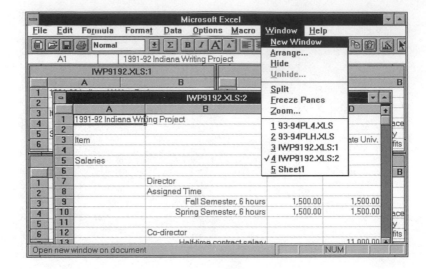

MDI applications provide options on the Window menu for arranging document windows on the workspace. The most common options are Tile and Cascade.

The Tile option arranges the document windows side-by-side like tiles on a wall (see fig. 5.65).

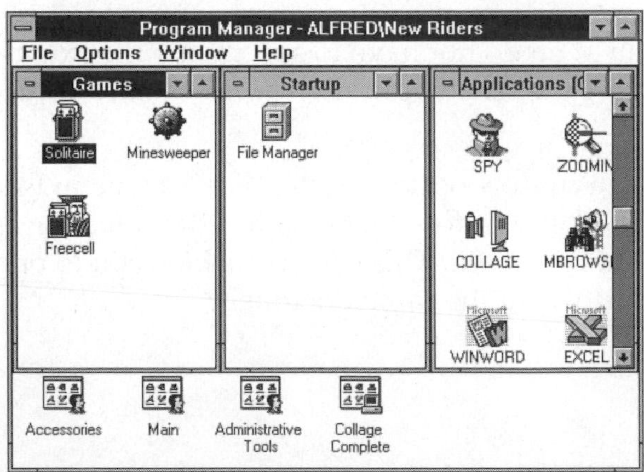

Figure 5.65:
The results of the Tile command in Program Manager.

The Cascade option tumbles the document windows down the workspace from upper left to lower right (see fig. 5.66).

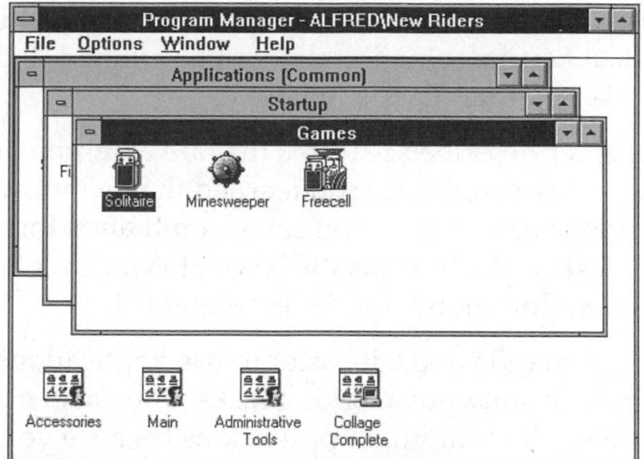

Figure 5.66: *The results of the Cascade command in Program Manager.*

Summary

When users first see Windows NT, their initial impression is how different it looks from the typical DOS, OS/2, or UNIX environment. As they begin to use Windows NT, they start to comment on the differences in the way things are done. Windows NT is based on a process of selecting an object to manipulate and then performing an action. Although Windows NT can be used entirely from the keyboard, most users find it easier to use the mouse for performing many tasks. These mouse actions can be used to control the various windows on the screen.

One of the most important aspects of the Windows NT environment is its consistency between applications. The objects that are manipulated within programs are based on a small set of general item types. The most obvious item used for controlling programs is the Windows menu structure. Menu items are selected to perform tasks, to select between settings, and to display dialog boxes.

This consistency is balanced by the fact that Windows NT offers a variety of ways to perform the same task. You can select an item from a menu by using the mouse, the keyboard, or a combination of both. Most menu items (as well as items within a dialog box) have a series of accelerator keys that can be used to select them. In addition, many items have a shortcut key combination that can be entered with a single keystroke to select the menu item.

This chapter described features that are common to all Windows NT programs. You learned that Windows NT applications have a common set of commands for performing similar tasks, which forms the basis of Windows NT's adherence to the Common User Access standard.

These commands make it easier to use applications because you can focus on your working tasks. They also make it easier to use less-familiar applications because you can easily guess the way an application works from having worked on other applications under the same framework.

In the next chapter, you become even more familiar with the Windows NT interface. You explore the desktop metaphor that organizes the operating system and gain practice of the skills you have mastered.

Mastering the Windows NT Desktop

In the earlier chapters, you learned the basics of the way Windows NT works. You also became familiar with the Windows interface and common elements of application windows and their functions. This chapter introduces you to the Windows NT desktop.

In character-based environments, such as MS-DOS and UNIX, you type commands at the command-line prompt to accomplish tasks. In Windows NT, you typically issue commands to the Windows NT desktop by using your mouse to accomplish many of the same tasks. This chapter covers the following topics:

- Getting to know the desktop
- Introducing the application groups
- Working in Program Manager

- Running applications
- Running multiple applications

Getting To Know the Desktop

After you launch Windows NT and successfully log in, you are presented with the desktop. System commands are represented by pictures on the Windows NT desktop. These pictures take the form of icons, buttons, controls, and parts of application and document windows. You communicate by acting on one of these pictures, clicking a mouse button, or pressing a key.

In MS-DOS and UNIX, you often use command-line switches to define the action the command is to take. Windows NT assigns the same information for a command by using option buttons, check boxes, list boxes, and combination boxes in a dialog box.

When Windows NT requires information about command options, a dialog box containing various controls appears. As discussed in Chapter 5, dialog boxes are Windows NT's pictorial way of representing familiar command-line options. A key difference between working at a command prompt and working on the Windows NT desktop is that you do not have to remember the exact command switches—you just have to specify the options you want in the dialog box.

In Windows NT, you also can run a command-prompt session by double-clicking on the Command Prompt icon in Program Manager. The set of commands available is similar to that in MS-DOS.

If you are familiar with character-based environments, you may find working on the desktop awkward at first. After you understand the parts and get used to the rhythm, however, you probably will find the desktop more comfortable than other operating systems' command lines.

Parts of the Desktop

The Windows NT desktop is organized into three layers: the background layer, the wallpaper layer, and the application layer. As figure 6.1 shows, each layer has particular functions attached to it.

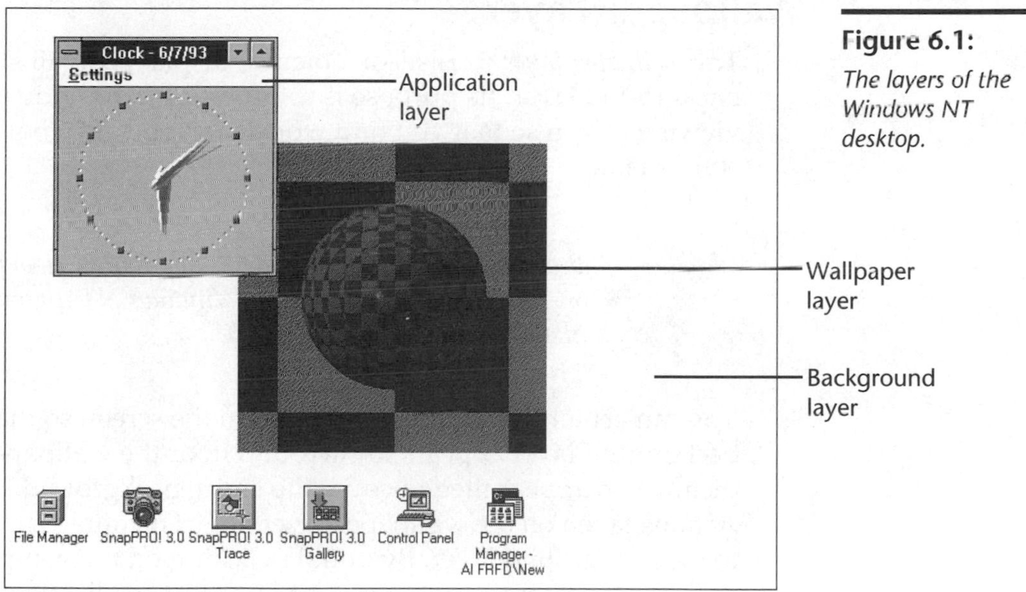

Figure 6.1: *The layers of the Windows NT desktop.*

Background Layer

The *background layer* is the deepest of the three layers of the desktop. (That is, the other two layers sit on top of the background layer.) The background consists of a pattern repeated uniformly over the screen. Its purpose is to provide a comfortable viewing screen, against which the other two layers are contrasted. Although the background layer might appear as having no command function associated with it, double-clicking on the background gives you access to the Task List (see figure 6.19, later in the chapter), which controls the way the desktop is presented.

The Task List *contains a list of active applications. After you double-click on an application in the Task List, Windows NT launches that application. You also can arrange the desktop by using the buttons provided on the Task List.*

Wallpaper Layer

The *wallpaper layer* consists of a picture displayed against the background layer. Its purpose is to provide an individualized viewing screen so that you find working at your PC more comfortable.

Technically, wallpaper *is a bit map that is displayed on-screen and stored in your Windows NT directory in a file with a BMP extension.*

You can center the wallpaper picture on the screen so that the background layer appears to surround it, or the wallpaper picture can appear tiled to cover the entire background. Actions taken on the wallpaper layer are transmitted directly to the background layer. By double-clicking on the wallpaper or the background, you initiate the Task List application.

Application Layer

The *application layer* consists of any application programs you run. Application programs appear in a window. By clicking on these windows, you interact with the application and accomplish work, just as commands typed at an application command prompt enable you to accomplish the same work.

A key difference between DOS and Windows NT is that in Windows NT, you can run multiple applications simultaneously (*multitask*), and these applications communicate directly with one another as you are working.

See Chapter 2 for more information on multitasking.

Windows NT always presents at least one application window when it starts. This application is known as the *Windows NT shell*, and it functions like a DOS, OS/2, or UNIX shell program. It enables you to take many actions that you otherwise take by typing a command at the command prompt. The shell program that comes with Windows NT is called the Program Manager (see fig. 6.2).

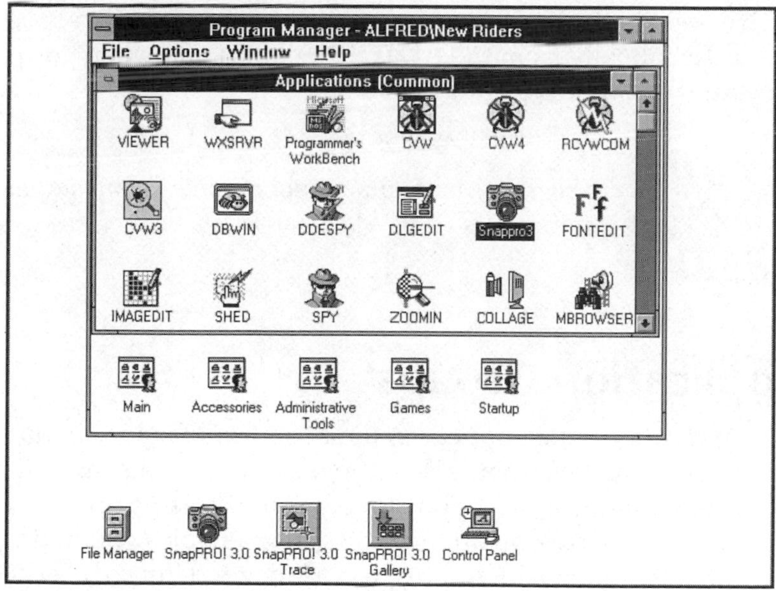

Figure 6.2:
The Program Manager, with added applications.

Program Manager

The *Program Manager* functions as the command and control center of your NT desktop. Because it acts as your shell, it always is present as you work in Windows NT. Program Manager displays groups of icons representing applications on your computer system, and enables you to run these applications or group them together into functional categories, called *application groups.*

This Windows NT feature of creating functional groups combines the command-prompt RUN command available in many operating systems with the capability of grouping related programs into subdirectories that are owned by a single parent directory.

The Program Manager also enables you to automatically launch applications with the launch of Windows NT by using the StartUp group (explained later in this chapter). This process is similar to the way you can activate programs automatically from the AUTOEXEC.BAT file when you launch your system under DOS.

Program Manager does not provide file-management capabilities—File Manager serves that purpose.

Application Groups

Application groups appear in the Program Manager in the application layer of the desktop (see fig. 6.3). Just as you can group related applications together in the same directory on your hard drive, an application group enables you to do the same thing visually in Program Manager. *Grouped applications* are programs that you place in the same group; they can be used at the same time.

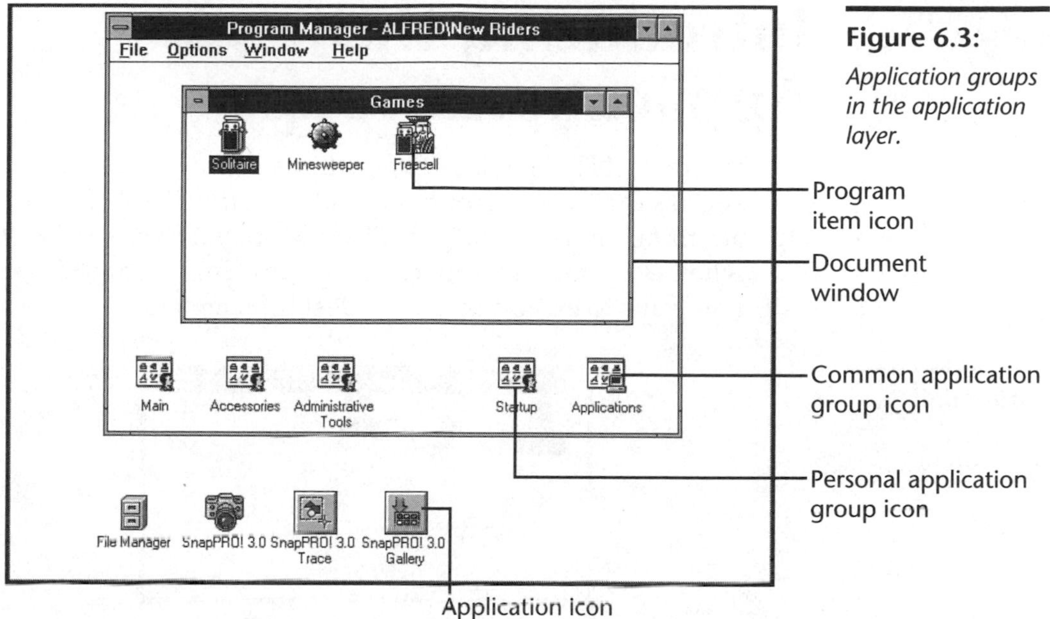

Figure 6.3:

Application groups in the application layer.

An application group appears in two ways. The most common is as a *group icon*, arranged along the bottom edge of the Program Manager window. If you double-click on the group icon, however, the application group opens to take on its other appearance: as a *document window* (also called a *group window*), which contains icons that represent the application programs in the group.

Windows NT includes two types of program groups. The *common groups*, which show a small computer in the lower right corner of their icons, appear for every user of a Windows NT system. *Personal groups*, which show a person's head in the lower right corner of their icon, appear only for an individual user. Thus, although the common groups remain the same for all users of the system, each individual user can group programs together into personal groups that reflect her personal working style.

Introducing the Application Groups

Windows NT organizes applications into application groups, such as the Games group illustrated in figure 6.4. To do anything on the Windows NT desktop, you have to decide whether to open an application group. This section shows you ways to exploit this basic desktop element.

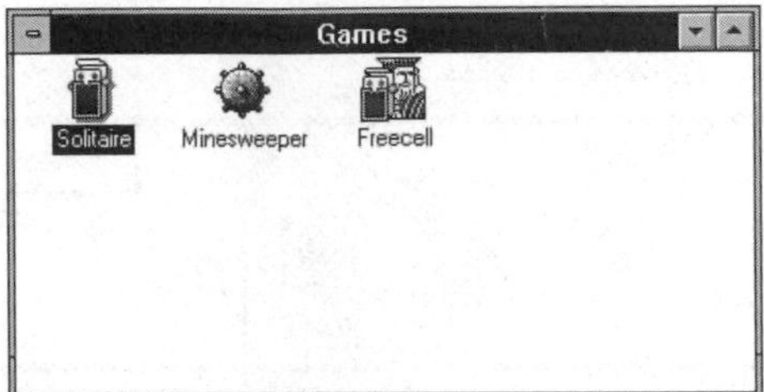

Figure 6.4:
The Games application group.

When you work at your desk, you have certain tasks that you typically perform as part of your job. You also have tools with which you perform these tasks. You might, for example, have a calculator, a notepad, some reminder notes, and some pencils that you use to work up a sales report. It is handy to have these items grouped together on your desk so that you have easy access to them as you work on your report.

Windows NT application groups enable you to organize the application programs you use into a document window that represents that task. If you want to work on a sales report, for instance, double-click on the sales report group icon. The application group window that opens contains all the programs you need for that task. You might have your spreadsheet, calculator, word processor, notepad, and network mail programs grouped together, for example. To access the tool you need at the moment, double-click on the program item icon.

Use a reasonable number of application groups on your Windows NT desktop. Create groups that represent the major tasks you perform. Keep in mind that creating large numbers of application groups takes resources away from working applications. Later in this chapter you are shown the way to add items to application groups.

Several application groups can contain the same program item icon, which enables you to create groups that represent the tasks you commonly perform at your PC (and have as many groups as you want). Your writing group, for example, might contain your word processor, style checker, dictionary, thesaurus, and encyclopedia programs. Your leisure group might contain various game programs, as well as the same word processor and encyclopedia. As you change tasks, you open the application group representing that task. All your tools are at hand and ready to go.

Windows NT creates six application groups when you install it: Main, Accessories, Games, StartUp, Administrative Tools, and Applications. These groups are explained in the following sections.

The Main Group

Just as you have tools you use to organize the way you work (such as a desktop calendar or a to-do list), Windows NT includes application tools you can use to organize its environment. These tools are in the *Main* application group, as shown in figure 6.5.

You find the following applications in the Main group:

- **File Manager.** Enables you to perform many file and disk operations, including running applications, formatting disks, managing file directories, and so on.
- **Mail.** Enables you to send and receive mail across your network.

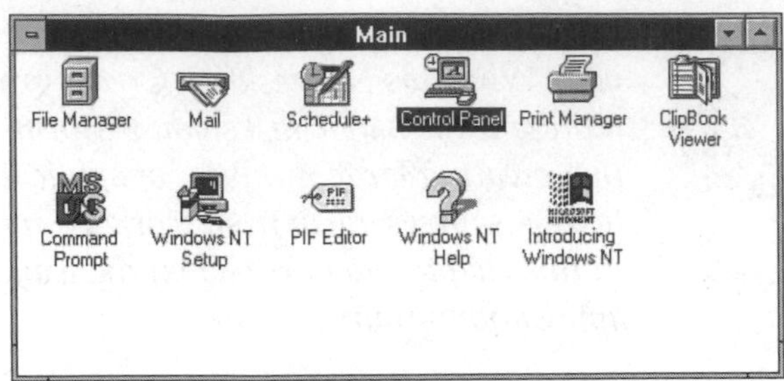

Figure 6.5:
The Main group.

- **Schedule+.** Enables you to maintain a calendar for yourself and to schedule meetings by accessing the calendars of other people on your network.
- **Control Panel.** Enables you to set up many of Windows' features by using various utilities provided by Windows NT.
- **Print Manager.** Enables you to manage Windows NT's print spooler. You can begin and stop print jobs, and change print-job priorities here.
- **ClipBook Viewer.** Serves as a "transfer agent" to move data from one Windows NT application to another, including programs running on different networked computers.
- **Command Prompt.** Enables you to open a command-line window to perform operations.
- **Windows NT Setup.** Enables you to modify some of the basic Windows NT operational parameters. You can, for instance, change video-display resolutions by using the Setup program.
- **PIF Editor.** Enables you to establish special settings so that DOS applications run correctly under Windows NT. These settings are established in a program information file (PIF).
- **Windows NT Help.** Provides help on all aspects of using Windows NT.
- **Introducing Windows NT.** Presents a tutorial on using Windows NT and its features.

The Accessories Group

The *Accessories* application group is shown in figure 6.6.

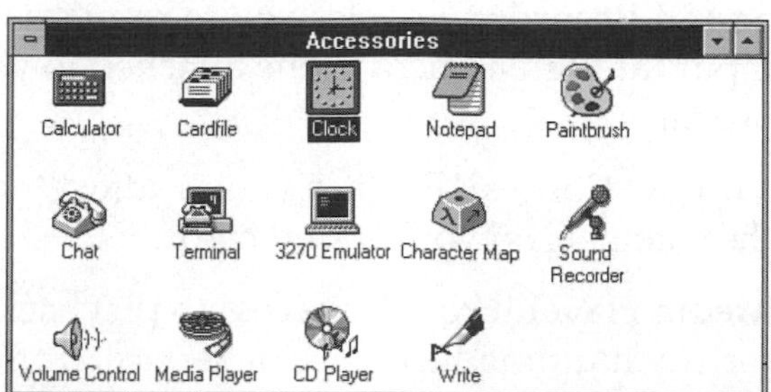

Figure 6.6: *The Accessories group.*

You find the following accessory application programs in the Accessories group:

- **Calculator.** Provides an on-screen calculator for math operations.
- **Cardfile.** Provides the same functionality as a desktop card file.
- **Clock.** Displays the time in both analog or digital form.
- **Notepad.** Provides a quick, easy-to-use ASCII editor for composing short notes or editing small ASCII files.
- **Paintbrush.** Provides a basic drawing package that enables you to produce graphics suitable for inclusion in documents produced by Windows NT applications. Supports PCX, BMP, and MSP formats.
- **Chat.** Enables you to conduct a "live" conversation with another user of your network.
- **Terminal.** Provides basic terminal-emulation capabilities and enables you to access other computers by modem or serial-port connection.
- **3270 Emulator.** Emulates an IBM 3270 terminal for users who need to access data on mainframes that expect this type of terminal.

- **Character Map.** Enables you to insert characters not found on most keyboards, such as extended characters and special characters provided in symbol fonts.
- **Sound Recorder.** Enables you to record sounds that are input through a microphone attached to your sound board.
- **Volume Control.** Enables you to adjust the volume of the channels on your sound card.
- **Media Player.** Provides access to playback capabilities for any multimedia device or service, from sound files to Video for Windows files.
- **CD Player.** Enables you to play audio CDs by using the sound services of your computer. Of course, you must have a CD-ROM drive to use this applet.
- **Write.** Provides a basic word processor with selectable fonts, a search-and-replace function, and other basic features.

You can use the preceding accessories to perform standard work tasks as soon as you install Windows NT. You probably will find it necessary, however, to augment these basic applications with more powerful, off-the-shelf applications. If you plan on doing extensive word processing, for example, Write probably will not suit your needs. Instead, a word processor with more features than Write provides—such as Word for Windows, WordPerfect for Windows, or Ami Pro—is required.

Administrative Tools

The *Administrative Tools* group contains tools that enable you to perform system-level tasks on your computer, such as adding users, configuring hard drives, backing up the system, and monitoring security.

As an individual user, you probably do not use these tools because Windows NT grants the privilege of using most of the features to the system administrator.

The Administrative Tools group is shown in figure 6.7.

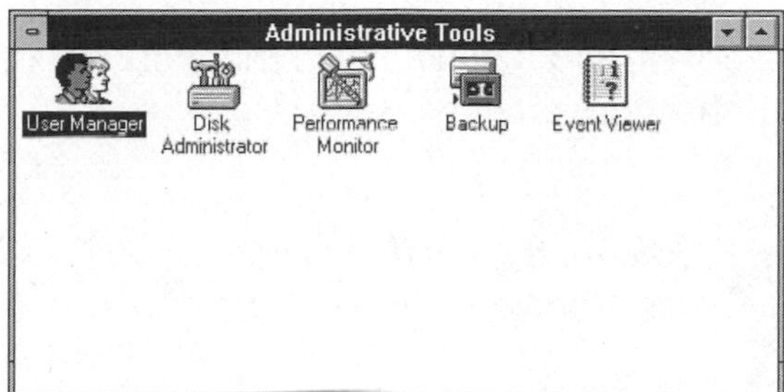

Figure 6.7:
The Administrative Tools group.

You find the following programs in the Administrative Tools group:

- **User Manager.** Enables you to add user logon accounts to the system and to grant user privileges.
- **Disk Administrator.** Enables you to configure hard drives, set up partitions, assign drive letters, and create fault-tolerant disk mirroring.
- **Performance Monitor.** Enables you to represent the speed performance of each segment of the system and operating system graphically so that you can troubleshoot potential performance problems.
- **Backup.** Enables you to back up data to a tape drive.
- **Event Viewer.** Provides a view of the event log, which lists everything that happens on the system. This application enables you to review potential security problems or system problems by examining relevant actions taken by the operating system.

Games

The *Games* application group (as shown in figure 6.4) contains the following three games: Solitaire, Minesweeper, and Freecell.

Besides their recreational function, these games also can help you practice basic Windows NT skills, such as using the mouse, and help you become familiar with Windows NT buttons, boxes, and scroll bars so that you can use other applications more effectively.

Microsoft notes that Solitaire is the most thoroughly tested program they ever produced!

The StartUp Group

The *StartUp* application group is where Windows NT places applications that begin automatically. As figure 6.8 illustrates, Windows NT does not automatically install any programs in this group. Add to this group any applications that you want to run automatically whenever Windows NT starts up. The StartUp group, therefore, serves much like the DOS AUTOEXEC.BAT file.

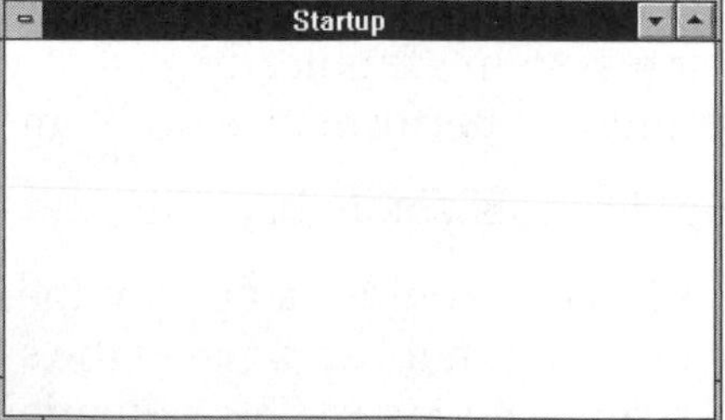

Figure 6.8:
The StartUp group.

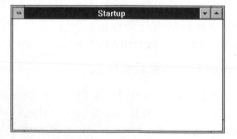

File Manager is a good application to add to the StartUp group, especially if you use it often. Loaded automatically, File Manager analyzes your hard drive's directory structure during start-up. The next

time you access File Manager after start-up, File Manager does not have to repeat this analysis. If you start File Manager from its application group each time you need it, you have to wait while File Manager analyzes your drive's directory structure every time.

The Applications Group

The *Applications* group, as shown in figure 6.9, is where Windows NT places all of the application programs it finds already installed on your hard disk. Windows NT searches your drives and sets up the application files it finds in this group. If Windows NT misses one of your applications, you have to set it up on your own. You probably want to reorganize the applications you find here into other groups that more accurately reflect your working tasks.

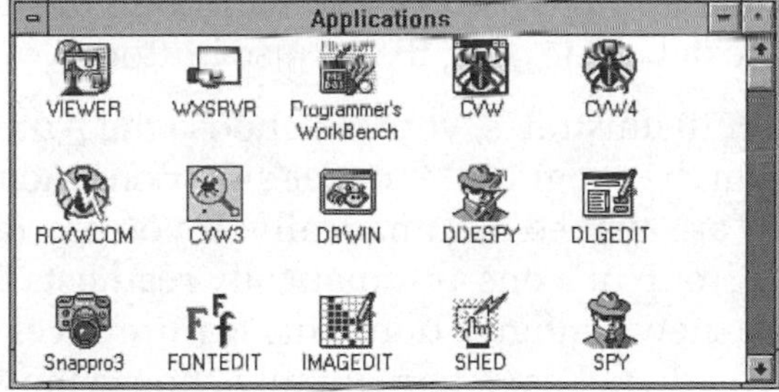

Figure 6.9: *The Applications group.*

Working in Program Manager

When you set up Windows NT, Program Manager initially sets up program groups and their associated icons. You can customize or add to these groups as desired. This section discusses the ways in which you work with Program Manager groups and icons.

Moving an Icon

If you are not satisfied with the location at which Windows NT has installed a program item icon, you can move it to another group quite easily. Set the mouse pointer on the icon you want to move, click on the mouse and hold it down, and drag the icon over the group window or group icon where you want to put it. Drop the icon by releasing the mouse button. If you drop the icon into a group window, the icon appears at the location in the window where you dropped it. If you drop it on a group icon, the relocated icon appears in the opened application's group window as the last icon.

Rearranging Icons

If you do not like the arrangement of the program item icons in an application-group window, you can rearrange these icons. Point to the icon you want to move with the mouse. Press the mouse button and drag the icon to the new location. Drop the icon by releasing the mouse button.

As figure 6.10 illustrates, you can choose the Auto Arrange option from the Program Manager's Options menu so that your icons are aligned automatically. If you rearrange icons, the entire group of icons automatically readjusts to accommodate the new configuration. This feature saves you time because you do not have to manually choose the Arrange Icons option from the Window menu after you have rearranged the icons in the group.

Adding an Icon

To add an application to an application group, follow these steps:

1. Select the Program Manager's File menu, then choose the New option.
2. Select the Program Item option radio button, then choose OK.

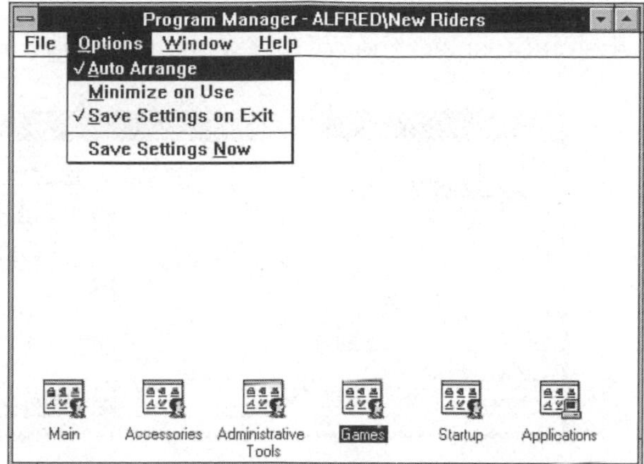

Figure 6.10:
*The **A**uto Arrange option in the Options menu.*

3. Type the name you want to appear under the program item icon in the Description text box. In figure 6.11, for example, the name `Excel` is intended to appear under the program item.

Figure 6.11:
Adding a new application to an application group.

4. Type the command line used to launch the application in the Command Line text box. (You can include switches and file names.)

   You also can use the **B**rowse button to enter the name of the application in the Command Line text box. To do this, select **B**rowse and choose the name of the application in the Browse dialog box (see fig. 6.12). Use the scroll bar to view the list of applications, select the application you want to add to your application group, and choose OK.

5. Type the name of the directory you want the application to use as a working directory in the **W**orking Directory

text box (see fig. 6.11). Again, you can use Browse to help you select the correct working directory.

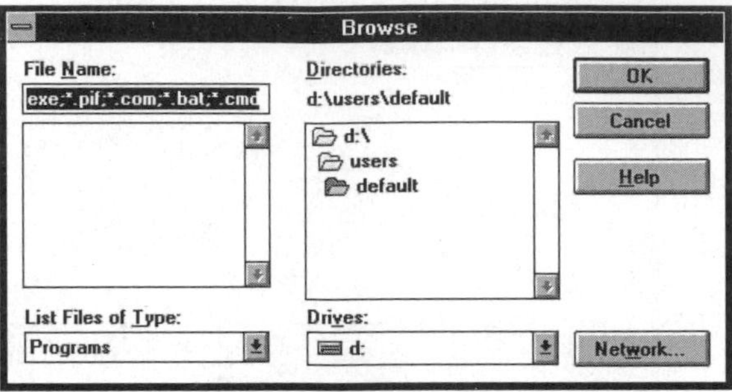

Figure 6.12: *Adding a new application by using the* ***B****rowse option.*

6. Enter the shortcut-key sequence by moving the pointer to the Shortcut Key text box and typing the key sequence you want to use.
7. Check the Run Minimized check box if you want the application to always begin as an icon.
8. Click on the OK button to create the new program item.

You also can add applications to a group by dragging them from the File Manager window. To do this, follow these steps:

1. Open File Manager by double-clicking on its program item icon in the Main application group.
2. Arrange your screen by dragging the title bars so that the File Manager and the Program Manager windows both are visible. You need to have only the group to which you want to add the application visible. Use the Tile button in the Task List application to arrange the windows quickly.
3. Locate the executable file for the application program you want to add in the File Manager.
4. Point to the file name with the mouse pointer. Press the mouse button, and drag the application file to the Program Manager window.

5. Drop the application file into the application group window or onto the group icon by releasing the mouse button.

6. Windows NT adds a program item icon for the application to the application group you select.

In Windows NT, the Program Manager enables you to manage application groups easily. You decide the way you want to represent your typical working tasks. You easily can create new groups, size and reposition groups, and delete outdated groups. By using the Program Manager, you can readily change your application groups to meet the demands of the changing tasks you face.

You can open a specific document or worksheet when an application is opened by placing the file name as a parameter in the Command Line text box. For example, the following command line opens Word for Windows along with the KENDRA.DOC document:

```
S:\WINWORD\WINWORD C:\SALES\KENDRA.DOC
```

Creating a New Group

You do not need to work with only the default groups Windows NT creates for you. Instead, you can create application groups that reflect your working style. To create new groups, follow these steps:

1. Select Program Manager's File menu, and choose the New option.

2. Select the Personal Program Group option button or the Common Program Group option button, depending on the type you want to create, and click on the OK button. (If you do not have the privileges to create a common program group, Windows NT informs you of this fact.)

3. Type the name you want to give the group in the Description text box, as shown in figure 6.13. This text then

appears under the group icon and in the title bar of the group document window.

4. Click on the OK button to create the group.

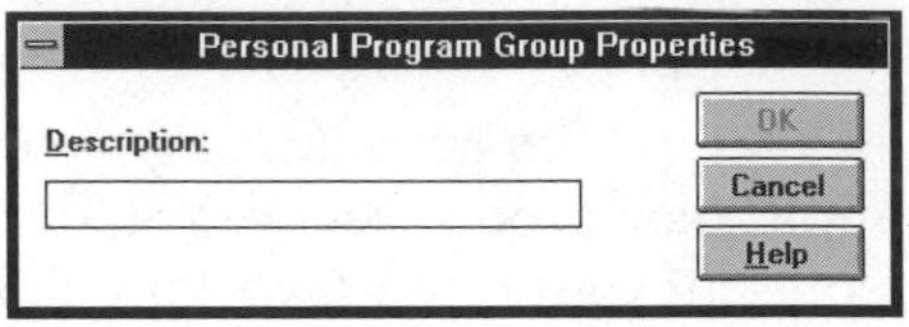

Figure 6.13: *Making a new application group.*

Personal Program Group Properties

Description:

OK

Cancel

Help

Modifying an Application Group

When you open a group icon in the Program Manager window, the application group window appears in the same position it held the last time it was opened. If this position is not convenient, several methods for moving and resizing the window are available.

If you want to move the window, point to its title bar with the mouse pointer, press the mouse button, and drag the window anywhere in the Program Manager's workspace. After the window is in position, release the mouse button.

If you want to change the application group window's size, point at one of its borders with the mouse pointer. After the pointer changes to a double arrow, press the mouse button down, and drag the border to increase or decrease the window's size. You see an outline representation of the new size as you drag. After the window is the size you want, release the mouse button.

If you want to arrange several open application group windows to get better access to the contents, use the Tile or Cascade options on the Window menu (see fig. 6.14).

The Tile option arranges the open windows edge to edge, like tiles on a wall. The Cascade option arranges the windows so that they fall from the upper left corner of the workspace toward the lower right corner. Each window's title bar and Control menu box is visible so that you easily can select a new application group window.

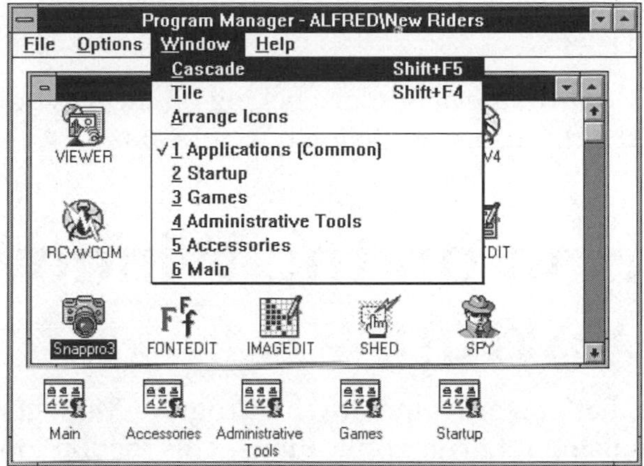

Figure 6.14:
*The **W**indow menu.*

Deleting an Application Group

As your working tasks change, an application group can become obsolete. As shown in figure 6.15, you can use the Delete option from the Program Manager's File menu to delete outdated groups.

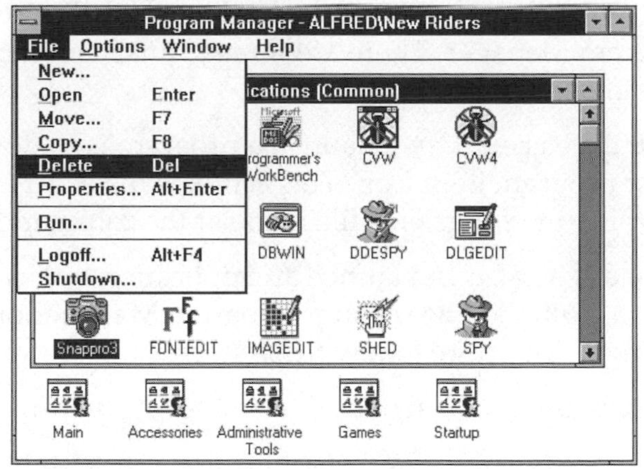

Figure 6.15:
*The **D**elete option.*

To delete an application group, follow these steps:

1. Highlight the group icon or group window you want to delete by clicking on it with the mouse.

2. Select the Program Manager's **F**ile menu, and choose **D**elete.
3. Confirm the action by clicking on the Yes button after the confirmation dialog box appears.

Working on the Windows NT Desktop

Now that you are familiar with Program Manager, you can begin using it to run applications. This section looks at how you can run single and multiple applications in Windows NT and how to work among them.

Running Applications

Program Manager and File Manager provide the same capability as the operating system command line for running programs. You can run any program that you can run from the MS-DOS or UNIX command line from Windows NT Program Manager. There are three primary methods of running an application.

First, the easiest way to launch a program is to double-click on its program item icon. This action is the exact equivalent of typing the program's file name at the command prompt.

Second, you also can launch an application by using the **R**un option from the **F**ile menu of Program Manager or File Manager. To do so, follow these steps:

1. Choose the **R**un option from the **F**ile menu.
2. Type the name of the application's executable file in the **C**ommand Line text box (see fig. 6.16). Include the directory path if the program is not in a directory on your system's search path.

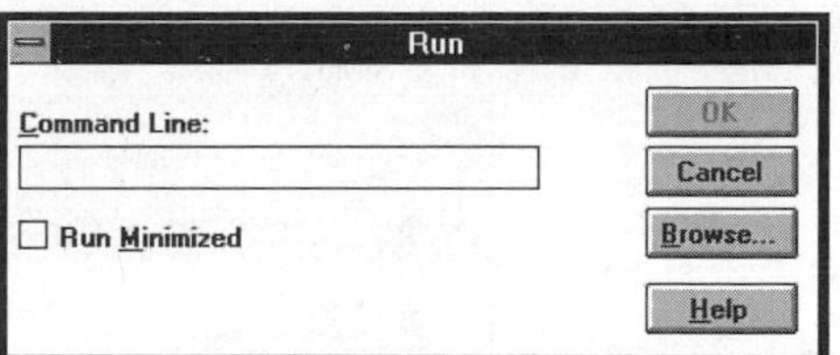

Figure 6.16: *Running a program by using the **Run** command.*

You also can select the **B**rowse button in the Run dialog box to display the Browse dialog box. (Note that the Run dialog box in File Manager does not include a Browse button.) Then, indicate the file you want to run in the File Name text box, and click on OK. This places the name of the application you want to run in the Command Line text box.

3. Click on the OK button.

*The **R**un option in the **F**ile menu is equivalent to entering a command at the command prompt. You can include a data file name and command-line switches.*

Third, you can launch applications from the File Manager window. Double-click on any program file name (those ending in EXE, COM, PIF, or BAT); Windows NT starts up the program.

If the extension of a data file (such as TXT) is associated with a particular application (such as Notepad), double-clicking on a data file runs the associated program and then opens the data file in the application window.

Exiting Applications

You can close most applications by choosing the Exit option from the File menu, as shown in figure 6.17. The application shuts down in an orderly way.

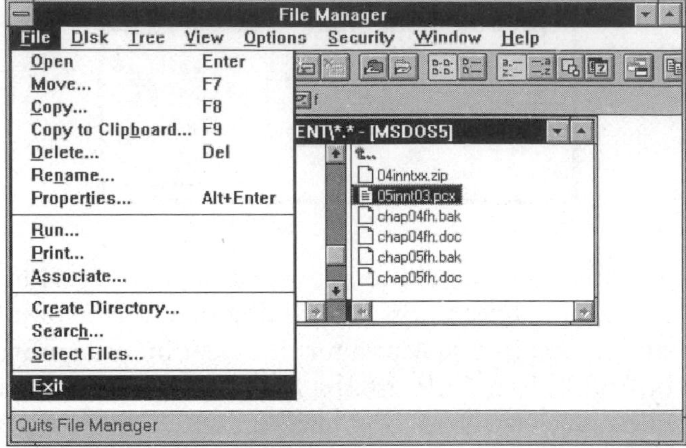

Figure 6.17: *Stopping an application by choosing Exit from the File menu.*

Before exiting, the application checks whether all data has been saved. If not, the application prompts you to save the data. After the data is saved (or you have chosen not to save), the application frees all its memory and resources and stops execution.

Windows NT provides a second method of exiting any application. (For applications such as Calculator, which do not provide an exit option, this is the only way to exit an application.) Click on the Control menu box and choose Close from the Control menu (see fig. 6.18).

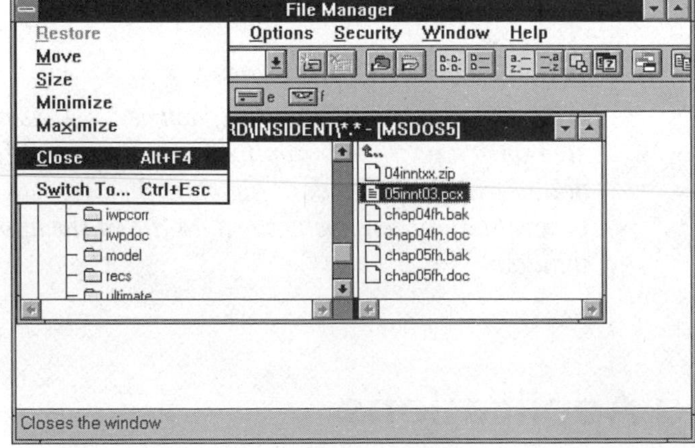

Figure 6.18: *Closing a window from the Control menu.*

An even quicker method is to simply double-click on the Control menu box. Before exiting, the same prompt to save data might appear.

The Windows NT Task List application (fully explained later in the chapter) provides another way to close an application. Launch the Task List by double-clicking on the background layer of the desktop or by selecting the S**w**itch To option from any application's Control menu. This method is useful if your screen is cluttered, and you want to reduce the clutter by exiting applications you are no longer using.

Bring up the Task List by double-clicking on the desktop. As illustrated in figure 6.19, click on the name of the program you want to execute in the list box. Click on the End Task button. The same prompt to save data then appears.

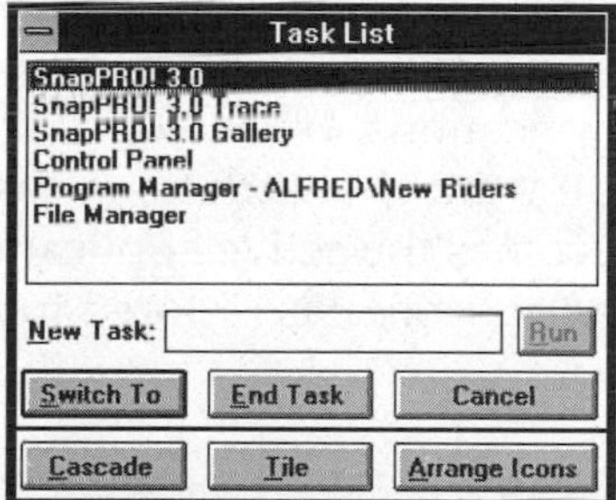

Figure 6.19: *Stopping a program from the Task List.*

Running Multiple Applications

One of the principal advantages of a windowed environment is its capability to run several applications at once. Windows NT makes it easy to switch between applications and also to find out which applications are running.

The method of multitasking used by Windows NT provides an advantage over Windows 3.1. Windows NT gives each program its own slice of time, shifting the timeslice *around among all the programs so they*

continues

all have a fair chance to execute. As a result, while one program works, so do all other programs.

In Windows 3.1, however, each program has to wait for the others to voluntarily yield the computer's resources before it can run. One busy application can prevent all applications from accomplishing work.

The easiest way to switch among applications is to click anywhere on the application window of the application you want to activate. The application's title bar is highlighted, and the application window moves to the top of the stack of running windows. The application is ready for input and commands.

You also can use the Alt+Tab key combination to switch between windows. While pressing this key combination, a box appears in the center of your screen (see fig. 6.20), listing the name of another opened application. Repeatedly pressing Tab while holding down Alt cycles you through the names of all running applications. When you reach the name of the application you want to switch to, release the Alt key. That application becomes the active application. If this application was running as an icon, it is restored to its original size and screen position.

Figure 6.20: *Switching among applications by pressing Alt+Tab.*

The second option is Alt+Esc. This option works like Alt+Tab, except that no dialog box appears. You move among the applications on the desktop. Each press of the key combination (Esc, while you hold down Alt) activates the next application on the list of running tasks. The application window or application icon is highlighted. Its open or minimized status does not change when the new task is made active, however. Icons become active, but they are not restored.

The third option is to use the Task List application. To initiate the Task List, double-click on the desktop or press Ctrl+Esc. (You also can select the Switch To option from any Control menu.) You can switch to any running application from the Task List by double-clicking on the application's name in the list box, or by clicking on the application's name and clicking on the Switch To button. The application, whose name is highlighted in the list box, becomes the active application. If it was minimized, its window is restored.

Windows NT links task-switching to mouse actions because clicking or double-clicking is much more efficient. If you can see your destination task on the screen, you can move to it visually by moving the mouse pointer.

If you can see the desktop background, you can move to the Task List by moving the mouse pointer. By enabling you to guide your interaction with your PC, Windows NT enables you to follow the natural flow of your thinking and working. Also, by attaching complex events to the mouse pointer, Windows NT enables you to focus more on the natural rhythm of your thoughts and less on the commands that perform the task.

Summary

This chapter introduced you to the key parts of the Windows NT desktop, including the background, the wallpaper, and the application layer. The functions associated with each also were identified.

This chapter also explained the way Program Manager provides a powerful substitute for the command-line prompt. The concept of building application groups that represent your working style suggests that you can be more productive in Windows NT than at the operating-system prompt.

You learned that you can arrange the applications that help you accomplish your work the way you want on your desktop. Procedures for running and exiting applications also show that Windows NT can provide great flexibility as you work.

7

CHAPTER

Configuring and Customizing the Windows NT Desktop

The Windows NT interface is very different from the DOS, OS/2, or UNIX command line. Although you can change some of the characteristics of a character-mode operating system interface, the extent to which you can customize it is limited. With some difficulty, you can change the screen colors, system prompt, and a few other characteristics. Windows NT, on the other hand, offers a number of controls to enable you to fully customize both its appearance and performance.

In this chapter, you discover ways to make Windows NT look and perform the way you want. In typical Windows NT fashion, you can make most of the changes with the click of a mouse button.

The changes you make might be for aesthetic reasons, such as adding a wallpaper to your background or changing colors of some of your interface components. Other changes can improve productivity. If you prefer to use the mouse with your left hand, for example, you can swap mouse buttons. (See "Controlling the Mouse" later in this chapter for instructions about swapping mouse buttons.)

This chapter covers the following topics:

- Changing colors by using the color icon
- Controlling fonts and ports
- Controlling the mouse
- Controlling the desktop
- Controlling printers by using the Printers icon
- Working with the Program Manager
- Replacing the Program Manager as the Windows NT shell
- Customizing the File Manager

Introducing the Windows NT Control Panel

You can make nearly all changes to Windows NT by using the Control Panel, which is a typical Windows NT application (CONTROL.EXE) that has a number of tools for controlling and changing the Windows NT interface.

The Control Panel does more than help you put a pretty face on Windows NT, however. It includes tools for adding and customizing your printer, setting the system date and time, and controlling multitasking.

Figure 7.1 shows the Control Panel. Your Control Panel might appear slightly different, depending on your hardware configuration.

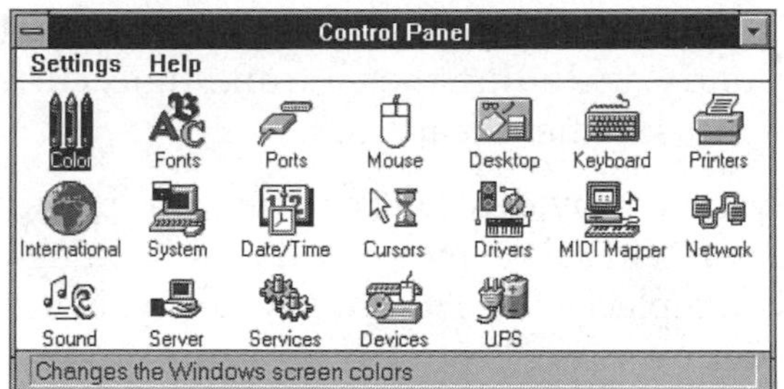

Figure 7.1: *Windows NT Control Panel.*

You can change only those elements of the Windows NT operating system that your system administrator has given you the privileges to change.

Each icon in the Control Panel enables you to control or customize a particular aspect of Windows NT. The following list describes the controls available in the Control Panel:

- **Color.** Controls the colors of the Windows NT interface components, including the workspace, background, and borders.
- **Fonts.** Enables you to view installed fonts, install new fonts, and delete existing fonts.
- **Ports.** Provides controls for setting baud rate and other communication parameters for each of your system's COM ports.
- **Mouse.** Enables you to swap left and right mouse buttons and adjust mouse sensitivity.
- **Desktop.** Controls a number of desktop features: wall-paper, background pattern, icon spacing, window-border width, and cursor-blink rate.
- **Keyboard.** Controls the keyboard repeat rate or sensitivity.
- **Printers.** Provides a full range of tools for adding, configuring, and removing printers.

- **International.** Controls many features that vary by country, including the date and time, currency, and unit of measurement features.
- **System.** Provides control over your path, boot configuration, virtual memory, and multitasking options. This icon replaces the 386-Enhanced icon in other versions of Windows.
- **Date/Time.** Sets the system date and time.
- **Cursors.** Enables you to change the mouse cursors (or mouse pointers) used by Windows NT to display different systems' events relating to the mouse, including animated cursors.
- **Drivers.** Enables you to install, configure, and remove hardware drivers. Many users do not have the privileges to use this icon, and have to rely on their system administrator to perform these services.
- **MIDI Mapper.** Enables you to adjust the settings for the Musical Instrument Device Interface on your sound card.
- **Network.** Controls network features when Windows NT runs on a networked workstation. Many users do not have the privileges to use this icon, and must rely on their system administrator to perform these services.
- **Sound.** Assigns sounds to various events for systems with sound boards; provides warning beeps for those without sound boards.
- **Server.** Enables you to configure your computer as a network server. Many users do not have the privileges to use this icon, and have to rely on their system administrator to perform these services.
- **Services.** Enables you to start, stop, pause, and configure the elements of the Windows NT operating system known as *services*. Many users do not have the privileges to use this icon, and have to rely on their system administrator to perform these services.

- **Devices.** Enables you to start, stop, and configure the hardware and software devices that make up your system. Many users do not have the privileges to use this icon, and have to rely on their system administrator to perform these services.
- **UPS.** Controls the behavior of an uninterruptable power supply attached to your system. Many users do not have the privileges to use this icon, and must rely on their system administrator to perform these services.

Changing Colors by Using the Color Icon

After you double-click on the Color icon, the Color dialog box appears (see fig. 7.2). The basic Color dialog box includes controls for selecting a predefined color scheme for the Windows NT interface, adding a new color scheme, and removing a color scheme. A large display area shows an example of the interface as you change color schemes or individual interface components.

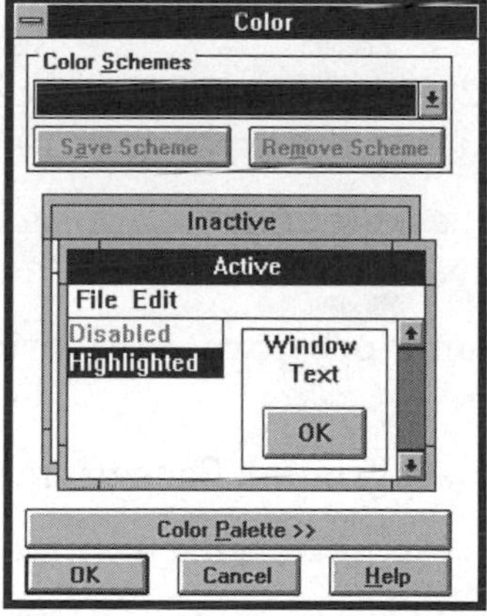

Figure 7.2:
The Color dialog box.

Windows NT has 23 predefined color schemes to suit a wide range of preferences. To choose one of the schemes, select the drop-down list button in the Color <u>S</u>chemes list box. A list of available color schemes drops down. Pick a scheme; you can view it in the sample display. If you like the color scheme, select OK for your selection to take effect.

Some of the colors in the predefined schemes may not be exactly what you want. The Color dialog box includes a Color Palette button, which, when selected, expands the Color dialog box to include a list of screen elements you can selectively customize. Figure 7.3 shows the expanded Color dialog box.

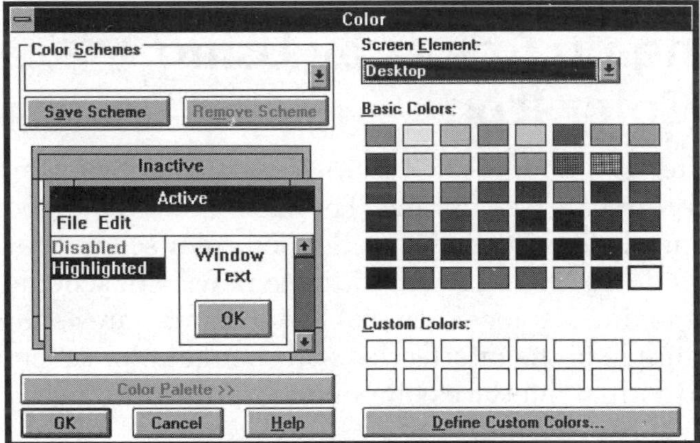

Figure 7.3:
The expanded Color dialog box.

The following 21 Windows NT interface components can be customized by using the expanded Color dialog box:

- **Desktop.** Background that appears behind all Windows NT.
- **Application Workspace.** Area inside an application's window.
- **Window Background.** Background for each window.
- **Window Text.** Text inside a window.
- **Menu Bar.** Menu bar at the top of each window.
- **Menu Text.** Text in each menu bar.
- **Active Title Bar.** Active window's title bar.

- **Inactive Title Bar.** All inactive windows' title bars.
- **Active Title Bar Text.** Text in the active window's title bar.
- **Inactive Title Bar Text.** Text in the inactive window's title bar.
- **Active Border.** Active window's border.
- **Inactive Border.** All inactive windows' borders.
- **Window Frame.** All window frames.
- **Scroll Bars.** All horizontal and vertical scroll bars.
- **Button Face.** Face of control buttons.
- **Button Shadow.** Shadow around the bottom and right edge of control buttons.
- **Button Text.** Control button text.
- **Button Highlight.** Highlight at left and upper edge of control buttons.
- **Disabled Text.** Dimmed text in menus.
- **Highlight.** Highlight bar in a menu.
- **Highlighted Text.** Menu text when the item is highlighted.

To change the color of one of these items, select it from the drop-down list box. Then pick the color you want the selected interface component to be from the color-selection menu. After you finish changing colors, save the color scheme by name. If you do not want to save it, select OK for the new scheme to become active.

If you want to save the color scheme, select the Save Scheme button in the Color Schemes group box. You are prompted to enter a name for the new color scheme. Enter a name, and choose OK. After you finish making changes, select OK again to exit the Color dialog box.

Using Custom Colors

The Color Palette in the expanded Color dialog box includes 16 spaces in which to store defined colors. To define a color, select the Define Custom Colors button. The Custom Color Selector dialog box appears (see fig. 7.4).

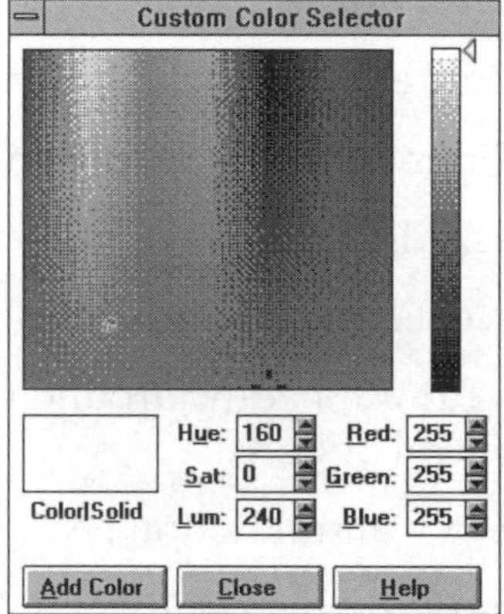

Figure 7.4:
The Custom Color Selector dialog box.

The Custom Color Selector dialog box gives you a choice of controls to create custom colors. You can either click the mouse inside the Color display box to get a rough estimate of the color you want, or drag the cursor in the Color display box until you get the color you want. Then use the slider controls for hue, saturation, and luminosity to fine-tune the color.

To add the color to the Custom Colors menu, select the box in which you want to store the new color. Then click on the Add Color button, and the color is applied to the selected box. To create a new color, return to the Color display box and use the same method to define your new color. After you have defined as many custom colors as you want, select the Close button to close the Custom Color Selector dialog box. To close the Color dialog box, click on the OK button.

Controlling Fonts

The Fonts icon in the Control Panel enables you to view installed fonts, add new fonts, and remove fonts. After you select the Fonts icon, the Fonts dialog box appears (see fig. 7.5).

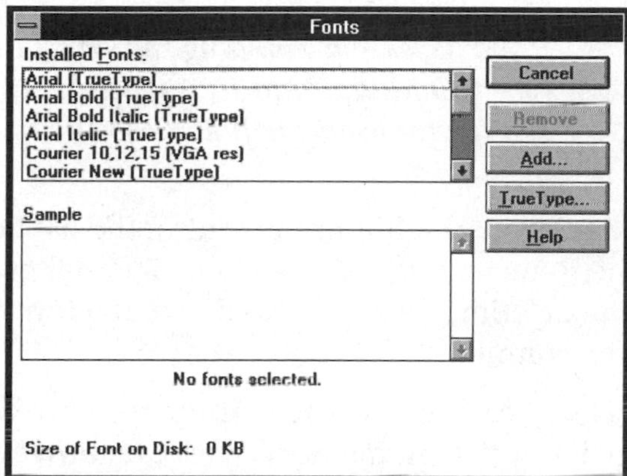

Figure 7.5:
The Fonts dialog box.

The list box in the Fonts dialog box displays all fonts currently installed for Windows NT applications in the *Registry*, which is the database that replaces the Windows 3.1 initialization files in Windows NT. To view a font, select it from the list box. A sample of the font appears in the Sample box. You can use this sample to identify fonts you no longer need or to identify a font you want to use in a document.

Some of the fonts listed in the Fonts dialog box have the description (TrueType) listed after their font name. TrueType fonts are scalable fonts. Unlike raster fonts, such as the MS Serif font, TrueType fonts can be resized to any point size without a loss of print quality. You use TrueType fonts by selecting one when you need it.

In addition to TrueType scalability, other advantages of using TrueType fonts are the many available shareware and public-domain TrueType fonts. For little or no cost, you can add many new fonts. One source of TrueType fonts is the

Windows NT forum on CompuServe. To access the Advanced Windows NT forum on CompuServe, type **GO WINNT** at any ! prompt.

Microsoft often reorganizes its support forums on CompuServe, and is likely to do so again as Windows NT moves from a beta product to a shipping product. If you have trouble finding the Windows NT forum, type ***GO MSCON*** *to access the Microsoft Connection, and use the menus to find the forum.*

To remove a font, highlight the font in the list box and then select the **R**emove button. The Control Panel prompts you to verify the deletion. Select **Y**es to delete the font or **N**o to cancel the command.

If you select **Y**es, the reference for the font is removed from the Registry and from memory. You can, however, add the font later without copying the definition file from the Windows NT distribution disks. If you prefer to delete the font file as well, check **D**elete Font File from the Disk check box when you confirm the deletion.

Use the **A**dd button to add a font. A file list box appears, which you can use to find the font-definition file (it usually has a FON or FOT file extension). After the file has been added, a sample appears in the Sample of Font box, and you can use it in your applications.

The **T**rueType button controls the way TrueType fonts are treated. Selecting the **T**rueType button brings up the TrueType dialog box. If you want to work only with TrueType fonts and exclude all others, select the **S**how Only TrueType Fonts in the Applications check box. Only TrueType fonts then appear in your application menus when you choose fonts.

Controlling Ports

The Ports icon displays a dialog box that you can use to set up the system's communication ports. Select the port to change from the Ports dialog box, and then click on the Settings button. The Settings for COM*x* dialog box appears, which enables you to set the baud rate, data bits, parity, stop bits, and flow control used by the selected port. The Ports and Settings for COM*x* dialog boxes are shown in figure 7.6.

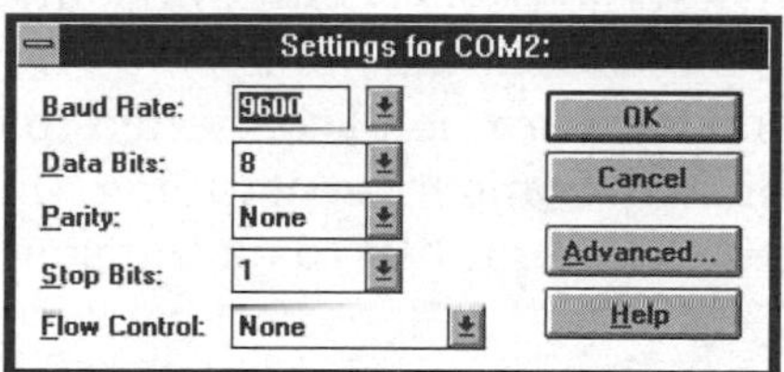

Figure 7.6:
The Ports and Settings for COMx dialog box.

Setting Baud Rate

The *baud rate* controls the number of signals (per second) sent down the line. Because various devices use standard baud rates, you can make your selection from preset baud rates in the Settings for COM*x* dialog box. To choose a baud rate, select the drop-down list button beside the Baud Rate box. The Control Panel responds with a list of possible baud-rate values. Select the one you need from the list. If the baud rate you need is not displayed, enter the value directly into the Baud Rate box by typing from the keyboard.

Various devices require different baud rates. The sending and receiving devices must use the same baud rate. If you dial an information service that uses 2400 baud, for example, you cannot use 9600 baud on your system and increase performance. You must use whatever the device on the other end of the line is expecting.

Modems typically use baud rates between 1200 and 9600. Plotters and printers often run at 9600 baud. Computers connected by a null-modem cable can often use 19,200 baud, and some can go as high as 115,200 baud. Control Panel only lists baud rates to 19,200. To use 115,200 baud, you must enter it from the keyboard.

Setting Data Bits, Stop Bits, and Parity

Your system's serial ports (COM ports) are *asynchronous devices*. This means that the information flowing between the computer and the peripheral connected to the COM port is not synchronized. Some form of timing, therefore, must be implemented in order for the data transfer to take place properly.

The information is broken into packets of a specific number of bits. A *bit* is the smallest unit of information a computer understands. The data is transferred down the line as a word made up of four to eight bits. Most often, the word is made up of seven or eight bits.

To synchronize the data, the actual data (represented by data bits) is framed by a *start bit* and a *stop bit*, which enable the receiving device to know when it has received a word.

To specify the number of data bits, select the appropriate option from the Data Bits drop-down list in the Settings for COM*x* dialog box. To set the number of stop bits, choose the appropriate number. Again, the values you select must match what the other device is expecting.

The Parity setting controls the way systems handle error checking. The available parity options are Even, Odd, None, Mark, and Space, as described in the following list:

- **Even parity.** A parity bit is added to the data stream and switched on or off to ensure that the total number of on (1) bits is always even. The receiving system checks the number of bits, and if it finds an even number, it assumes no transmissions were lost. If the receiving device finds an odd number, however, it assumes a transmission has been lost, and directs the sending device to resend the data.

- **Odd parity.** The parity bit is switched on or off to make sure that the total number of on bits is always odd. The receiving system checks the total number of bits to make sure that it is odd.
- **Mark parity.** The parity bit is always turned on. Mark parity provides only limited error checking because it does not check to see whether a bit was lost in transmission. Mark parity does, however, provide a pattern for the receiving system to look for.
- **Space parity.** The parity bit is always turned off. Again, this provides a pattern for the receiving system to recognize, but it does not provide for error checking.
- **None.** No parity checking is implemented.

Setting Flow Control

Flow control coordinates data transfer between two systems by providing a means for the receiving system to tell the sending system that it is ready to receive more information. Flow control also is called *handshaking*.

The three options for flow control in the Settings for COM*x* dialog box are Xon/Xoff, Hardware, and None, as follows:

- **Xon/Xoff.** A software method by which the Xon character (11 hex, DC3, or Ctrl-Q) is used to signal that the system is ready to receive. The Xoff character (13 hex, DC1, or Ctrl-S) is used to signal that the sending system must stop transmitting until it receives the Xon character again.
- **Hardware.** A dedicated line in the cable connecting the two devices is used to coordinate data transfer.
- **None.** No method of flow control is used.

After you determine the proper setting, select it in the Flow Control drop-down list. When all settings are in place, click on the OK button to implement the changes. You then can set values for each of the other ports in your system.

Controlling the Mouse

The Mouse icon displays a dialog box that enables you to control mouse response with two variables: tracking speed and double-click speed. It also enables you to swap the function of the left and right mouse buttons.

Changing the tracking speed alters the response of mouse movement as you move it across the desktop. The mouse has two levels of acceleration that accelerate the cursor when the mouse moves more than a certain distance over a given period of time.

To reduce mouse acceleration, slide the button in the Mouse Tracking Speed slider bar to the left or use the left scroll button. To increase mouse acceleration, move the slider to the right or use the right scroll button.

The *double-click speed* defines the maximum time between clicks that the two clicks are recognized as a double-click. If the amount of time exceeds the double-click speed limit, the two clicks are recognized as individual clicks.

If you increase the setting by moving the slider to the left or by using the left scroll button, you increase the amount of time that can pass between the two clicks of a double-click. If you move the slider to the right or use the right scroll button, you decrease the time that can pass between the two clicks of a double-click.

The Swap Left/Right Buttons check box enables you to switch operation of the left and right mouse buttons. If you are left-handed and prefer to use the right mouse button as the select button, you can swap mouse buttons by checking this box.

Another situation in which you might prefer to swap buttons is if you are using a spreadsheet such as Excel. You can select cells with your left hand while entering numbers on the numeric keypad with your right hand.

Controlling the Desktop

The Desktop icon gives you a number of controls to define the appearance of the Windows NT desktop. After you select this icon, the Desktop dialog box appears (see fig. 7.7).

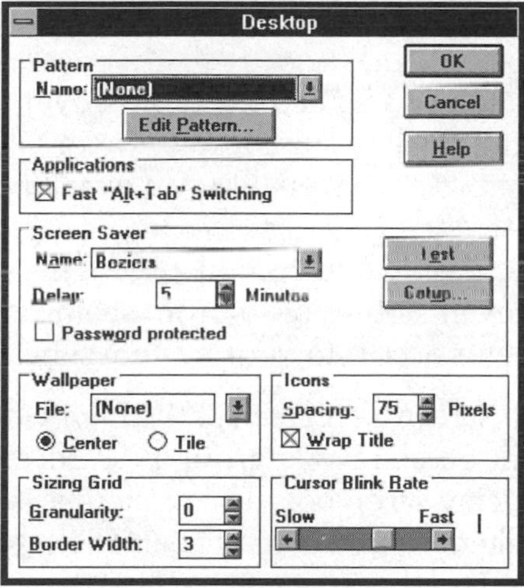

Figure 7.7:
The Desktop dialog box.

The Pattern group box sets the background pattern that appears over the desktop. You can select from 13 predefined patterns by using the drop-down list button. If you prefer, you can edit an existing pattern or create a new one.

If you select the Edit Pattern button, the Desktop-Edit Pattern dialog box appears. You use this dialog box to create new patterns and add them to the list of available patterns. You also use it to remove a pattern from the list. (A pattern uses little additional memory.)

Using a Screen Saver

The next group in the Desktop dialog box is the Screen Saver box. A *screen saver* is a memory-resident program that monitors keyboard and mouse activity. When no activity occurs for a user-defined time span, the screen saver blanks the screen and, optionally, displays a dynamic pattern, such as a moving star field.

The VGA displays required by Windows NT do not generally need a screen-saver program to prevent burn-in. On VGA displays, a screen saver is more of a novelty than anything else.

One reason to use a screen saver, however, is to prevent the unauthorized use of your computer workstation. The Windows NT screen savers enable you to set a password that must be entered to regain access to the system after the screen saver has blanked the display. This serves two purposes: it prevents other users from seeing confidential data, and it prevents access to your system when you are away.

To choose a screen saver, select the N**a**me drop-down list button in the Screen Saver group box. Set the delay time by using the **D**elay scroll box. The *delay time* is the amount of time the system can be inactive before the screen saver blanks the display. To set a password, check the Passw**o**rd protected check box.

To set options for the screen saver, select the Set**u**p button. A configuration dialog box tailored to the saver you have selected appears (see fig. 7.8), enabling you to set parameters for the screen saver and to specify a password. If you want to test the screen saver, return to the Desktop dialog box and select the T**e**st button.

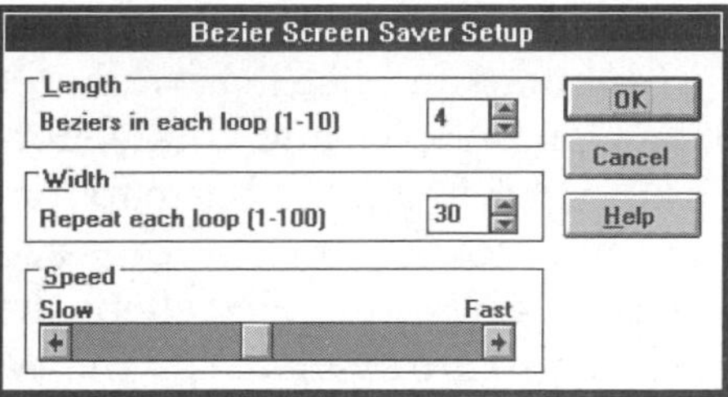

Figure 7.8:

The Screen Saver Setup dialog box.

Using Wallpaper

The next group box in the Desktop dialog box is the Wallpaper group, which enables you to set up a wallpaper bit map. *Wallpaper* appears over the desktop pattern, and the wallpaper image comes from a standard Windows NT bit-map (BMP) file.

Although there are a number of standard bit maps to choose from, you can create your own bit maps in Paintbrush or another application that creates Windows NT bit-map files.

To use a new image as wallpaper, copy it to the Windows NT directory, and then select it by using the Desktop dialog box. Figure 7.9 shows one of Windows NT's standard wallpaper images.

Figure 7.9

A standard Windows NT wallpaper image.

You can convert graphics files, in various formats, to a Windows NT bit map and use it as wallpaper. The Windows NT forums on CompuServe and GEnie, in particular, have a number of wallpaper images in bit-map format that you can use. Many graphics forums on CompuServe offer images in GIF (pronounced "jif") format. Excellent shareware utilities, such as WinGIF, also are available on the Windows NT forums. These utilities enable you to view GIF files in Windows NT and convert them to other formats, including the Windows NT bit-map format. After converting a GIF file to bit-map format, you assign it as your wallpaper in the same manner as described previously.

Windows 3.1 bit maps can be used with Windows NT.

Remember that wallpaper uses more memory to display than a desktop pattern. If you find your system is running short of memory, consider removing your wallpaper to see whether it clears up the problem.

Controlling Icon Spacing and Window Placement

The Desktop dialog box also contains the Icons group box, which contains two controls, Spacing and Wrap Title. The Spacing option enables you to set the default spacing between icons. The value, in pixels, is the distance from one point on an icon to the corresponding point on the next (for example, from bottom right corner to bottom left corner). You can set icon spacing to any value between 32 and 512. After setting icon spacing, you must use the Arrange Icons command in Program Manager to update the desktop. Only the icons in the active window are rearranged (see fig. 7.10).

Figure 7.10: *Icons brought closer by using a smaller icon spacing value.*

The width of a typical icon is 32 pixels, so setting icon spacing to 32 and rearranging them causes the icons to touch one another.

Another consideration when you set icon spacing is the length of program descriptions that appear under your icons. Although the icons do not overlap, the descriptions, if they are too long, still might overlap and be difficult to read.

To shorten the description under an icon, select the icon by clicking on it. Then select the File and Properties commands from Program Manager's menu. Enter the new program description in the Description field of the Program Item Properties dialog box, and choose OK.

Another option is to wrap the icon title. *Wrapping* causes multiple-word descriptions under an icon to wrap, or flow, to more than one line. To wrap icon titles, check the Wrap Title check box.

The Sizing Grid group box controls the placement of windows on the desktop. The Granularity option specifies a grid, in multiples of 14 pixels, used to locate windows when you drag them across the display or open new windows. The grid gives you an easy way to line up windows and organize the display.

By default, Granularity is set to 0, meaning that no grid is used, and you can position windows anywhere on the desktop.

In general, a granularity setting of 1 is best if you want to use the grid to align windows. Higher settings do not provide much flexibility in window placement.

Border width is another parameter you can change in the Sizing Grid group box. Border Width specifies the width of borders around the windows on the desktop. Although border width is a matter of personal preference, changing border width serves some functional purposes. As the border decreases in size, it becomes harder to grab window borders. If the border is too small, resizing a window can become a difficult task.

The border size you select depends on both your personal preference and your dexterity with the mouse. No one value gives you the best results, so experiment with border width until you find one you like.

The Desktop dialog box also offers the Cursor Blink Rate control. This slider bar controls the speed at which the cursor blinks.

Although the cursor blink rate is primarily a matter of personal preference, it can help you find a cursor in an application window. You may find a slower cursor blink rate useful for making the cursor more visible on LCD displays.

Controlling Printers by Using the Printers Icon and Print Manager

The Printers icon in the Windows NT Control Panel gives you the tools necessary for installing and configuring printers to use in Windows NT. When you select it, the Print Manager application begins (see fig. 7.11).

The Print Manager window lists any currently installed printers, the default printer, and the status of the currently selected printer, and includes buttons and menu commands for tasks such as adding and configuring a printer.

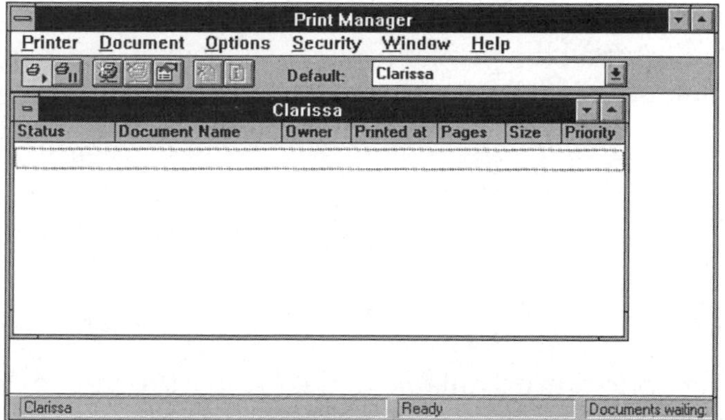

Figure 7.11:

The Print Manager window.

If you have not installed your printer yet, select the Create Prin<u>t</u>er option on the <u>P</u>rinter menu to choose from a list of supported printers. The <u>D</u>river drop-down list box lists all available printers (an extensive list). If your printer is listed, select it. If you have a third-party driver to install for your printer, select the last option, Other.

Print Manager then prompts you to identify the driver file for the printer. Specify the name of the file to install as a printer driver. (The file generally is provided on a disk that comes with the printer.)

After you install your printer, it must be configured. To configure a printer, select <u>P</u>roperties from the <u>P</u>rinter menu. The Printer Properties dialog box appears (see fig. 7.12).

Printer Properties
Printer Name: Clarissa
Driver: HP LaserJet IIP
Description: HP LaserJet IIP on LPT1:
Print to: LPT1:
Share this printer on the network
Share Name:
Location:
OK
Cancel
Setup...
Details...
Settings...
Help

Figure 7.12:

The Printer Properties dialog box.

The controls and buttons in this dialog box enable you to set defaults for all the printer options. In general, you can use the default time-out values (usually accessed from the Setup button) unless you experience problems with the printer.

If you experience problems, try raising the time-out values.

Other options are available in the Printer Properties dialog box; they vary according to the type of port to which the printer is connected. If connected to an LPT port, the Settings button provides at least the time-out setting. If connected to a COM port, however, the Settings button is used to set communication parameters for the selected port.

If you select Settings, the Settings for COM*x* dialog box appears. Use the dialog box to set communication parameters for the port, including the baud rate, data bits, parity, stop bits, and flow control. You also can control the base I/O address for the port, and its interrupt.

If your printer is connected to a network, you can select the Connect to Printer option from the Printer menu. Choosing this option brings up the Connect to Printer dialog box (see fig. 7.13).

Figure 7.13:

The Connect to Printer dialog box.

Any existing network queue connections are shown in the Shared Printers list box. To connect to an existing queue, select the queue, and choose the OK button. After you establish proper connections for the device, set options for your printer, as discussed for the Printer Properties command. Set the options required for your printer, and then choose OK to activate the changes (see fig. 7.14).

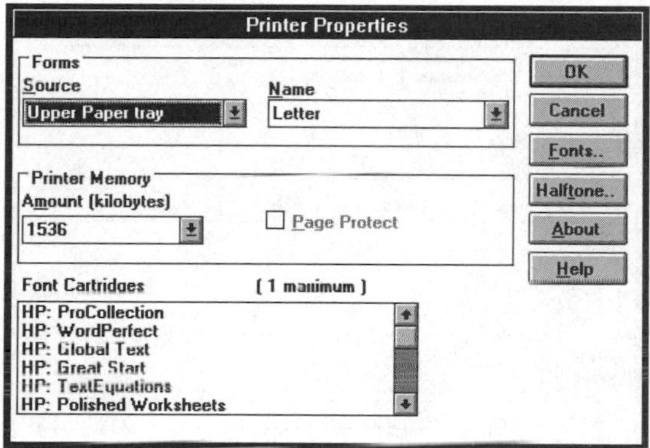

Figure 7.14:
The options dialog boxes for the HP LaserJet IIP.

When you are satisfied with the setup for your printer, exit the Print Manager.

In Windows NT, all print jobs are scheduled through the Print Manager. The Print Manager enables you to reschedule print jobs that are pending in the print queue. You can move a print job in front of another if you decide it has a higher priority, for example. In addition, you can remove a pending print job from the queue if you decide you do not need to print it. Because Windows NT includes networking features, Print Manager enables complete, efficient control over network print queues.

Controlling System Options

The System icon in the Control Panel provides a dialog box that gives you control over system functions (see fig. 7.15). This dialog box enables you to set environment variables, manage virtual memory, and prioritize tasks when *multitasking* (running more than one task at the same time).

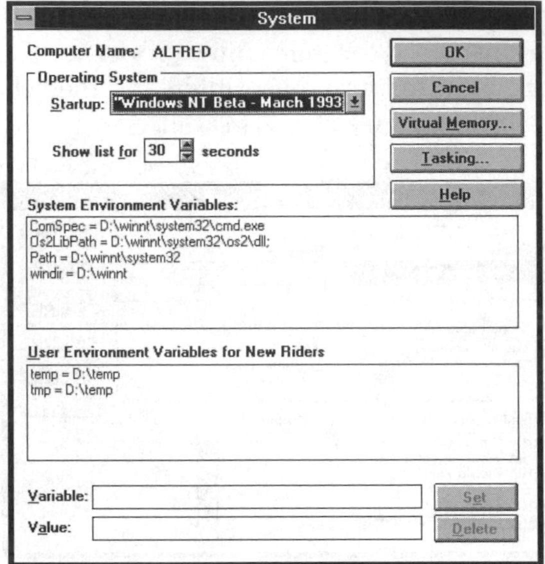

Figure 7.15: *The System dialog box.*

Setting Environment Variables

Windows NT enables you to define environment variables that it uses to find directories with which it works. When Windows NT installs, it defaults to the settings in the System Environment Variables list box. You can add your own environment variables, displayed in the **U**ser Environment Variables list box. You might want to set a `path` variable so the system knows which directories to search for executable and data files. You also might want to include values for the commonly used `temp` and `tmp` variables.

To set an environment variable, enter the variable name in the **V**ariable text box. Enter the value in the V**a**lue text box. Use the S**e**t button to set the value of the variable, and the **D**elete button to delete unwanted variables. (You can modify only the **U**ser Environment Variables.) The values of the variables are stored as a part of your logon profile.

Controlling Virtual Memory

The Virtual Memory button in the System dialog box enables you to control the way Windows NT handles *disk paging*, which refers to Windows NT's capability to simulate memory by using a portion of your hard disk. This technique enables Windows NT to run very large applications or many applications concurrently. After you select the Virtual Memory button, the Virtual Memory dialog box appears, as shown in figure 7.16.

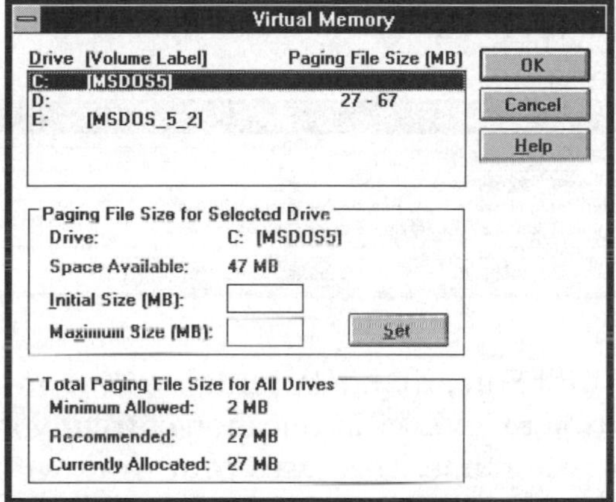

Figure 7.16: *Virtual Memory dialog box.*

To set up the paging file, select the drive that contains the file in the Drive [Volume Label] list box. Windows NT shows the amount of space available in the Space Available display in the Paging File Size group. It also places recommended file sizes (the defaults) in the Initial Size and Maximum Size text boxes.

You can enter your own settings, but it is best to accept the defaults.

Current paging file information is displayed in the Total Paging File Size for All Drives group of controls. To set up the paging file, click on the Set button, then click on the OK button.

Controlling Multitasking

Multitasking refers to the computer's capability to run more than one application (task) at a time. During multitasking, the computer services each task for a brief period of time, cycling through the tasks quickly, so it appears that the computer is doing more than one job at a time. It is not, however—it is just switching back and forth too quickly for you to notice.

You can prioritize various applications by using the three settings in the Tasking dialog box, which you access by clicking on the Tasking button (see fig. 7.17).

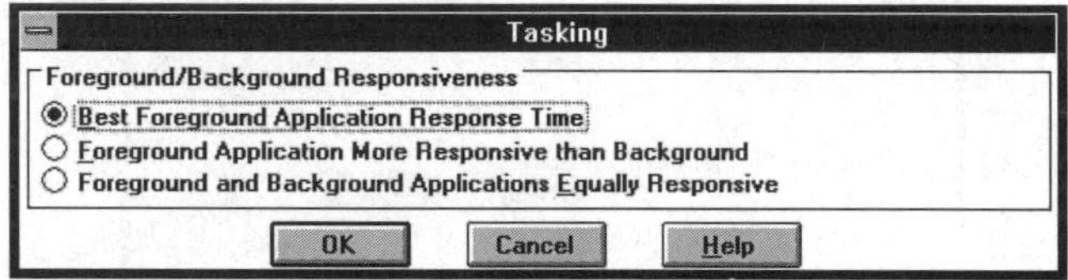

Figure 7.17: *The Tasking dialog box.*

Select the Best Foreground Application Response Time option button to give the application currently in focus the most processing time. This eases your work with the current application, making it run as fast as possible.

Select the Foreground Application More Responsive than Background option button if you want to allocate more time to applications running in the background, but still want the primary application to run quickly.

Select Foreground and Background Applications Equally Responsive option button if you need to devote more time to background applications, and you do not mind slower performance in the current application. Windows NT provides these options to simplify prioritizing your applications. Experiment to see what best suits your working style.

Controlling Other Settings with the Control Panel

The Control Panel includes five other icons that control a range of options: International, Keyboard, Date/Time, Cursors, and Sound.

Using the International Icon

The International icon enables you to control many environmental settings that usually vary by country. These settings include the language used for case-sensitive tasks and sorting, the keyboard layout, unit of measurement (English or metric), date and time format, currency format, and number format. You select these settings using drop-down list boxes. Figure 7.18 shows the International dialog box.

Figure 7.18:
The International dialog box.

You can change many settings globally by selecting a different country setting. If you switch from United States to United Kingdom, for example, the Measurement, Date Format, Time Format, and Currency Format options change.

You can also adjust the Date Format, Currency Format, Time Format, and Number format individually. To do so, click on the Change button next to the format you want to change. Adjust the controls in the dialog box that appears to suit your needs, then click on the OK button. By adjusting these formats individually, you can alter a particular country setting to suit specialized needs, such as a preference for Day-Month-Year date order in a U.S.-based business.

Using the Keyboard Icon

The Keyboard icon performs two tasks—it enables you to change the response rate of your keyboard and to control key response time. If you select the Keyboard icon, the Keyboard dialog box appears (see fig. 7.19), with a scroll bar to change the key Repeat Rate and Delay Before First Repeat.

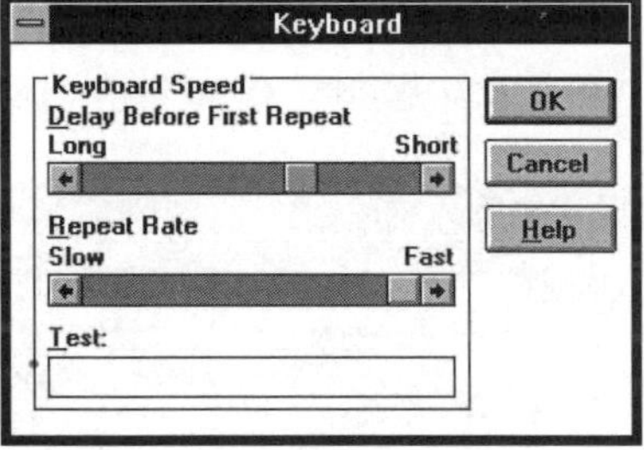

Figure 7.19:
The Keyboard dialog box.

You decrease or increase the keyboard key repeat rate by moving the Repeat Rate slider to the left or right. Below the scroll bar is a text box in which you can test the change in repeat rate.

The Delay Before First Repeat slider controls the amount of time a key can be down before it begins to repeat. You can increase the time, for example, so that you can hold the key down longer without repeating characters.

If you are a "heavy-handed" typist, you might want to increase this setting. If you prefer a light touch on the keyboard, decrease this setting.

Using the Date/Time Icon

The Date/Time icon is very simple—all it does is set the system's date and time. In the dialog box (see fig. 7.20), you can use scroll arrows to change the date and time, or you can enter the new date and time directly. You also must set your Time Zone in the drop-down list box and decide whether to check the Automatically Adjust for Daylight Savings Time check box.

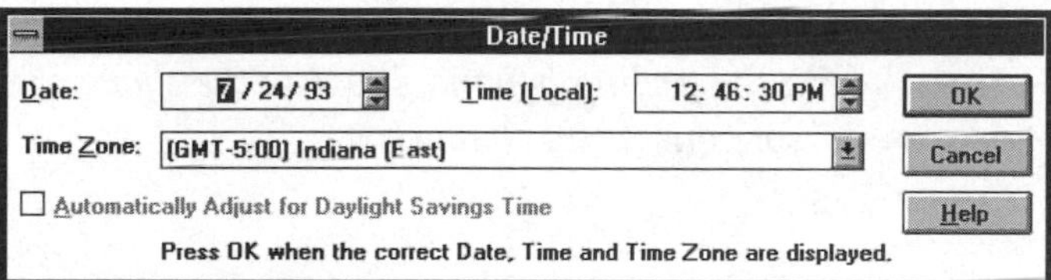

Figure 7.20:
The Date/Time dialog box.

Using the Cursors Icon

The Cursors icon enables you to choose which mouse cursors appear in Windows NT. For instance, if you prefer to replace the hourglass as the wait icon, select the hourglass in the System Cursors list box (see fig. 7.21).

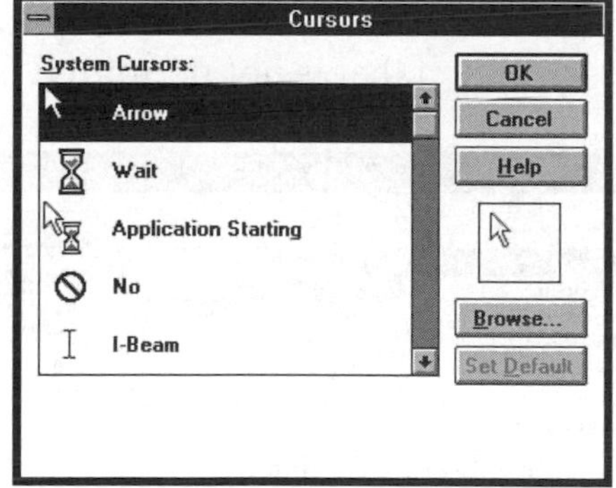

Figure 7.21:
The Cursors dialog box.

Next, click on the Browse button to select an alternative cursor by file name.

When you choose a file name in the list box, the cursor represented by that file appears in the preview box. Click on the OK button to substitute the cursor you chose for the hourglass. (You always can reset to the system default cursors by clicking on the Set Default button.)

In Windows NT, you can have animated mouse cursors. You can replace the hourglass, for example, with a self-peeling banana, or a barber pole that spins. These cursors are fun, but they might not be useful as substitutes for the cursors you use to take action. It is hard to see the hot spot for clicking and double-clicking with the peeling banana, because the shape of the cursor constantly changes.

Using the Sound Icon

The Sound icon enables you to assign sounds to various system events if your system includes a sound card. Windows NT includes four synthesized sounds, and you can add other sound files by copying the new sounds' WAV files to the Windows NT directory.

If your system lacks a sound card, the Enable System Sounds check box enables/disables a warning beep that sounds when you try an action that is not permitted (see fig. 7.22).

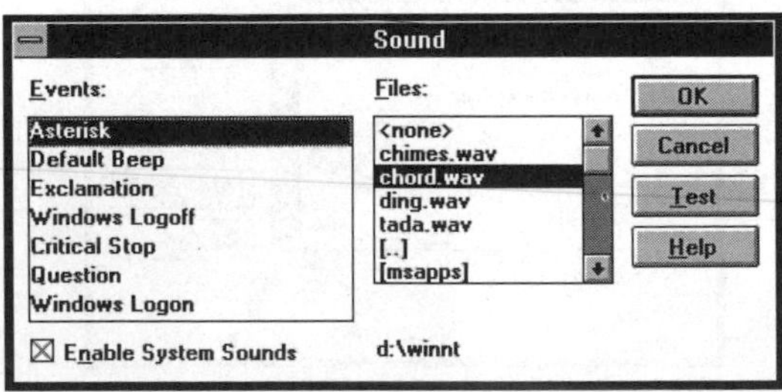

Figure 7.22:
The Sound dialog box.

Although the Control Panel often offers the quickest and simplest way to customize Windows NT's appearance and behavior, it is not the only way. In the next section, you examine some of the ways you can change the appearance and behavior of Windows NT's shell, Program Manager.

Working with the Program Manager

Although Windows NT acts as an interface between you and your computer, it uses a shell program to act as an interface between you and itself. By default, the standard Windows NT shell is the Program Manager, which is what many new users think of when they think of "Windows NT." The Program Manager gives you program groups and other aspects of the Program Manager interface that most users associate with Windows NT.

You have four options for controlling the way the Program Manager functions. All four appear in the Options menu in Program Manager's menu bar (see fig. 7.23).

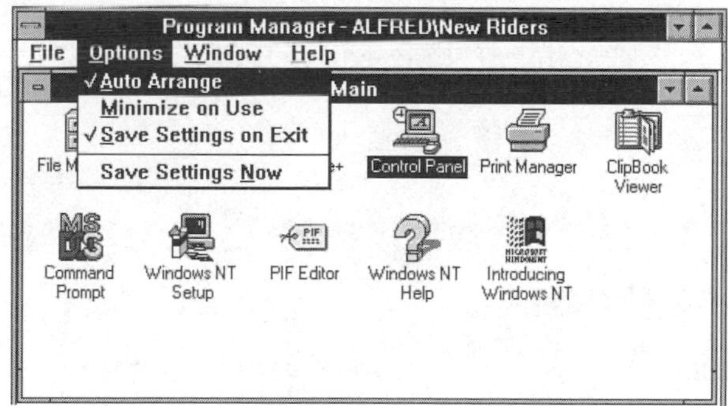

Figure 7.23: *Program Manager's **Options** menu.*

The four options are as follows:

- **Auto Arrange.** Controls the way Windows NT handles icons in a group. If Auto Arrange is active, you see a check mark beside it. Auto Arrange causes the Program Manager to automatically rearrange item icons inside a group window when you open or resize the window. If Auto Arrange is disabled, icons remain stationary as you manipulate the window.

- **Minimize on Use.** Controls whether the Program Manager window automatically reduces to an icon when you run an application. If enabled, Program Manager shrinks to an icon when you select an application from a program group. If Minimize on Use is not enabled, the Program Manager window remains on the screen.
- **Save Settings on Exit.** If enabled, this option saves changes to the desktop when you exit Windows NT. If, for example, you move groups or group icons around on the desktop and want to save your changes for the next session, check the Save Settings on Exit option before you exit Windows NT.
- **Save Settings Now.** Saves the Program Manager's settings immediately without exiting the Windows session. This option prevents you from having to log off and then abort it in order to save settings for Program Manager.

These options are the only direct ways to customize the Program Manager. You can do a number of things indirectly, however, and many of them relate to the use of Program Manager.

Working with Program Groups and Program Items

A *program group* is a collection of program item icons that resides inside a group window. The group window can be resized, moved, minimized to an icon, or maximized to fill the display. Each of the program items inside the group window is represented by an icon.

Usually, the program item is an executable file, such as an EXE, COM, or BAT file. You also can use document files and macro files (really document files) as program items, as well as PIFs (program information files).

Some of the ways you can customize your Program Manager shell include creating groups, eliminating groups, and moving items from one group to another.

Creating a New Group

Many Windows NT applications create their own groups when you install the application, ensuring that all programs available with the new application are added to your Windows NT environment.

You also can create your own groups. You can, for example, place some of your existing applications in a common group for easier access. You can include the spreadsheet, the word processor, the Control Panel, the DOS icon, and a few other program items in the group. You can then keep only this group open on the desktop and still have access to all your main applications and tools.

Another reason to create a program group is to gather selected document files. You can associate a document file type with an application; open the application along with a document file simply by clicking on the document file's icon. You learn how to associate a file type with an application a little later. First, you need to learn how to create a program group.

To create a new group, select the New command from Program Manager's File menu. You see the New Program Object dialog box. Select the Personal Program Group option or the Common Program Group option and click on OK. (Personal groups appear only during Windows sessions during which you are logged on. Common groups appear for all users logged on to your system.) The Program Manager generates a new dialog box, called Program Group Properties, in which you supply the group description. The Personal Program Group Properties dialog box is shown in figure 7.24.

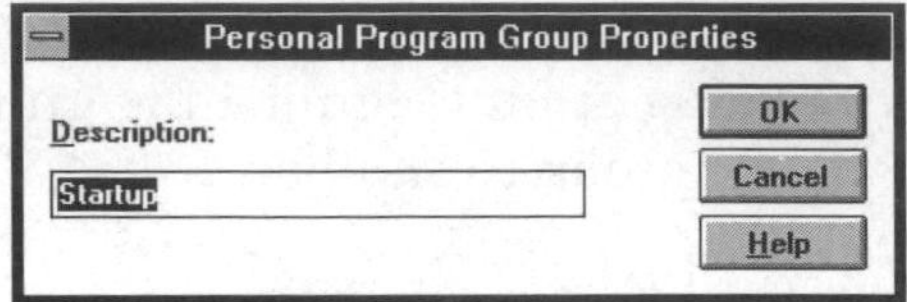

Figure 7.24:
The Personal Program Group Properties dialog box.

The Description field appears underneath the group's icon on the Program Manager desktop. After you supply a description and file name, choose OK. The Program Manager adds the group to the Registry and adds the new group window to the desktop. The new group is now ready to have program items added.

Creating a Program Item

As you read earlier, a program item can be an executable file—such as an EXE, COM, or BAT file—or it can be a document file or PIF. Regardless of the type of file it represents, a program item icon in a group only represents a file of some kind; it is not the file itself. If you delete an icon from a group, for example, only the reference to the file is deleted—the file itself is still intact.

To create a program item of any type, use the New command in the program Manager's File menu. Click on the Program Item option button, and click on OK. The Program Manager displays the Program Item Properties box, which you use to supply information about the new item. The Program Item Properties dialog box is shown in figure 7.25.

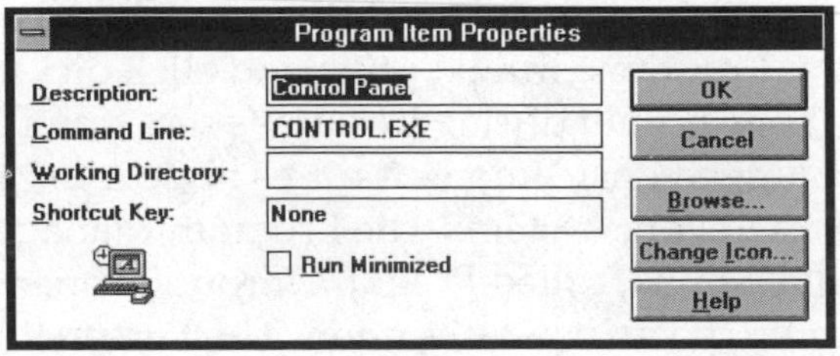

Figure 7.25:
The Program Item Properties dialog box.

As you can see, the Program Item Properties dialog box is similar to the one you use to create a program group. The description in the Description field is used as the description under the program item icon when it appears in a group window.

If your description is too long, it can overlap another item's description. A way to avoid overlapping is to turn on icon title wrap by using the Desktop icon in the Control Panel.

The Command Line field specifies the command to invoke when the program item is selected. If the item is an executable file, enter the name of the file, including the extension, in the Command Line field. If the directory containing the file is on the path, you can omit the drive and directory. It is a good idea, however, to always include the absolute path, including the drive, for the file. This eliminates potential problems.

You can enter any arguments required by the program on the command line as well. *Arguments* are characters following the file name that tell the program how to behave when it starts. The most common argument is the name of a file to load. Type arguments after the file name separated by blank spaces.

You also can enter the name of a PIF if the item is a DOS application that includes a PIF file or a DOS application for which you intend to create a PIF file. It is always a good idea to use a PIF for DOS applications you run under Windows NT and to specify the PIF for the program item, instead of the program's executable file. This ensures that the settings in the PIF are always used, which saves memory and avoids potential problems with video display and other characteristics.

In addition to executable files and PIFs, you can specify a document file in the Command Line field, even if you have not associated the file type with the application. (See "Associating Document Files with Applications" later in this chapter for more information.) This arrangement offers one of the easiest ways to launch an application and load a document file—click on the icon attached to the document, and the application loads automatically.

The Working Directory setting specifies the directory that becomes active when the application is started. If you keep the application's document files in a specific directory, set Working Directory to point to the document directory. If you leave the setting blank, the directory that has the program file becomes the working directory.

You also can assign a shortcut key to the application by using the Shortcut Key setting. A *shortcut key* is a combination of the Ctrl+Alt, Ctrl+Shift, or Ctrl+Shift+Alt keys with another key, such as A, B, C, or F6. If you have an application running in the background that has been assigned a shortcut key, press the shortcut-key sequence to bring the application to the front of the desktop (make it active).

Browsing for a File and Changing Icons

If you do not recall the location of a file you wish to enter into the Program Item Properties dialog box, use the Browse button to find it. Select Browse, and use the list box to find the file.

You also can use the Program Item Properties dialog box to change the icon associated with a program item. If you select the Change Icon button, the Select Icon dialog box appears. Enter the name of the executable (EXE) file, Dynamic Link Library (DLL) file, or individual icon file (ICO) that contains the icon. The icons display in a scrollable viewing box. Select the icon you want, then choose OK for the change to take effect. The file PROGMAN.EXE contains several icons you can use for your new item.

Associating Document Files with Applications

For a document item icon association to work, the file extension must be associated with an executable file or a PIF. To associate a document file type with a program or PIF, open the File Manager and locate a document file of the type you want to associate with the application.

Select the file, and then select the Associate command in the File Manager's File menu. A dialog box appears, prompting you to enter the name of the application with which to associate the document type. Include the drive and path to the executable or PIF file, and then choose OK. File Manager adds an entry to the Registry for the new document association, which makes the association effective for future Windows NT sessions.

Replacing Program Manager as the Windows NT Shell

Alternative shell programs have been very popular for Windows 3.1. As Windows NT launches, however, no third-party shells have been announced for Windows NT. Inevitably, replacements for Program Manager will appear. More than likely, they will install themselves into the Registry when you run the setup programs and provide a means of uninstalling themselves.

The shell for Windows NT is set by using a line in the Registry database. You can view the setting in the HKEY_LOCAL_MACHINE on Local Machine window. It is in the SOFTWARE\Microsoft\Windows NT\Current Version\Winlogon entry. You should not adjust this setting without expert help. A mistaken setting can leave your system without a shell, and you with no way to access commands and programs in Windows NT.

At present, trying to change your shell gives you no advantage. It is very unlikely that you have this privilege. When third-party shells become available, use the facilities they provide for changing shells.

Customizing the File Manager

Just as you can customize the Program Manager, the File Manager includes a few parameters you can customize. For example, you can have the File Manager minimize automatically whenever you invoke an application by clicking on its file in the File Manager. To set this option in the File Manager, select the Options menu and check the Minimize on Use command. The next time you execute a file by clicking on it in the File Manager, the File Manager minimizes to an icon after it executes the application.

Other Settings in the Options Menu

Other settings in the Options menu are Confirmation, Font, Customize Toolbar, Toolbar, Drive Bar, Status Bar, Open New Window on Connect, and Save Settings on Exit.

- The Font option enables you to specify the font to be used to display directory and file listings. Select the font name, style, and size from the list boxes. The Display Lowercase for FAT Drives check box controls whether the entries in a directory window are displayed with upper- or lowercase letters for drives using the FAT file system. If it is not checked, files and directories are listed in capitals. If you want to display lowercase on NTFS and HPFS drives as well, check the Display Lowercase for All Drives box as well.
- The Customize Toolbar option opens a dialog box that enables you to select which File Manager commands appear as buttons on the toolbar. Highlight the predefined buttons in the list boxes, and use the Add and Remove buttons to change which items are on the toolbar. If you need to reset to the factory default, click on the Reset button. Clicking on the Close button activates your changes.

- The Status Bar option controls whether File Manager displays a status bar at the bottom of the parent window. Depending on the type of information you display in File Manager, the status bar lists the current drive letter, available disk space, number of files selected, and number of bytes used by the selected files. Although this information is helpful, it takes a little additional time for the File Manager to calculate and display. If speed is an important consideration and you do not need to see the information in the status bar, you can turn the Status Bar option off (see fig. 7.26).
- The Toolbar and Drivebar options control whether these items are displayed (a matter of preference). No performance advantages are associated with displaying or not displaying these items.
- The Confirmation option controls the way File Manager handles file and directory deletions, among other tasks. The Confirmation dialog box has six check boxes you can use to control whether File Manager requires confirmation of certain actions before they are carried out. Unless you are an experienced user, consider leaving all of the options checked for safety. They make it more difficult for you to lose data.

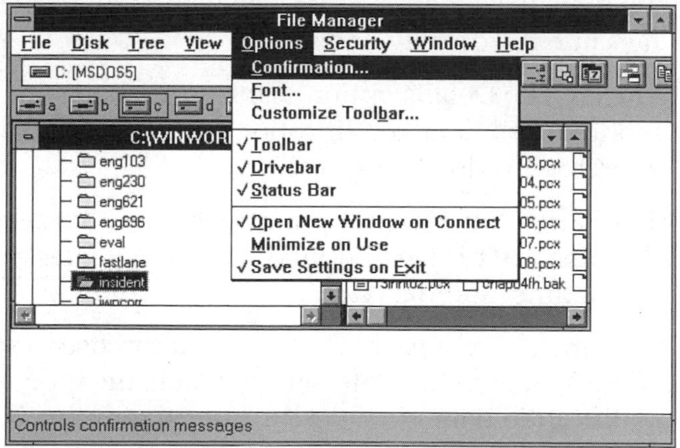

Figure 7.26:
File Manager's options.

- The Open New Window on Connect option controls whether a shared directory is displayed in a new document window when you connect to it. Leaving this setting checked is a convenience. When you connect to a shared directory over the network, you have visual confirmation that the connect has taken place.
- The Save Settings on Exit option controls whether File Manager saves the settings in the current session. After you go to the trouble of setting your preferences for the File Manager, save them so they take effect every time you use File Manager. When you select Exit from the File menu, File Manager saves your preferences in its initialization file (WINFILE.INI). The next time you launch File Manager, the same settings are in place.

Controlling File Display Information

You also can control the type of information that File Manager displays about the files in each directory. The View menu includes three options: Name, All File Details, and Partial Details. These options control the type of information displayed about each file:

- The Name option displays only the name of each file in the directory—nothing else—enabling you to fit more files into the display window.
- The All File Details option displays the file name, size, modification data, modification time, and file flags (such as archive, hidden, and so on).
- The Partial File Details option enables you to select any combination of size, last modification data, last modification time, and file flags.

The View menu includes parameters you can use to sort the file listing. You can choose to sort by name, file type, size, or last modification data.

The By File Type option in the View menu enables you to set the types of files to be displayed in a directory window. You can choose any combination of directories, programs, documents, or other files, as well as hidden/system files.

Summary

Although this chapter does not cover all the facets of customizing the Windows NT interface, you now have an overview of the types of preferences you can change and a good understanding of the methods you can use. You have seen how to change the color scheme, control fonts and ports, customize the mouse, change the desktop settings, control your printer, and customize both Program Manager and File Manager.

Many of the changes you make to the Windows NT interface are purely aesthetic—they do not affect performance. These changes still can increase your overall productivity by giving you a more useful and comfortable tool.

Take a half hour to go through the Windows NT interface and set it up as you prefer. Even if your only gain is comfort, the time is well spent.

Using Windows NT Applets

The usefulness of Windows NT lies in its 32-bit architecture and 32-bit commercial applications that are designed to run on the Windows NT platform. There are also some useful, albeit relatively simple, applications that come with Windows NT. These applications—which typically are scaled-down versions of more sophisticated, off-the-shelf applications—are commonly referred to as *applets*.

This chapter looks at Windows NT applets, and discusses the following:

- Surveying single-user applets
- Exploring multiuser applets
- Using administrative tools

Surveying Single-User Applets

There are several single-user applets included with Windows NT. Most of these are identical to their Windows 3.1 counterparts; some are enhanced versions of the Windows 3.1 applets; and some applets are new. These Windows applets are described in the following sections.

- **3270 Emulator.** New to Windows NT, the 3270 Emulator is a basic terminal-emulation program that enables connection to an IBM 3270 mainframe. Emulating an IBM 3178/79 terminal, this applet enables you to connect to the host computer in one of the following three environments: Virtual Machine/Conversation Monitor System (VM/CMS), Time Sharing Options (TSO), and Customer Information Control Systems (CICS). The 3270 Emulator is shown in figure 8.1.

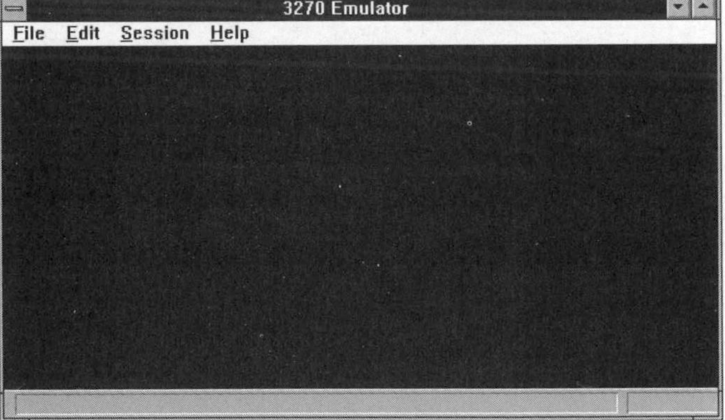

Figure 8.1: *3270 Emulator adds built-in communications power to Windows NT.*

- **Calculator.** Calculator provides the basic functions of a normal hand-held calculator. You can optionally change its display to that of a scientific calculator to provide additional capabilities.

- **Cardfile.** Cardfile features a simple flat-file database that stores addresses and other commonly accessed information. Because it has no querying capability, its usefulness is primarily for small amounts of data.

- **CD Player.** New to Windows NT, CD Player enables you to play audio CDs on your CD-ROM drive. This applet enables you to create a CD database to define CD and track titles, define the order of play, and set a variety of related options. After you have defined the title and/or tracks of a CD, CD Player automatically recognizes the CD when you place it in the CD-ROM drive. CD Player is shown in figure 8.2.

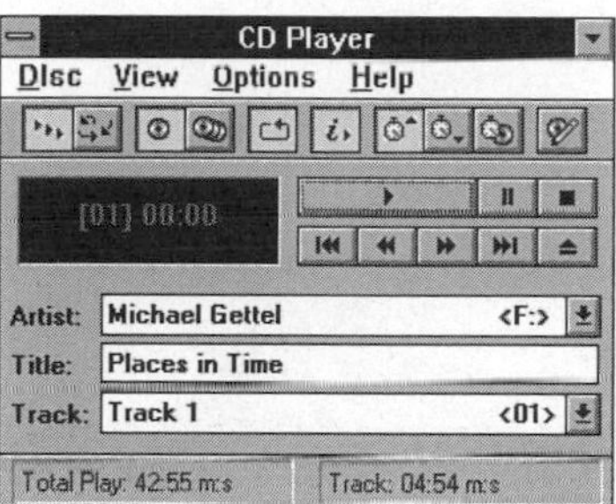

Figure 8.2:
CD Player.

- **Character Map.** Character Map contains a grid that displays the entire character set for a specific font. This applet is useful when you need to use a special "high-ANSI" character, and do not know the Alt+num keyboard equivalent. Use Character Map to copy special characters to the Clipboard and paste them into other Windows applications.
- **Clock.** Displays an on-screen digital or analog clock showing your PC's system time.
- **File Manager.** Enhanced in Windows NT, File Manager is used to perform file management tasks within Windows NT. File Manager eliminates the need to perform command-line operations on such activities as creating and deleting directories, moving and copying files, and running EXE files. File Manager is shown in figure 8.3.
- **Media Player.** Media Player is used to play multimedia files, such as WAV and MIDI sound files, and AVI (Video for Windows) video clips. It also can be used with any Media Control Interface (MCI) connected to your PC.

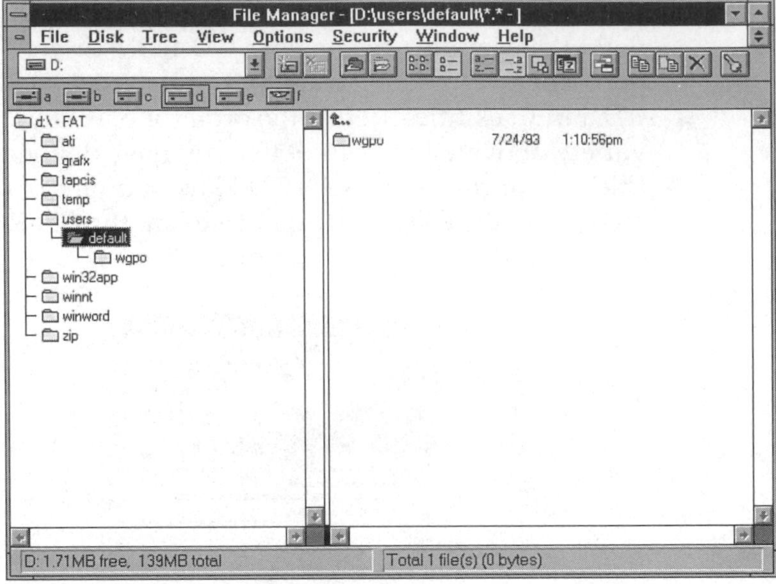

Figure 8.3:
File Manager.

- **Notepad.** Notepad is a basic text editor for working with ANSI text files. It provides limited editing features similar to DOS's EDIT utility.
- **Paintbrush.** Paintbrush is a useful paint program for working with BMP or PCX graphics. Although its tool palette and features are much more limited than commercial paint applications, Paintbrush is very useful for basic bit-map manipulation.
- **PIF Editor.** PIF Editor is a special utility that creates and edits program information files (PIFs).

Program information files (PIFs) *are used by Windows NT to run character-based DOS applications.*

- **Sound Recorder.** Sound Recorder is like an on-screen audio tape recorder. It enables you to record, play, and even edit WAV sound files.

- **Terminal.** Terminal is a basic communications program that enables you to connect to remote computers, on-line services (such as CompuServe), bulletin-board services, and mainframes. This applet provides TTY, DEC VT-100, and DEC VT-52 terminal-emulation support.
- **Write.** Write is a basic word processing program you can use to write letters and view WRI documents.

Exploring Multiuser Applets

Windows NT also includes four multiuser applets. They are called *multiuser* because they can be used by a workgroup as well as by a single individual.

For example, although the Windows 3.1 Clipboard enables you to exchange data between applications on a single desktop, the Windows NT ClipBook Viewer enables you to exchange data between desktops as well. The following sections look at the four Windows NT multiuser applets: ClipBook Viewer, Mail, Chat, and Schedule+.

ClipBook Viewer

Windows NT users probably work daily with more applications on their desktop than do users of most other operating systems (especially those that do not support multitasking).

A key factor is the ease at which data exchange can be carried out in the Windows NT environment. Windows NT uses a storage area known as the *Clipboard*, which enables you to send data from one application and insert a copy of that data into other applications.

Windows 3.1 has a utility, called the Clipboard Viewer, to view the contents of the Clipboard. Windows NT provides a much more powerful tool: the *ClipBook Viewer*, which is an expanded workgroup version of the Windows 3.1 Clipboard Viewer.

Although you can use the ClipBook Viewer to view, save, and delete data contained in the Clipboard, you also can use it to exchange data between desktops within your workgroup.

The actual storage area for your data is not the ClipBook Viewer. The Clipboard is a much more ethereal entity: a class of Application Programming Interface (API) functions located in the USER library that manage the exchange of data between applications. The ClipBook Viewer is simply a window to that data.

Using the Clipboard

As introduced in Chapter 5, nearly all Windows applications use the Clipboard. To use it, you need to choose one of three commands found under the Edit menu. These commands are described as follows:

- Cut removes the selection from the active window and places it in the Clipboard.
- Copy duplicates the selection from the active window and places it in the Clipboard.
- Paste inserts the contents of the Clipboard into the active window at the position of the cursor.

The capability to exchange data between Windows NT applications is not as simple as it may appear. To understand this complexity, think about the unique data types of the applications you use (see table 8.1).

Table 8.1
Variety of Available Data Types

Application	*Works primarily with*
Word for Windows or Ami Pro	Formatted text
Notepad	Unformatted text
WordPerfect for DOS	OEM text
Excel or Quattro Pro for Windows	Spreadsheet data (including numbers and formulas)
Paintbrush	Bit-map graphics
Micrografx Draw or Aldus Freehand	Vector graphics
Microsoft Sound System	Sound

The variety of data types that exists between applications can lead to some potential problems. For instance, how can you transfer formatted text from WordPerfect for Windows to Notepad (which accepts only unformatted text)? If you have ever tried to open up a WordPerfect file (or another word processing file) with Notepad (or another text editor), you know that the result is garbled: text is sandwiched between formatting specifications.

Does this same logic carry over to Clipboard data exchange between WordPerfect and Notepad? No. WordPerfect data is not pasted as unintelligible text into Notepad because of the way in which the source application (WordPerfect), the Clipboard, and the receiving application (Notepad) work together.

The contents of the Clipboard are always treated as a single unit. You can never paste part of the Clipboard contents into a document.

When you copy data to the Clipboard, the source application sends data in as many formats as it is able to send. For example, among the formats WordPerfect transfers to the Clipboard is Text (consisting of unformatted characters). Notepad is able to accept the WordPerfect data because it also supports Text format, and is thus able to paste it correctly into a document.

The source application ultimately is in control of the way the data is formatted. The source application determines the type of formats to support; the receiving application makes a determination about which format to accept when it pastes the data. As a result, some of the formatting or information on the data may be lost if the same data formats are not supported in the receiving application.

There is no ceiling on the amount of data you can store in the Clipboard. In fact, you are limited only by the amount of memory your computer has. As a result, imagine the lag on system resources that would result if the source application had to supply the Clipboard with multiple formats of the same data. To get around this problem, most applications tell the Clipboard which types of formats they support, and furnish data in that format when a receiving application requests it from the Clipboard.

You have no control over the formats being copied and pasted. The source application determines which formats to send to the Clipboard; the receiving application looks at the available formats and accepts the highest available format. In other words, you cannot force Notepad to accept RTF—Notepad alone makes that determination.

Using the Clipboard Window

When you start the ClipBook Viewer by double-clicking on its icon in the Main group of Program Manager, the ClipBook Viewer appears with two child windows: Local ClipBook and Clipboard.

Use the Clipboard window to work with data on your desktop. Remember that the Clipboard window is not the Clipboard—it is only a window showing the contents of the Clipboard. As a result, the ClipBook Viewer does not need to be running to be able to use the Clipboard.

You can perform the following tasks by using the Clipboard window:

- **Clearing the contents of the Clipboard.** To delete the contents of the Clipboard, activate the Clipboard window and choose the Delete option from the Edit menu or press the Del key. You are asked to confirm this deletion by clicking on the Yes button in a message box.

An alternative method of clearing the contents of the Clipboard does not require you to open the ClipBook Viewer at all. Instead, it can be done within the application in which you are working.

For example, if you are in a word processing application, select a space, and then choose the Copy command from the Edit menu. The space is inserted into the Clipboard, overwriting its previous contents.

- **Viewing data in different formats.** The View menu for the Clipboard window lists the data formats sent by the source application to the Clipboard. To change the display of the data, select one of the formats from the list. You will notice that Default Format is initially checked. This setting signifies that the Clipboard window has automatically selected the format being displayed from the list of available formats. If the source application is running, Default Format displays the contents of the Clipboard window in the format preferred by the source application. If it is not running, the ClipBook Viewer selects the best format left available.
- **Saving the contents of the Clipboard.** You may need to save data in the Clipboard for a later time. There are two ways to save Clipboard data.

You can save the contents of the Clipboard as a page to the *Local ClipBook*, which is a permanent storage area for data that you can recall later or share with other workgroup members. To save to the Local ClipBook, select the Local ClipBook window and choose the Paste option from the Edit menu. In a dialog box, you are asked to name the page you are creating, and you have the option to declare it as a *shared item* (available for use by others). Click on the OK button.

You cannot save formatted text in the Local ClipBook or as a CLP file. When you paste the formatted text into a Local ClipBook page or save it as a CLP file, it immediately is converted to Text format (even if the source application is still running).

You also can save the contents of the Clipboard to a Clipboard file (as in Windows 3.1). To do so, choose the Save As option from the File menu. Enter a file name in the Save As dialog box, and click on OK. Clipboard files have a default extension of CLP.

Under most circumstances, you will want to use the Local ClipBook to store contents of the Clipboard. The Local ClipBook enables you to view and share such data much more easily than by working with CLP files.

When you shut down a Windows NT session, Windows NT saves any contents remaining in the Clipboard as a CLP file. You can access that data during a later session.

Using the Local ClipBook

The Local ClipBook is a centralized storage location of Clipboard items. Each separate entry into the Local ClipBook is called a *page*. Pages can be viewed in a list (by choosing the Table of Contents option from the View menu), in Thumbnail view (by choosing the Thumbnails option), or as a display of their actual contents (by choosing the Full Page option).

Figure 8.4 shows the Local ClipBook, displaying its pages in Thumbnail view.

Figure 8.4:
Local ClipBook.

Sharing Data by Using ClipBook

Although the ClipBook Viewer is a useful and powerful tool for an individual desktop, it also can be used to exchange data between desktops. Because all members of your workgroup that run Windows NT have their own ClipBooks, you can access remote data from their ClipBooks, and others can access your Local ClipBook.

Sharing Data from Your Local ClipBook

To enable other users to share your local data, check the Share Item Now box as you paste a new page into your Local ClipBook. If you check the share box, a second dialog appears for you to set specific options.

- **Start Application on Connect.** Checking the Start Application on Connect box causes the source application to start whenever another user accesses this data. This option is useful when creating dynamic links between applications.

Dynamic data exchange is discussed in Chapter 11.

- **Run Minimized.** Checking the Run Minimized box forces it to run in a minimized state.
- **Permissions.** Clicking on the Permissions button displays the ClipBook Page Permissions dialog box. In this dialog box, you can set the type of access you want other users to have to the ClipBook page. You can designate the following levels of access: Full Control, Change, Read and Link, Read, and No Access.

After setting these options, other users can connect to, and work with data in, your ClipBook.

Accessing Remote ClipBook Data

You can access shared data on other users' computers and copy it to your Clipboard. To do so, you need to connect to the remote computer's ClipBook by choosing the Connect option from the File menu.

In the Select Computer dialog box, specify the computer you want to connect to by entering the name or selecting a name from the Computers list. After clicking on the OK button, a new window opens in your ClipBook Viewer window, displaying the remote ClipBook.

You work with the shared pages of the remote ClipBook in the same way that you work with your Local ClipBook.

To disconnect from another computer, choose the Disconnect option from the File menu.

Mail

One of the best business tools of the information age is electronic mail (e-mail). The use of e-mail within offices can make business communication much more efficient and useful than past forms of written communication.

An e-mail package is a standard element of a typical local area network. Windows NT includes Mail, which is a simplified version of Microsoft Mail. Mail enables you to send and receive electronic mail (both text messages and files) across your workgroup.

Setting Up Mail

To run Mail, double-click on its icon in the Main group of Program Manager. As Mail loads up for the first time, it prompts you to designate a postoffice.

A postoffice *contains information about user accounts for a workgroup and also functions as a depository for the workgroup's messages.*

You can create a new postoffice or connect to an existing one. If the administrator has not already established an account for you in the postoffice, you need to create the account.

A postoffice is used by the workgroup, not by a single individual. Thus, all workgroup members have mailboxes within a central postoffice.

Typically, a postoffice has already been set up for your use by the administrator. If so, choose the Connect to an Existing Postoffice in the Welcome to Mail dialog box.

The Network Disk Resources dialog box appears. Select the desired postoffice by typing its path in the Network Path text box. Alternatively, you can locate the appropriate path by selecting a computer from the top box and the desired path in the lower box.

After clicking on the OK button, Mail asks if you currently have an account in the postoffice. If so, click on the **Y**es button and you are prompted for your password. If you do not have an existing account, click on the **N**o button. A dialog box appears, asking for the following information about you:

- **Name.** Enter your full name (up to 30 characters in length). [Required]
- **Mailbox.** Enter a name (up to 10 characters) that you will use as a log-on name to Mail. It is recommended that you use your Windows NT user name to avoid the necessity of remembering several user names. [Required]
- **Password.** Enter a password (up to 8 characters) for use as you start Mail. Be sure to choose a password that you can remember. [Required]
- **Phone #1.** Enter your primary phone number.
- **Phone #2.** Enter a secondary phone number.
- **Office.** Enter your office number or location identifier (up to 32 characters).
- **Department.** Enter your department name (up to 32 characters).
- **Notes.** Enter any additional information in this field (up to 128 characters).

After entering this information, click on the OK button. Mail displays the Inbox window. You now are ready to begin using Mail.

If you do not connect to an existing postoffice, you can create a new postoffice by choosing the Create a new Workgroup Postoffice option from the Welcome to Mail dialog box. You are required to administer the postoffice if you create it, however.

Sending a Message

To send a message to one or more users on your network, click on the Compose button from the Mail window, or choose the Compose Note option from the Mail menu. The Send Note window appears, as shown in figure 8.5.

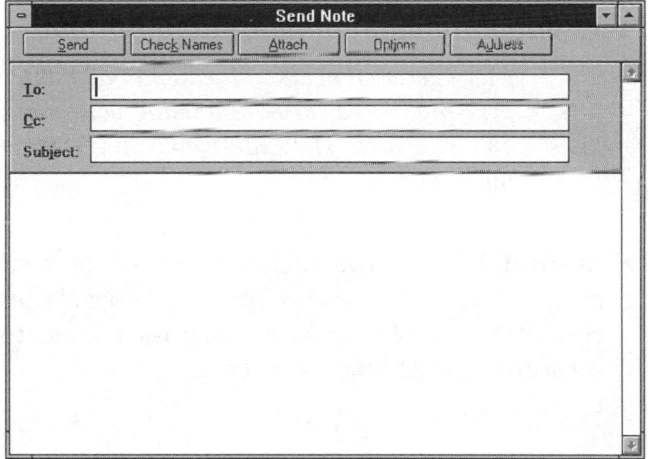

Figure 8.5:
The Send Note window.

When you send a message, you have to define the following three elements:

- **Recipient.** Declare the users to which you want to address the message. You can send a message directly to other workgroup members or send it as a carbon copy (cc:).

A carbon copy (cc:) *is a carryover from traditional written business communications, in which a copy of a letter is sent to all interested parties.*

Enter the user name of the person(s) in the To text box. If you want to view an address list of users in the workgroup, click on the Address button. The Address dialog box appears.

Select the name of one or more persons from the list, and click on the To button. (Alternatively, you can double-click on a name in the Directory box.) After you have selected the appropriate names, click on the OK button to return to the Send Note window.

If you want to send a carbon copy of the message to another user, enter the user name in the Cc text box. You can click on the Address button to add user names to the cc: list as well.

Move between fields in the Send Note window by pressing the Tab key or by using your mouse to click on a new field. The Enter key is not used for this purpose.

- **Subject.** Declare a subject of the message so that the recipient understands the message's basic purpose and content before she reads it. Enter the subject for the message in the Subject text box.

Keep in mind that e-mail tends to be less structured or formal than standard paper letters. Because you typically are sending text, formatting and page layout is immaterial.

- **Message.** Enter the actual text of the message. Use the large box at the bottom of the window as your area for writing the message. The actual text-editing capabilities in the message area are meager (roughly parallel to Notepad), but you can use the standard cut, copy, and paste commands.

You can view the message area in a proportional or fixed font. Use the Change Font option on the View menu to switch between them.

Before sending the message, you may want to set options for the message. Click on the Options button to display the Options dialog box. Set the desired options, as follows:

- **Return receipt.** If this box is checked, you will be notified when the message recipient(s) reads the message.
- **Save sent messages.** If this box is checked, Mail saves a copy of your message for you. This option enables you to keep a log of your correspondence.
- **Priority.** Electronic messages can have priority levels. Set your message to the appropriate level by choosing the High, Normal, or Low options. The recipient of the message sees the priority of the message in his Inbox.

When you have completed the message and set the desired options, click on the Send button to send the message over the network to the mailbox of the addressee.

Reading a Message

When you receive an e-mail message from another workgroup member, it is placed in your Inbox, as shown in figure 8.6.

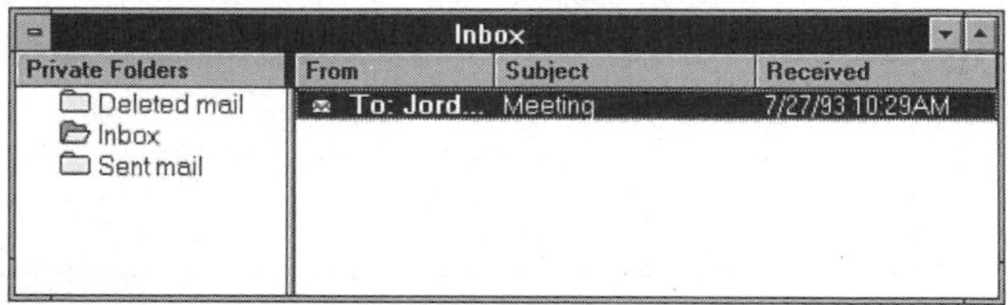

Figure 8.6: *Inbox with incoming mail.*

Notice that an unread message has a closed envelope icon beside it. To read the message, double-click on the message entry from the Inbox, or select the entry and press Enter. Your message appears in a message window.

The left side of the Inbox displays a list of available folders. You can store your e-mail in a variety of folders just as you store written correspondence in a filing cabinet.

To view the contents of a folder, click on the appropriate folder icon. Also, by double-clicking on the button at the top of the window, you can switch between private and shared (public) folders.

Responding to a Message

After you read an e-mail message, you might want to respond to that message. Instead of having to create a new message and then reentering the recipient name and subject, you can reply to the existing message.

To reply, click on the Reply button from the toolbar, or choose **R**eply from the **M**ail menu. The message window appears (see fig. 8.7).

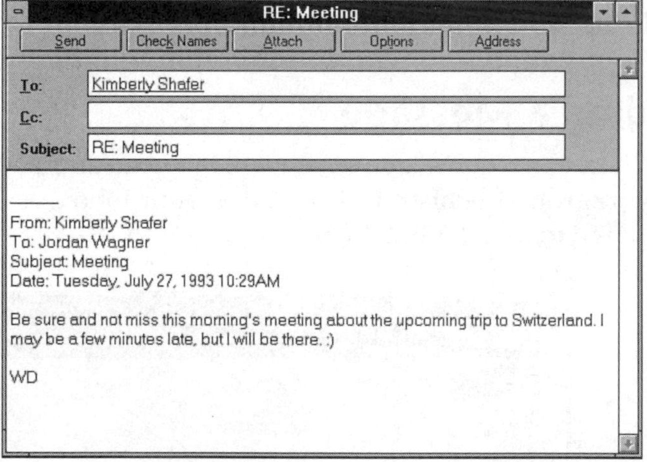

Figure 8.7:

Replying to a message.

Mail automatically addresses the letter, adds `"RE: "` to the subject of the message, and provides the original text of the message in the message area below a line.

When you choose the **R**eply command, your response is sent only to the person who sent you the message. If other users are receiving carbon copies of the message, you probably want to send your reply to them as well. To do this, click on the Reply All button, or choose Reply to All from the **M**ail menu.

Removing Messages

To delete messages from your mailbox, select the desired message from the Inbox list, and click the Delete button on the toolbar. Mail moves the message to the Deleted mail folder (see fig. 8.8), where it is deleted as you exit Mail.

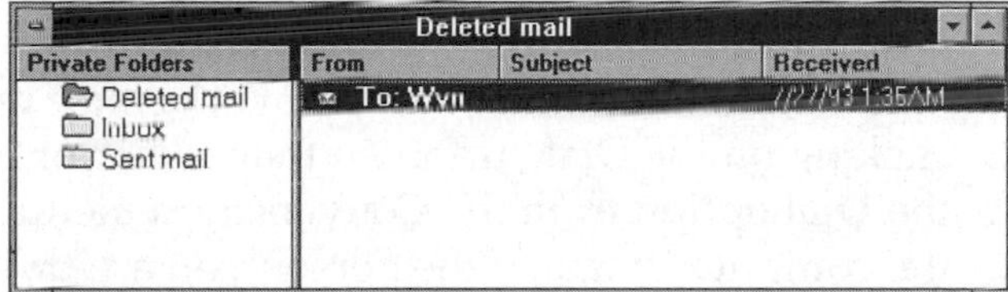

Figure 8.8:
Deleted messages are placed in the Deleted mail folder.

If you decide to undelete the message before you exit Mail, click on the Move button to move the message to a different folder.

Chat

Chat is a tool you can use to have a "live" conversation with another workgroup member over the network. To run Chat, double-click on the Chat icon in the Accessories group of Program Manager. The Chat window appears, as shown in figure 8.9.

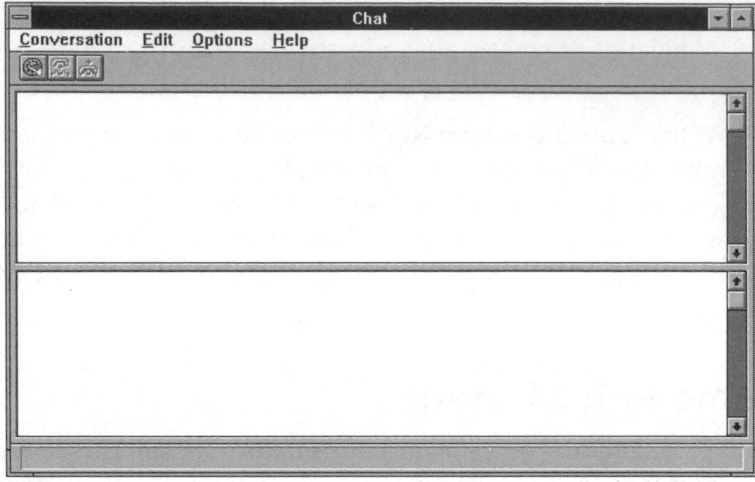

Figure 8.9:
Chat window.

Think of Chat as a different type of phone, and a Chat conversation as a different kind of phone call. To conduct a Chat conversation, do the following:

- **Call another user.** Call another workgroup member by clicking on the Dial button on the toolbar or by choosing the Dial option from the Conversation menu. Choose the computer name of the person you are trying to call, and click on OK.

  Chat then calls the computer you choose, and waits for the person for whom you are calling to answer. The status bar at the bottom of the Chat window notifies you of the call's status.

Think of the computer name as a phone number, because each phone number has a physical location to which it is associated.

- **Conduct a conversation.** If a user answers the Chat request, the caller can begin typing in the top window while the receiver can type in the bottom window. A conversation need not be unidirectional: you both can type information simultaneously if needed.

- **Hang up.** When you are finished with the conversation, you or the other workgroup member is free to hang up and terminate the conversation. To do so, click on the Hangup button from the toolbar, or choose the Hangup option from the Conversation menu. When the person with whom you are conversing hangs up, you are notified by Mail in the status bar.

If another workgroup member calls you and requests an on-line Chat conversation, you can answer the call by clicking on the Answer button from the toolbar or by choosing the Answer option from the Conversation menu. If Chat is not open, Windows NT automatically starts it for you.

Schedule+

Schedule+ is a miniature personal scheduling manager for use in scheduling appointments and tasks, jotting notes, and maintaining a calendar book.

Schedule+ also can be used as a workgroup scheduler. Using Schedule+, workgroup members can have a public schedule to help with setting meetings and viewing others' schedules. To run Schedule+, double-click on its icon in the Main group of Program Manager.

Schedule+ is much more advanced than the limited Calendar applet provided in Windows 3.1.

Schedule+ uses the same user name and password as Mail. If you already have established these in Mail, you do not have to do so again in Schedule+. Instead, enter your user name and password in the Password dialog box. The Schedule+ Appointment List window appears (see fig. 8.10).

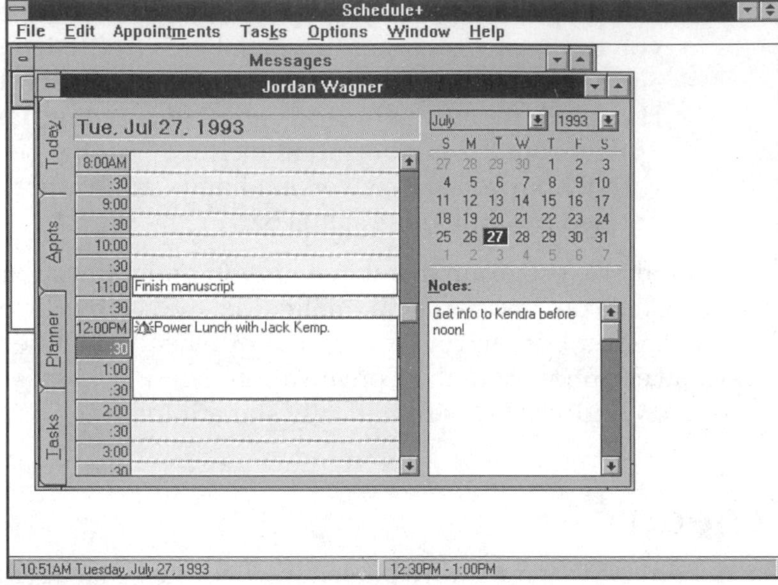

Figure 8.10:
Schedule+ window.

The Schedule+ window can be divided up into the following four areas:

- **Tabs.** The tabs on the left of the window enable you to view different pages of Schedule+. Click on one of the four tabs to switch between page views.
- **Calendar.** The monthly calendar shows the current month by default. To view a different date, select the appropriate month and year from the list boxes above the calendar, and click on the date in the calendar.
- **Daily schedule.** The main part of the window is a daily schedule for the date specified above it (and in the calendar beside it). Enter appointments and block out activities in this box.
- **Notes.** Enter any miscellaneous comments related to the current day in this box.

Scheduling an Appointment

To schedule an appointment in Schedule+, designate the block of time for the activity by selecting an initial time

(12:00 p.m., for example), and drag the mouse to the end time (2:00 p.m.).

From the Appointments menu, choose the New Appointments option. The Appointment dialog box appears (see fig. 8.11).

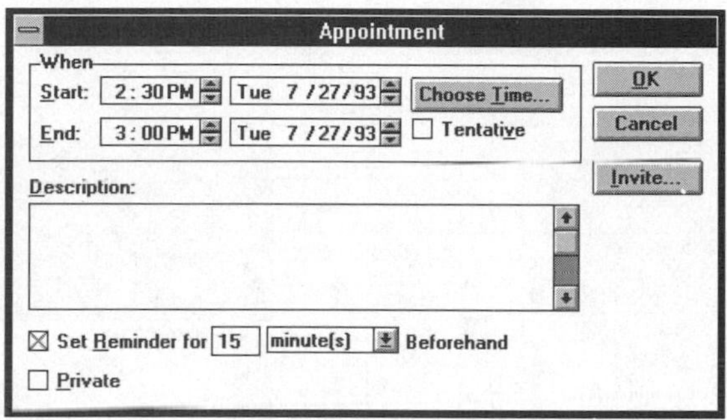

Figure 8.11: *Appointment dialog box.*

Set the following appointment details in this dialog box:

- **When.** In the When box, your Start and End times for the appointment already have been set. Modify them if necessary. You can declare the appointment as tentative by checking the Tentative box.
- **Description.** Enter text in the Description box to describe the appointment. Use as much space as necessary. Schedule+ places this text in the time block that you specify in your daily schedule of the main Schedule+ window.
- **Reminder.** Check the Set Reminder check box if you want Schedule+ to issue a reminder before the time of an appointment. Enter the amount of time before you want the reminder issued in the space provided.
- **Private.** If you want to keep the description of your appointment private from other workgroup members, check the Private box.
- **Invite.** Click on the Invite button to invite other workgroup members to attend the appointment. In the Select Attendees dialog box, choose the persons you want to invite from the postoffice list.

Using the Planner

The Planner window (see fig. 8.12) displays the times you and other workgroup members have set appointments.

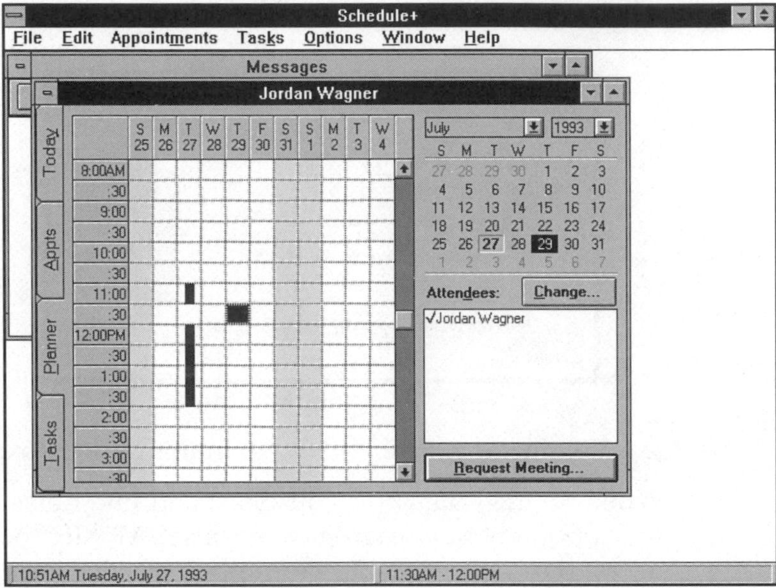

Figure 8.12:
Planner window.

The Planner window can be divided into the following four areas:

- **Tabs.** The tabs on the left of the window enable you to view different pages of Schedule+. Click on one of the four tabs to switch between page views.
- **Time slots.** The main part of the window is an appointment grid, displaying the time slots of set appointments. To view an appointment, double-click on its time slot in the Planner window. Schedule+ displays the Appointment Book window of the person who scheduled the appointment.
- **Calendar.** The monthly calendar shows the current month by default. To view a different date, select the appropriate month and year from the list boxes above the calendar, and click on the date in the calendar with your mouse.

- **Attendees.** The Attendees box displays the names of the workgroup members whose appointments are shown in Schedule+. To change the list, click on the Change button, and choose the desired workgroup members from the Select Attendees dialog box. In addition, if you want to send a meeting request to each of the attendees, click on the Request Meeting button.

Using the Task List

You can use the Task List to list and prioritize activities you need to perform. Access the Task List by clicking on the Tasks tab of the Schedule+ window (see fig. 8.13).

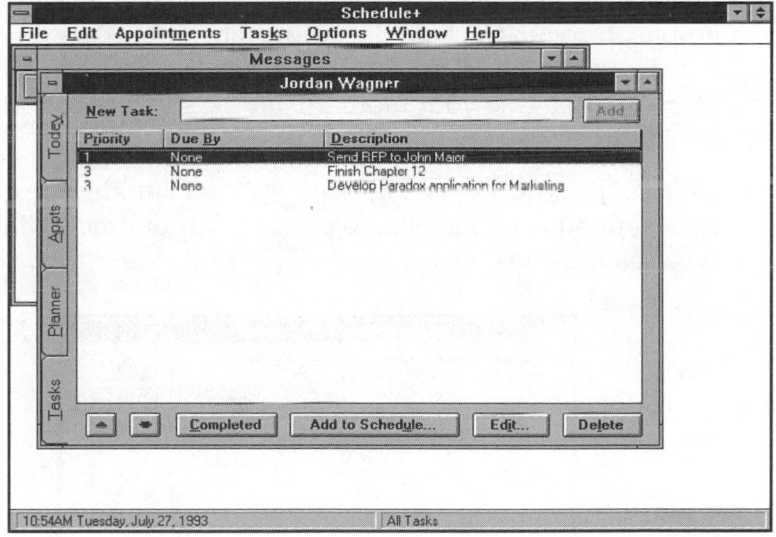

Figure 8.13: *Tasks window.*

The Task List has the following options:

- **Add task.** To add a new task, enter its description in the New Task text box and click on the Add button (or press Enter). The new task is added to the Task List.
- **Edit task.** You can edit a task after it has been placed on the Task List by double-clicking on the list item (or by selecting the item and clicking on the Edit button). The Task dialog box appears, enabling you to change the task's description, project, due date, and priority.

- **Add project.** Schedule+ enables you to group tasks by project. To add a project, choose the New Project option from the Tasks menu. In the Project dialog box, enter a project name in the Name text box. Check the Private box to prevent other workgroup members from seeing the contents of this list.
- **Completed task.** When a task is completed, remove it from the list by selecting it and clicking on the Completed button.

Scheduling a Recurring Appointment

Schedule+ can automatically schedule a recurring appointment (a board meeting every Friday at 10:00 a.m., for example), for you. Click on the Appts tab, and set the desired date by using the calendar. Next, select the desired time block by dragging your mouse from the starting time to the ending time.

Choose the New Recurring Appt option from the Appointments menu to display the Recurring Appointment dialog box (see fig. 8.14).

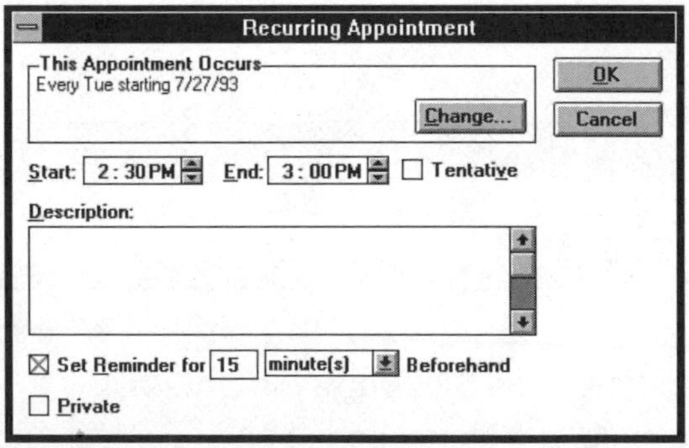

Figure 8.14: *Recurring Appointment dialog box.*

Click on the Change button to display the Change Recurrence dialog box. Select the desired pattern by setting its occurrence (daily, weekly, biweekly, monthly, yearly), day of week, and duration.

Using Administrator Tools

A new set of applets, called Administrator Tools, is provided in Windows NT to help administrators configure and monitor their Windows NT networks. These tools, discussed in the following sections, include the Disk Administrator, User Manager, Performance Monitor, Event Viewer, and Backup.

These utilities are not for everyone's use—they are usable only by users with administrator-level rights on the network.

Disk Administrator

The Disk Administrator is a powerful tool that is used to configure local and networked hard drives. It enables you to work with any physical or logical FAT (File Allocation Table, used by DOS); HPFS (High Performance File System, used by OS/2); and NTFS (NT File System) drives. It does not, however, currently support drives compressed using MS-DOS 6.0's DoubleSpace.

To run Disk Administrator, double-click on the Disk Administrator icon in the Administrative Tools group of Program Manager. The Disk Administrator window appears, as shown in figure 8.15.

Disk Administrator enables you to perform many of the same tasks as DOS's FDISK utility. Although it may seem strange to perform such low-level functions on your disk in a graphical environment, Disk Administrator is much more powerful than its DOS counterpart.

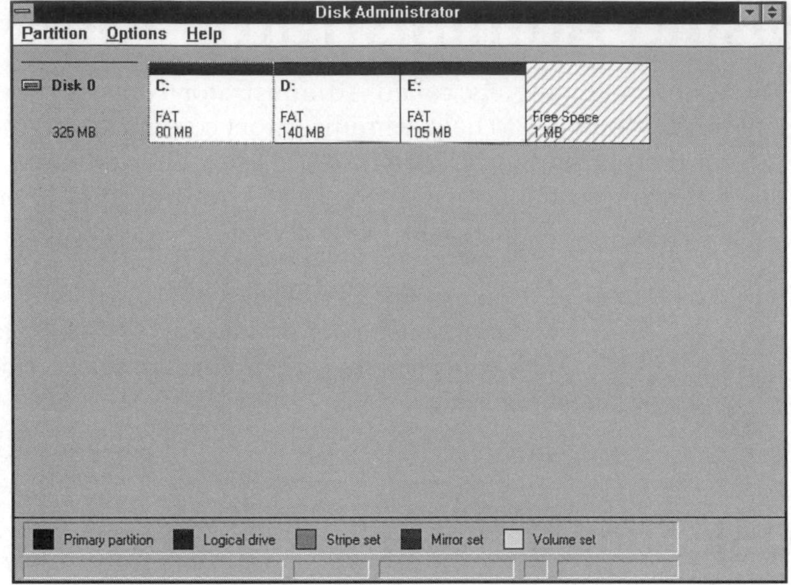

Figure 8.15:
Disk Administrator.

*Disk Administrator does not provide the capability to convert FAT drives to NTFS. This command must be performed by using the command-line utility CONVERT. Formatting a drive must also be performed by entering **FORMAT** at the command prompt.*

User Manager

User Manager is used by the administrator to manage user accounts on the Windows NT network. To run User Manager, double-click on the User Manager icon in the Administrative Tools group of Program Manager. The User Manager window appears, as shown in figure 8.16.

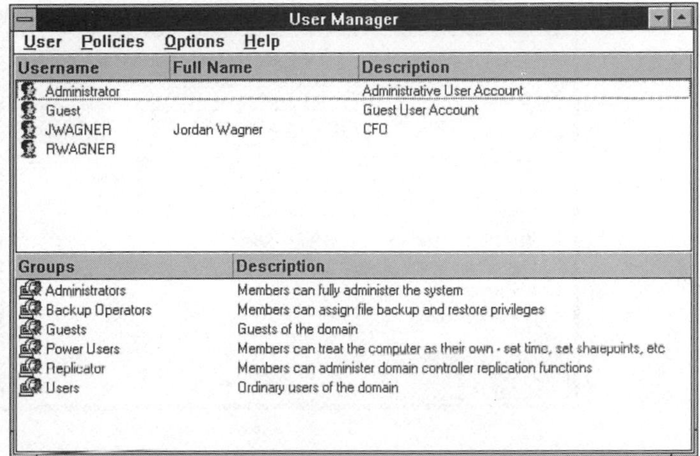

Figure 8.16:
User Manager.

The top portion of the window displays a list of user names for the entire system. Data tracked includes the following:

- **Username.** Refers to the log-on name that you enter as you log on to the system.
- **Full Name.** Used to enter the complete name of the user. Although this data is not used by Windows NT, it is helpful for the administrator to work with full names rather than cryptic user names.
- **Description.** Used to enter optional comments about a particular user (such as title or position in the company). This is another field not required by Windows NT.

You can view or modify additional information on a specific user by double-clicking on the entry in the Username list. The User Properties dialog box appears, as shown in figure 8.17.

Although the administrator can modify some of the settings, such as Full Name and Description, she cannot change or view the password. A password is proprietary to each individual user.

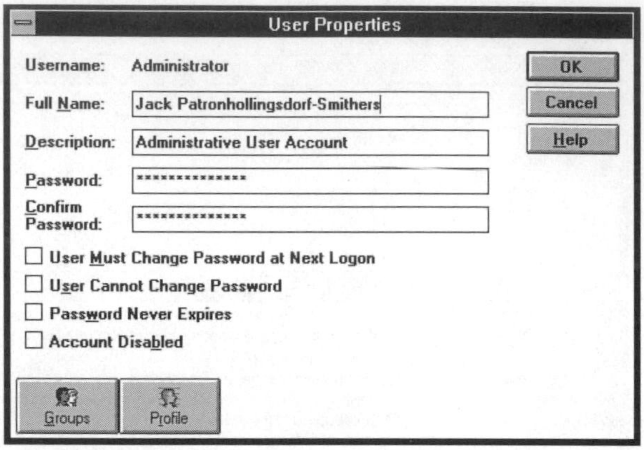

Figure 8.17: *User Properties dialog box.*

When a new account has no password, or an existing account's password has expired, the administrator can add a password to the account. The administrator can view or modify additional information about the user by clicking on the Groups or Profile button. As you finish working with a user account, click on the OK button to return to the User Manager window.

The lower portion of the User Manager window lists the user groups that are defined for the system. You can double-click on each of these entries to display additional information about each group. When you double-click on an entry, the Local Group Properties dialog box appears (see fig. 8.18), in which you can enter a description of the group as well as view all of the members of the group in the Members list.

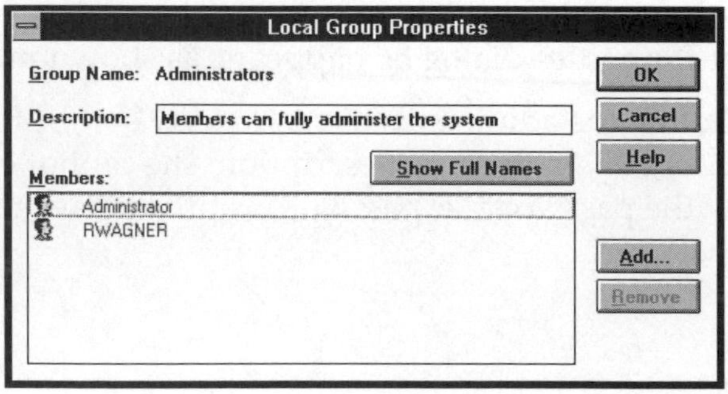

Figure 8.18: *Local Group Properties dialog box.*

Add additional users to the group by clicking on the **A**dd button. Delete a user from the group by selecting a user name from the Members list and clicking on the **R**emove button.

Performance Monitor

Performance Monitor enables the administrator to track the performance of the system. To run Performance Monitor, double-click on the Performance Monitor icon in the Administrative Tools group of Program Manager. The Performance Monitor window appears, as shown in figure 8.19.

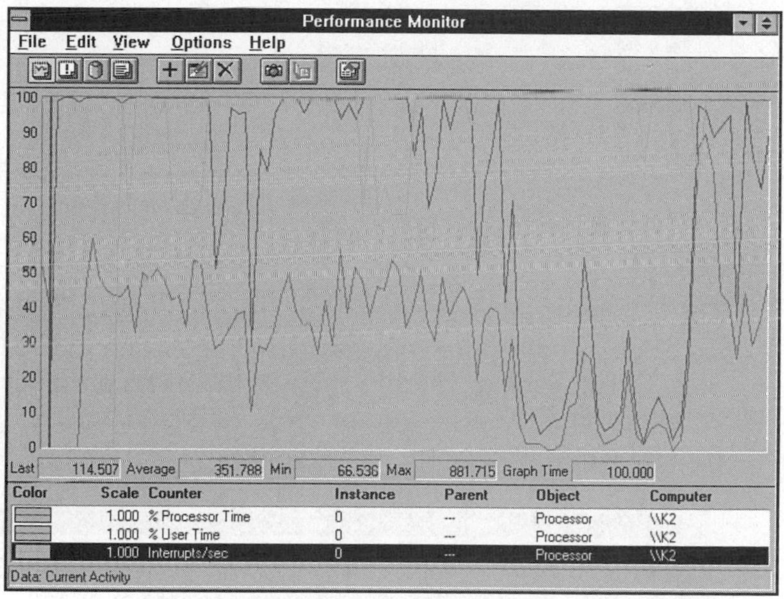

Figure 8.19:
Performance Monitor.

Event Viewer

Event Viewer is another tool that can be used by the administrator to track system-operation logs kept by Windows NT. The system logs document-system events (for example, errors and warnings encountered), application events (such as crashes), and security events (such as invalid password entries).

To run Event Viewer, double-click on the Event Viewer icon in the Administrative Tools group of Program Manager. The Event Viewer window appears, as shown in figure 8.20.

Figure 8.20:

Event Viewer.

Event Viewer - System Log on \\K2

Log View Options Help

Date	Time	Source	Category	Event	User	Computer
7/27/93	10:59:43 AM	Print	None	10	N/A	K2
7/27/93	10:59:26 AM	Parallel	None	15	N/A	K2
7/27/93	2:15:15 AM	Service Control Manager	None	7023	N/A	K2
7/27/93	2:15:15 AM	LanmanServer	None	2503	N/A	K2
7/26/93	9:53:30 PM	Service Control Manager	None	7024	N/A	K2
7/26/93	9:53:30 PM	Service Control Manager	None	7026	N/A	K2
7/26/93	9:53:30 PM	Service Control Manager	None	7001	N/A	K2
7/26/93	9:53:30 PM	LanmanWorkstation	None	3113	N/A	K2
7/26/93	9:53:27 PM	NetDDE	None	13	N/A	K2
7/26/93	9:53:27 PM	NetDDE	None	204	N/A	K2
7/26/93	9:53:23 PM	Serial	None	25	N/A	K2
7/26/93	9:53:20 PM	Service Control Manager	None	7002	N/A	K2
7/26/93	9:53:20 PM	Service Control Manager	None	7000	N/A	K2
7/26/93	5:43:01 PM	Service Control Manager	None	7026	N/A	K2
7/26/93	5:43:01 PM	Service Control Manager	None	7001	N/A	K2
7/26/93	5:43:01 PM	Service Control Manager	None	7024	N/A	K2
7/26/93	5:43:00 PM	LanmanWorkstation	None	3113	N/A	K2
7/26/93	5:42:58 PM	NetDDE	None	13	N/A	K2
7/26/93	5:42:57 PM	NetDDE	None	204	N/A	K2
7/26/93	5:42:53 PM	Serial	None	25	N/A	K2

Backup

The final tool is Backup, which, as its name implies, is used to back up and restore volumes, directories, and individual files. To run Backup, double-click on the Backup icon in the Administrative Tools group of Program Manager. The Backup window appears, as shown in figure 8.21.

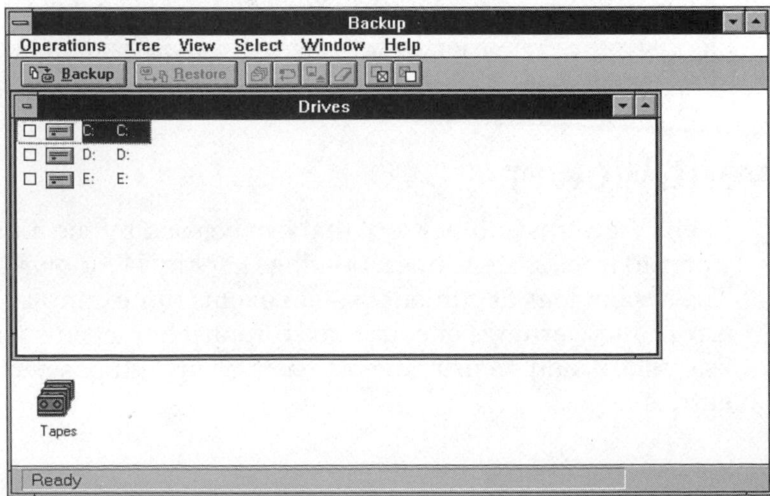

Figure 8.21:

The Backup window.

Summary

Although the acceptance of the Windows NT operating system is not based on the applets that are included with it, these mini-applications do play an important role for users of the environment. This chapter looked at the applets that come with Windows NT, and divided them into three groups: single user, multiuser, and administrative.

The single-user applets make up the largest group of NT applets. Most in this group are identical to those included with Windows 3.1. Some, such as File Manager, have been enhanced; a few, such as 3270 Emulator and CD Player, are new applets designed for Windows NT.

Multiuser applets are workgroup-based. They include ClipBook Viewer, Mail, Chat, and Schedule+. These applets facilitate workgroup data exchange, communication, and schedule coordination.

The final group is a set of Administrative Tools, including Disk Administrator, User Manager, Performance Monitor, Event Viewer, and Backup. These tools can be used only by users with administrator-level rights.

Printing and Managing Fonts

Managing fonts on your desktop has never been easier than in Windows NT. You can create and print professional-looking documents by using the fonts included with Windows NT on virtually any output device.

If you think back to earlier versions of Windows, recall that it always has been a much friendlier environment in which to manage fonts than DOS. Fonts are dealt with at the operating-environment level rather than at the application level. With third-party font managers, users worked with text that would look the same on-screen when printed out. Windows NT, however, has become much more sophisticated than earlier Windows versions by seamlessly integrating a scalable font technology into its environment.

Additionally, Windows NT makes printing easier, more seamless, and more painless than previous 16-bit versions of Windows or DOS. In fact, once you get your printer configured the way you want it, Windows NT frees you from worrying about the printing process. Instead, you can think about the quality of your printer's output.

As this chapter looks at the world of fonts and printing in Windows NT, it focuses on the following topics:

- Introducing fonts in Windows NT
- Using TrueType Fonts
- Embedding fonts
- Substituting fonts
- Comparing TrueType fonts with PostScript Type 1 fonts
- Installing and removing fonts
- Using other screen fonts
- Installing and configuring printers
- Managing print jobs with Print Manager

Although typeface and font are used interchangeably in PC circles, a distinct difference exists between the two. A typeface *is the basic design of characters; a* font *is the complete set of characters for a given typeface at a particular point size and style.*

Introducing Fonts in Windows NT

As you work in Windows NT, you'll become acquainted with the following four distinct groups of fonts:

- **Bit-map or raster fonts.** These fonts are created by arranging pixels in a particular pattern to appear and print in a fixed point size. A unique bit map must be created for each character, point size, and type style.

Windows 3.0 fonts, such as Helvetica or Times Roman, are bit-map fonts that come in 8-, 10-, 12-, 14-, 18-, and 24-point sizes. A separate file is needed for each point size and style (normal, bold, italic, and bold italic). These screen fonts cannot be downloaded to printers; as a result, these screen fonts usually are different from what actually is printed by the printer.

- **TrueType fonts.** These fonts, known as *outline fonts*, are generated by using mathematical calculations. An outline font is a set of mathematical instructions for each character that contain a series of points to form an outline. An outline font is scalable because you can increase or decrease the point size of a font by multiplying or dividing by the desired factor.

  An outline font can be scaled in a wide range of sizes, from 2 to nearly 700 points (although many Windows NT applications may limit this actual range). All mathematical instructions for a font can be stored in a single file rather than in multiple bit-map files. TrueType fonts are compatible with all devices except plotters.

With TrueType support, font management in Windows NT is very similar to Windows 3.1.

- **Device-specific fonts.** *Device-specific fonts* are either installed on the printer or downloaded, and are controlled more by the device than by Windows NT. Windows NT does not map device-specific fonts; instead, it relays the logical font request to the device—printer or software—whose job it is to map the fonts properly. PostScript fonts are considered device-specific fonts.

- **Vector fonts.** *Vector fonts* are scalable fonts, consisting of tiny dots and line segments. Vector fonts typically are used only when outputting to a plotter, although a few dot-matrix printers support vector fonts. Windows NT comes with three vector fonts: Modern, Roman, and Script. Because of their makeup, vector fonts do not have the same quality as the other types of fonts. Thus, most Windows NT applications do not even display vector fonts in their font lists.

Using TrueType Fonts

Windows 3.1 introduced a breakthrough in font technology on the PC platform. Before Windows 3.1, you had to purchase a third-party font manager, such as Adobe Type Manager (ATM), to achieve identical screen and printer output. Without ATM, you probably worked with Helvetica and Times Roman on-screen, and found your documents looking quite different when you printed them out. Not so in Windows 3.1, which integrated the scalable font technology known as TrueType into the operating environment. Windows NT incorporates this same TrueType font technology into its operating environment.

TrueType was developed jointly by Apple and Microsoft. The TrueType fonts included with Windows NT match those of Apple System 6.0.5, and can be used on the Macintosh without conversion. The basic TrueType fonts included with Windows NT (see fig. 9.1) are designed to match the core PostScript fonts.

The 14 standard TrueType fonts in Windows NT were made by Monotype, one of the major font foundries. These fonts have been widely praised for their outstanding quality; in fact, many consider them superior to their PostScript Type 1 counterparts.

Arial
Arial Italic
Arial Bold
Arial Bold Italic

Courier New
Courier New Italic
Courier Bold
Courier Bold Italic

Times New Roman
Times New Roman Italic
Times New Roman Bold
Times New Roman Bold Italic

αβχδεφγηιφκλιμνοπτλωψαψ (Symbol)
♋♌♍♎♏♐♑♒♓♎⊠◆♓○& (WingDings)

Figure 9.1:
TrueType fonts included with Windows NT.

Although TrueType is the new kid on a block traditionally dominated by PostScript, its acceptability has been widespread. This acceptability centers on four factors, which can be summarized as follows:

- **Ease of use.** One of the greatest strengths of TrueType is that it is closely integrated in the Windows NT environment. In fact, the Windows NT Graphical Device Interface (GDI) was designed specifically for this purpose. No other font manager is as easy to use. Installing, removing, and working with TrueType fonts is effortless. Even applications designed for Windows 3.0 can use TrueType fonts because of the way Microsoft integrated TrueType into the GDI. Moreover, new TrueType Application Programming Interface (API) functions give applications greater control over the placement and manipulation of characters.

TrueType can be used in Windows 3.0 applications, but the printed document may not be exactly WYSIWYG in the same way that Windows 3.1 and Windows NT documents are.

- **Identical screen and printer output.** TrueType enables you to work with fonts that appear the same on the screen as they will on the printer.

TrueType is almost WYSIWYG. Because of the differences in dots-per-inch between your monitor (usually around 96,120 dpi) and printer (usually 300,600 dpi), no font technology is absolutely identical.

- **Scalable.** No longer do you need to design your document around the sizes of the Windows NT bit-map fonts (8, 10, 12, or 14). If you use bit-map fonts with point sizes other than the built-in ones, they look jagged as they are resized. TrueType fonts are scalable fonts that can be displayed and printed in virtually any size above two points. Figure 9.2 shows the letter "Q" in Arial typeface at 12 and 62 points. As you can see, the two are directly proportional.

Figure 9.2:
TrueType fonts are scalable.

- **Portable.** TrueType fonts are printer portable, meaning that a TrueType document prints identically on any output device, regardless of the printer's page description language (PDL), such as PostScript or Hewlett-Packard's PCL. TrueType is portable also across platforms so that a document created in Windows NT can be seamlessly moved to a Macintosh.

How Windows NT Handles TrueType Fonts

Although TrueType looks identical on the screen and printer, the process that Windows NT goes through to display TrueType on these various devices is different.

Suppose you start Word for Windows and begin typing an office memo. Based on the character specifications—such as font, point size, and style—Word asks Windows NT for the appropriate bit map to represent each character in the document.

Windows NT finds the appropriate TrueType font file, based on the information provided by Word, and sends it to the TrueType rasterizer. The TrueType rasterizer converts the outline instructions into a bit map, and returns the bit map to the GDI to display. This bit map then is sent to the device driver for displaying on-screen. This process is shown in figure 9.3.

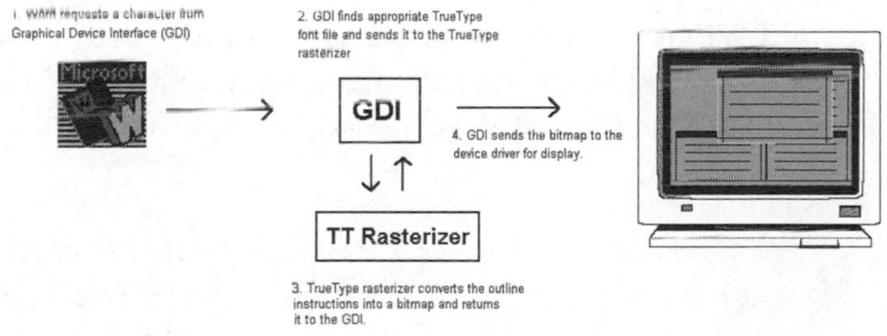

Figure 9.3:
The process of displaying a TrueType font.

As shown in figure 9.3, TrueType font outlines are converted to a bit map to appear on-screen (as well as to print), based on the result of mathematical instructions for a particular point size. TrueType outlines are device-independent, and thus are an ideal representation of the font. However, 96-dpi screens and even 300-dpi laser printers do not have enough resolution to display or print the character properly because the size of a pixel is too large.

If nothing is done to correct this, diagonal lines and curves within a font outline look jagged because the optimum outline of a character is in units smaller than a pixel. A diagonal line might need only part of a pixel to represent it, for example, but because the pixel is the smallest unit of measure, the pixel needs to be either on or off. If the pixel is on, the line looks too wide; if the pixel is off, the line is too narrow.

To prevent this from happening, before TrueType creates the bit map, it first optimizes the bit map by using *hints* (instructions that optimize the look of the scaled outline character by changing its outline to produce a better-looking character).

Without hints, a lowercase "m" or "n" may have different widths for each of its legs. Hinting distorts the original outline characters so that the "m" and "n" bit maps displayed have identical legs, regardless of the number of pixels available.

Hints are less important when the font is larger and the resolution is greater on the output device. Although hints are needed when printing or displaying on devices below 800dpi, new 600-dpi laser printers, such as the HP LaserJet IV, can produce the desired results with fewer hints.

Both TrueType and PostScript support hinting, but they use different techniques. PostScript Type 1 hints are a set of instructions given to the rasterizer, telling it how the character can be modified. The PostScript rasterizer then is responsible for carrying out these instructions. In contrast, TrueType hints are carried out by the font itself rather than the TrueType rasterizer.

The significance of this difference may not be obvious, but it can affect the performance and quality of the hint. First, TrueType hints are faster because they are performed by the font producer during the development of the font instead of at run time by the rasterizer. Second, built-in hints can improve the quality of the generated TrueType font because the font designer, not the rasterizer, is in control of the final appearance of the font. Third, potential hinting problems can be resolved during the development process instead of at run time. As a result, the TrueType font rasterizer is quicker and more efficient at executing the font code.

A PostScript rasterizer interprets PostScript hints; a TrueType rasterizer simply processes the TrueType font's hints. PostScript can be thought of as a high-level interpreted language; TrueType can be considered a low-level assembler-like language.

When you print your TrueType document, the way the fonts are dealt with is based on the type of printer being used. On LaserJet and compatible printers, TrueType generates LaserJet soft fonts and downloads only the characters needed by the printer to print the text, instead of entire font files being sent. (Typical soft fonts require downloading entire character sets.) Characters are printed as text, not as graphics.

On PostScript printers, TrueType downloads smaller characters (14-point characters and below) as Type 3 fonts (bit map), which is faster than downloading an outline font. For larger fonts, TrueType sends a Type 1 outline for each size that needs to be rasterized by the PostScript printer.

On dot-matrix printers, TrueType sends text as graphics for each pass of the printhead. Although printing TrueType on a dot-matrix printer is slow, the quality is remarkably good.

TrueType Font Embedding

TrueType solves the problem of transferring Windows 3.1 and Windows NT documents between computers. Before TrueType, a document created on a computer with a specific set of fonts could not be properly displayed or printed on a second computer without the same set of fonts being installed. As a result, document sharing within an office environment was limited to those workstations that were equipped with identical fonts and font managers. When sending a document to a typesetter, you also had the legal dilemma of whether to include copyrighted font files on the disk to ensure that their output was identical to that of the service bureau.

TrueType eliminates these problems through a technology called *font embedding*, which embeds the fonts in the document so that they still can be displayed and/or printed when opened on a computer without those fonts installed. A font is specifically coded by the developer to have one of the following three embedding qualities:

- **No embedding.** If a font allows no embedding capabilities, the source application does not embed the font in a document when it is saved. The receiving computer is forced to make a font substitution when the document is opened on the computer. PostScript and most other current non-TrueType fonts are in this class.
- **Read-only.** If a document contains one or more read-only fonts, you can read and print the document, but the receiving application does not allow you to edit it until every read-only embedded font has been removed.
- **Read/Write.** The read/write option enables you to read, modify, and print the document with the embedded TrueType fonts. Moreover, the application in which you open the embedded document asks you whether you want the font installed permanently. The standard TrueType fonts that come with Windows NT are all read/write fonts (as are the fonts that come in the TrueType Font Pack). If a font is read/write enabled, you can distribute an embedded document to whomever you choose; there are no copyright restrictions placed on you.

The actual significance of font embedding will be felt in forthcoming versions of major Windows 3.1 and Windows NT applications. Currently, the 16-bit version of Microsoft PowerPoint is the only Windows application that supports font embedding.

Windows NT Font Mapping

If you have worked with fonts for any length of time, you know a vast number of fonts are available that are virtually identical in appearance, but have copyrighted face names. Font mapping eliminates any possible confusion by Windows when it searches for exact face names.

Windows NT enables you to substitute fonts that are not found on your system with installed fonts. This process is known as *font mapping*. When you open an existing document or create a new one, an application requests a font from Windows NT by listing its face name and other characteristics. If there is no exact match with a physical font (a font that can be transferred to the printer and screen), Windows NT must try to map that request to the closest possible physical font.

Windows NT advanced font-mapping capabilities are available in Windows 3.0. Both Windows 3.0 and 3.1 have a core-mapping facility, which selects the physical font that most closely matches the requested font. Windows 3.0 requires that all font requests go to the core mapper—even when a font request has a match. Windows NT speeds up the process considerably by making an "end-around" the core mapper when an exact match is found (that is, the core mapper is not even accessed).

When an application requests a font from Windows NT, Windows NT has to decide which font to use, based on the following conditions:

- **Font does not exist.** If the name of the font does not exist, Windows NT always selects the appropriate TrueType font by matching the font characteristics (point size, serif/sans serif, monospaced/proportional).
- **Font matches a bit-map font.** To ensure compatibility with Windows 3.0, a bit-map font is used and stretched when needed for displaying at all point sizes if the name of a font matches only a bit-map font.
- **Font matches a bit-map and TrueType font.** If the name of a font matches a bit-map and TrueType font, the bit-map font is used at the point sizes for which there is a bit map; the TrueType font is used at the remaining point sizes.
- **Font has a duplicate face name.** If two or more fonts have the same name, most applications list only the font name once. TrueType fonts are always listed first.
- **Font does exist.** If the name of the font exists, Windows NT ignores the substitution table and uses the specified font. This action may seem obvious, but it is very useful.

Comparing TrueType with PostScript

Microsoft is nothing if not a giant killer. Although the big battles include the one between Microsoft and IBM over operating-system dominance (Windows NT versus OS/2), there are other technologies that Microsoft is not content to leave alone. Before Windows 3.1 and Windows NT, PostScript was the unquestioned leader of scalable font technology. With TrueType's introduction into Windows 3.1 and now Windows NT, however, the landscape has changed considerably. PostScript still dominates the high-end desktop publishing, graphics design, and typesetting markets, but TrueType is making inroads into these territories. No longer does a business have to look to a PostScript printer to print professional-looking documents.

PostScript is a page description language (PDL) developed by Adobe and Apple in the mid-1980s that quickly became the standard PDL used by serious typographers. Type 1 fonts are the industry standard and are used by every service bureau. PostScript printers have a set of Type 1 fonts built into them: often Helvetica, Times Roman, Palatino, and Avant Garde, to name a few. There are two major kind of PostScript fonts: Type 1 is a set of scalable typefaces; Type 3 fonts typically are bit-map fonts used primarily for printing text at small sizes.

A page description language *(PDL), such as PostScript or Hewlett-Packard's PCL, is a set of instructions used to manipulate fonts, graphics, and color, and to set printer options. PDLs are resident in a printer or printer cartridge.*

Although TrueType font technology is built into Windows NT, PostScript (through Adobe Type Manager) is integrated into OS/2 2.1.

The debate now rages over which scalable font technology you should use: TrueType or PostScript. Table 9.1 lists the major differences between the two font technologies. PostScript is still the best choice for desktop publishing and graphics design because of its universal support by service bureaus. TrueType is the best choice for normal use and in standard business communications. Thus, if your chief concern is to produce professional-quality documents, you cannot go wrong with TrueType.

Table 9.1
TrueType vs. PostScript Type 1

Category	*TrueType*	*PostScript*
Operating System Integration	Windows NT	OS/2 2.*x* (Adobe Type Manager)

continues

Table 9.1
Continued

Category	*TrueType*	*PostScript*
Scalable font technology	Yes	Yes
Universally available for all Windows NT users	Yes	No
Hinting instructions carried out by Rasterizer	Font	Font
Industry standard for typesetters/ service bureaus	No	Yes
Estimated number of fonts available	2,500	Over 20,000
Overall level of typeface sophistication	Mixed	High
Printer portability	Virtually any printer	With ATM, virtually any printer
Platform portability	PC, Mac	All major platforms

The fast rise of TrueType and the affordable quality fonts in the TrueType Font Pack have created a price war between the major font foundries. The result is that never before have there been as many quality TrueType and Type 1 fonts available at such reasonable prices.

Although PostScript has a much richer library of available fonts, the number of quality TrueType fonts is growing rapidly with the success of Windows 3.1 and anticipated success of Windows NT. Microsoft introduced the

TrueType Font Pack for Windows, which contains 44 typefaces. These fonts are designed to be combined with the standard TrueType typefaces to make an equivalent to the standard set of PostScript fonts. Many new CD-ROMs also are available that contain TrueType fonts.

One of the best sources for free or shareware fonts is the DTPFORUM on CompuServe. You can find hundreds of TrueType (and PostScript Type 1) fonts in Library 9. Although some are of dubious quality, there are many decorative fonts that can enrich your font library.

Working with Fonts

Windows NT provides the Font section of the Control Panel to enable you to install and remove TrueType, bit-map, and vector fonts. It also allows you to set TrueType options. The Fonts dialog box is shown in figure 9.4.

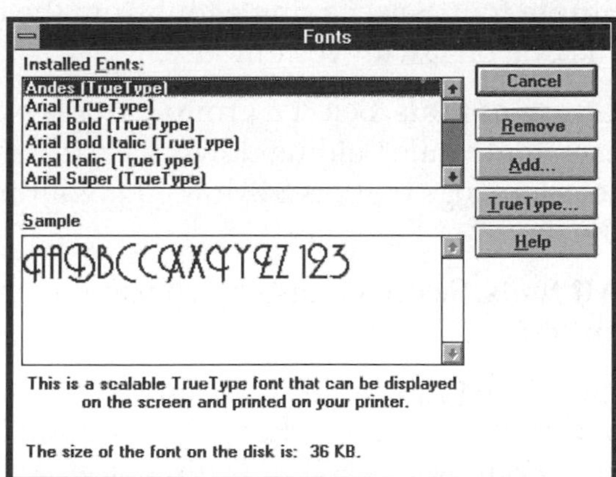

Figure 9.4:
The Fonts dialog box.

Installing Fonts

The process of installing fonts in Windows NT is straight forward. To install TrueType, bit-map, or vector fonts, click on the Fonts icon in the Control Panel to display the Fonts dialog box (see fig. 9.4). Click on the Add button to display the Add Fonts dialog box, as shown in figure 9.5.

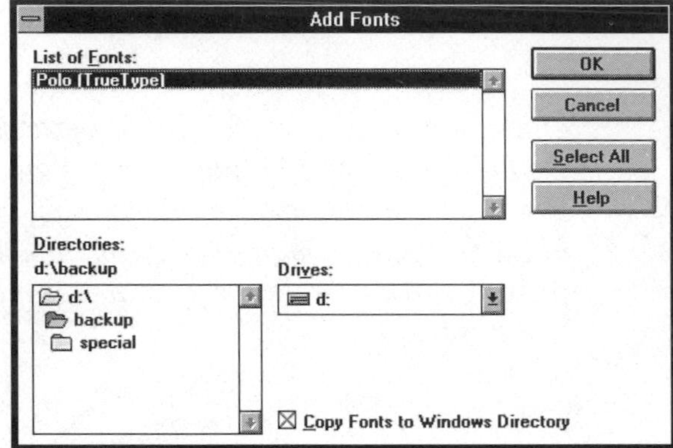

Figure 9.5:
The Add Fonts dialog box.

Use the Drives and Directories controls to select the path that contains the font files you want to install. When you change directories, Windows NT looks for font files located in the path and lists the font names in the List of Fonts box. You have a choice of the following fonts to install:

- **Single font.** Select a single font from the fonts list by clicking on it with your mouse.
- **Group of fonts.** Select a group of fonts by clicking on each font while holding down the Ctrl key. You also can select a range of fonts by dragging your mouse down the list.
- **All fonts.** Select all fonts by clicking on the Select All button.

By default, the Copy Fonts to Windows NT Directory box is checked. With this option checked, Windows NT copies each font to the WINNT\SYSTEM32 directory.

It usually is best, from a font management point of view, to centralize all your fonts into a single location. If you have large numbers of fonts located on a CD-ROM or network drive, however, you can save space on your hard drive by keeping the fonts at the other location. Remember, though, if you do not copy the file to the WINNT\SYSTEM32 directory, Windows NT needs to access the CD-ROM or network to use it. Windows NT prompts you to insert the disk containing the fonts when required.

Avoid using fonts stored on a network disk because you add to the network traffic each time Windows NT accesses that font.

When you are ready to add the selected fonts, click on the OK button.

Although you may want to have as many fonts as possible available to you when you are working, installed fonts slow the time it takes to load Windows NT and most applications, and they drain memory. You probably do not notice much of a difference unless you have at least 100 fonts installed.

The general rule of thumb is to install only the fonts you use regularly. You can always remove a font from Windows NT without deleting the font file, and add the font later if you need it.

Removing Fonts

To remove a TrueType, bit-map, or vector font from Windows NT, click on the Fonts icon in the Control Panel to display the Fonts dialog box. Select the font(s) from the Installed Fonts list and click on the Remove button. The Remove Font dialog box appears (see fig. 9.6), asking you to confirm your action.

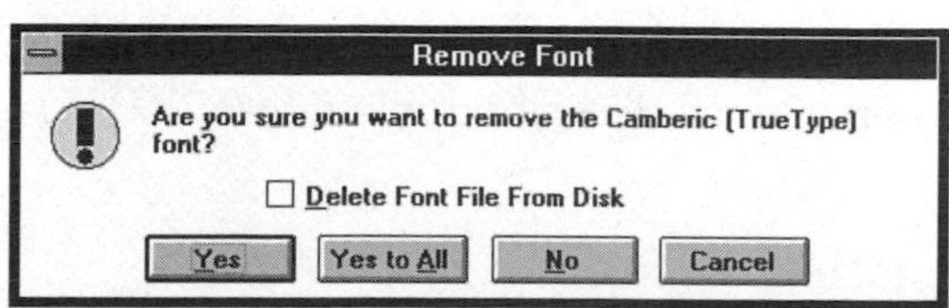

Figure 9.6: *The Remove Font dialog box.*

In the dialog box, you also have the option of deleting the font file from your hard drive by checking the Delete Font File From Disk box. Click on the Yes button to remove the specified font. (If you are deleting a group of fonts, click on the Yes to All button to avoid confirming the removal of each font.)

Setting TrueType Options

The Font section of the Control Panel also enables you to specify that you want to use TrueType exclusively on your machine. To set this option, click on the TrueType button in the Fonts dialog box.

The TrueType dialog box appears (see fig. 9.7), and displays the Show Only TrueType Fonts in Applications check box. If you work with TrueType exclusively, you can restrict applications from listing all other available fonts.

Figure 9.7: *The TrueType dialog box.*

This option applies only to Windows applications that support TrueType. You cannot use TrueType fonts in a DOS or POSIX application, for example.

Understanding Bit-Map Fonts

Windows NT includes five bit-map fonts that are available for screen use, as described in table 9.2.

Table 9.2
Windows NT Screen Fonts

Font	*Point Sizes Supported*	*Font File Name (? = A-F)*
Courier	10, 12, 15	COUR?.FON
MS Sans Serif	8, 10, 12, 14, 18, 24	SSERIF?.FON
MS Serif	8, 10, 12, 14, 18, 24	SERIF?.FON
Small	2, 4, 6	SMALL?.FON
Symbol	8, 10, 12, 14, 18, 24	SYMBOL?.FON

These fonts are essentially the same set of bit-map fonts from Windows 3.0 (although Windows NT changed the names of two of them: Helv instead of MS Sans Serif; Tms Rmn instead of MS Serif). They are exactly the same as the fonts in Windows 3.1.

These fonts are not listed in all your applications (Word for Windows, for example). Many applications list only those fonts that can be printed to the default printer. Consequently, they are listed if you have a dot-matrix printer as the default, but not if a laser printer is set as the default printer. Some applications, such as ObjectVision or Paradox for Windows, enable you to design a document for either the screen or printer; their font lists can vary.

Understanding System Fonts

System fonts are used in various parts of the Windows NT interface, such as dialog boxes and menus. Each of the following three fonts are required by Windows NT:

- **System font.** The *system font* is the default font used by Windows NT in menus, dialog boxes, window titles, and caption bars. The system font is proportional, and it is based on the type of display you are running. The system font varies, depending on the display on which you run Windows NT.

- **Fixed font.** The *fixed font* is a monospaced font, and it was the former default font for 16-bit Windows versions (prior to 3.0). Some applets (Notepad, for example) and applications that require a monospaced font use the fixed font.

- **OEM font.** The *OEM font* is a monospaced font based on the code page by the system. The OEM font plays several roles—it determines the height of dialog boxes, and is used by the ClipBook Viewer to display OEM Text.

Understanding DOS Session Fonts

Windows NT enables you to change the fonts of your DOS applications that run in a windowed DOS session. Variable-sized fonts enable you to customize the size of the text and window to a size that is suitable for you. *DOS session fonts* are based on the code page of the computer.

To change the font in your DOS-based application, open the program in a window, and choose the Fonts command from the window's control menu. In the Font Selection dialog box (see fig. 9.8), select the appropriate font size from the Font list: 4×6, 5×12, 6×8, 7×12, 8×8, 8×12, 10×18, 12×16, or 16×8.

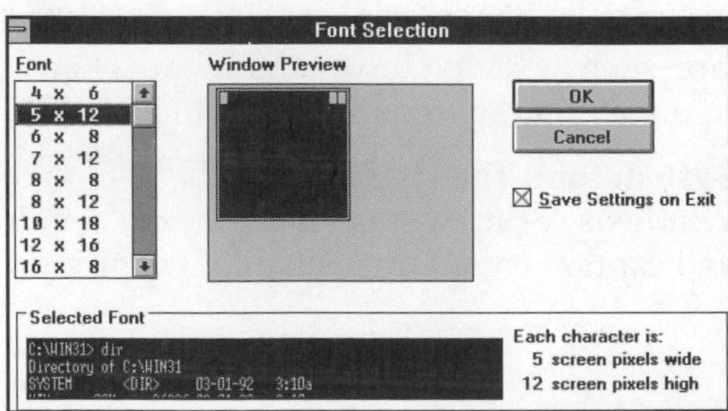

Figure 9.8:
The Font Selection dialog box.

Use the Window Preview and Selected Font to see what the window and font will look like. If you want every windowed DOS session to have the same configuration, check the Save Settings on Exit box, and click on OK.

Using the Windows NT Print Manager To Configure Printers

Windows NT print-management capabilities are more extensive than previous 16-bit versions of Windows. The Print Manager utility in Windows 3.1 and earlier was a basic manager of print jobs and did little else. In fact, some 16-bit Windows applications bypassed the Print Manager altogether and managed printing by itself.

In contrast, Windows NT controls printing much more tightly so that all printing must be done through its Print Manager. Windows NT also integrates the printer-setup commands into Print Manager so that all printer controls are accessible through the Print Manager window.

Installing and Configuring Printers

When you are ready to install or configure a printer, open Print Manager—from either the Control Panel (double-click on the Printers icon) or the Main group of Program Manager (double-click on the Print Manager icon). The Print Manager window appears, as shown in figure 9.9.

Print Manager displays a child window for each of the installed printers, and shows the name of the default printer at the top of its window in the Default list box. In addition to displaying printers, the Printers dialog box enables you to perform a number of operations, including configuring your printer connection, setting up your printer options, and installing and removing a printer.

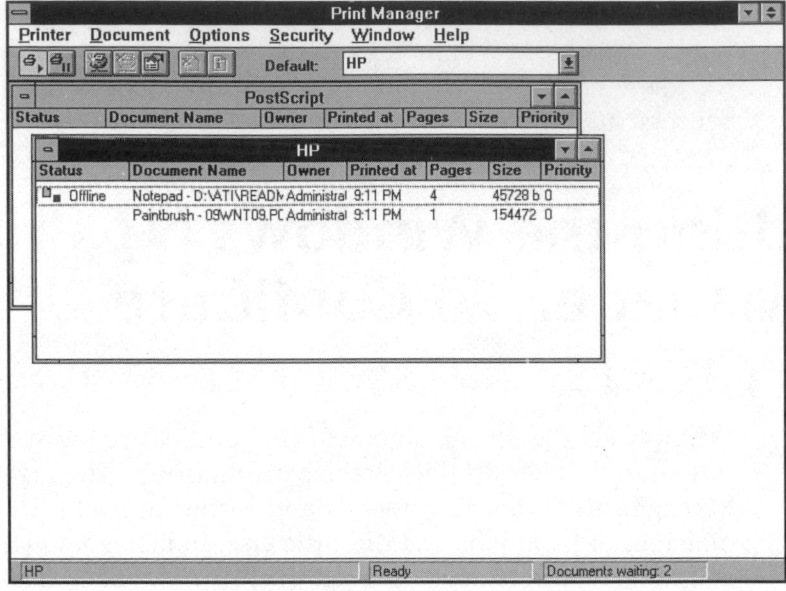

Figure 9.9: *Windows NT Print Manager.*

If you want to install a new printer, choose the Create Printer option from the Printer menu. The Create Printer dialog box opens, as shown in figure 9.10.

Create Printer
Printer Name: PostScript
Driver: Apple LaserWriter II NT v47.0
Description:
Print to: LPT1:
Share this printer on the network
Share Name:
Location:
OK
Cancel
Setup...
Details...
Settings...
Help

Figure 9.10: *The Create Printer dialog box.*

The Create Printer dialog box offers several options:

- **Printer Name.** Enter a name (fewer than 32 characters) to be used to identify the printer in Print Manager and Windows NT dialog boxes.

- **Driver.** Select the desired printer from this list.
- **Description.** Enter a description to inform users about the printer.
- **Print to.** Select a destination for your print job. You can choose one of the following options:

  LPT1–LPT3. These names identify your computer's parallel ports. Most printers use LPT1. If you select an LPT port, you can click on the Settings button to specify how long the Print Manager waits for a printer to come back on-line and accept information. (A printer might not accept transmissions following an error condition or during a large print job.)

  COM1–COM4. These names identify your computer's serial ports. If you select a COM port, you can click on the Settings button to specify additional information. The Ports dialog box appears (see fig. 9.11), displaying a list of valid ports you can configure. Choose one and click on the Settings button.

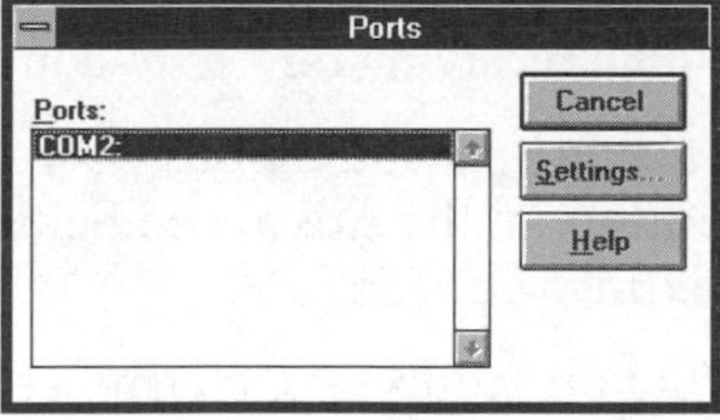

Figure 9.11:
The Ports dialog box.

Most printers support the default COM port settings; if yours does not, refer to your printer manual to determine the correct configuration for the COM port.

The Settings for COM2 dialog box is shown in figure 9.12.

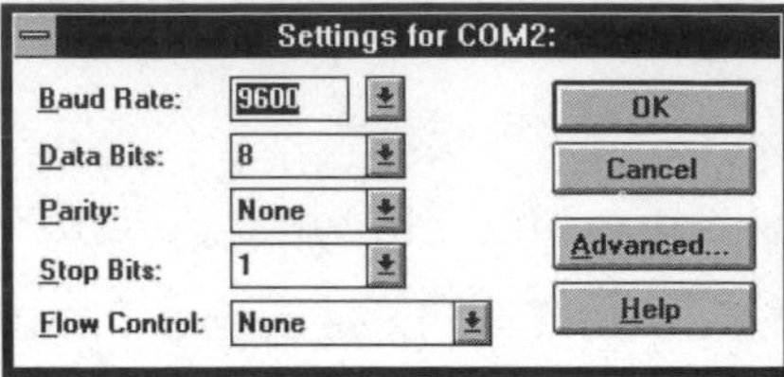

Figure 9.12:
The Settings for COM2 dialog box.

In the Settings for COM2 dialog box, you can configure the following five settings:

- **Baud Rate.** Determines the speed at which characters are sent through the port.
- **Data Bits.** Determines the number of data bits used to represent each character.
- **Parity.** Determines the method used for error checking. This setting checks to ensure that the correct number of bits has been received.
- **Stop Bits.** Determines the amount of time between transmitted characters.
- **Flow Control.** Determines the handshaking method used by the receiving device to control the flow of data.

If you need to configure advanced port settings, click on the Advanced button. In the Advanced Settings dialog box, two additional settings appear:

- **Base I/O Port Address.** Determines the address used by the port in your computer's I/O address space.
- **Interrupt Request Line (IRQ).** Determines the interrupt used by the COM port.

There may be no user-configurable advanced settings for your COM port. If not, Windows NT notifies you, and returns you to the Settings for COMx dialog box.

Under most circumstances, do not make any changes to the default settings configured by Windows NT. If you have problems, first try to change your hardware configuration to match the defaults used by Windows NT.

- **FILE.** Tells Windows NT that print jobs will be sent to a file rather than a printer.
- **Network Printer.** Enables you to specify a route that is not listed. When you select this option, the Print Destinations dialog box appears, as shown in figure 9.13.

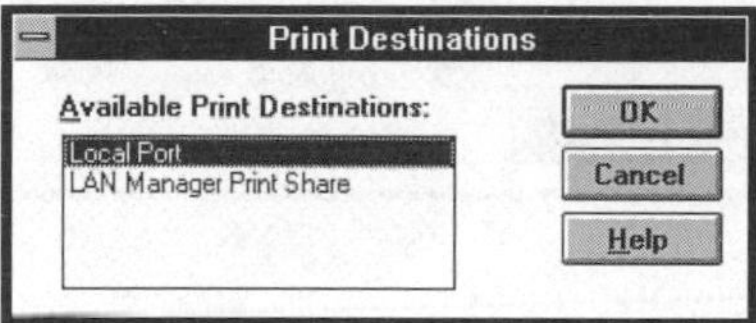

Figure 9.13: *The Print Destinations dialog box.*

The list of available options depends on the network to which you are attached. By default, there are two options: Local Port (adds the name of a port); and LAN Manager Print Share (adds a LAN Manager print share—versions 2.*x* of LAN Manager).

- **Share This Printer On The Network.** Click on this box to make the printer available to others on the network. Windows NT automatically creates a DOS-compatible share name, and places it into the Share Name text box (see fig. 9.10). Edit as needed. In addition, you can edit a description of the location of the printer in the Location text box.

Another option available in the Create Printer dialog box is the Details button, which, when clicked on, will display the Printer Details dialog box (see fig. 9.14).

In the Printer Details dialog box, there are several options you can specify for the printer:

- **Available From.** Specifies the hours you want the printer to be available for printing.

- **Separator File.** If you want to send a file to be printed before each new print job, enter the file in this text box. Clicking on the ellipsis button enables you to browse through the directory tree for a specific file.

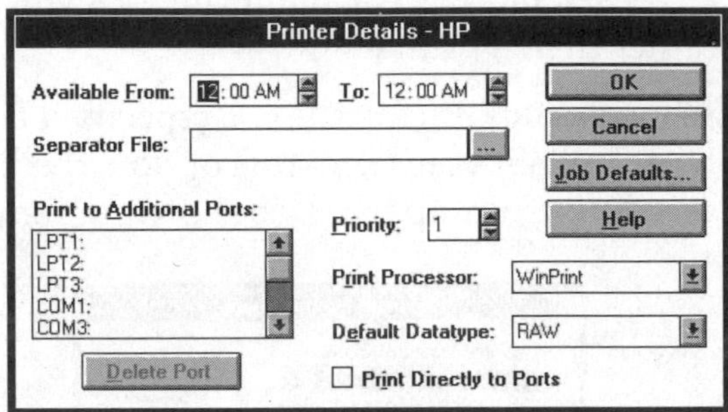

Figure 9.14: *Printer Details dialog box.*

Separator files *enable you to print a page at the beginning of each document so that you easily can separate printed documents. These files also enable the printer to switch between PCL and PostScript printing.*

To specify either of these options, enter the name of one of the separator files (DEFAULT.SEP, PSLANMAN.SEP, PCL.SEP, or PSCRIPT.SEP) that are included with Windows NT in this text box.

Windows NT's default separator file is DEFAULT.SEP. Use this file to print a blank page before each new print job.

- **Print to Additional Ports.** If you want to pool one or more printers together with your current printer, select the port(s) to which the other printer(s) is attached. The printer then sends the job on to all other selected printers each time a print job prints on the current printer.
- **Priority.** Specifies the priority of print jobs sent to the printer. Enter a number between 1–99 (the higher the number, the higher the priority).

Suppose you would like to use different priority levels for your printer, depending on the specific document you are printing. Instead of manually adjusting this setting each time in Print Manager, you can create two or more instances of the same printer (using different printer names), and set each printer to a different priority level.

When you need to print a document quickly, you print to the "Extraordinarily Urgent" printer. For normal use, you can use the "Just Plain Average" printer, tagged with a lesser priority. Finally, if you have a document with no priority for printing, you can choose the "Maybe Next Year" printer, tagged with the lowest priority setting.

- **Print Processor.** Provides the capability to change the print processor if a specific application requires this option. Most applications use the WinPrint processor.
- **Default Datatype.** Enables you to specify a different default datatype. This is another option you normally do not need to change from the default setting. Options include RAW, NT JNL 1.00, and TEXT.
- **Print Directly to Ports.** Check this box to eliminate print spooling and transfer data directly to the printer.
- **Job Defaults.** Clicking on this button displays a dialog box that enables you to set default settings for printed documents. The actual dialog box depends on the printer you are configuring.

After you have defined all options for your printer, click on the OK button. When you add a new printer, Windows NT copies the driver file from your driver disk into the Windows NT SYSTEM directory. The driver is then used to communicate between Windows NT and your printer.

If the printer driver is not already on your system, Windows NT prompts you to insert the appropriate CD-ROM or floppy disk (one of the Windows NT distribution disks or an updated driver on a separate disk) into a CD-ROM or floppy drive. When you insert the disk and click on OK, the driver file is copied onto your system.

Windows NT enables you to install the same printer several times. Multiple configurations of the same printer are helpful if you frequently change the port to which your printer is attached, or if you frequently need to print to both a printer and a file by using the same printer.

Suppose, for example, that you frequently do desktop publishing work, and that you use a PostScript printer in your office. You also need to print to a file when you take a job to your typesetter.

You might call a printer "Legal" if you want it to use legal-size paper. You might call the same printer "Envelope" when printing envelopes. You can change the settings for each print job, or name the printer differently to retain all the settings. If you change printer setups often, giving the printer different names saves you a lot of time.

Although you can use a single installed PostScript printer and change port settings between printer and file output, a much easier solution is to install two instances of the same printer driver. Configure one (such as LPT1) to your printer port, and configure the second to FILE. You then can switch between the two printers.

If you install a printer more than once, Windows NT does not need to reinstall the printer driver. Instead, Windows NT uses the printer driver installed the first time.

Setting a Default Printer

You easily can set the default printer in Print Manager by selecting one of the installed printers from the Default list box at the top of the Print Manager windows (see fig. 9.9).

Removing a Printer

If you are no longer using a printer and want to remove it from your printer list, select the printer window or icon in Print Manager, and choose the Remove Printer option from the Printer menu. Print Manager asks you to confirm that you want to delete the printer before doing so.

When you remove a local printer, Windows NT does not actually delete the printer driver file on your hard disk. Instead, it only removes the printer's name from the list of available printers.

If you want to add the printer again to the list, you can use the Create Printer option to re-create your printer setup. Because the driver you intend to use still resides on your hard disk, you do not have to use the Windows NT distribution disk (CD-ROM or floppy) to copy the driver file onto your computer.

Setting Up a Printer

After you install and connect a printer, you still might need to set up some settings specific to your particular printer. You have two ways to set up a printer, depending on where you are working within Windows NT:

- **Print Manager.** Click on the Setup button in the Create Printer dialog box (accessed by choosing the Create Printer option from the Printer menu).
- **Windows NT Applications.** Virtually all Windows applications enable you to print text or graphic data.

If so, then they also should have a Print Setup command on their File menu that displays installed printers. Click on the Setup button in that application's dialog box.

The exact setup options depend on the type of printer you are using. The most popular printer options include LaserJet and PostScript laser printers, and dot-matrix printers.

Configuring a LaserJet Printer

The most popular laser printers available today are HP LaserJet or compatible printers. If you have a LaserJet, configuring it is a relatively straightforward process. Click on the Setup button in the Printers dialog box, or choose Print Setup from the File menu of most Windows applications to display the dialog box shown in figure 9.15.

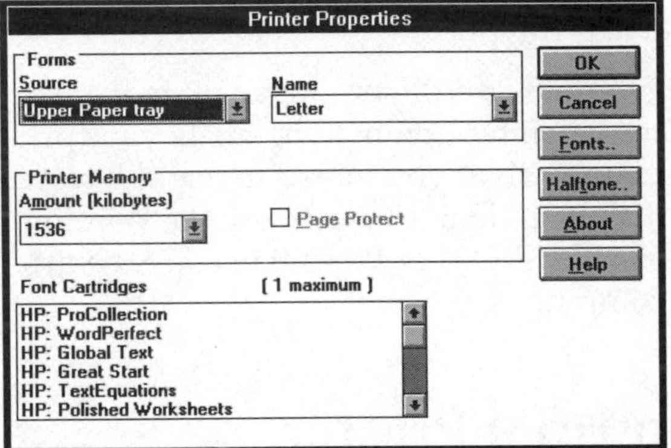

Figure 9.15:
The HP LaserJet dialog box.

Even though most laser printers print at 300 dpi, more advanced printers, such as the LaserJet series, have resolution-enhancement capabilities. With special software, LaserJet printers can vary the size of the ink dots printed on a page. (The LaserJet IV uses Resolution Enhancement Technology and prints at 600 dpi.) These features improve dramatically the gray-scale output and sharpness of photos and art.

Configuring a PostScript Printer

To print PostScript fonts, you need a PostScript-compatible printer, which involves more options than any other type of printer. To set these options, your PostScript driver dialog boxes can lead you through as many as four levels of nested dialog boxes. To display the initial setup dialog box, click on the Setup button in the Printers dialog box after you select your PostScript printer, or choose Print Setup from the File menu of your Windows application.

The initial dialog box, shown in figure 9.16, provides the basic paper source, size, and orientation, as well as the number of copies.

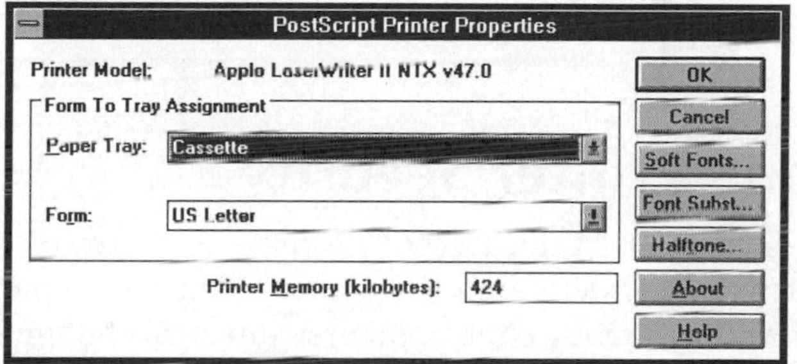

Figure 9.16:
The PostScript Printer Properties dialog box.

You do not have to have a PostScript printer to use the PostScript printer driver. You can set up the PostScript settings as usual, and print the job to a file. This can be useful if you want to print a PostScript file on a printer that is not attached to your system, or if you need to submit a PostScript file to a service bureau for typesetting.

If you want to print a PostScript document to a file, choose FILE as your destination when you connect your printer.

Configuring a Dot-Matrix Printer

A dot-matrix printer has fewer available options to configure. If you have a dot-matrix printer, click on the Setup button in the Printers dialog box after you select the dot-matrix printer in Print Manager. Figure 9.17 shows a dialog box for an Epson 24-pin dot-matrix printer.

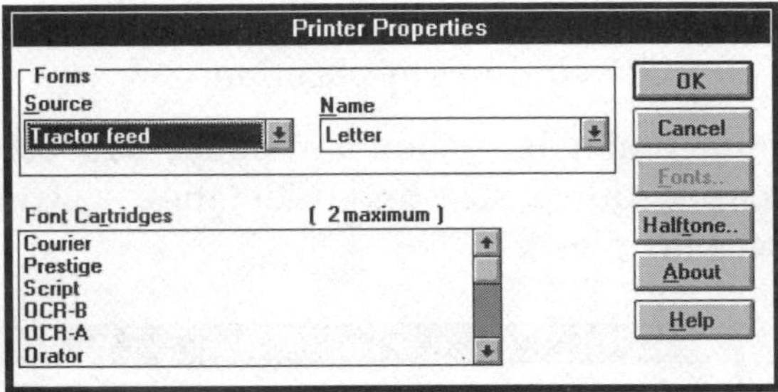

Figure 9.17: *The Epson LQ-850 dialog box.*

Setting Printer Security

You can restrict the access that users and groups of users have to a printer. Such restrictions include the permission to print documents, control printer settings, change printing orders, and pause the printer. To do so, choose the Permissions option from the Security menu in the Print Manager window. Windows NT displays the Printer Permissions dialog box.

You can specify access restrictions for each user or group by making selections from the Type of Access list box. Possible options include Full Control, Manage Documents, Print, and No Access. In addition, you can add to the list of users or groups by clicking on the Add button.

Owning a Printer

Owners can change access permissions for a printer. You can take ownership of a printer if you have Full Control access or are a member of the Administrators group. To own a printer, choose the Owner option from the Security menu in Print Manager. The Owner dialog box is displayed, as shown in figure 9.18. Click on the Take Ownership button.

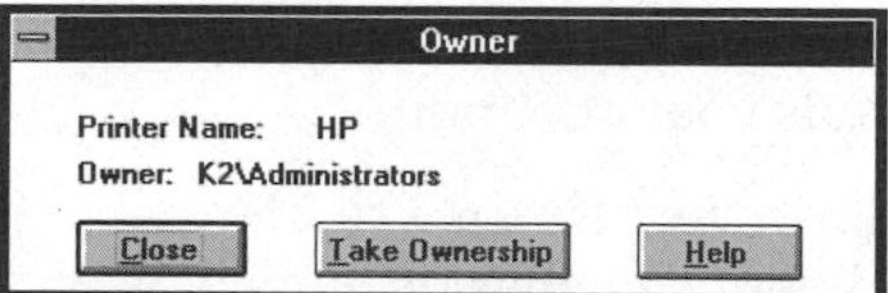

Figure 9.18:
Owner dialog box.

Connecting to Remote Network Printers

To access a remote network printer, your computer must be connected to it. You can do this by clicking on Connect To Printer in the Printer menu in Print Manager. Windows NT displays the Connect to Printer dialog box, which lists the remote printers available to you in the Shared Printers box.

To select a shared printer, enter its name in the Printer text box. If the Expand by Default box is checked, you can select a remote printer from the Shared Printers list.

If the Expand by Default box is not checked, double-click on a network in the Shared Printers list; it expands to show the domains or workgroups on that network. Double-click on the domain or workgroup name to display the names of its remote printers. When you are ready to connect, click on the OK button.

Managing Print Jobs with the Print Manager

In addition to installing and configuring printers, the actual management of Windows NT print jobs also is done through the Print Manager. Print Manager acts as a print-spooling utility that, when activated, receives print jobs from all Windows NT applications, logs them into a queue, and sends the jobs to one or more printers at the appropriate time.

The Print Manager icon is located in the Main group of Program Manager, but you do not have to run it to be able to use it. When you print a document from an application, Print Manager opens automatically until the print job is over; then it closes automatically. Print Manager stays open only if a printer needs your attention.

You can, however, use the Print Manager to view the print queue and perform other print management tasks.

Changing the Print-Queue Order

You can change the order of files in the print queue. This capability is helpful if you are printing a number of documents and you want to print a lower-priority document first.

To move a print job, select the desired job from a printer window with your mouse, then drag and drop it into a new position. Figure 9.19 shows the print queue for the printer named "HP".

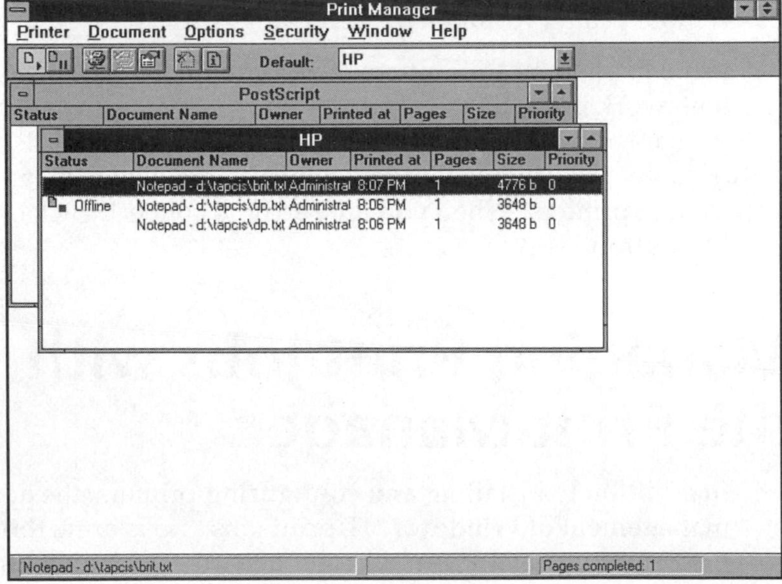

Figure 9.19: *Print Manager queue.*

There are two limitations to changing the queue order. First, you cannot move a job that is currently being printed. Second, you cannot move a print job from one printer to another.

Deleting a Print Job

If you want to cancel a pending or current print job, select the job from the print queue and choose Remove Document from the Document menu. A message box confirms your action.

Setting Document Details

By double-clicking a document in a print queue or selecting a document and choosing Details from the Document menu, you can view the Document Details dialog box.

This dialog box enables you to view specific details about the print job, such as its title, status, number of pages, and size (in bytes). It also enables you to set various options for the document, including:

- **Notify.** Specifies the user name notified when a document has printed. The default name is the document owner.
- **Priority.** Determines the priority the document is given in the print queue. Highest numbered priorities are printed before lower numbers. Values range from 1–99.
- **Start Time.** Specifies the time at which to start the print job. Note that because there are no date settings, a print job must print within 24 hours.
- **Until Time.** Specifies the time at which you would like a document to cease printing.

Troubleshooting TrueType Printing

Although TrueType is an innovative font technology, there always are compatibility problems with the scores of printers and printer drivers available today. In time, these problems will be solved by Microsoft and the printer manufacturers.

Overall, the single best thing you can do with a printer problem under Windows NT is to get the latest driver available. The best resources for this are the printer manufacturer's forum, the Microsoft Software Library on CompuServe, or the Microsoft Download Service (MSDL): (206) 936-6735.

Summary

With the integration of TrueType technology into Windows NT, printing is easier and more seamless than ever before. The type quality of TrueType is matched only by PostScript and other advanced font technologies.

This chapter discussed TrueType fonts and how they can be used in Windows NT. It also described other fonts used by Windows NT for on-screen use.

You learned about the Windows NT Print Manager, which is a powerful, integrated print-management facility. (Print Manager is a far cry from its weak Windows 3.1 counterpart.)

Using Print Manager, you can install, configure, and remove printers; connect to network printers; and set levels of authorization for users on your network. You also can use it to control document queues, including prioritizing print jobs, setting document details, and removing documents from the queue.

Windows NT brings a whole new level of sophistication to printing on the PC platform. With TrueType and the new Print Manager, printing can be as simple or detailed as you require.

Creating Solutions through Integration

Running DOS, OS/2, and POSIX Applications

Exchanging Data between Windows Applications

Using Object Linking and Embedding

PART 3

Running DOS, OS/2, and POSIX Applications

When you move to Windows NT from DOS, character-mode OS/2, or UNIX, you need not abandon your existing applications. You can run DOS, OS/2, and POSIX-compliant applications from within Windows NT, sometimes with better performance. You even can access a command prompt from within Windows NT. If you have previous Windows experience, this information is nothing new—Windows users always shell out of Windows to DOS.

POSIX *is a standard developed by a consortium of UNIX vendors designed to bring order to the various UNIX environments available, each of which is slightly incompatible with the others. POSIX-compliant UNIX applications can run on Windows NT.*

In Windows NT, you can operate more than one DOS, OS/2, or POSIX session simultaneously, and each session is an emulation of a *x*86 microprocessor with its own memory, devices, and environment variables. Because each session is an emulation of a different *x*86 machine, the term *virtual* is used. These multiple virtual machines are all preemptively multitasked, just as is any other program running under Windows NT.

This chapter shows you the way to set up and run your DOS, OS/2, and POSIX applications with Windows NT. You learn to manage character-mode windows, switch between character-mode tasks, and cut-and-paste among applications. In the last part of this chapter, you explore the customization options available for configuring the Windows NT multitasking environment for use with DOS programs.

This chapter provides more hands-on instruction for using Windows NT with DOS, OS/2, and POSIX applications. In particular, this chapter covers the following topics:

- Setting up a DOS, OS/2, or POSIX application by using Setup
- Setting up a DOS, OS/2, or POSIX application by using the Program Manager
- Setting up terminate-and-stay-resident (TSR) programs
- Using the Program Information File (PIF) Editor to create PIFs that customize your DOS applications
- Starting DOS, OS/2, and POSIX applications under Windows NT
- Switching among non-Windows NT applications
- Cutting-and-pasting data among non-Windows NT applications

Setting Up a Non-Windows NT Application

Sometimes you want to run a non-Windows NT application under Windows NT. What is a *non-Windows NT application*? The five categories of non-Windows NT applications are as follows:

- Windows applications written for Windows versions 3.1 and older
- Character-mode OS/2 applications
- POSIX-compliant UNIX applications
- DOS applications
- Memory-resident DOS programs (TSRs)

If you have an older Windows application (written for Windows 3.1 or 3.0), contact the manufacturer to obtain an updated version. Because Windows NT is a 32-bit operating system, and Windows 3.1 is a 16-bit operating system, you will obtain great performance benefits if you update your program. Windows NT runs almost all Windows 3.1 and 3.0 applications, but it must emulate Windows 3.1's 16-bit operating system by using software. This additional software layer between the program and the operating system may slow performance.

Windows NT should run all of the software for the operating systems with which it is compatible. Because Windows NT is a secure operating system, however, it does not allow any program to have direct access to the hardware. Some programs may seek direct access to the hardware, attempting to bypass the operating system to gain speed advantages. Programs that are created by using these techniques may not be fully compatible with Windows NT.

The rest of this chapter discusses running the other four types of non-Windows NT applications: OS/2 applications, POSIX applications, DOS applications, and TSRs. From the first, you have read that DOS, OS/2, and POSIX applications run under Windows NT. This is worth repeating: you need not do anything out of the ordinary to run such applications under Windows NT. In fact, most of the techniques described in this chapter pertain to both non-Windows NT and Windows NT applications. Only certain techniques (editing PIFs or loading TSRs, for example) are specific to DOS applications, and even these processes are for special cases.

For the purposes of this chapter, assume that your DOS, OS/2, and POSIX applications are already installed on your hard disk, but have not been set up to run under Windows NT. If you have never installed such an application, it is not particularly difficult, but it is time-consuming.

Almost every application comes with an installation guide that leads you through the installation process. One installation disk usually is labeled the *setup* or *install* disk; start with that disk. The setup program almost always is called SETUP.EXE or INSTALL.EXE (the file may have a BAT file extension). To install the application, type the name of the setup program, press Enter, and off you go. The program prompts you to answer a list of fairly easy questions; usually, the default responses to these questions work fine.

After the application is on your hard disk, you must set it up to run under Windows NT. Again, this is a straightforward process. You have two options: you can use the Windows NT Setup program, or you can let Program Manager set it up for you when you add it to a program group.

The following sections describe ways to set up your DOS, OS/2, and POSIX applications to run under Windows NT by using each of these two options.

Using Setup To Set Up an Application under Windows NT

When is it best to use Windows NT Setup rather than the Program Manager? Suppose you do not yet have Windows NT on your PC, but you already have a lot of DOS applications. When you install Windows NT for the first time, the Setup program searches your hard disk, finds all your applications, and sets up the applications you want—including setting up a PIF (program information file) for each DOS application. (PIFs are discussed later in the chapter.)

You also may prefer to use Setup rather than Program Manager if you have already installed Windows NT, and there are a number of applications that you did not set up when you initially installed Windows NT. Using Setup in this situation is faster than using Program Manager.

To set up applications by using the Windows NT Setup program, make sure that the Program Manager and the Main group are active. (The Windows NT Setup program is located in the Main group, unless you have moved it. If you moved the program to another group, make that group active.) After the Program Manager and the Main group are active, follow these steps:

1. Double-click on the Windows NT Setup icon.
2. Select the Options menu, and choose Set Up Applications. The dialog box shown in figure 10.1 appears.

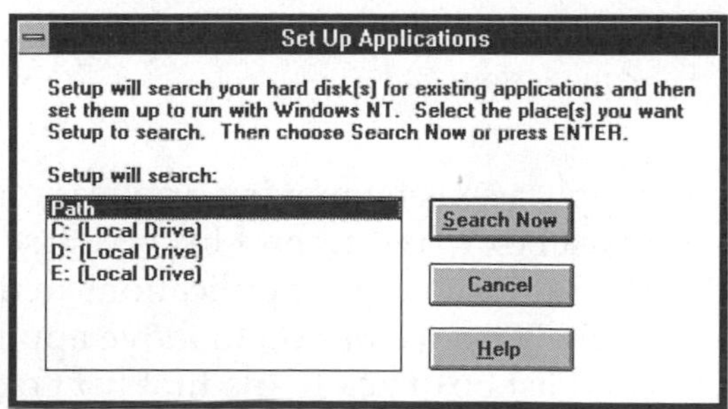

Figure 10.1: *The Set Up Applications dialog box.*

3. Select whether you want to search the Local Drive or the Path by choosing either a Drive or Path from the Setup will search list box. Click on the **S**earch Now button.

You can set a personal path variable by using the System icon in the Control Panel.

4. After the search is complete, another Set Up Applications dialog box appears, as shown in figure 10.2. The first list box in the dialog box shows the applications that Setup has found.

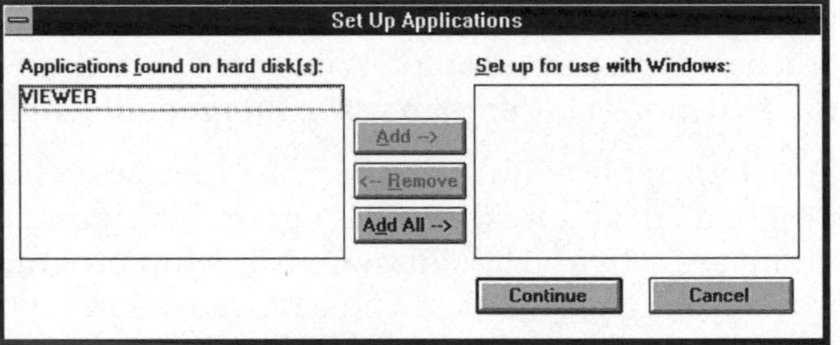

Figure 10.2: *The second Set Up Applications dialog box.*

If you closely watch the results of the search in the dialog box that appears before this one, you can cancel the search if you see that Windows NT Setup has already found the application you want to set up. To cancel, click on the Cancel button in the dialog box. You get the same results by canceling the search after it has found the application as by letting it continue to completion.

5. Set up applications by moving application names from the first list box to the second list box. Use the **Ad**d or A**d**d All buttons to move applications to the second list box; use the **R**emove button to move applications from the second list box back to the first list box.

6. Click on Continue when all applications you want to set up under Windows NT are listed in the second list box. The applications are added automatically to the Applications program group on your Windows NT desktop.

If you run Setup under DOS (or under earlier versions of Windows) and you are interrupted before completing the task, you ruin your system's configuration and have to start over. With Windows NT, you are not penalized for running Setup. Your program groups do not change unless you want them to, and your Windows NT installation is not ruined. After you correctly set up Windows NT once, you can cancel any application's setup operation before completion without the risk of destroying everything you set up.

Using Program Manager To Set Up an Application under Windows NT

Instead of using Setup, you can use Program Manager to install a DOS, OS/2, or POSIX application under Windows NT. Program Manager examines the selected application, and it determines the best way to run it. Because Program Manager does the work, there is not much to setting up applications with the Program Manager.

Program Manager can only make a guess at the proper running parameters (for instance, how much memory to allocate) for a DOS application—sometimes there is an error. The DOS program may run too slowly, or be unable to print or display graphics correctly. If this happens, you can create a PIF for the DOS application, which describes the DOS environment that Windows NT provides for the DOS application.

To use Program Manager to set up DOS, OS/2, and POSIX applications under Windows NT, follow these steps:

1. Activate Program Manager.
2. Choose New from the File menu. The New Program Object dialog box appears.

3. Select the Program Item option button, and click on OK. The Program Item Properties dialog box appears.
4. Fill out the edit fields, as described in the following list:
    - **Description.** The name you want to see under the icon.
    - **Command Line.** The complete path, including the executable file name and extension, plus any optional arguments (such as the file you want to open when the application starts up).
    - **Working Directory.** The name of the directory in which the application looks for data files.
    - **Shortcut Key.** The key combination you want to press to start the application. If you use the application frequently, it is much quicker to assign a shortcut key to the application than to click on its icon with the mouse.

    You can use the **Browse** button to make a selection from the Browse list box; the command-line parameters then appear in the correct field.
5. Click on OK when everything is the way you want it. The dialog box disappears.

Where did the new program item go? The new program item for the DOS application you just set up appears in the program group that last was active.

Setting Up Memory-Resident Programs under Windows NT

The last category of non-Windows NT applications is that of DOS *memory-resident programs (TSRs)*. These programs do not run like regular DOS applications, so they are categorized separately. Memory-resident programs expect a single-task environment; they also expect to address memory directly. Unlike most DOS applications, however, they expect to be loaded when the PC boots. These programs run only while other applications are running. When you close them, memory-resident programs are not unloaded from memory (thus, they are called *terminate-and-stay-resident programs*). TSRs are used for the following two functions:

- **Utilities.** TSRs function as *utilities*, such as device drivers, that run only when certain pieces of hardware are accessed. Two common examples of this type of TSR utility are network software (protocols) and mouse drivers.
- **Pop-ups.** TSRs function also as pop-ups, whose menus become visible only when a special key combination is issued. This type of TSR is used as communication programs or personal-information managers. When you access them, they momentarily suspend the operation of any other DOS application being used.

In one sense, the pop-up TSR was a multitasking pioneer. Before the wide availability of the graphical user interface, it was the best way to interrupt activities in one application to take care of other business.

TSRs often create unusual side effects when they run in an environment, such as Windows NT, that is already set up for multitasking. Because you may need to run an application that requires a utility TSR—for example, a mail program—you will learn how to set up a TSR shortly. Pop-up TSRs that emulate multitasking are of less value because their functions are probably duplicated in Windows NT.

Although Windows NT enables you to use your favorite TSR, you should avoid using TSRs, if possible.

Under Windows NT, you should not load TSRs from AUTOEXEC.BAT or CONFIG.SYS. Although Windows NT maintains two files with these names so that you can configure your DOS environment, you should include only the commands necessary to make the DOS environment functional for you, such as essential device drivers.

If you load additional programs in AUTOEXEC.BAT and CONFIG.SYS, Windows NT makes a copy of them to serve each DOS session you start. This reduces the total amount of memory available for running applications. Instead, start TSRs from a batch file that contains the commands for all the TSR programs you plan to use with the application you are starting. After placing all the TSR commands in the batch file, follow them with the command to start the application. Then save the batch file. You should make a PIF for this batch file, and install the PIF into Program Manager, as described earlier in this chapter. (See "Understanding Program Information Files for DOS Applications" later in this chapter for more information on PIFs.)

The TSR probably requires a special key combination to start it. If this combination is reserved by Windows NT (for example, Windows NT reserves Ctrl+Esc to open the task switcher), you must edit the TSR's PIF to enable the key combination to be used to start the TSR. After you edit the TSR's PIF, Windows NT can no longer use that reserved key combination. You cannot access a TSR from either the Windows NT desktop or a Windows NT application; you can access it only from a DOS application.

Use Program Manager to run a TSR by itself. Because Windows NT treats a pop-up TSR like any other DOS application, you can use Windows NT Setup or Program Manager to add the TSR's executable file to a program group. An icon representing the TSR is inserted in the active program group. (You also can use Program Manager to run the TSR's executable file directly, as described later in this chapter.)

Now you know the way to set up non-Windows NT applications. Most of the time, setup is totally automatic. In every case, Windows NT detects that you are setting up a DOS application and takes the appropriate steps.

By now, you probably have some sense of what a PIF is; the following section gives you a closer look, in case you ever have to change one.

Understanding Program Information Files for DOS Applications

Windows NT requires a *program information file (PIF)* to optimize the DOS environment for each DOS program you run. Many common DOS applications come with customized PIFs to optimize their performances under Windows NT. Under Windows NT, each DOS application inherits the DOS environment you define when you configure Windows NT. PIF parameters customize the DOS application's environment and issue a command to execute the DOS application itself. In that respect, PIFs are like DOS batch files.

The difference between batch files and PIFs is that you have to create the batch file to customize a DOS environment and run a program. On the other hand, Windows NT can install the DOS application's own PIF, create a custom PIF for you, or use the Windows NT default PIF, _DEFAULT.PIF.

If you are familiar with Windows 3.1, you know that you can run a DOS program without creating a PIF. If you do so in Windows NT, the DOS environment set up for the program will be based on default values that might not suit the program. Under Windows NT, it is best to create a PIF for each DOS application.

The following three ways enable you to install a PIF for a DOS application that you want to run under Windows NT:

- Let Windows NT Setup provide the PIF automatically when you install an application. This normally is done when you first install Windows NT, but it can be done any time you want to add a DOS application to a Windows NT program group.
- Create a custom PIF manually by using the PIF Editor.
- Use the default PIF, _DEFAULT.PIF, and use the PIF Editor to modify it to suit the DOS application.

Editing a PIF is not usually a daily occurrence. Once a PIF is established, there are few reasons to change it. Because you may encounter a situation where you want to edit one, however, a little how-to advice is in order. The following sections explain how to use the PIF Editor, how to edit both a standard and an imported PIF, how to provide multiple PIFs for the same application, and how to provide lists of the PIF options for standard and 386-Enhanced modes.

Windows NT uses only 386-Enhanced settings (and it does not use even all of those). The standard-mode options are included in the PIF editor, however, in case you need to create PIFs that are compatible with other versions of Windows. A system administrator, for instance, may need to create PIFs to run on the wide variety of machines attached to a network, some of which might be running Windows 3.1 in Standard mode because they contain an 80286 microprocessor.

Starting the PIF Editor

The PIF Editor looks like (and works like) all other Windows NT applications. You can find it in the Main program group. Start the PIF Editor in the usual manner—by double-clicking on its icon. Alternatively, run it from Program Manager by choosing **R**un from the **F**ile menu and supplying the following command-line parameters:

```
C:\WINNT\SYSTEM32\PIFEDIT.EXE
```

After you start the PIF Editor, the PIF Editor screen for 386-Enhanced mode appears because Windows NT runs DOS applications in this mode. Figure 10.3 shows the 386-Enhanced mode PIF Editor dialog box. (The PIF Editor dialog box for Standard mode is shown in figure 10.5, later in this chapter.) You learn about each of the dialog-box options later in this chapter.

Figure 10.3:

The PIF Editor dialog box for 386-Enhanced mode.

You can create PIFs for both standard and 386-Enhanced modes. The PIF Editor Mode menu contains the items Standard and Enhanced; the current operating mode is checked. You can edit a PIF for either mode, regardless of the fact that Windows NT is running in 386-Enhanced mode. If you select Standard mode, a warning appears—the PIF you are about to create has the wrong type of parameters for the current mode. You can, however, proceed with your PIF editing session.

Editing a Standard Windows PIF

Windows NT contains several DOS applications, and each has its own PIF. One of these applications is QBasic, which has its own PIF. This section uses this PIF to show the way in which to edit an existing program information file.

Suppose that you like to work with QBasic when you make the transition to Windows NT. If you work with such a DOS application often, perhaps to maintain simple programs that you use exclusively in your office, you can optimize this PIF for your purposes. You might, for instance, want to change QBasic's working directory to a directory that holds only your QBasic programs.

This section makes the assumption that you have set up QBasic in a Program Manager group.

First, determine which PIF is associated with QBASIC.EXE by restoring Program Manager and looking at the QBasic application's properties under the File menu.

Follow these instructions to look at the properties of a DOS application (in this case, the QBasic application):

1. Open the Main program group, and find the QBasic icon.
2. Highlight the title of the application.
3. Select Properties from the File menu. Notice the command-line argument QBASIC.PIF, which is the name of the PIF that Windows NT executes to run the DOS Prompt application. You can edit this PIF.
4. Click on Cancel to dismiss the Program Item Properties dialog box.

Now you are ready to edit the PIF file associated with the DOS application. Follow these instructions to edit the DOS Prompt PIF:

1. Start the PIF Editor.
2. Select Open from the File menu.
3. From the list box that contains several PIFs, select QBASIC.PIF. The dialog box shown in figure 10.4 appears.

Figure 10.4:
The PIF Editor dialog box, with the QBASIC.PIF file.

4. Enter a name in the Startup Directory text box.
5. Save the PIF by selecting File and then choosing Save.

Many DOS applications have their own PIFs that enable them to run under Windows NT. You can import an application's PIF and edit it with the PIF Editor. The PIF Editor can edit old PIFs.

Using Multiple PIFs for the Same Application

Suppose that you frequently multitask with a project-management application that runs under DOS. You want to minimize its use of resources under Windows NT most of the time you use it, but you have one special project data file that requires all available memory. Whenever you use this special project data file, you need at least 512K of memory. The PIF you use specifies only 256K of memory, which is usually enough, but not when using the large project data file. You can create a customized PIF specifically for your project.

Follow these instructions to create a second PIF for this DOS application:

1. Start the PIF Editor and open PROJ.PIF.
2. Under the File menu in the PIF Editor, use the Save As option instead of Save. This option enables you to assign a new name to the PIF you are editing. Name the special PIF **SPECPROJ.PIF**. You now can make editing changes to SPECPROJ.PIF, instead of to the original PIF.
3. For the Memory Requirements parameter, set both the KB Required and KB Desired options to **512**.
4. Add the file name of your special project to the Optional Parameters edit field so that the project file is opened automatically.

   Anything you enter in the Optional Parameters field is passed to the DOS project manager, as if you entered the text on the DOS command line. If you start the project management application by entering PROJECT SPECPROJ.DAT, for example, enter **specproj.dat** in the Optional Parameters field.
5. Change the Window Title field so that you can distinguish between the special project icon and the normal one. For example, enter **Special Project**.
6. Save the new PIF by selecting Save under the PIF Editor's File menu. Windows NT adds the new PIF in the Windows NT directory on the hard disk.

Now that the PIF for the special project has been created, use the Program Manager to add Special Project to a program group. Follow these steps to add a newly created PIF to a program group:

1. Make Program Manager the active application.
2. Open the program group in which you want to place the special project's icon.
3. Select File, and choose New.
4. Choose the Program Item option. The Program Item Properties dialog box appears.

5. Enter **Special Project** in the Description edit field.
6. Enter the path and name of the new PIF in the Command Line field (the name of the PIF is SPECPROJ.PIF).

A PIF usually is located in your default user directory. Unless you created the PIF in another directory, you don't have to specify a path in the Command Line field.

The preceding exercises introduced you to some typical PIF-editing sessions. The PIF Editor dialog box also has a number of other variables that you can manipulate. These variables change, depending on whether you are targeting the PIF for standard or 386-Enhanced mode.

Unless you do a lot of work with DOS applications, you may never have to modify a PIF beyond what you've done so far. If you use DOS applications under Windows NT frequently, however, you will appreciate the complete lists of PIF parameters provided in the following sections.

Examining PIF Options for Standard Mode

Figure 10.5 shows the PIF Editor dialog box for Windows NT Standard mode.

Table 10.1 presents the PIF options available in Standard mode, with a description of each option.

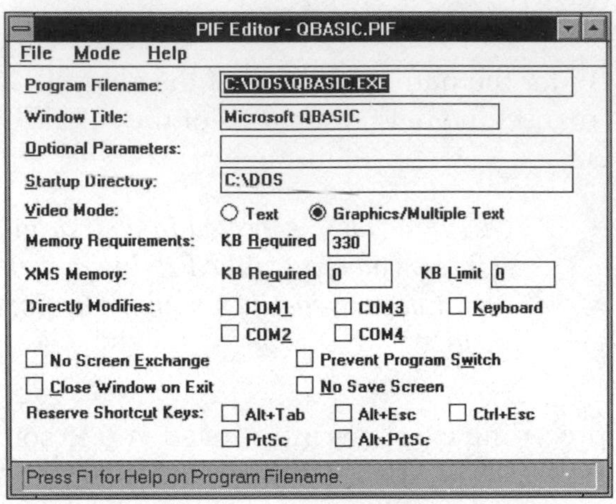

Figure 10.5: *The PIF Editor dialog box for Standard mode.*

Table 10.1
Basic PIF Options in Standard Mode

Option	*Description of Function*
Program File Name	The name and path of the file that starts the DOS application, including the file extension. An example is C:\WORD\WORD.EXE. You can specify an environmental variable by using the SET command and % parameters.
Window Title	Appears below the icon and in the title bar at the top of the window (if the application runs in a window instead of full-screen). It is optional—if you leave it blank, the application's name is used.
Optional Parameters	Accepts the same information you enter on the DOS command line to pass to the DOS application when it starts. This optional field has 62 characters, and typically is used to specify a file to be opened at start-up.

Option	*Description of Function*
Start-up	Becomes current on start-up; it is Directory where the application looks for data files.
Video Mode	Selects how much memory is needed to save and restore your DOS application's screen contents. The options are Text and Graphics/ Multiple Text. (The Text option uses less memory and should be checked if your DOS application normally runs in text mode.)
Memory Requirements	The number in the KB Required option specifies the minimum amount of conventional memory that must be available to start the DOS application (128K is recommended). If less than this amount is available, Windows NT displays a message recommending that you try to free some memory. Regardless of the amount of memory you specify here, Windows NT gives the DOS application as much memory as it has available.
XMS Memory	Allocates extended memory to a DOS application. The KB Required option specifies the minimum amount of XMS needed. The KB Limit option specifies the maximum amount of memory to be allocated—an important option if you are multitasking with DOS applications in a memory-limited environment. Refer to the manufacturer's specifications for the application's memory-usage requirements.

continues

Table 10.1
Continued

Option	*Description of Function*
Directly Modifies	Excludes other applications from accessing certain system resources while the DOS application is active, thus giving the DOS application exclusive use of the PC hardware while it is running.
No Screen Exchange	Saves memory in a memory-limited situation. It disables the capability to save screen contents with the Alt+PrtSc or PrtSc keys.
Prevent Program Switch	Saves memory in a memory-limited situation. It disables Windows NT's task-switching capability. This option requires you to exit the DOS application in order to switch back to Windows NT or a Windows NT application. Normally, you can use Alt+Esc to switch back to Windows NT or a Windows NT application that is running at the same time. Because this option makes operating inconvenient, do not use it unless you have severe memory limitations.
Close Window on Exit	Closes the application's window when it finishes. If left unchecked, Windows NT maintains an inactive window with the last screen full of information from the application. In this situation, you have to manually close the window.
No Save Screen	Frees more memory for the DOS application by disabling screen saving. There is some risk, however, of introducing unwanted side effects if the DOS application does not maintain its own screen contents.

Option	Description of Function
Reserve Shortcut Keys	Warns Windows NT that Windows NT cannot use the selected key combination during the operation of this DOS application. The selected key combinations are reserved for use with the DOS application for the duration of the DOS session.

Examining PIF Options for 386-Enhanced Mode

Unless you are supporting users on a network who need Standard-mode PIFs, you need to create PIFs for 386-Enhanced mode. In this mode, you have two types of PIF options: *basic options*, similar to the Standard-mode options listed in the preceding table, and *advanced options*.

From the PIF Editor dialog box for 386-Enhanced mode, click on the Advanced button; the Advance Options dialog box shown in figure 10.6 appears.

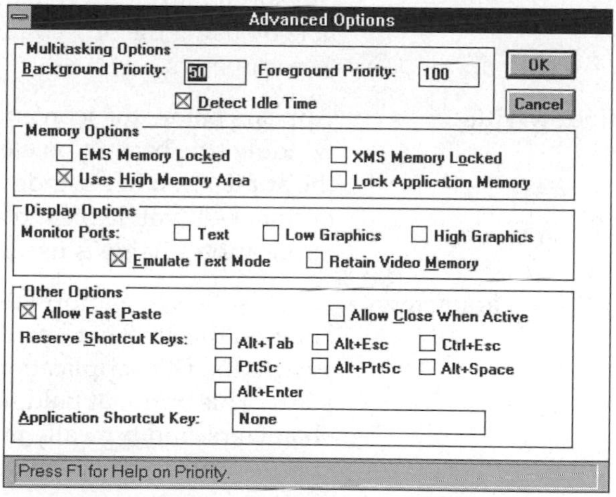

Figure 10.6:

PIF Editor Advanced Options dialog box for 386-Enhanced mode.

The Windows NT button next to the Advanced button opens a dialog box containing two text boxes that enable you to enter the name of the CONFIG.SYS and AUTOEXEC.BAT files to use with this program. You can use these options to specify custom configuration files to use with the program you are running. You should base these files on the AUTOEXEC.NT and CONFIG.NT files that Windows NT uses to establish the basic DOS environment for all DOS programs. To do so, edit these files and save them using a new name.

The advanced parameters affect special features, such as preemptive multitasking, use of the HMA, and virtual memory. Table 10.2 lists the basic 386-Enhanced PIF parameters; table 10.3 lists the advanced 386-Enhanced parameters.

Table 10.2
Basic PIF Options in 386-Enhanced Mode

Basic Option	*Description of Function*
Program File Name	The name and path of the file that starts the DOS application, including the file extension. An example is C:\WORD\WORD.EXE. You also can specify an environmental variable by using the SET command and % parameters.
Window Title	Appears below the icon and in the window title bar (if you elect to run the application in a window). It is optional—if you leave it blank, the application's name is used.
Optional Parameters	Accepts the same information you enter on the DOS command line to pass to the DOS application when it starts. This optional field has 62 characters, and typically is used to specify a file to be opened at start-up.

Basic Option	*Description of Function*
Start-up Directory	Becomes current on start-up; it is where the application looks for data files.
Video Memory	Selects the amount of memory needed to save and restore your DOS application's screen contents. The options are Text, Low Graphics, and High Graphics. The Text option uses the least memory (less than 16K). Low Graphics corresponds with CGA resolution and consumes about 32K; High Graphics is suitable for EGA and VGA, but it requires about 128K of memory.
Memory Requirements	The number in the KB Required option specifies the minimum amount of conventional memory that must be available to start the DOS application (128K is recommended). If less than this amount is available, Windows NT displays a message, recommending that you free some memory. KB Preferred enables you to set the limits for the amount of memory that the application can use (up to a maximum of 640K; specify less memory if you want other applications to have more memory available to them). Regardless of the amount of memory you specify here, Windows NT gives the DOS application the memory it has available.
EMS Memory	Emulates expanded memory for those DOS applications that require it (few do). Some older applications run better if they have access to EMS. You can set the KB Required and KB Limit values as specified in the preceding entry.

continues

Table 10.2
Continued

Basic Option	*Description of Function*
XMS Memory	Allocates extended memory to a DOS application. The KB Re**q**uired option specifies the minimum amount of memory needed (usually 0, because most applications do not require XMS to run). The KB L**i**mit option specifies the maximum amount of memory to be allocated. In limited-memory situations, prevent Windows NT from using XMS by setting both options to 0. Refer to the manufacturer's specifications for the application's memory-usage requirements.
Display Usage	Specifies whether you want the application to start the session in a full screen (F**u**ll Screen) or a window (**W**indowed).
Execution	**B**ackground specifies that execution of this application can take place concurrently while other applications maintain the foreground focus. **E**xclusive suspends the execution of all other DOS applications while this session has foreground focus.
Close Window on Exit	Leaves the window up after the DOS application terminates (useful if the DOS application displays output before terminating—the output remains so that you can read it).

Windows NT does not use the Close Window on Exit PIF option. If you need the DOS window to stay on-screen after a program exits, start the DOS window and run the program from the DOS command prompt in the DOS window.

Table 10.3
Advanced PIF Options in 386-Enhanced Mode

Advanced Option	*Description of Function*
Multitasking Options	
Background Priority	Determines what portion of the processor's attention this application receives when it operates in the background. Enter a value from 1 to 10,000; the value is compared to the values given to all other DOS applications' foreground and background processing values, and represents a proportion of the sum of all the values.
Foreground Priority	Determines what portion of the processor's attention this application receives when it operates in the foreground. Enter a value from 1 to 10,000.
Detect Idle Time	Gives up resources during idle time. Turn this option off for communications programs that need to remain active in order to detect activity on the communication line.
Memory Options	
EMS Memory Locked	Expanded memory is not swapped to the hard disk.

continues

Table 10.3
Continued

Advanced Option	*Description of Function*
XMS Memory Locked	Extended memory is not swapped to the hard disk.
Uses High Memory Area	Windows NT loads the application in HMA whenever HMA is available, freeing memory for other DOS applications. If the application cannot be loaded in HMA, you have no adverse effects.
Lock Application Memory	Disables memory swapping to the hard disk. Although this option may speed up some applications, it consumes memory and slows down the multitasking environment in memory-limited situations.
Display Options	
Monitor Ports	Experiment with this option if your display shows irregularities when you switch tasks to and from the session.
Emulate Text Mode	Speeds up the display of text; particularly useful with word processing applications.
Retain Video Memory	If your application switches display modes (from text to graphics, for example), select this option. It ensures that Windows NT holds enough memory in reserve to accommodate your application's video requirements as you switch between applications. Otherwise, Windows NT gives the application's allocated memory to the application

Advanced Option	Description of Function
	that needs it most. The memory given to another application may not be available when you return to graphics mode.
Other Options	
Allow Fast Paste	Disable this option if you paste from the Clipboard into the application and nothing happens.
Allow Close When Active	Choose this option if you want Windows NT to automatically close the application when you exit Windows NT. Normally, Windows NT does not close any active DOS application when you exit Windows NT. By selecting this option, you incur the potential for loss of data.
Reserve Shortcut Keys	This option warns Windows NT that, during the operation of this DOS application, Windows NT cannot use the selected key combination; the selected key combinations are reserved for use with the DOS application for the duration of the DOS session.
Application Shortcut Key	Enter the key combination that causes this application to become the active application when pressed.

Windows NT does not actually use many of the PIF settings available in the PIF Editor. Check the Help file, included with the PIF Editor, for the latest information about which settings Windows NT uses. All these settings are included for compatibility with other versions of Windows.

Operating DOS, OS/2, and POSIX Applications

The following sections describe how to start, switch, and cut-and-paste among DOS, OS/2, and POSIX applications running under Windows NT. Some of the details described may seem complicated, but they are things you need to know to begin a deeper exploration of Windows NT. Remember that the normal operation of non-Windows applications under Windows NT is not complicated; with minor exceptions, these applications intermingle seamlessly with Windows NT applications and with other non-Windows applications.

Starting DOS, OS/2, and POSIX Applications

After you set up non-Windows applications under Windows NT, you start them like any other Windows NT application—by double-clicking on the icons. The following list describes the options for running DOS, OS/2, and POSIX applications under Windows NT:

- Double-clicking on the icon to run the application as it was set up automatically by the Windows NT Setup program. For DOS applications, this method runs the PIF that was created by Windows NT when you set up the application.
- Selecting **R**un from the Program Manager's **F**ile menu. Generally, this is the method you use to run the application's EXE file directly, but you can call the PIF for DOS applications from the Program Manager in this way, too.
- Double-clicking on the application's EXE file name from the File Manager. You also can execute a PIF in this way.
- Starting the Command Prompt application and running the application from the command line.

- Running the application automatically when Windows NT starts up. You can do this by moving the application's icon into the StartUp program group.

Windows NT has two other important features that involve loading a data file when you start a non-Windows application. In command-line interfaces, you can call an application and pass the application a data file name by including the file name on the command line (for instance, PROJECT SPECPROJ.DAT). This loads the data file as you start the application. Windows NT enables you to do this in the following ways:

- Create a program item for the data file by using the File and New commands in Program Manager. Program Manager then presents you with the Program Item Properties dialog box, in which you enter the name of the data file's executable (EXE) parent in the Command Line input field, as well as the name of the data file. This method creates an icon in the active program group that represents the data file (discussed in more detail later).

- Open File Manager, and locate the data file. Click on the data file's entry in File Manager, drag the data file over its parent EXE or PIF file, and drop it.

- If you have associated the data file's extension with the application by using File Manager's File Associate command, you can double-click on the data file name in File Manager. File Manager automatically starts the appropriate application, and loads the data file (this procedure also works for Windows NT applications and data files).

It was suggested previously that you can use Program Manager to create an icon for the data file. Consider the following example. Suppose you have a text file called PHONE.TXT, and you add it to Program Manager as a new program item (by using the File and New commands). The new program item's icon is the Notepad icon with PHONE.TXT as the icon label. (The procedure for creating program items with the Program Item Properties dialog box is outlined earlier in this chapter.) You can change the icon, but leaving it as the Notepad icon is a reminder of the data file's parent application.

The new program item is executable—you can double-click on its icon to start Notepad and load PHONE.TXT. By making data files into program items that you can start with a double-click, you really access the power of Windows NT's graphical user interface!

You also can use this program-item approach for organizing data files with their parent applications for grouping project data. First, create a program group for the project, and then add the project's data files as program items.

Switching among DOS, OS/2, and POSIX Applications

Being able to run more than one DOS, OS/2, or POSIX application concurrently brings a new dimension of productivity to Windows NT. You probably are familiar with formatting a floppy disk while running another application. It is just as simple to use a communications program that sends and receives data over a modem, or a terminal-emulation program with an active session to a mainframe or UNIX server. Running two non-Windows applications concurrently is as easy as clicking four times. As always, however, there are some finer points to discuss.

Start your applications, as described in the preceding section. You can start as many applications as you have available memory. Once you start a DOS, OS/2, or POSIX session, it becomes the active one until you switch from it. Windows NT provides the following options to switch among non-Windows applications:

- If the active application is running in a windowed session, click on another window or icon to change the focus. If your DOS, OS/2, or POSIX session is in a full screen, make the session windowed by pressing Alt+Enter.
- Press Alt+Tab to switch to the most recently active application, regardless of whether it is a Windows NT

application or a non-Windows application. Hold the Alt key and press the Tab key multiple times to cycle through your running applications.

- Start the Task List, and select the task you want to switch to from the list box.
- Minimize all running applications into icons, and select the one you want from these icons. Although this is not the best way to switch tasks, it works, and it can come in handy.
- Use a shortcut-key combination to start another application. Remember that you can specify shortcut keys in the Program Item Properties dialog box.

Because it is so easy to run DOS, OS/2, and POSIX applications, you may start several that you are planning to use sometime during your day when you start your computer. Besides cluttering up your display, they all cut into system resources, which can be a serious problem. (System resources include devices as well as memory.)

Do not start applications of any type that you do not use right away. Although Windows NT is a multitasking environment, and you are encouraged to run more than one application, the more applications, the less memory and resources available to a single application.

Adjusting Run-Time Characteristics by Using the Control Menu

Several characteristics of the way in which a DOS, OS/2, or POSIX application runs can be controlled from the Control menu. For example, start a windowed DOS session, select the Control menu's Settings option, and examine the parameters as they are reviewed in the following list. The changes you make from the Control menu are in effect only during the application's session; they do not change the settings in the DOS application's PIF. The parameters are as follows:

- **Display Options.** This parameter controls whether the DOS session runs in a window on the Windows NT desktop or in full-screen DOS mode.
- **QuickEdit Mode.** Enables you to select and edit information displayed in a DOS window using the mouse.
- **Save Configuration.** Causes the configuration information for the DOS session to be saved on exit.

In addition to these PIF Editor parameters, the Control Settings menu offers a Terminate option. This option terminates the DOS session that has crashed (does not respond to commands typed from the command prompt), and enables you to abandon an unresponsive session and return to Windows NT.

Use the Terminate option only as a last resort. It causes the loss of unsaved information.

Each of these options works for OS/2 and POSIX sessions as well. The DOS session was used as an example.

A difference between Windows NT and Windows 3.1 is that Windows NT can survive a Terminate operation much more successfully. Although it is unlikely that you will destabilize the operating system by using Terminate under Windows NT, do not use it frequently.

Freeing Up System Memory

Do you see an `Out of Memory` error message when you run DOS applications? Everybody can use more memory, and, as you learned earlier in this chapter, memory is one of the cheaper PC hardware resources these days. If your DOS applications operate slowly on your PC, try to get more memory for your system.

As the number of applications that open under Windows NT grows, you may get an `Out of Memory` error message when you try to start another application, regardless of the number of memory chips you have. When this happens, close any applications—Windows NT or DOS—that you are not using. If you still continue to see the message, try the following maneuvers:

- Minimize any Windows NT applications that you are not directly working with but need to keep running.
- Cancel any background processing that is not needed (for instance, a background print job).
- If your DOS, OS/2, or POSIX application is running in a window, try running it full-screen.
- Clear the Clipboard.
- Set the Desktop's Wallpaper option to None (some wallpaper bit-map images are large files and require CPU cycles to display properly).

A number of memory-management techniques have been presented for DOS, OS/2, and POSIX applications, but hardly anything has been said about memory management for Windows NT applications. Windows NT applications are very cooperative about their use of memory. They ask for it when they need it, use it, and give it back when they are done; the memory management is handled by Windows NT. Non-Windows applications, on the other hand, do not expect to run with any other applications, so they require a certain amount of memory when they start up, and they keep it while they are running.

Pasting Data among Non-Windows Applications

DOS, OS/2, and POSIX applications operate slightly differently than Windows NT applications in their use of the Clipboard. There are several methods for moving data from the application to the Clipboard, depending on the mode in which the application is running. These methods, illustrated in the remainder of this section, work for DOS, OS/2, and POSIX applications. (For purposes of illustration, these examples use a DOS application.)

If the DOS application is running in a full screen, you can move the entire screen contents only to the Clipboard—the normal Windows NT cut/copy/paste editing tools are not available. For a DOS application running in a window, you have the following options for moving information to the Clipboard:

- Move selected material only
- Move the contents of the DOS-session window
- Move the entire desktop

The following example shows ways to exchange data from a full-screen DOS session to the Clipboard. If you do not have a standard DOS application, such as Word or Lotus 1-2-3, on your computer, don't worry. The following example works from the DOS command prompt:

1. Start a DOS command-prompt session, and make sure that it occupies a full screen.
2. Issue the DOS directory command by typing **DIR** and pressing Enter. The directory list for the current directory appears. Remember that, in a full-screen DOS session, your only option is to copy the entire contents of the screen to the Clipboard.
3. Copy the contents of the screen to the Clipboard. To do this, press PrScr. Your display may flicker for a moment.
4. Switch back to Windows NT and view the Clipboard (select ClipBook in the Main program group and

examine the Local Clipboard document window). You should be satisfied that PrScr really does copy the full screen to the Clipboard.

In the next exercise, you exchange data from a windowed DOS session to the Clipboard. If you viewed the contents of the Clipboard in the preceding exercise, your session is probably running in a window at this point. If it is not, press Alt+Tab to switch to the full-screen DOS application, and then switch it into window mode by pressing Alt+Enter.

1. Select Edit from the session's Control menu. Use the mouse or press Alt+space bar to open the Control menu.
2. Select Mark. Notice that the cursor appears in the upper left corner of the window. Find the text you want to select by moving the cursor with the mouse or the arrow keys.
3. Select the text by holding Shift and moving the arrow keys, or by holding the left mouse button and dragging. If you are used to the way a word processor marks text with the arrow keys—in consecutive characters, words, or lines—the behavior of the Control menu's marking mechanism may be a little foreign. Text is marked in rectangular columns, with no regard for verbal content. You mark a block of characters from a matrix of characters.
4. Complete the copy operation by pressing Enter or by choosing Copy from the Edit menu.

The other two ways to copy text from a windowed DOS session are as straightforward as full-screen mode. To copy the entire contents of the windowed DOS session, press Alt+PrScr. To copy the entire desktop, press PrScr.

After you have some data cut to the Clipboard, you paste it into a DOS session by selecting Paste from the Edit menu. This command works a little differently, depending on whether the target session is windowed or full-screen.

To copy from the Clipboard into a windowed DOS session, make sure that you have something in the Clipboard, and that your DOS session is in a window. If you still have the

DOS Prompt session in a window on the screen, move the cursor to a point in that session where you want the text in the Clipboard to be inserted. Select Paste from the Control Edit menu. The new text appears, beginning at the cursor. You cannot cut and paste formatted text among DOS applications; the formatting is lost when you move it into a DOS session.

To copy from the Clipboard into a full-screen DOS session, make sure that what you want to paste is already in the Clipboard. The Clipboard is harder to view when an active full-screen DOS session is in progress. Switch the DOS Prompt session into a full screen, and place the cursor where you want the insertion to go. Now, minimize the full-screen session by pressing Alt+Esc. Click once to open the Control Edit menu, and choose Paste. Double-click on the session's icon to restore it. The text is inserted at the point at which the cursor was located before the paste.

Summary

The complexity of computers always expands to meet your ability to understand them. Working with DOS, OS/2, and POSIX applications under Windows NT is no exception. As far as running these applications under Windows NT is concerned, the 20 percent that does the 80 percent is transparent to the Windows NT user. It is no more difficult to set up, start, or switch tasks with one of these applications than it is to do the same things with a Windows NT application.

As you conclude this chapter, take a moment to reflect on what you have learned about Windows NT so far. If you have been following the examples, you should be getting used to the logic as well as the rhythm and pace of the graphical user interface. By now, you've used the basic application templates: the File and Edit menus, the list boxes, and the dialog boxes that focus your attention and make it easy to do complicated tasks. In the next few chapters, you increase your knowledge of Windows NT applications greatly.

Exchanging Data between Windows Applications

There are many ways in which the Windows NT environment makes it easier and faster to do common (and uncommon) tasks. The most important of these are integration and interoperability. Windows NT's *Dynamic Data Exchange (DDE)* is a powerful tool that enables the user to dynamically exchange information between applications.

Object Linking and Embedding (OLE), *another feature of Windows NT, enables the user to create compound documents that contain information (objects) from a number of sources and seamlessly integrate the information into a single document. By using OLE, the compound document can contain objects from any source, including nontraditional document sources.*

By using DDE, graphs that are produced in a Windows NT application can be truly data-driven; when the data changes at the source, the graphic changes at the destination. Documents can be kept up-to-date automatically, thus reducing errors and downtime for maintenance. The best feature of DDE is its inherent ease of use; most DDE links are no more complicated to create than is pasting data from the Clipboard.

This chapter covers the following topics:

- Cutting-and-pasting
- Linking and embedding
- Understanding end-user DDE
- Understanding programmable DDE

Examining Traditional Cutting-and-Pasting

Under Windows NT, the user no longer has a "glass cage" (a web of proprietary data formats) around each individual application, as she did under character-based operating systems. In a character-based system, each program maintains its data in a proprietary format. Given the proper conversion program, the information from one program can be translated into a format that can be used by another program. Alternatively, because most programs can read and write ASCII files, users can convert one application's information to plain text and import it into another application. When this is done, however, all original formatting is lost.

With most character-based applications, inserting graphics into a document is, at best, a cumbersome and time-consuming enterprise. The graphic is often represented by a reference to the image file and can be seen pictorially (if it can be seen pictorially at all) only in a preview mode.

Even under the most favorable circumstances, transferring data from one application to another is a chore. Although your character-mode application might enhance the operating system by compensating for these difficulties, each of your applications must use the same conventions for extending the operating system; otherwise, they cannot communicate or share data. With rare exceptions, you cannot maintain an open channel of communication through which data can regularly pass from one program to another.

To prepare a document that requires information developed in several different programs—for example, a proposal that calls for narrative text written in a word processor, financial data created in a spreadsheet, and illustrations from a drawing or paint program—you must get a hard copy of each of the elements and then sit down with scissors and a paste pot to create a composite. You then photocopy or print the composite by using offset techniques.

Some character-mode programs incorporate the scissors-and-paste-pot metaphor into their feature set. Earlier programs had a text *buffer* that enabled the transfer of text from one application to another. Other programs use the metaphor of the *clipboard*.

Whatever name is used for that holding area, users can mark a piece of text for copying or cutting to the buffer or clipboard, perform the copy or cut, and then paste that text back into the document at another place. The text buffer (or clipboard) serves much like a temporary scratch pad to hold text data during a transfer operation.

This clipboard is merely used to move text from one part of the same document to another, however; when the document is closed, whatever data is on the clipboard or in the buffer is lost. You cannot carry over the data from one program to another.

WordPerfect for DOS, by using its Library and Office DOS shell applications, moves the user a bit further in a more advanced direction. The shell's Clipboard holds

continues

the cut or copied information, enabling the user to paste it into another program's document—but only if that program has a cut-and-paste feature that the WordPerfect shell recognizes.

Impatience with the impenetrable glass cages that surround individual applications has grown, thus creating innovation. Software developers came up with the idea of the *integrated program*, which gives the user a word processor, database, spreadsheet, and communications module in one package. Each module can function independently, but the true strength of integrated applications lies in the capability of the application modules to work together and exchange information. An integrated program gives a consistent interface across several modules in the package. Data created in one module in the integrated program usually can be used in another module.

Lotus Symphony, Alpha Works (now Lotus Works), Enable, and Microsoft Works are integrated programs of this kind.

For the most part, however, these integrated programs also are enclosed by a glass cage. To use the data in any program outside of the integrated modules (except perhaps in other programs from the same vendor), you will be subject to the same constraints imposed by traditional stand-alone programs.

With the advent of Windows 3.0 (and especially with Windows 3.1 and Windows NT), problems with proprietary data formats are ending. As you learn in this chapter, applications under Windows NT can be integrated tightly. Perhaps even more significant, applications can be *interoperable*: they are capable of exchanging information and running simultaneously in the same computer. You benefit from access to multiple applications that are available with one keystroke—each application exchanges data with the others.

The day is approaching when computing no longer will be *program-centric*. Traditional character-based applications are characterized by the many arcane keystroke commands that are required to perform various functions. Many word processors, for instance, require a complex series of keystrokes to mark a block of text and to change the blocked text's typeface to bold. There is no way to represent all the commands and command sequences on the screen; the user requires help from keyboard templates, users' guides, and other printed materials.

The model that integration and interoperability give is *document-centric*, in which the document is the center of attention and the applications that create the documents are only tools. Document-centric applications are inherently more intuitive and require less time to learn, leaving more time for using the application.

In Windows NT, a document can be a text document, a spreadsheet, a database, a drawing or picture, or the output from different Windows NT applications.

Even within the Windows NT environment, degrees of integration and interoperability exist. You can achieve the most seamless flow of information at the highest end by using stand-alone programs such as Microsoft Word, Lotus Ami Pro, Microsoft Excel, and Polaris PackRat. These programs have or support Windows macro languages and incorporate OLE and DDE.

An integrated program, such as Microsoft Works for Windows, gives you flexibility to share data among its modules and with other programs that are running under Windows NT. Integrated programs also offer a convenient way to gain access to tools when disk space is at a premium, as it can be on a laptop or small computer.

At the lower end, the desktop accessories that come with Windows NT—Write, Schedule+, and Cardfile—enable you to perform limited data sharing. To take advantage of integration and interoperability in the Windows NT environment, however, you need more robust tools.

Examining Linking and Embedding

For the DOS or UNIX user who is just getting started with Windows NT, the appeal of the graphical environment lies in its attractiveness as a shell and in its capability to multitask DOS and POSIX applications. Windows NT, however, offers much more than task switching and cutting-and-pasting among DOS and POSIX applications and among DOS, POSIX, and Windows NT applications.

You cannot fully realize the enormous power of Windows NT until your core applications are Windows-specific applications, especially those that support the Windows functions known as linking and embedding.

Linking and embedding *is an umbrella term for the methods that enable users to share functionality and integrate data across diverse applications.*

The technical specifications for both DDE and OLE protocols are still evolving, and so is the jargon. Early on, the industry used DDE and OLE as separate terms.

Both DDE and OLE enable you to share data among Windows NT applications. They are extensions of the data sharing discussed in the sections on the Clipboard.

This chapter and the next help you become familiar with the differences and similarities between static data exchange with the Clipboard and dynamic exchange of data using DDE and OLE. These chapters also show you ways to take advantage of these Windows NT features.

Windows NT offers two different ways to implement Dynamic Data Exchange. The first, *interactive DDE,* uses the regular interface of the application you use to manually create a link. The commands you need to create links between one application and another are accessible directly from the applications' menus.

The second method, *scripted DDE,* requires writing code in the application's macro language to establish a link. Each method is discussed in this chapter.

A macro *is a set of instructions that can be invoked with a single keystroke. Macros are used to automate a series of frequently performed repetitive tasks.*

A macro may be nothing more than a collection of simple commands, such as applying a particular style to a paragraph in a document; or it may provide an entirely new function in the application, such as retrieving data from a database and inserting it into a spreadsheet.

A macro also can be a "program" to perform a specific task, such as a link with an application to retrieve data.

DDE enables you to share information and also to send commands from one application to another to control the behavior of the receiving application.

OLE currently is available only through the Clipboard's copy-and-paste metaphor. Everything you require to accomplish an OLE task is part of the application's standard menu interface. The commands are on the menus; you do not need to do any macro programming.

Dynamic Data Exchange (DDE)

Dynamic Data Exchange is an internal communications protocol that Windows NT uses to enable one application to talk to or exchange data with another application. Although DDE normally is used to transfer information between applications, it also can be used within an application. DDE is a powerful tool for the user who needs to exchange information between applications.

DDE creates a communication channel through which data is sent from one application to another. This channel is known as a *link*. DDE links normally are live; when there are changes in data within the originating application, the other application is updated through the link—automatically or on demand, depending on whether you have created an automatic or a manual link.

Links can be established in several different ways. Later in this chapter, you are shown various methods for linking applications.

As you work in an application, you may need to gather data from another source; you can include a table of spreadsheet data in your word processing document, for example. To do this, you can use a DDE link to the other application. Typically, you choose a DDE link between applications when one or more of the following situations occurs:

- You want to access data that resides in another application on your system.
- You want to have access to the information in its native, stand-alone application.
- You want to share the information in more than one instance within a document or use it as an element in more than one document.
- You want DDE to take over a server application by remote control to perform a task.

Suppose, for example, that you regularly prepare a summary sales report that you send, at specific intervals, to managers in your company—once a week to sales managers, twice a month to department heads, and once a month to the chief financial officer. These reports are based on sales figures you track and total every day in Microsoft Excel. You can create a boilerplate report in Microsoft Word and include in it a link to the range of your Excel worksheet that shows the running sales total.

As you update the figures in Excel every day, the updated total automatically is piped to the report document through the DDE link. Every time you open the Word document to print it out and send it to the managers, it reflects the latest data from your Excel worksheet.

Object Linking and Embedding (OLE)

Object Linking and Embedding does not create a simple link, as does DDE. A DDE link always is connected to the source document; the information never really is contained in the destination document. OLE, on the other hand, embeds information that you generate in another application into your current document, and that data becomes a part of the current document. The current document "owns" the embedded data, which then cannot be shared directly with other documents or applications.

OLE objects can be linked or embedded, depending on the capabilities of the OLE server.

The real power of OLE is that it not only embeds the data in your document, but it also identifies to Windows NT the application in which the data was created. When you want to edit the embedded information (see *object* in table 11.1), you double-click on it; the source application, with all its tools and attributes, appears on top of the current document. When you exit from the source application, you are returned to the current document, and the embedded object is updated to reflect your changes.

In OLE 2.0, the source application will substitute its menu for the menu of the container application. A second window does not open.

Updating an OLE object does not occur automatically. Because the data is contained within the destination document, you must explicitly send updated data from the source document after you have made changes to it.

DDE and OLE Terminology

Table 11.1 defines some standard DDE and OLE terms that are used throughout this chapter and the next, as well as related terms that you may encounter in other discussions.

By using the terminology in table 11.1, *linking* (DDE) refers to creating data in one application (the source application), such as a spreadsheet, and linking it to the destination document created in another application, such as a word processor. When you change or update the information in the source document, the change is reflected at the same time in the destination document. The item is stored in the source document, and can be linked to several different destination documents.

Table 11.1
Standard DDE and OLE Terms

Term	*Related terms*	*Meaning*
Object	Data, information	Any piece of data that can be manipulated as a single unit, such as a picture, chart, spreadsheet range, or section of text.

Term	*Related terms*	*Meaning*
Source	Server application	The application in which a application linked or embedded object is created, such as Microsoft Excel or WordPerfect for Windows. Also, the application that sends data requested by another application via DDE.
Source document		The document, in the source application, in which the data (object) was created. Also, the sending end of a data transfer through a DDE link.
Destination application	Client application	The application whose document will receive an object. Also, the application that requests data from another application by DDE.
Destination document	Target, client, or host document	A document that contains embedded or linked data (see also *Container document*). Also, the receiving end of a data transfer through a DDE link.
Compound document		A single document made up of parts created in more than one application.
Container document	Target, client, or host document	A document that contains either embedded or linked data (objects). (See also *Destination document*.)
Automatic link	Hot link	A link that automatically updates the destination document when the source document is changed.

continues

Table 11.1
Continued

Term	*Related terms*	*Meaning*
Manual link	Warm link	A link that requires user intervention to update the destination document when the source document is changed.
Cold link		Data that is transferred once (by a straight cut or copy and paste, or by a one-time DDE request) and cannot be updated dynamically. The term *cold link* is a misnomer—the described function is not really a link at all.

By using the terms in table 11.1, you can further define *embedding* (OLE) as creating an object in the source application, which you then can access directly from the container document. The object created is said to be embedded in the container document. When the object requires editing, Windows NT immediately returns you to the source application, in which you make the necessary changes. (You do not have to open or switch to the source application; Windows NT takes care of that for you.) Windows NT then updates the container document to reflect those changes, and the object is stored in the container document.

Applications that Support DDE

Almost 2000 Windows applications are on the market, but not all of them support DDE (some do not need to support it). A screen saver or font manager, for example, does not need DDE capability.

An application can support DDE as a client, server, or both. DDE support can be found in the high-end word processors, spreadsheet programs, database applications, fax-generating applications, desktop publishing programs, communications programs, and electronic mail packages. Consult an application's documentation or on-line help to determine if it supports DDE.

You should consider updating your DOS or POSIX applications to Windows NT applications. Updating enables you to take greater advantage of multitasking in the Windows NT environment, as well as DDE and OLE. (This option will be especially attractive when OLE 2.0 arrives on the scene.) The time you save sharing data and switching between applications is worth the upgrade cost.

To find out if the Windows NT application you are using (such as Word, Excel, PageMaker, or Works) has interactive DDE capabilities, pull down the menus and look for commands such as Paste **L**ink or Paste **S**pecial. Usually, these commands are on the **F**ile or **E**dit menus (see fig. 11.1).

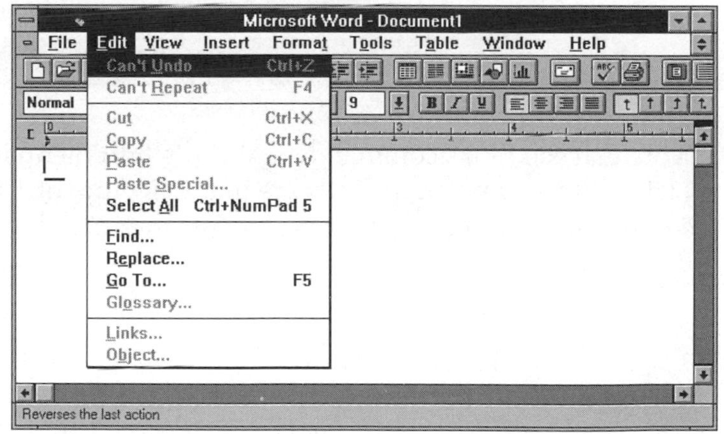

Figure 11.1:
*The Paste **S**pecial command in Word's **E**dit menu.*

The Paste Special command in Microsoft Excel and the spreadsheet module of Works do not refer to DDE. The Paste Link command does. When you select the Paste Special command in Word and the word processing module of Works, you are offered the further option of Paste Link when appropriate.

In addition, a command called **Links** might appear on the menu, as shown in figure 11.2. This command enables you to edit or update the links. If you see these commands, you can be sure your application supports at least one form of DDE.

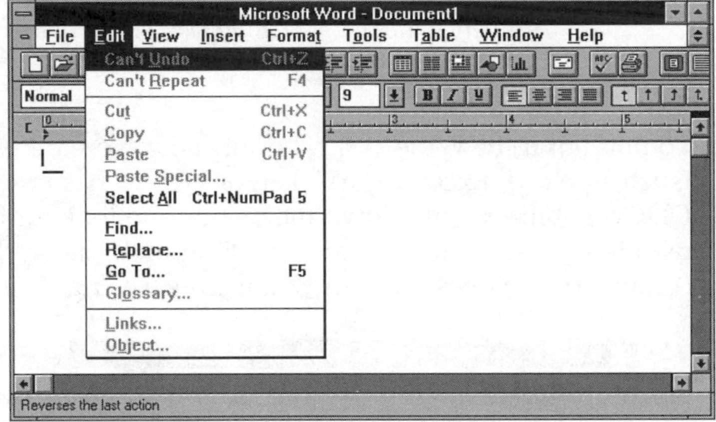

Figure 11.2:
*Word's **E**dit menu, showing the **L**inks command.*

Note that the **Links** command on Word's **Edit** menu in figure 11.1 is dimmed when no links are in the document. The **Links** command also might appear on the **File** menu, as it does in PageMaker.

Do not be intimidated by the prospect of setting up a DDE function. After you know how to use the Clipboard—in other words, after you can cut, copy, and paste—you have what you need to create DDE links.

A second application of DDE is through the use of macros. You must consult the application's documentation to see if your application supports DDE macros, which are available only in applications that have (or understand) a macro language.

You can, for example, create a macro in Word's macro language (sometimes called WordBasic) that requests data from or passes data to Polaris PackRat. Even though PackRat itself does not have a macro language, it understands the DDE commands that it receives by macros from Word, Excel, Ami Pro, and other applications.

Although this chapter includes discussions and examples of DDE macros, a full discussion of programmable DDE is beyond the scope of this book. Each application that supports programmable DDE has its own variations of syntax, and you must turn to the vendors of the respective applications for documentation on their specific DDE code.

Refer to Ultimate Windows 3.1, *available from New Riders Publishing, for application-specific DDE information.*

Applications That Support OLE

OLE is a newer technology than DDE, and fewer applications support it. Because of its power and ease of use, however, it has been an instant hit with end users. Full support for OLE is an intrinsic part of Windows NT, making OLE a standard that developers are likely to support. Many high-end applications include OLE 1.0 support now, with OLE 2.0 support coming in their next releases.

In most applications, the menu options Paste Link and Paste Special are found under Edit. Some applications, however, do not follow this convention. In Microsoft PowerPoint, for instance, the Insert command is under the File menu. When you choose it, you see a

continues

list of all types of objects available on your system that can be embedded. If you are learning a new application and you want to use DDE or OLE, look first under Edit for Paste Link or Paste Special, then check under File or Insert for other options that indicate link operations.

You can recognize OLE-compliant applications by looking for another set of commands on the menus. These commands, usually found on the Insert or Edit menu, refer to inserting objects, as shown in figure 11.3.

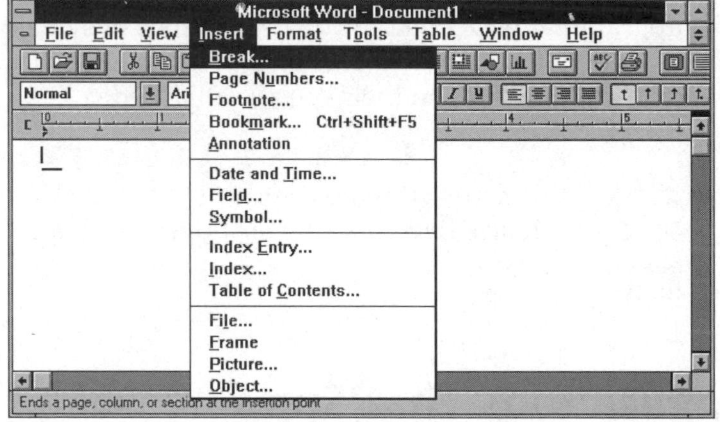

Figure 11.3:
The Object command on the Insert menu in Word.

Microsoft now is shipping several applications that are designed specifically to create or edit embedded objects. These so-called embedding applications *include the Equation Editor, which creates the notation of scientific and mathematical formulas; MS Draw, for pictures created in or convertible to the Windows NT Metafile Format (WMF); MS Graph, which produces sophisticated graphs from tabular figures without requiring a separate spreadsheet program; Note-It, which inserts pop-up notes anywhere in your document; and WordArt, which enables you to create special text effects for formats, such as logos and headlines.*

Some of these embedding applications are bundled with Windows NT, including those applications that comprise the Multimedia Extensions. Others are bundled with individual Microsoft applications. No single application comes with all of them. After you install an embedding application on your system, however, its parameters are written into the appropriate section of the Registry database (see fig. 11.4). This enables any application that supports OLE to recognize and use the embedding application.

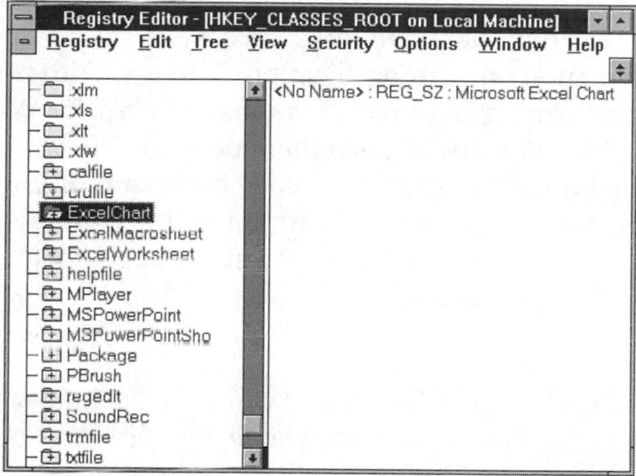

Figure 11.4:
Listing the objects that are available for embedding.

You can embed worksheet ranges and charts created in Excel; entire documents created in Word; other word processors, such as Ami Pro for Windows NT; and bit maps created in Paintbrush.

Cardfile and Write, two of the desktop accessories that come with Windows NT, both support OLE. By choosing the Object command, you can see a list of the objects available. (In Cardfile, you must choose Picture on the Edit menu to have this option.) In figure 11.5, for example, text that was created in PowerPoint is embedded in a Cardfile card.

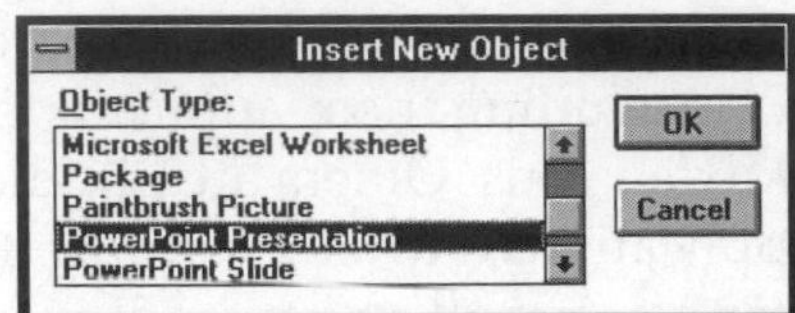

Figure 11.5:
The Insert New Object dialog box.

Understanding Interactive Dynamic Data Exchange

You learned that DDE links are easy to set up by using commands on your applications' menus, with no macro programming required. If you have Word for Windows and Excel for Windows, open them now so you can work through the following examples on your computer. If you do not have these programs, you still can follow the examples to learn ways to use DDE links and what to expect from other applications that support DDE links.

A hot link *automatically updates the receiving document when the data in the source changes.*

A warm link *notifies the user that a change has been made, but the user must specifically make a request to the server to update the data.*

When a DDE link is created in a document, it needs to know the following things about the source to which it is going to be linked:

- The name of the source application
- The name of the source document (file name)

A document can be a text document, a graphic, a portion of a graphic, or a spreadsheet range.

- Specific reference to the data to be linked, such as a spreadsheet range or text in a word processor

You do not need to name the range in Excel. If you have several links in one document and want to examine or edit them, however, it is easier to know which one is which if the links refer to named ranges rather than to row-and-column designations.

The following example shows you the way to link a named range in Excel to a document in Word.

First, create a range in Excel, name it, and save the Excel worksheet. In the following steps, you can substitute other names and numbers for the names and numbers provided. Remember, however, that a DDE link must include the name of the source document. If you do not name and save the worksheet now, later you will need to edit the links to show the worksheet's name. Of course, you are required to assign the spreadsheet a name the first time you save it.

1. Create a six-cell matrix in Excel. In cells from A1 to C1, label the columns **First**, **Second**, and **Third**. In the row beneath the labels, in cells A2 to C2, enter the numbers **1000**, **1500**, and **1750**.

2. Highlight the range, and define its name as **Range1**. Define the range name by choosing the Define Name option under the Formula menu.

3. Save the worksheet as **EXAMPLE1.XLS**. Until you save the worksheet, it has no name.

4. Highlight the range, select the Excel Edit menu, and choose Copy.

5. Open a new document in Word. Select Word's Edit menu (see fig. 11.1), and choose the Paste Special command. The Paste Special dialog box appears (see fig. 11.6). The name of the source document is automatically included in the link field that is inserted into the Word document.

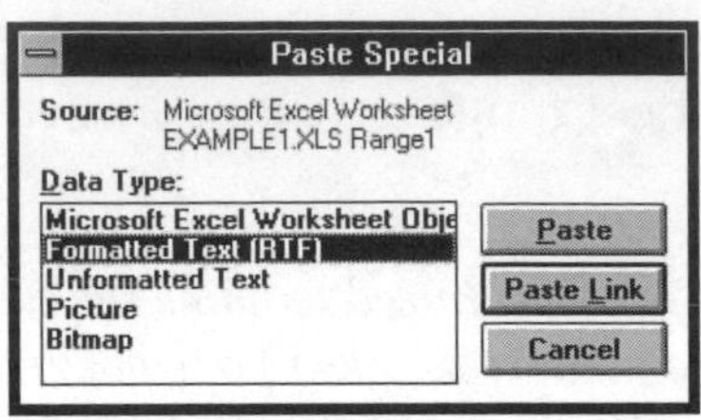

Figure 11.6:
Word's Paste Special dialog box.

In figure 11.6, Word automatically identifies the source application (`Microsoft Excel Worksheet`), the source document (`EXAMPLE1.XLS`), and the name of the range (`Range1`).

Remember that the Clipboard maintains the data that you place there in several different formats, which are supported by the source application, the destination application, or both.

In figure 11.7, for example, the View menu in the ClipBook Viewer displays the available formats, with those that the running applications support activated. (Those not supported are grayed out.) ClipBook Viewer displays the formats currently available for the item on the local clipboard.

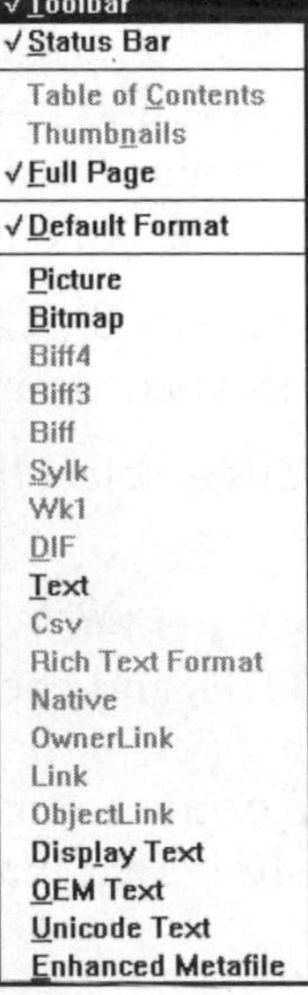

Figure 11.7:
The ClipBook Viewer View menu.

You now need to create a connection between the worksheet and the document. You do this by highlighting any choice in the Data Type list box except Microsoft Excel Worksheet Object (see fig. 11.6). This activates the Paste Link button. By clicking on the Paste Link button, Windows NT establishes a DDE connection between the Word document and the named range in the Excel worksheet, and places the data from Excel into your Word document, as displayed in figure 11.8.

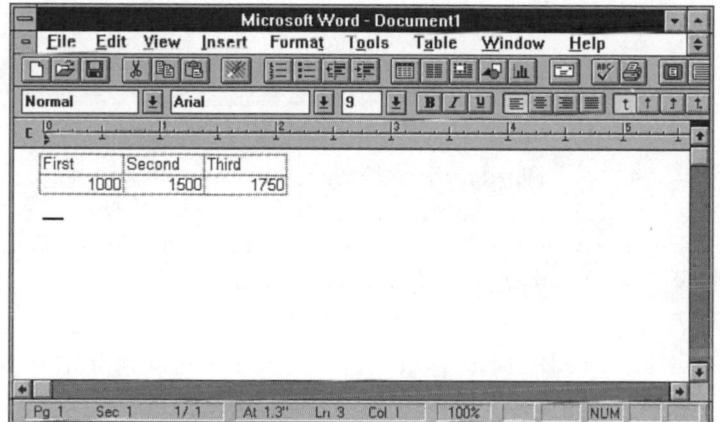

Figure 11.8:
The Excel range, after being placed in Word.

If you choose the Microsoft Excel Worksheet Object in the Paste Special dialog box, Windows NT embeds the range in your document as an OLE object, instead of creating a DDE link from your document to the range in the worksheet.

You now have a link field in Word, pointing to the range in the Excel worksheet. You can examine the syntax of the link by placing the cursor in the table, selecting the View menu, and then choosing Field Codes (see fig. 11.9). You also can press Shift+F9.

You can switch back to the contents of the link—the table—by pressing Shift+F9 again. In figure 11.9, the switches indicate the formatting that you chose in the dialog box, in this case, `\r` and `\a`. The `\r` switch denotes a Rich Text Format switch; the `\a` switch denotes an automatic switch.

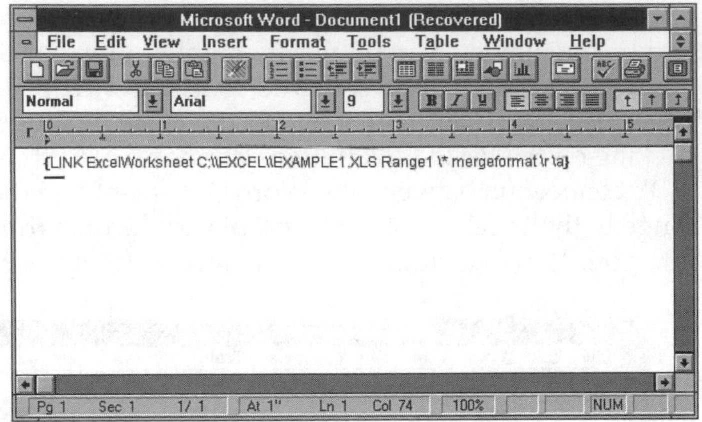

Figure 11.9: *The syntax of Word's `LINK` field.*

Word automatically puts the switch `\*mergeformat` into the field, which tells Word to format the results of the field. For more information on this switch, consult your Word documentation.

Make sure that the pointer still is somewhere in the table, and then select the Edit menu. A new option is on the menu—the Microsoft Excel Worksheet Link option (see fig. 11.10). Choose this option to make Excel the foreground application and to see the worksheet to which the Word document is linked. The linked range is highlighted.

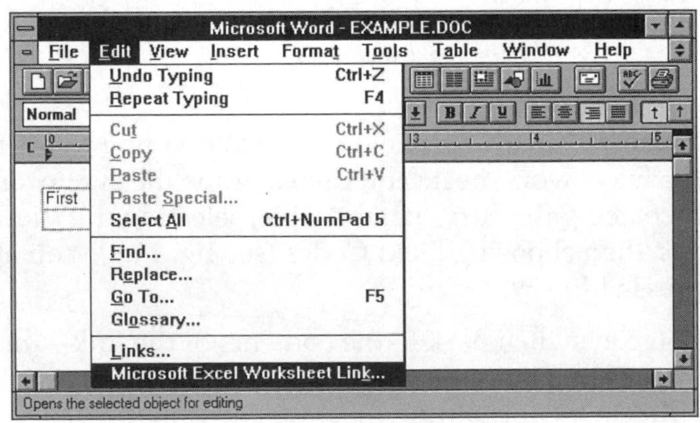

Figure 11.10: *The Word Edit menu, showing the Microsoft Excel Worksheet Link option.*

To further demonstrate the linking feature, create two more ranges—one on the same worksheet and the other on a new worksheet. On the EXAMPLE1.XLS worksheet, create a two-cell matrix, and insert the numbers **12345** and **67890**. Name the matrix **Range2**. Follow the previous steps to create a link to your Word document.

Next, create a new Excel worksheet, save it as **EXAMPLE2.XLS**, and create a six-cell matrix on it. Label three columns **AAA**, **BBB**, and **CCC**; in the row beneath the labels, insert the numbers **111**, **222**, and **333**. Name it **Range3**. Again, follow the preceding steps to create a link to your Word document.

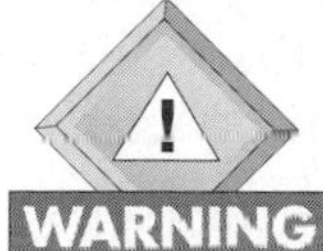

Be sure to save your Excel worksheets.

You now should have three Excel ranges in your Word document, as shown in figure 11.11.

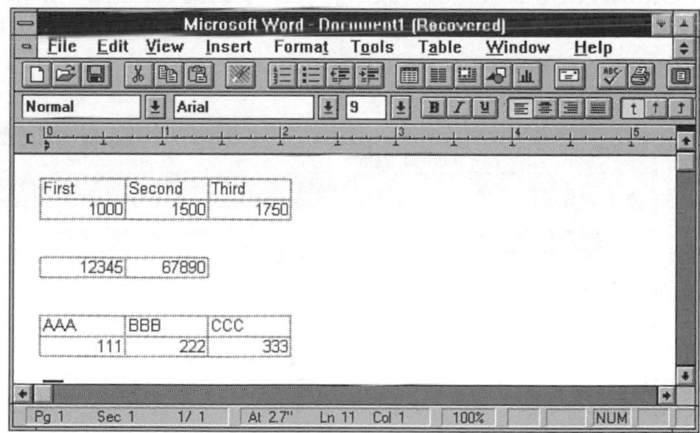

Figure 11.11: *Three live links to Excel.*

Switching between Applications

As you learned in earlier chapters, Windows NT enables you to move back and forth between applications in various ways. In the preceding examples, you did the following to switch between Word and Excel:

- Selecting the Control menu (or using Ctrl+Esc to start the Task List dialog box), highlighting the desired application, and choosing the Switch To command. You can click on the Control menu icon (directly to the left of the title bar), or use Alt+space bar to activate the Control menu.
- Minimizing the current application and maximizing the other.
- Pressing Alt+Esc to cycle through the applications on your desktop.
- Pressing Alt+Tab to cycle through the open applications.

You also can move between applications by taking advantage of the link between the two applications. Place the pointer in any of the three Word tables that are linked to the Excel worksheets, and then choose Excel Worksheet Link from the Edit menu. This moves you instantly to the linked range on the Excel worksheet and highlights the range.

The name of the Excel worksheet appears in the document's title bar, as shown in figure 11.12. Later, you see how this compares to what appears on an Excel document's title bar when you use embedded objects.

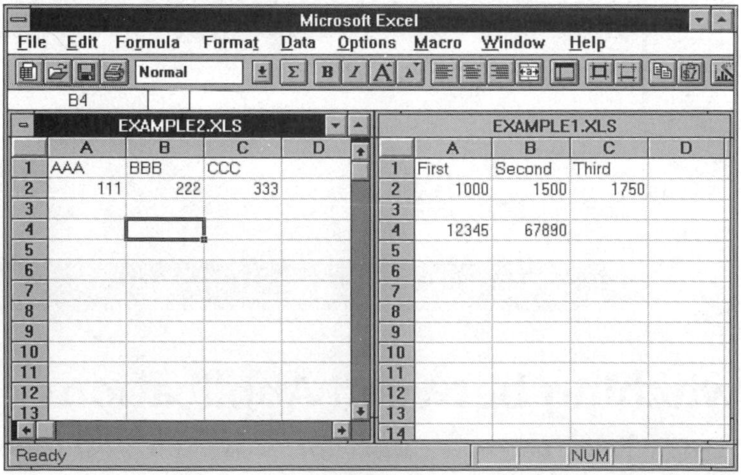

Figure 11.12:

Excel worksheet names EXAMPLE2.XLS and EXAMPLE1.XLS in the title bars.

You also can examine and edit the links. You need to edit the links if you rename your Excel worksheets or move them to another directory, for example.

You can edit a link by choosing the Field Codes option in the View menu and making the changes in your document. You also can use the Links dialog box, which you access by choosing the Links option under the Edit menu (see fig. 11.13).

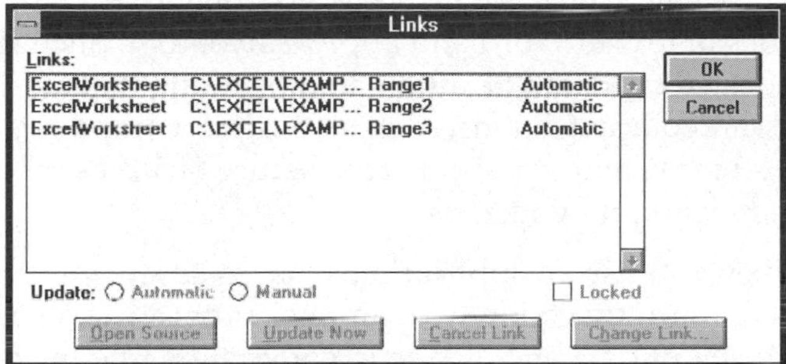

Figure 11.13:
The Links dialog box.

If you move or rename a source document, you must edit the link to reflect the change, or Word does not know where to find the linked data.

To edit a link, select it in the list and click on the Change Link button. The Change Link dialog box appears (see fig. 11.14).

Figure 11.14:
The Change Link dialog box.

In the Change Link dialog box, you can edit the three elements that DDE needs to know to maintain the link: the application name (`Excel Worksheet`, in this example), the path and file name (of the source document), and the data item (the unit of information—a named range in this example).

Understanding Advanced DDE

You probably repeat tasks when you use an application such as Excel or Word. For instance, you may frequently mark a block of text in Word and apply a style to it. Such frequently repeated tasks can be automated by using macros. Most advanced applications, such as Word for Windows, Lotus 1-2-3 for Windows, and Excel, feature facilities for creating and maintaining macros.

When you use an application's macro language to manage DDE communication with another program, you enable transfer of data and also send commands that make the other program do something. From within a Word macro, for example, you can send a series of commands that start Excel, ask it to open a particular worksheet, enter data in the worksheet, make Excel create a chart from that data, and finally copy the chart and paste it into the Word document. You can program all types of tasks in other applications without ever leaving the word processor.

In the following example, Word and Excel act as the front end to a database program. DDE commands issued by Word or Excel cause the database program to perform some of its native functions—such as a search—by remote control.

Using Macros To Access Information

Polaris PackRat is a Windows *personal information manager (PIM)* that is used as a contact database, an appointment calendar, and a project manager. It is an example of a program that, although it has no accessible DDE functions on its menus, understands and can respond to DDE commands from other applications. PackRat is shipped with a number of macros that are written in the macro languages of Word, Excel, Ami Pro, and others.

These macros enable programs to engage in a two-way conversation with PackRat. Through the mechanism of these macros, PackRat can receive commands and data from applications and send data to other applications when requested to do so. It cannot, however, initiate the DDE communication with another program because it has no macro language of its own.

Other programs can be accessed through DDE, but PackRat is used in these examples because it represents a new generation of Windows add-ins.

An add-in *is a program that adds specific functions or capabilities to an existing application. Add-ins for DOS programs have existed for some time and have become available for Windows NT applications. In addition to behaving as an add-in to applications such as Word and Lotus 1-2-3, PackRat also operates as an independent Windows NT application.*

The prerequisites for a DDE link include the name of the source document and a reference to the data within the source document. In general, Windows NT recognizes the source application of DDE data when the DDE link is created. When manipulating DDE links through a macro language, however, you have to explicitly provide Windows NT with the source application's name.

As explained earlier in this chapter, a DDE link represents a channel for the exchange of data between applications. These channels are managed by Windows NT and normally are invisible to the user. When you created the Excel-to-Word DDE links in the previous example, Windows NT established the DDE channel, through which Excel and Word can exchange data. When you work with DDE through macros, you deal directly with DDE channels and messages.

Each macro language has its own DDE syntax. Because the details of application macro languages differ, not everything discussed in this section may make sense if you have not worked with the macro language. Thus, the following examples are intended only to give you an overview of different macros. Although a complete discussion of macro languages is beyond the scope of this book, the brief discussion given here may point the way to further work.

A Sample Macro

The DDE commands most often found in macro languages include the following:

- **Initiate.** The Initiate command—in WordBasic, DDEInitiate()—begins a DDE communication with another application. This command opens a channel to the external application and passes the application information required to begin a DDE dialog.
- **Poke.** The Poke command is used by the client application to send a value to a data item in the server application.
- **Request.** The Request command is used by the client application to retrieve the value of a data item in the server application.
- **Terminate.** The Terminate command is sent by the client application to the server application to immediately end the conversation.

The arguments to the command are the other application's name (usually its commercial name, such as "PackRat") and a word indicating the source of the data Word wishes to access (in the case of PackRat, the source is "System"). The command returns a numeric value—the number of the communication channel—that DDEInitiate opens. The following example demonstrates the DDEInitiate macro command:

```
ChanNumFN = DDEInitiate("PackRat", "System")
```

In the preceding syntax, the user assigns a variable name—`ChanNumFN`—to the channel number that is returned by the `DDEIntiate` call.

The following lines are from a WordBasic macro that enables the user to search PackRat's Phone Book facility for a name and address. If the search is successful, the name and address then are imported into the Word document at the current location of the cursor.

```
DDEPoke(ChanNumFN, "STARTSEARCH", "P")
DDEPoke(ChanNumFN, "FULLNAME", dlg.Nam$)
DDEPoke(ChanNumFN, "COMPANY", dlg.Comp$)
DDEPoke(ChanNumFN, "ENDSEARCH", "")
```

In the preceding syntax, `DDEPoke` sends PackRat the search criteria that the user has entered in the dialog box. The `"STARTSEARCH"` entry in the first `DDEPoke` command puts PackRat in search mode; the next two `DDEPoke` commands tell PackRat the data to retrieve (`dlg.Nam` and `dlg.Comp`). The last `DDEPoke` turns off PackRat's search mode.

Because these examples are very application-specific, do not worry about what `dlg.Nam$` or `"ENDSEARCH"` means. Look at the overview of data-exchange possibilities with DDE.

In the following lines, `DDERequest` is the command that tells PackRat to retrieve the data and send it back to the user:

```
LName$ = DDERequest$(ChanNumFN, "LASTNAME")
FName$ = DDERequest$(ChanNumFN, "FIRSTNAME")
```

The first data retrieved from PackRat is `LASTNAME`; it is assigned to the WordBasic variable `LName`. The second bit of information returned from PackRat is `FIRSTNAME`; it is assigned to the variable `FName`. These values then can be inserted by Word into the active document, for instance. The WordBasic variables can be used later in the macro as needed.

If you have PackRat on your system, you can look at these macros in detail. The WordBasic macros are contained in a Word template file called PACKRAT.DOC.

Getting Used to DDE

Some users do not like DDE because the commands that invoke DDE are not uniform across all the applications that support it. You have seen this in the Word and Excel menus. In Excel, the Edit menu has the Paste Special option, which has nothing to do with DDE, and the Paste Link option, which does invoke DDE. In Word, on the other hand, you must select the Edit menu and choose Paste Special to get to the Paste Link option.

This inconsistency between applications makes users think that DDE is too complicated or too obscure to use. You will be comfortable using DDE links if you remember the following points:

- Pasting a DDE link is really a Clipboard function.
- If interactive DDE is available in an application, a reference to links appears on a menu—usually under Edit, File, or Insert.

The difficulties in using DDE are disappearing as applications evolve. Many users, for instance, would feel overwhelmed writing macros in WordBasic because they are not programmers. WordBasic, as is obvious from the preceding example, is very much like a programming language. Developers now are finding very clever ways to make users feel more comfortable with tasks that many users feel should be reserved for programmers, however.

MicroPhone II is an example of a communications program that has a very powerful macro language included with it. You can write macros to automate any MicroPhone II function, including DDE transactions with other programs.

You do not have to master programming, however, to use the macro language. Any command in the language can be created from the Script Manager dialog box, which you access by using the Edit Scripts command on the Scripts menu (see fig. 11.15).

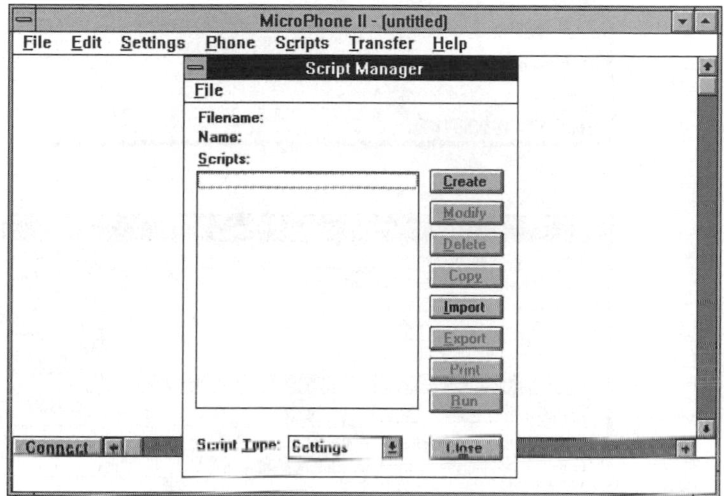

Figure 11.15: *MicroPhone II's Script Manager dialog box.*

To create a DDE transaction, click on the Create button to start writing a script in the macro language. This action causes the Create Settings Script dialog box to appear, as shown in figure 11.16. Each command in the macro language is described by an English term in the list box that appears in the lower left corner of the dialog box. To initiate a DDE transaction, scroll through the list box until you find the DDE command and select it by clicking on it, as shown in figure 11.16.

After you have selected the DDE command, the second list box immediately to the right becomes active (also shown in figure 11.16). This list box shows you the possible DDE actions you can take.

When you select Initiate to start a conversation, a text box appears directly below this list box. You enter the application and the data source for the DDE conversation in this text box (see fig. 11.17).

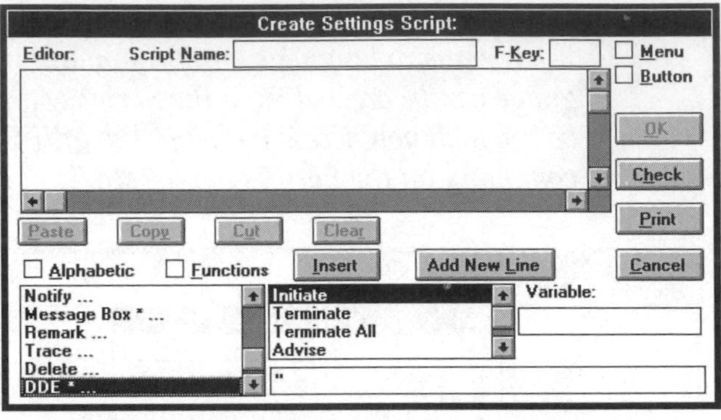

Figure 11.16: *Selecting the DDE command in the list box.*

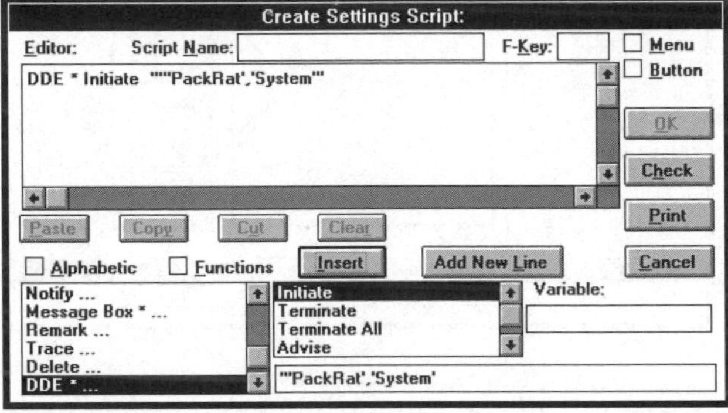

Figure 11.17: *Entering the application and data source for a conversation.*

Enclose these items in single quotes, as shown. MicroPhone II supplies all other necessary elements of the syntax. The only parts of the command you need to type are the arguments for the Initiate command, enclosed in single quotes and separated by a comma. To insert the comma in the script, click on the ***I****nsert button just above the second list box.*

The other DDE commands illustrated in the previous WordBasic script can be created in the same way. You need to know only that you want to create a DDE command and express that in the left list box. You need to choose a DDE action in the right list box, and you need to be able to fill in the arguments for the command, if any. To build a DDE macro correctly, you need a working knowledge of the seven DDE actions and what arguments they take.

Each of the actions and the necessary arguments are explained in detail in the Help file that accompanies MicroPhone II. (Figure 11.18 shows the screen that explains the Initiate command.) You access this Help file by selecting the <u>D</u>DE option on the <u>H</u>elp menu.

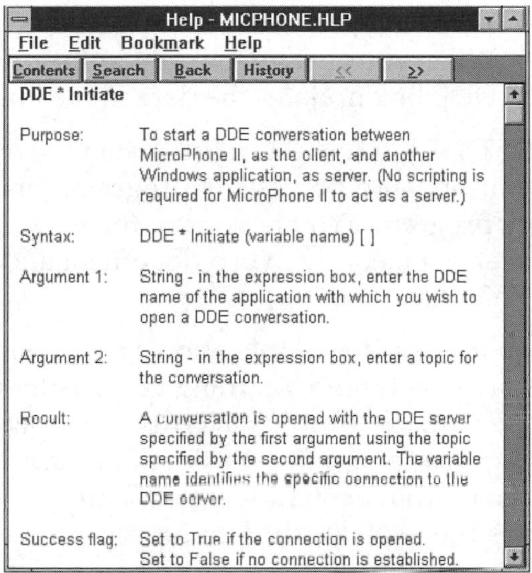

Figure 11.18: *The Help screen for the DDE Initiate command.*

Using DDE is becoming easier and easier. By the time you update to the next version of your applications, the menu items that enable you to work with DDE will have become fairly standardized. You also will find that developers have created automated ways to script macros for working with DDE. Getting used to DDE is something that all users should do, because it makes you work much more productively.

Although interactive DDE probably will be emphasized less by vendors when OLE 2.0 is released, scripted DDE still performs tasks (such as control other applications) that OLE cannot do.

Summary

Windows NT has eliminated the glass cage that has surrounded character-mode applications for many years. It now has the capability to share data between applications without losing vital formatting and time. Dynamic Data Exchange enables you to create a live link between one application and another. When you change the data in the original application, the DDE link updates the data in the linked application.

By using DDE links, you can link data in spreadsheets, documents in word processing programs, and pictures in graphics programs. You have seen the way an Excel worksheet is linked to a Word document and to a PowerPoint file.

Through the use of an application's macro language, you can automate many time-consuming tasks. Although it is outside the scope of this book, the reader is encouraged to investigate DDE macro programming further. *Integrating Windows Applications*, from New Riders Publishing, offers many examples and explains the key concepts in detail.

Using Object Linking and Embedding

You saw in the last chapter that Windows NT enables you to share data between applications by using Dynamic Data Exchange (DDE). This chapter explains Object Linking and Embedding (OLE), which is a mechanism for inserting a vast amount of information and data into a document. The information and data are treated as *objects*—that is, collections of information that you can treat as a single unit and manipulate as a single unit.

Most of the examples in this chapter discuss fairly straightforward cases—the way to insert Excel spreadsheet fragments into a Word document, for instance. Windows NT also enables you to include multimedia in your compound document. *Multimedia* includes voice annotation, full-motion video, music, and other information. (To take advantage of Windows NT's multimedia capabilities, you must have the appropriate hardware for sound generation and video display installed on your computer.)

This chapter covers the following topics:

- Examining OLE
- Embedding non-OLE objects
- Understanding the Object Packager
- Introducing OLE client and server relationships

OLE is sure to play a major role in Windows NT software development in the near future, especially after version 2.0 is released in the fall of 1993. This chapter describes OLE and some practical applications.

OLE 2.0 is an update of the original OLE technology that offers many new features and capabilities.

Examining OLE

Windows NT offers an extended feature of Dynamic Data Exchange (DDE). *Object Linking and Embedding (OLE)* is a Windows feature that extends the Clipboard and DDE methods of data exchange to a new level. It enables the user to combine the services of various applications by placing information from the source application(s) into the receiving application's document. Although OLE's technical underpinnings are complex, you do not need to know what goes on under the surface of the interface.

A compound document *is a document that contains data elements created in more than one application. A classic example is a document that you create and manage with your word processor. The document becomes a compound document when you add a table you created by using your spreadsheet, a graphic you*

created by using your presentations graphic program, and a voice annotation you created by using the Windows Sound Recorder.

After you create a DDE link, the container document must keep track of the name of the source application, the name of the source document, and the identifier for the data to which the link points. Most applications enable you to examine and modify the links, so you also must be aware of the name of the source application, the source document, and so on. You also must have some idea of the way the linking mechanism functions.

OLE packages the data into an object that contains much more information than a DDE link. If you examine the syntax for an embedded object in applications that enable you to, such as Word and Excel, you see an indication of the kind of object. This indication of object type tells Windows NT what the source application is. The object (with information about its formatting, the way it is drawn, what colors it uses, and so on) is stored in the container document.

In DDE, the *container document* maintains information that points to data stored elsewhere. In OLE, the container document maintains the object. You do not need to know the source application's name; all you need to know is what kind of object you want to embed.

A linked *object is independent of the compound document; an* embedded *object exists only within the confines of the compound document.*

To demonstrate essential differences between DDE and OLE, the following exercise uses the EXAMPLE1.XLS Excel worksheet that you created in Chapter 11. In the following example, you embed DDE rather than use it to link the range named Range1. For this exercise, open both Word and Excel.

1. Begin with a new document in Word, switch to Excel, and open EXAMPLE1.XLS.
2. Select the Formula menu, and choose the Go To command.
3. From the list of named ranges, select Range1. This takes you to the range and highlights it for you.
4. Select the Edit menu, and choose Copy.
5. Switch back to Word, select Word's Edit menu, and choose the Paste Special option. The Paste Special dialog box appears (see fig. 12.1).

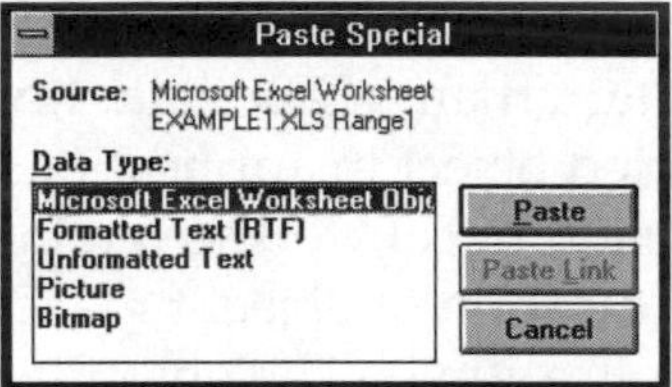

Figure 12.1: *Choosing the Microsoft Excel Worksheet Object option in the Paste Special dialog box.*

In Chapter 11, you were instructed not to choose the Microsoft Excel Worksheet Object item when the Paste Special dialog box appears. This item enables you to activate OLE embedding, not DDE linking. Now, however, choose Microsoft Excel Worksheet Object to continue this example.

6. Choose the Microsoft Excel Worksheet Object item in the Paste Special dialog box. Note that the Paste Link button becomes grayed out, meaning that you cannot activate DDE linking.
7. Click on the Paste button. An OLE object is created and embedded in your document because you selected the Microsoft Excel Worksheet Object item.

   You now see an embedded object in your Word document, as shown in figure 12.2.

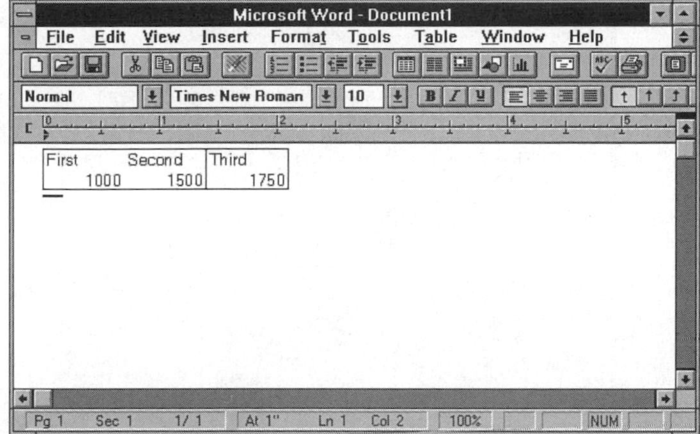

Figure 12.2:
The Excel range, embedded in the Word document.

If you click anywhere on an embedded object, sizing handles appear around the object. The following message appears in the status line at the bottom of the screen: `Double click to Edit Excel Worksheet.`

Sizing handles *are little squares around the perimeter of the object that enable you to change its dimensions.*

To examine the syntax of the embedded object, select the View menu, and choose the Field Codes option. You see the `EMBED` code appear; it references an Excel worksheet (see fig. 12.3).

To continue with this exercise, select Field Codes from the View menu again, which returns you to a normal view of your document.

Select Word's Edit menu. Note that, as illustrated in figure 12.4, a command is added: Microsoft Excel Worksheet Object. In Chapter 12, when you created a DDE link, this command was called Excel Worksheet Link.

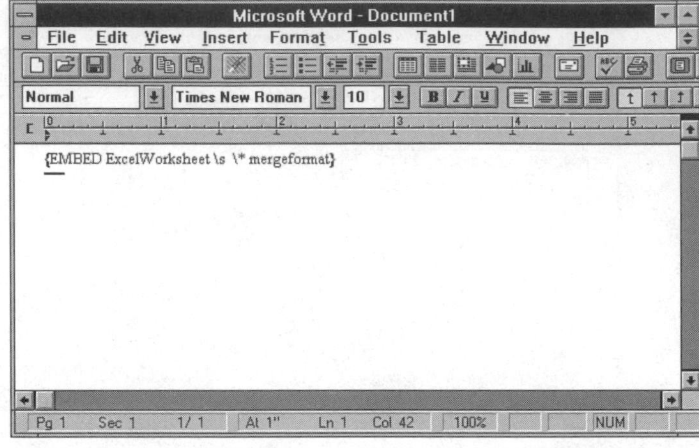

Figure 12.3:
The EMBED field tells you what kind of object is embedded.

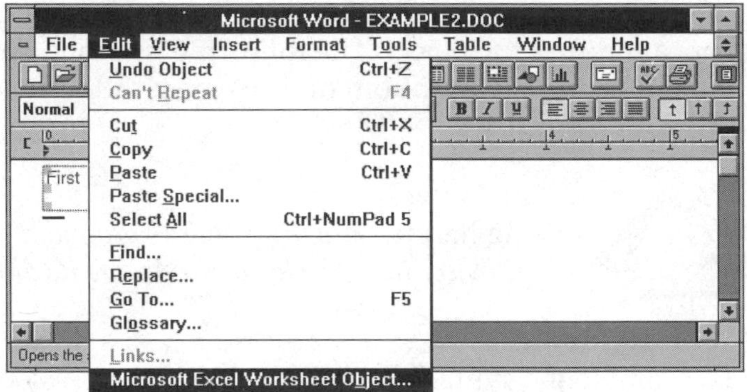

Figure 12.4:
*Word's **E**dit menu, showing the Microsoft Excel Worksheet O**b**ject option.*

You can make Excel the foreground application by choosing the Microsoft Excel Worksheet O**b**ject command or by double-clicking on the object. Windows NT launches Excel (if it is not already launched) and passes it the embedded spreadsheet data. After Excel is active, your embedded spreadsheet data is already in the open spreadsheet. Notice that the text in the title bar of the spreadsheet is different (see fig. 12.5). The title bar informs you that you are working with an Excel object that is part of your Word document.

Figure 12.5:
The Excel worksheet title bar shows that it is an object embedded in the Word document.

In OLE 2.0, double-clicking on an embedded object does not open a new window for the source application. Instead, the source application's menu bar replaces the container application's menu bar, enabling you to edit the object by using the services of the source application while still in the container application's window. This is called in-place editing *or* in-situ editing.

You cannot name this worksheet—the system automatically does it for you. The file also does not show up anywhere in your list of files. This worksheet does not exist as an independent entity; it exists only as an object in the Word document. You can still edit the worksheet as if it were a normal Excel worksheet.

If you are following along with this example, select **W**indow in the Excel menu bar, and choose EXAMPLE1.XLS. Compare the title bars of your embedded spreadsheet data and EXAMPLE1.XLS (see fig. 12.6).

With the XLS worksheet as the active window, select the **F**ile menu (see fig. 12.7). Note the **S**ave command. Make the worksheet object the active window, and again select the **F**ile menu.

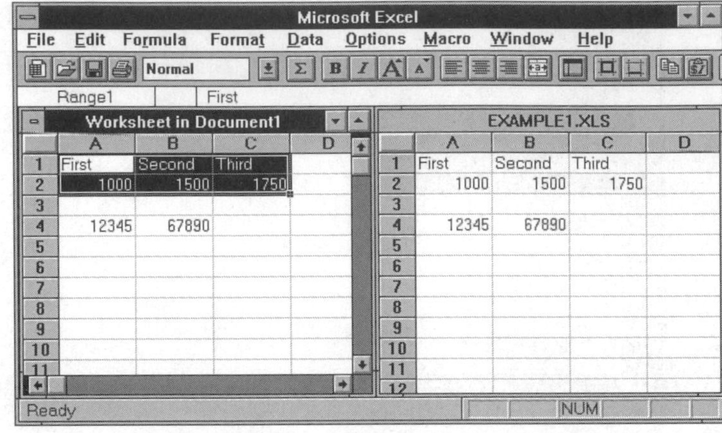

Figure 12.6: *The Excel workspace, showing the XLS worksheet and the Word worksheet object.*

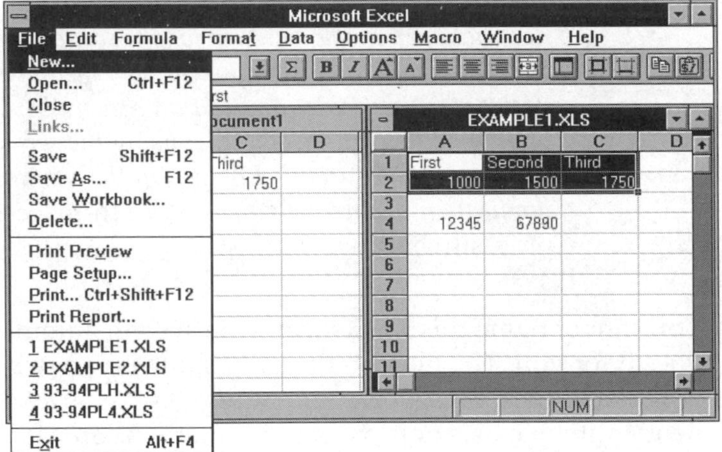

Figure 12.7: *The Excel **F**ile menu.*

Notice in figure 12.8 that the **U**pdate command replaced the **S**ave command on the menu.

You can experiment with updating the embedded data. From within Excel, make sure that the worksheet object is the active window. Experiment by changing one of the numbers in the six-cell matrix, and choose **U**pdate from the **F**ile menu. You then return to the Word document, the embedded worksheet object is updated, and Excel closes (if no other spreadsheets are open in Excel).

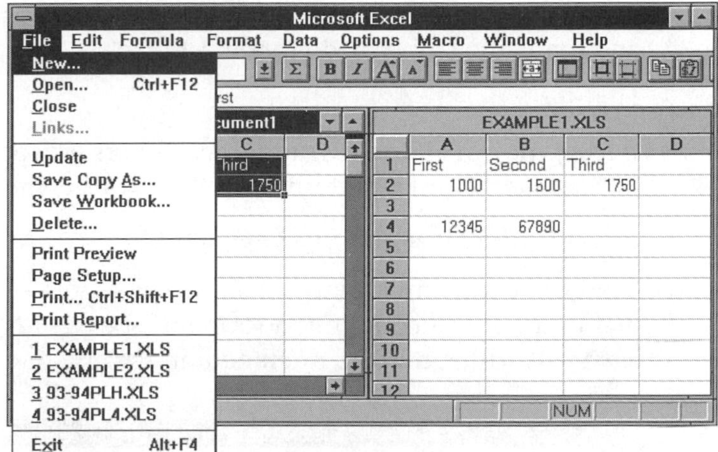

Figure 12.8:
*Excel's **F**ile menu and **U**pdate command when the worksheet object has the focus.*

Suppose, for example, you change the amount in the third column of the worksheet from `1750` to `2000`. The Word document automatically updates with the new number (see fig. 12.9) when you choose Update in the Excel File menu.

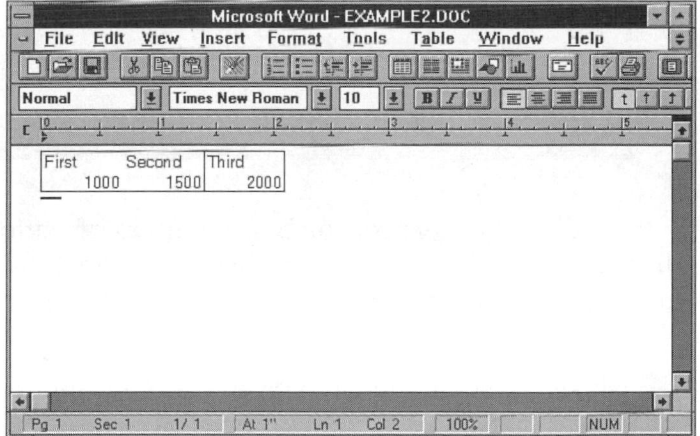

Figure 12.9:
The Word document, after the spreadsheet data is updated.

The Microsoft Excel Worksheet Object embedded in Word can be changed only by Excel. You can change the text face used for the numbers or the border around the numbers only by using Excel. Follow these steps:

1. Double-click on the embedded object. This opens Excel, and loads the embedded worksheet object.
2. Highlight the six-cell matrix.
3. Access the Forma**t** menu, and select a border from the **B**order menu and a pattern from the **P**atterns menu.
4. Select **U**pdate from Excel's **F**ile menu.

The changes you just made—by using Excel's tools—are reflected in the Word container document (see fig. 12.10). You have just edited a Word document in Excel!

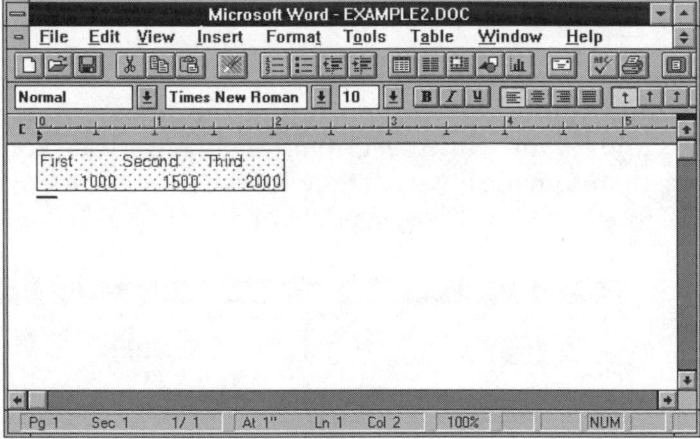

Figure 12.10:
The embedded object now has a border and a pattern.

In the preceding exercise, you began with information that already existed in an Excel worksheet. You can, however, create an Excel Worksheet object from scratch, directly from Word, by following these steps:

1. Make sure that you have Word running, and then create a new document by selecting **F**ile and choosing the **N**ew command.
2. Select the **I**nsert menu, and choose **O**bject (see fig. 12.11).
3. Select Microsoft Excel Worksheet from the Object list box (see fig. 12.12).

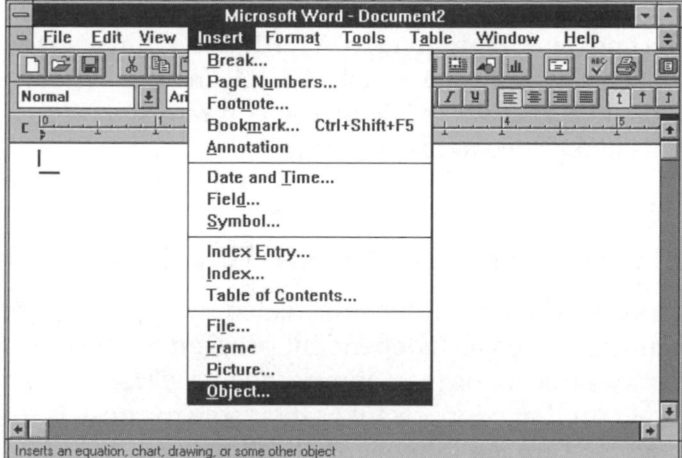

Figure 12.11: *Word's **I**nsert menu, showing the **O**bject command.*

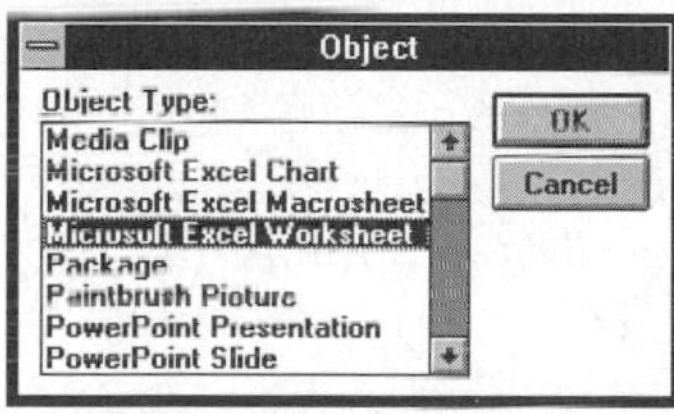

Figure 12.12: *Choosing Microsoft Excel Worksheet from the Object list box.*

Excel opens. Instead of Sheet1 appearing, however, a screen appears that has all the basic attributes of a normal Excel worksheet except for a different title bar. This title bar tells you that the worksheet is an object to be embedded in Word (see fig. 12.13).

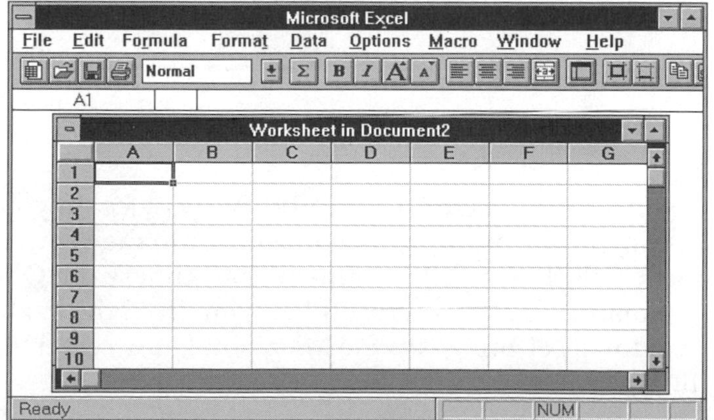

Figure 12.13: *The worksheet that appears after choosing Microsoft Excel Worksheet from the **O**bject command.*

Add some data to this worksheet. As before, enter **First**, **Second**, and **Third** in cells A1, B1, and C1, respectively. Enter **1000**, **1500**, and **2000** in cells A2, B2, and C2. When you select Update from Excel's File menu, you return to Word with new data embedded as an OLE object.

Embedding a Microsoft Draw Object

Embedded objects often are created by applications that cannot be used as independent programs. You only can call these applications (sometimes called *applets*) from within a program that supports OLE; their sole purpose is to produce objects to embed in other applications.

Some of these embedding applications are Microsoft's Note-It, WordArt, Microsoft Graph, and Microsoft Draw. These applications are classic add-ins, as described in Chapter 11.

If you try to run an embedding application, such as a stand-alone program like Microsoft Word (by clicking on the name of the EXE file in File Manager, for example), you receive a message such as the one shown in figure 12.14.

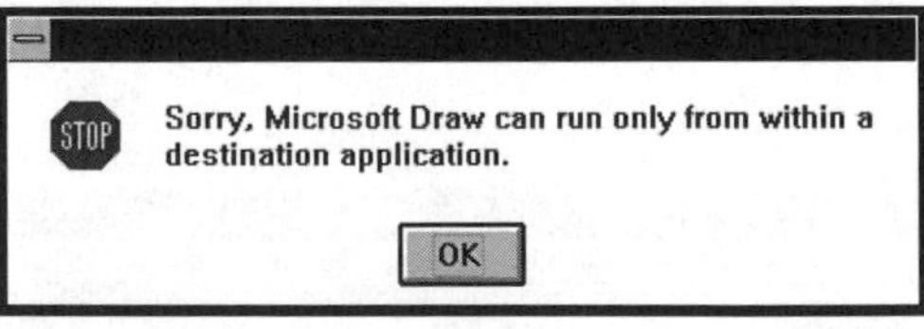

Figure 12.14: *The Windows NT error box appears when attempting to run an OLE server applet by itself.*

If you want to embed a Microsoft Draw object in your Word document, for example, you must do it in the Word document. Select Word's Insert menu, and choose the Object command. Choose Microsoft Drawing from the list box; Windows NT brings up the Microsoft Draw screen (see fig. 12.15).

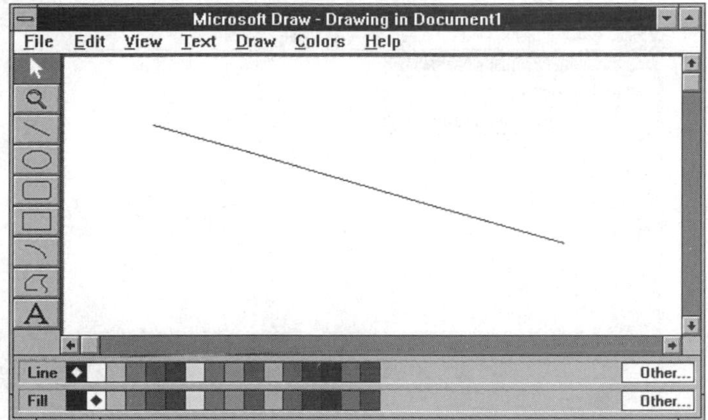

Figure 12.15:
The Microsoft Draw screen.

The title bar tells you that the object you create here is part of your Word document. You can use the functionality of the drawing program to create your object. You even can import a clip-art picture (or another graphic file into Draw, and use it as an OLE object), which you can modify. That piece of clip art becomes an embedded object after it passes through Microsoft Draw.

The Microsoft Draw File menu (see fig. 12.16) offers several options. You can import clip art by using the Import Picture command. You also can update the current object, stay in Microsoft Draw, and continue to edit the object by using the Update command. You can return to your Word document by using the Exit and Return to Document1 command. If you choose the last option, you are asked if you want to update the object in your Word document.

Notice that the Microsoft Draw File menu has no Save option. Remember, an embedding application can only produce objects for embedding in destination documents—you cannot save a graphic produced in Microsoft Draw as a file. The graphic becomes part of the destination document when you select Update or Exit and Return to Document in the Microsoft Draw File menu.

Figure 12.16:

The Microsoft Draw File menu.

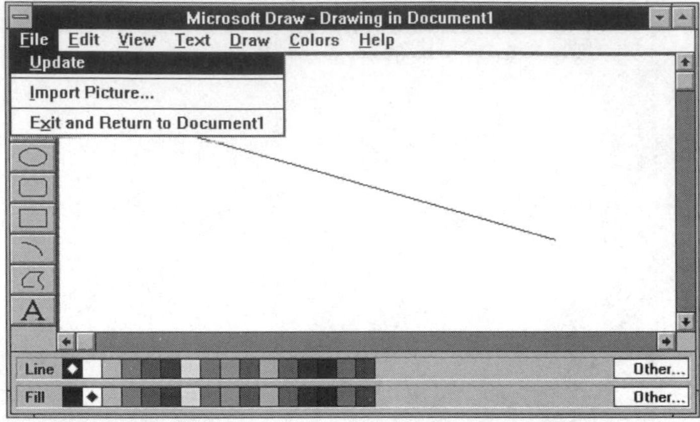

When you return to Word, select the View menu, and choose Field Codes; or click on the drawing object, and press Shift+F9 to see Word's field description of the object, as shown in figure 12.17.

Figure 12.17:

Word's EMBED field identifies the Microsoft Draw object.

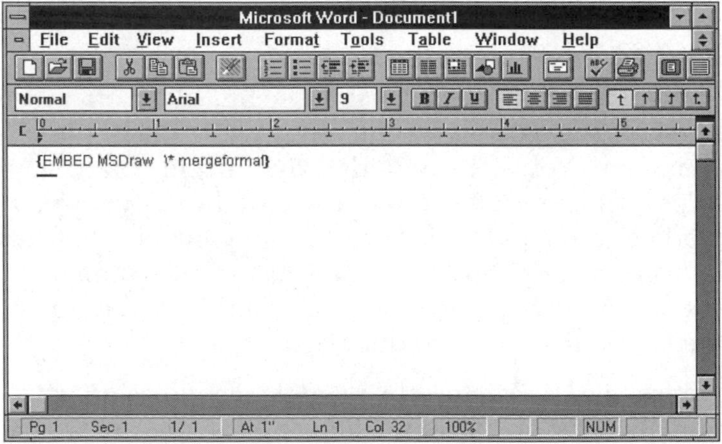

Follow these steps to edit an OLE object in Word's compound document in Microsoft Draw:

1. With the drawing object still highlighted, the following text appears on the status line at the bottom of the screen: `Double-click to Edit Microsoft Drawing.`

2. Double-click on the object, or select the Edit Microsoft Drawing command on Word's Edit menu to bring up the Microsoft Draw screen, with the object loaded.

3. Make any modifications by using Microsoft Draw's tools.

Embedding a Microsoft Sound Recorder Object

Microsoft Sound Recorder enables you to put a microphone graphic anywhere in your document and include a voice message with it. It differs from Draw in that it is a separate application. (For example, you can save WAV files by using SoundRec.)

Sound Recorder also can act as an OLE server.

To embed an object, follow these steps:

1. Select Object from the Word Insert menu, and choose Sound Recorder from the Object list box.

2. Click on the microphone button, speak your message into the microphone, and then click on the stop button.

3. To embed the voice note in your document, open the File menu, and select the Update option (see fig. 12.18).

Figure 12.18:
Creating and editing Sound Recorder objects.

To use the Sound Recorder application, you need to have a sound board and microphone installed on your computer.

If you double-click on the Sound Recorder object in Word, you do not return to Sound Recorder. Instead, Sound Recorder plays back the voice message you created.

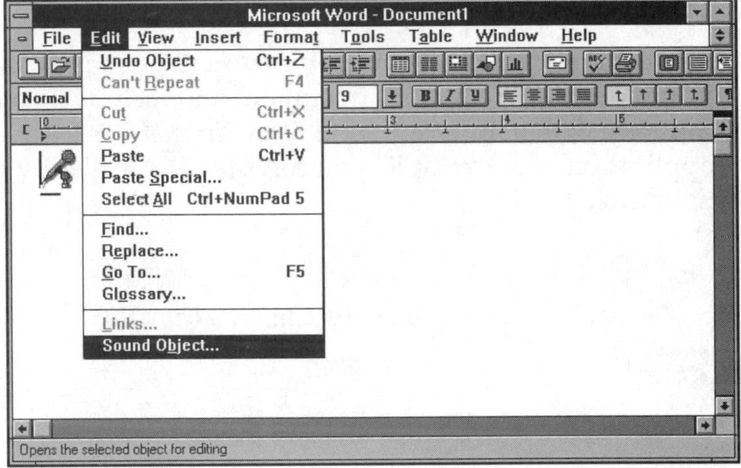

Figure 12.19: *Opening a Sound Recorder object embedded in a Word document.*

To return to the Sound Recorder, you must select Sound Object from Word's Edit menu, as shown in figure 12.19.

Embedding Non-OLE Objects

You might need to embed objects from applications that are not OLE-compliant. You may have a table derived from a non-Windows NT database, for instance, that you want to include in a report. Although you can export the database data in an ASCII-file format and import the ASCII file into your Word document, you lose the benefits of DDE and OLE.

Specifically, you have no way to return to the source application to view or edit the data. For Windows NT to apply OLE actions on the data, you must be able to somehow create an object from the data.

Windows NT has a way to create an OLE package data from non-OLE applications to make the data OLE-compliant. Normally, you only can embed data from OLE-compliant applications in a Windows NT document. Packaging data from non-Windows NT applications wraps the data so that Windows NT can perform OLE actions on it. The package contains the data and enough information about the source application. Windows NT can launch the source application to enable you to view or edit the data in its source application.

Object Packager

Windows NT provides a utility called the *Object Packager* that enables you to wrap non-OLE data in an object package and embed the package in your document. The package is represented by an icon that stands for the contents of the package. Object Packager gives you complete freedom to change the package's contents and appearance (the icon) in your document. To access the package, click on the icon with the mouse; Windows NT invokes the source application, which then displays the data.

Under Windows NT, you no longer have to be content simply reading a document. With the capability of OLE to embed information and data from a wide variety of sources, you can read some portions of a document, view full-motion video, and listen to voice or music recordings. Windows NT always gives you new ways to access information.

In addition to some rather obvious sources of data, you can package operating system commands, batch files, and data files. (Windows NT usually recognizes the source application by the file extension of the data file.)

Using the Object Packager

To package a non-OLE object, double-click on the Object Packager icon, which normally is found in the Accessories program group.

Windows NT may not install the Object Packager in a program group on installation. You can find its executable file, PACKAGER.EXE, in the \WINNT\SYSTEM32 directory if Windows NT does not undertake the installation.

The Object Packager is divided into two windows that are placed side by side. You specify the content of the package in the right window and the appearance of the package in the left window. The content window of the package normally displays a brief description of the package contents. The appearance window displays the icon that is used to represent the package when it is embedded in a document (see fig. 12.20).

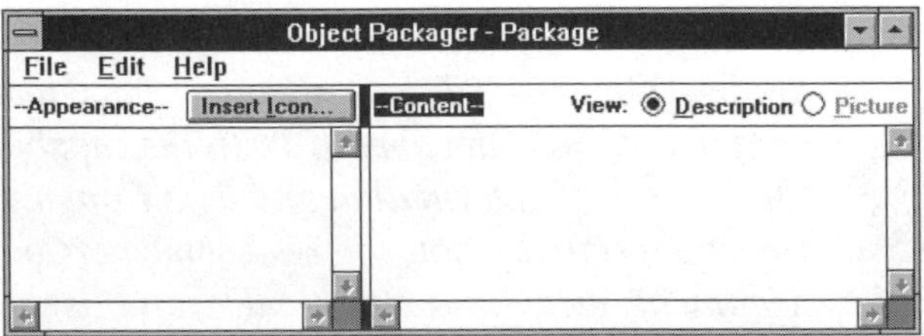

Figure 12.20: *The Object Packager.*

The process of creating a package with Object Packager is the following:

- Locate the data and add it to the content window.

- Determine the package appearance.
- Copy the package to the Clipboard.
- Embed the package in the destination document by pasting it from the Clipboard into the destination document.

Except for assembling the package in the first two steps, no difference exists between working with OLE packages and working with static data transfers by using the Clipboard.

In the following example, you see how easy it is to embed a DOS command in a document:

1. Double-click on the Object Packager.
2. Select the File menu, and choose the Import command.
3. Use the file-selection list to choose an executable file, such as the TREE.COM in the \WINNT\SYSTEM32 directory.
4. Select the file name by double-clicking on it. The Object Packager closes the file-selection list and puts a description of the package contents in the Contents window (see fig. 12.21).

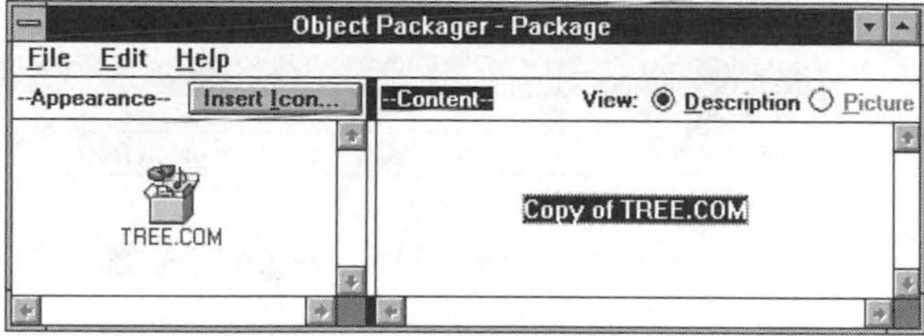

Figure 12.21: *The Object Packager with TREE.COM in the Contents window.*

The Object Packager selects an icon to represent the package and inserts the icon in the Appearance window. The selected icon in this example is the Windows NT icon for Object Packager. To change the icon, select the Insert Icon button at the top of the Appearance window.

Most Windows NT applications have icons bound into them. The bound icons are available to use for other applications.

Object Packager displays a dialog box with the name of the executable file providing the icon—in this case, PACKAGER.EXE. You can use the **B**rowse button to select another executable file to provide an icon. PROGMAN.EXE has many icons available. Figure 12.22 shows the selection of a knife icon to represent the package.

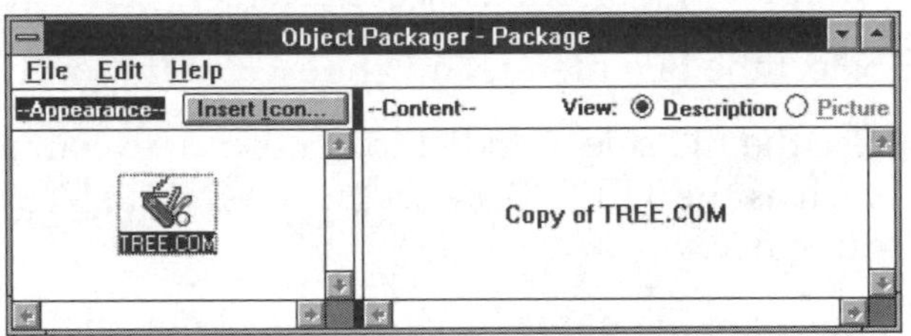

Figure 12.22: *The Object Packager with the knife icon in the Appearance window.*

5. Select the **E**dit menu, and choose the Copy Pac**k**age command to copy the OLE package to the Clipboard (see fig. 12.23).

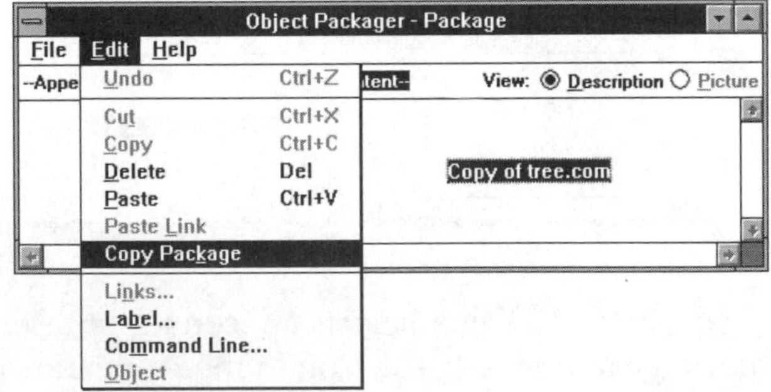

Figure 12.23: *The Object Packager **E**dit menu, showing the Copy Pac**k**age command.*

6. Switch to the document in which you want to embed the package. Move the pointer to where you want to embed the package.

7. Select Write's **E**dit menu, and choose **P**aste.

   Windows NT inserts the package and its icon in the document at the selected spot (see fig. 12.24).

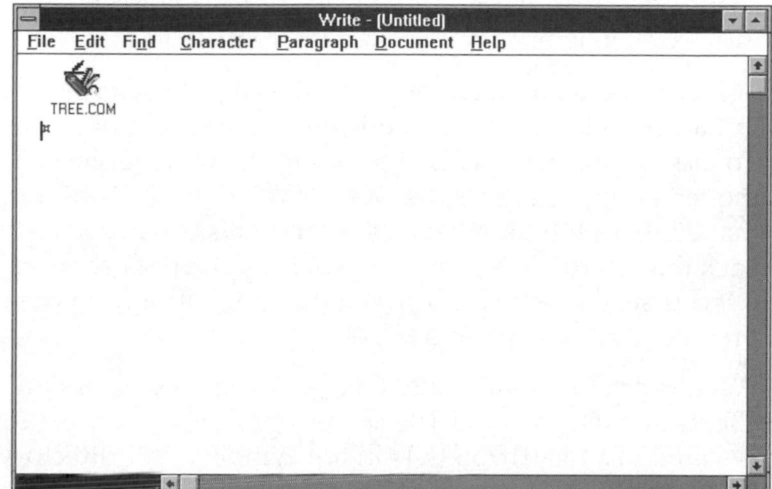

Figure 12.24: *The OLE package embedded in a Write document.*

Windows NT offers many ways to specify the content of the data you want to package. An in-depth discussion of OLE packaging and the many variations possible is beyond the scope of this book. For a comprehensive discussion of OLE, read Integrating Windows Applications, *from New Riders Publishing, which shows you how to embed DOS batch commands, image data, documents from non-Windows NT applications, and other sophisticated uses of OLE.*

Introducing OLE Client and Server Relationships

OLE follows a client-server model in the relationship between source applications and destination applications. In OLE, source applications act as the server that provides services to the client application that uses the services. When you use OLE to embed an Excel spreadsheet range in a Word document, for example, Excel (the server) provides spreadsheet services to Word (the client). When you want to view or change the spreadsheet data, the spreadsheet data is copied into Excel, in which you can work with the data.

Similarly, data packaged by using the Object Packager initially is obtained from a multitude of server applications. To use the preceding voice-recording example, for instance, the server application is the DOS or Windows NT program that digitizes the sound and saves it on disk. When you play back the recording, a program provides playback services. (Of course, the same DOS or Windows NT application can provide playback services.)

Windows NT maintains a database of known servers and clients that they service. The server-application information is stored in a file (REG.DAT) in the Windows NT directory. Windows NT also provides a registration information editor (REGEDIT32.EXE) that enables you to add new server applications to the database or to modify the characteristics of existing server applications.

In Windows NT, unlike other versions of Windows, editing the Registry database is a dangerous operation. All configuration information for Windows NT is contained in the database, not in the files SYS.INI and WIN.INI. Accidental changes to the Registry can render Windows NT inoperable. As Microsoft's own product support staff is fond of saying, you can really "hose your system."

Make certain that you know what you are doing before you open the Registry Editor. Use Windows NT Setup, Control Panel, and application setup programs to make the changes you need to make to your system before you use the Registry Editor.

Summary

The technologies of linking and embedding have propelled users toward the fulfillment of an old promise: the capability to manage many different kinds of information in a seamless flow.

In this chapter and Chapter 11, you learned that you can create links that enable data to be shared across applications with just a few keystrokes or clicks of the mouse. You have seen the way to use two powerful tools, DDE and OLE, merely by employing simple Windows NT techniques that you already know. You also learned ways to link a spreadsheet range with a word-processing document and ways to embed several kinds of objects, text, and graphics in a document.

This chapter took you on a brief tour of Object Linking and Embedding, which promises to bring even greater interoperability to many functions that previously were unreachable by users. OLE is a powerful tool for the informed user, and it will play a greater role in future Windows NT developments. This chapter has only touched upon the ultimate potential of Object Linking and Embedding.

So far, you have been exposed to a variety of ways that Windows NT can increase your productivity. But keep in mind that the concepts and ideas presented in a book cannot substitute for hands-on experience. Continue to work on as many examples as necessary to gain experience and become comfortable with your new Windows NT skills.

Managing the Windows NT Network

Exploring Networking with Windows NT

Understanding the System Registry

Exploring the Windows NT Advanced Server

PART 4

Exploring Networking with Windows NT

The vast majority of PCs used in business today are connected to a network. PC network packages, such as Novell NetWare and Microsoft LAN Manager, are sold as add-on products, with versions available for specific systems such as DOS and OS/2.

Since Windows 3.1, Microsoft has tried to integrate networking more closely into the operating system, presenting a standard interface for network management through a Network utility under the Control Panel. Just as Windows 3.1 depends on DOS for its underlying operating system functionality, it depends on an underlying DOS network package for its networking capabilities.

In Windows NT, Microsoft has fully integrated network services into the operating system. Full Microsoft LAN Manager functionality and (nearly full) interoperability comes standard. Extended, or replacement, software from other PC network vendors such as Novell will tie into the same Control Panel management and configuration facility.

In this chapter, you will examine Windows NT networking, including:

- Understanding Windows NT and Microsoft LAN Manager
- Understanding Windows NT networking architecture
- Using the Control Panel's Network utility

Understanding Windows NT and Microsoft LAN Manager

Although Microsoft has achieved a high degree of integration between the operating system and the network under Windows NT, the network interface is based on the LAN Manager model. Naming conventions, management by domains, Workstation and Server components, and the standard NetBEUI transport and Named Pipes IPC all are quite similar to elements of the LAN Manager.

LAN Manager Concepts and Terminology under Windows NT

A Windows NT computer is easily integrated into an existing LAN Manager network, and a Windows NT Advanced Server can act as the domain controller for LAN Manager clients. A Windows NT computer cannot join a LAN Manager domain if it is managed by an OS/2 server, however.

If a Windows NT computer is used in such a domain, you need to specify a workgroup name that is different from the domain name (see the section on using the Control Panel later in this chapter), and the Windows NT computer does not fall under the management of the domain. Provided that there is a domain account for the user name logged on at the Windows NT machine, it can attach to shared resources available on that domain and communicate by using IPC with computers in that domain.

Just how, and how well, a Windows NT computer integrates into a local area network (LAN) that is based on Novell NetWare (or other PC network operating systems) is still unclear. Windows NT is not yet in final release as this book is being written, and only preliminary software of limited functionality has been made available by Novell.

Windows NT Network Resources

The standard network interface for Windows NT is nearly the same as that of Microsoft LAN Manager's interface. Shared network disks or printers on other Windows NT computers or OS/2 LAN Manager computers can be attached to with the familiar NET USE command.

Named Pipes IPC and Universal Naming Convention (UNC) file access use the computer name specified on the top-level screen of the Control Panel Network utility. Workstation and server components exist that you can manage with the NET START and NET STOP commands.

One difference is that there is no NET LOGON—the username and password specified for the current Windows NT session is used. This is a consideration when integrating a Windows NT computer into an existing LAN Manager network. A Windows NT workstation integrates seamlessly into a Windows for Workgroups workgroup by specifying the appropriate workgroup name in the Control Panel.

A variety of Interprocess Communications (IPC) interfaces are provided to maximize connectivity with client-server applications. These include Named Pipes, Sockets, DCE-conformant remote procedure calls (RPC), DLC connectivity for SNA access to IBM mainframes, and a Remote Access Service package to enable access to Windows NT-based networks via telephony. Standard TCP/IP utilities also are provided, including `ftp`, `telnet`, and `rsh`.

Peer Networking

Windows NT provides full *peer-networking* capabilities. This means that it can act as both a server and a workstation on the network. It shares resources with other computers while enabling users to access shared resources on other computers.

Peer networking is not common under DOS and Windows 3.1, for which a distinct separation usually exists between client computers (although Windows for Workgroups has recently provided some of this capability). Under DOS and Windows 3.1, a distinct separation exists between client computers—which can access but not share remote resources—and server computers—which can share, but not provide access to resources.

On the other hand, peer networking is a standard feature of UNIX workstations, and is a feature of some OS/2 networking packages, such as Microsoft LAN Manager. Other OS/2 packages, such as the Novell NetWare Requester for OS/2, have only limited peer capabilities. The recent popularity of Windows for Workgroups has rekindled interest in peer networking among PCs.

Understanding NT Networking Architecture

Windows NT has a layered network architecture that enables great flexibility in combining various components. Numerous layered conceptual models exist, such as the ISO and IEEE standards, but for purposes of understanding Windows NT network architecture, it can be simplified to three distinct layers:

- A network adapter device driver, which provides the control functions for a specific network card
- A transport protocol layer, which provides one of several standardized formats and mechanisms for moving data across the network
- Higher-level services, such as the Server and Workstation software, for sharing resources such as disks or printers, IPC mechanisms such as Named Pipes or Sockets, and various network utilities

The power of the layered approach is the capability to "mix and match" among components at the three levels. You can install a variety of network adapters under Windows NT, regardless of the choices at a higher level, because the device drivers running these adapters conform to the NDIS standard first developed for OS/2 LAN Manager.

Similarly, you can use different transport protocols, such as TCP/IP or NetWare IPX. Because these transports are also written to established standards, they can interoperate among versions of the same transport protocol provided by different vendors. These transport protocols are accessed from higher-level network services via the Windows NT Transport Driver Interface.

Transport Protocols

Windows NT has three standard protocols:

- **NetBEUI.** This transport protocol, used by LAN Manager, is installed automatically in Windows NT and is a good choice for a departmental LAN. It does not support routing and is not suited for wide area networks (WANs), however.
- **TCP/IP.** This protocol is the industry standard routable transport protocol, and is provided for full WAN connectivity. TCP/IP also is the standard for UNIX computers. You can configure TCP/IP routing options from the Control Panel.
- **DLC.** This transport protocol is provided primarily to facilitate connectivity with IBM mainframe computers on SNA networks.
- Other standard protocols, such as Novell's IPX, will undoubtedly be made available by third-party vendors.

Under Windows NT, you can install multiple network adapter cards and their device drivers on a single computer. Additionally, you can use multiple transport protocols on a single card, and you can use the same transport protocol on multiple adapter cards. This capability is the essence of the flexibility provided by a layered architecture.

Setting up these connection pathways from adapter driver through transport protocol to network services is known as *binding*. The next section discusses the way choices are made among options for each of these layers, and the chosen packages are configured and bound together to form a full networking capability.

Using the Control Panel Network Utility

Windows NT network functionality is controlled by using the Network Control Panel utility. To use this utility, you must be logged on as a member of the Administrators group (see fig. 13.1).

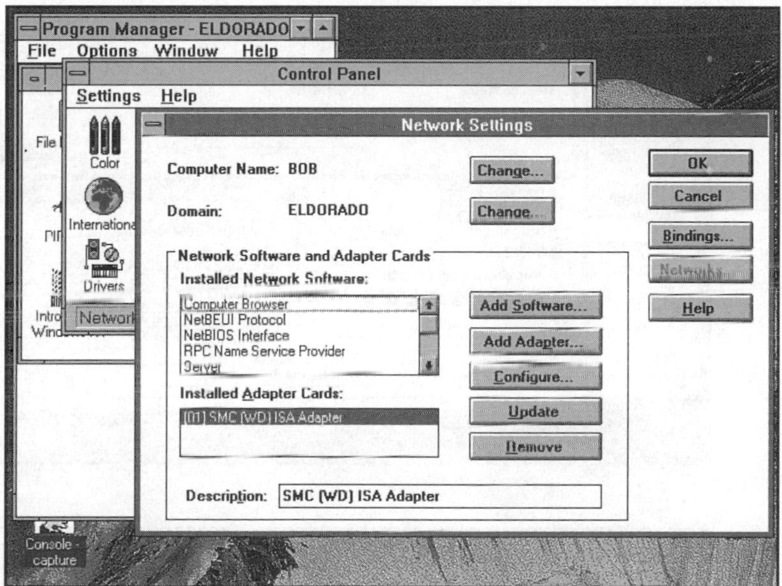

Figure 13.1:
Highest-level screen of the Network applet.

Network Name and Domain

The top two lines specify the computer's *network name* (the name by which it is known on the network) and the workgroup or domain to which the computer belongs.

The computer name must be unique within the workgroup or domain, and it cannot be the same as the workgroup name. Although a workgroup *is a group of computers listed together in the Network Browser, a* domain *is a managed group with a Windows NT Advanced Server that acts as the domain controller.*

To join a domain, the computer name being used must have an account on the Windows NT domain controller, or valid information must be entered in the Create Computer Account in Domain dialog box under the Domain Settings screen (see figs. 13.2 and 13.3).

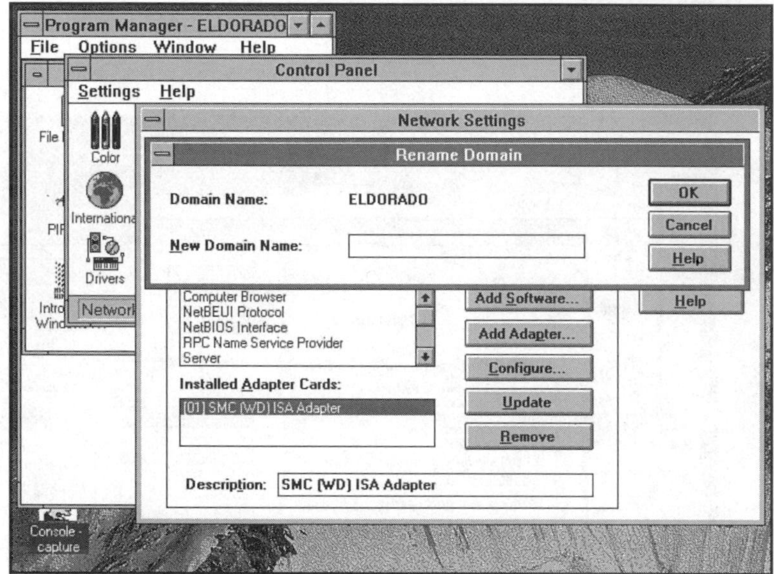

Figure 13.2: *Rename Domain dialog box.*

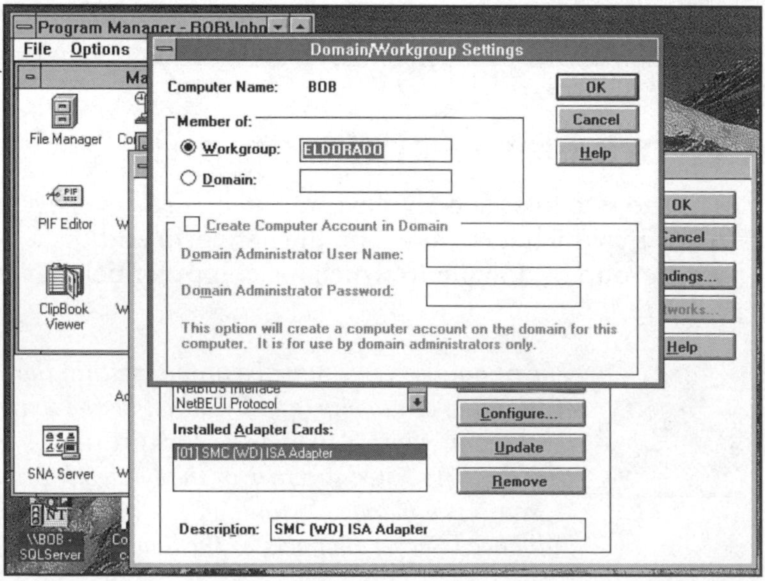

Figure 13.3: *Domain/ Workgroup Settings dialog box.*

If you are using the Windows NT Advanced Server, you must be either a member of, or domain controller for, a domain.

Network Software and Adapter Cards

Also found in the top-level screen are list boxes, showing Installed Network Software and Installed Adapter Cards. You can add new items to these lists by clicking on the Add Software or Add Adapter buttons.

In each case, there is an option to allow new choices not listed to be installed from disk. This is the way you can add a package such as Novell NetWare, or a device driver for a nonstandard network card, to a Windows NT computer. You can delete items in the list boxes by highlighting them and clicking the Remove button.

You specify configuration settings for an adapter by highlighting the adapter card in the Installed Adapter Cards list box and clicking on the Configure button. A screen that is specific to the network adapter type appears (see fig. 13.4). More than one network adapter can be installed in a Windows NT computer.

If you make incorrect choices for settings such as the adapter card IRQ, the network card might not function. Although Windows NT usually detects such errors and enables the user to make changes, it is still the user's responsibility to make sure that a network adapter has correct jumper settings and that no conflicts exist with other components in the system.

If problems still exist, use the Event Viewer to check the Event Log for relevant system messages.

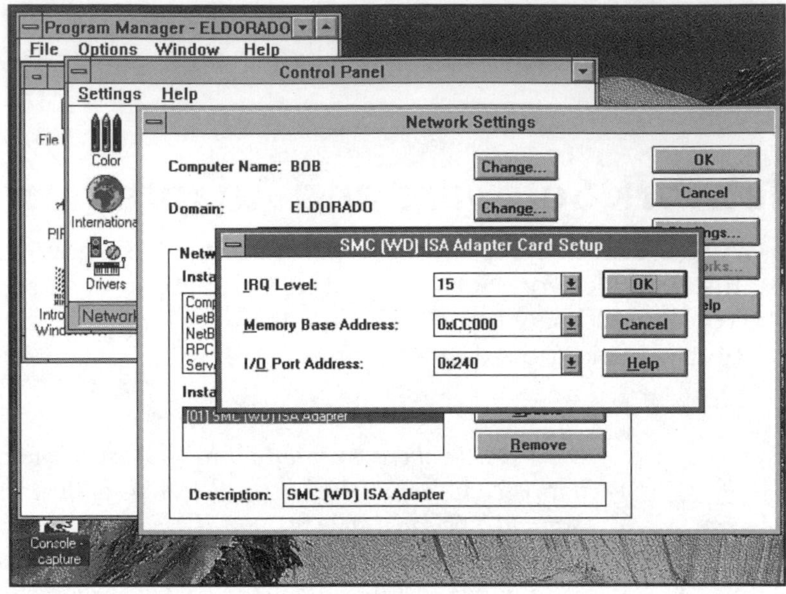

Figure 13.4: *Sample Adapter Card Setup dialog box.*

Similarly, you can set configuration parameters for network software by highlighting the software and selecting Configure. The dialog box for TCP/IP configuration is shown in figure 13.5; this is where parameters such as the computer's IP address, subnet mask, and default name resolution behavior are set. The latter two settings control TCP/IP routing, and should be set only by a network administrator familiar with TCP/IP.

A variety of other network-related software, including Remote Access Service (RAS), RPC, and DLC links, can be configured from this section also. In most cases, Windows NT will need to be rebooted for system-wide changes to become effective.

Bindings

Binding, the process of linking together software to form pathways through the three conceptual layers, is controlled from a screen brought up by clicking the **B**indings button. By default, all possible bindings are set up, and when new network adapters or transports are added, an automatic binding step occurs.

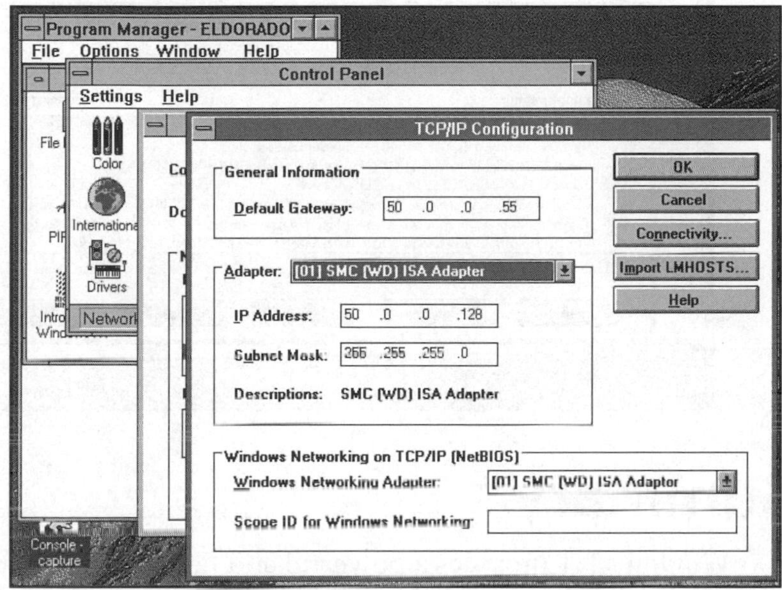

Figure 13.5:
TCP/IP Configuration dialog box.

It is possible to disable some bindings if they are not going to be used—for instance, if a Token Ring card is connected to a NetBEUI network only and an Ethernet adapter is connected to a TCP/IP network only. This is seldom necessary, however, and should only be done by a network administrator because incorrect bindings can disable network connectivity. The Bindings screen is chiefly of interest to a network administrator while troubleshooting. An example of the bindings dialog box is shown in figure 13.6.

Because you can connect a Windows NT computer to more than one network simultaneously, the question arises of which network to search first for a requested resource or service. You can control this from the Network Provider Search Order screen, accessed from the Network Settings screen, which is available on Windows NT computers that have more than one network installed.

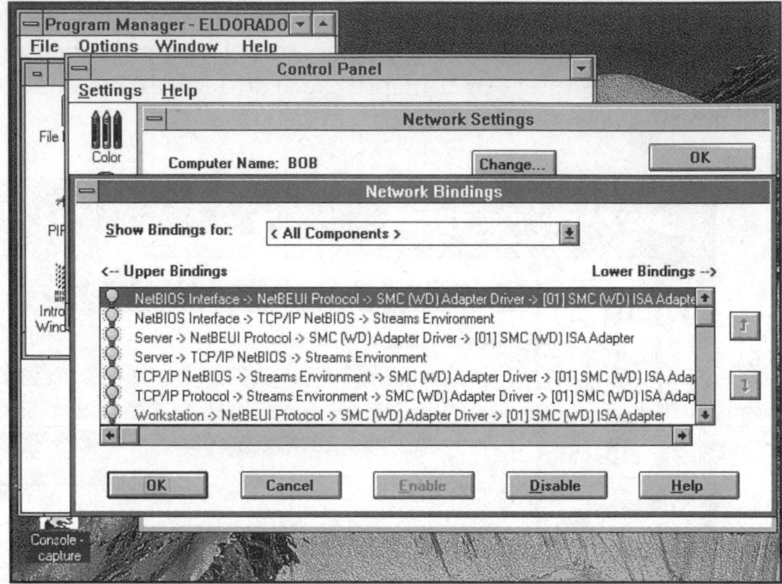

Figure 13.6:
Network Bindings dialog box.

Summary

Windows NT provides a powerful and flexible set of network services that are based on the LAN Manager model. Features include full peer networking, support for multiple network adapters and transports, and a complete set of IPC facilities.

Installation and configuration of these components have been unified under a single interface, the Control Panel utility. Windows NT is completely compatible with Windows for Workgroups, and full domain-management facilities are provided in the Windows NT Advanced Server. These features give Windows NT the most fully featured, and yet easy to use, network support available under any PC operating system.

Understanding the System Registry

Anyone who has ever installed a peripheral card or software package on a PC can appreciate the difficulties involved in system configuration. You encounter CONFIG.SYS entries, AUTOEXEC.BAT entries, and WIN.INI entries. Each of these file entries has its own format, is in its own location, and has various ways of interacting with the system.

Multiply the problem by several hundred—or thousand—PCs on a large network to understand the challenge faced by today's corporate information systems departments. Simplifying the process of system configuration is the basic concept behind the Windows NT System Registry.

The System Registry *provides a single storage point for configuration information, which controls all the hardware and software on a computer, with a standard structure and interface for access to that information.*

In addition, Windows NT permits remote Registry access across the network, enabling the configuration of all of a group's PCs from a single central point. You can control access to the Registry by using Windows NT's security system. Because the entire machine configuration is held in one place, backing up a system (and copying or moving it to another machine) becomes much simpler.

This chapter discusses the following:

- Understanding the Registry format
- Using the Registry
- Accessing the Registry with REGEDT32
- Exploring the four root keys
- Recovering the system with Registry backups

Understanding the Registry Format

The basic structure of the System Registry is similar to the familiar tree structure of a hierarchical file system, such as that found in DOS, OS/2, and UNIX.

The file system has the following components:

The *root directory* contains

some *files*, and

some *subdirectories*, each containing

some *files*, and

some *subdirectories*, each containing...

and so on.

The System Registry has the following components:

The *root key* contains

some *values*, and

some *subkeys*, each containing

some *values*, and

some *subkeys*, each containing...

and so on.

The Windows NT System Registry has four root keys. Following the preceding file-system analogy, you can think of the root keys as equivalent to file-system logical drives C, D, E, and F.

These root keys are referred to in Microsoft's documentation as predefined keys, *or* first-level keys.

The four root keys are described in table 14.1.

Table 14.1
Windows NT Root Keys

Root key	*Function*
HKEY_LOCAL_MACHINE	Shows information about the hardware and software on the computer. This information includes configuration data for the hardware and software installed on the computer, as well as the basic configuration of the computer itself (processor type, and so on).
HKEY_USERS	Shows information about all users active on the computer. It does not show all user IDs, only those currently active.

continues

Table 14.1
Continued

Root key	*Function*
HKEY_CURRENT_USER	Actually a subkey of HKEY_USERS, it shows information for the user examining the Registry information.
HKEY_CLASSES_ROOT	Included for Windows 3.1 compatibility and OLE support. Associates a file-name extension with an application package.

Each branching point, or *node*, of the Registry tree is a root key that has a name. As in a file system, the names are unique for all subkeys under a given key, so the full hierarchical name (or *Registry path*) of any node in the tree is unique.

Value names under a specific root key also are unique, both among themselves and among subkey names under that key, just as file names and subdirectory names are unique within the same directory. The similarity of structure between the Registry and a file system is further emphasized by Microsoft's use of the backslash delimiter for Registry paths.

Any specific value in the Registry has a unique full Registry path name, beginning with the name of one of the root keys, extending through subkey names, and ending in the value name, as in the following example:

```
HKEY_LOCAL_MACHINE\SOFTWARE\Microsoft\Windows
NT\CurrentVersion\InstallDate
HKEY_CURRENT_USER\Keyboard Layout\Active
```

Value names consist of the Registry name, which defines the value, a data type, and associated data. There are five predefined value data types, described in table 14.2

Table 14.2
Registry Value Data Types

Value data type	*Description*
REG_BINARY	Unstructured binary data.
REG_DWORD	A numeric value, stored in a 32-bit integer.
REG_SZ	A NULL-terminated string.
REG_MULTI_SZ	Multiple NULL-terminated strings, concatenated and terminated with a double NULL.
REG_EXPAND_SZ	A NULL-terminated string, meant to be taken as a file name, and which will be expanded when used into a fully qualified path name.

The size of value data for a Registry entry has a large (about 1M) limit. The Registry is not intended for storing large data items; you should store large data items in application-specific disk files, with the path name stored in the Registry.

Using the Registry

You can add or remove keys and values from the Registry, or edit value data, by using the Windows NT graphical utility REGEDT32. Microsoft recommends that you not use REGEDT32 to directly alter the Registry, but rather to use Windows NT utilities, such as Setup and the Control Panel (or an application-installation program), to make any modifications programmatically.

Because all machine-configuration information is stored in the Registry, an incorrect entry can be disastrous. The Windows NT API presents an interface for Registry manipulation, and Microsoft is encouraging software developers and makers of hardware peripherals to use this interface to store configuration data during installation. Until third-party products can correctly make all entries every time, which is unlikely in this imperfect world, those responsible for PC installation or configuration need to be able to use REGEDT32.

Windows NT is a very new operating system, and the acceptance of the convention of using the Registry for third-party configuration information remains to be seen. It is hoped that hardware and software manufacturers will make full use of the power and convenience of the Registry concept.

Accessing the System Registry with REGEDT32

You can launch REGEDT32 from a Windows NT command line, from the **Run** option of the Program Manager, or from its own icon. In the following section, REGEDT32 is used to examine some of the basic structures and features of the Registry.

Be careful not to change Registry values if you follow along on your own computer. As noted earlier, entering incorrect information in the Registry can cause serious problems.

After you launch REGEDT32 for the first time, you see a window for each of the four root keys (see fig. 14.1).

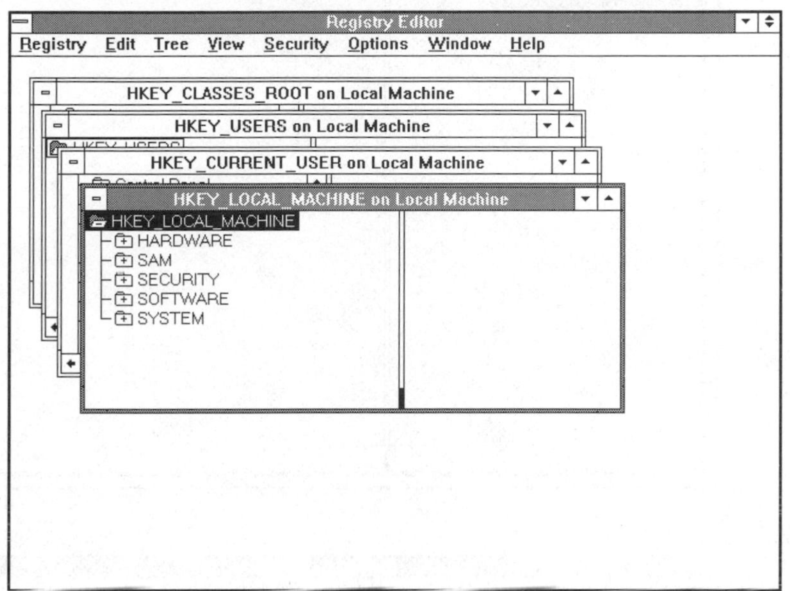

Figure 14.1:
Windows of the four root keys.

Within the window for each root key, key entries appear in a graphical tree structure on the left side of the screen, with one key highlighted. Values under the key are listed on the right side of the screen.

Each key has a file folder icon, which is marked with a + if that key contains further subkeys (see fig. 14.2).

Double-clicking on the key causes the subkey structure to appear, and it replaces the + with a - (see fig. 14.3).

Double-clicking on the key again closes the key.

You can edit values by double-clicking on them. If you double-click on a value, a dialog box appears that is specific to the data type for that value (see fig. 14.4).

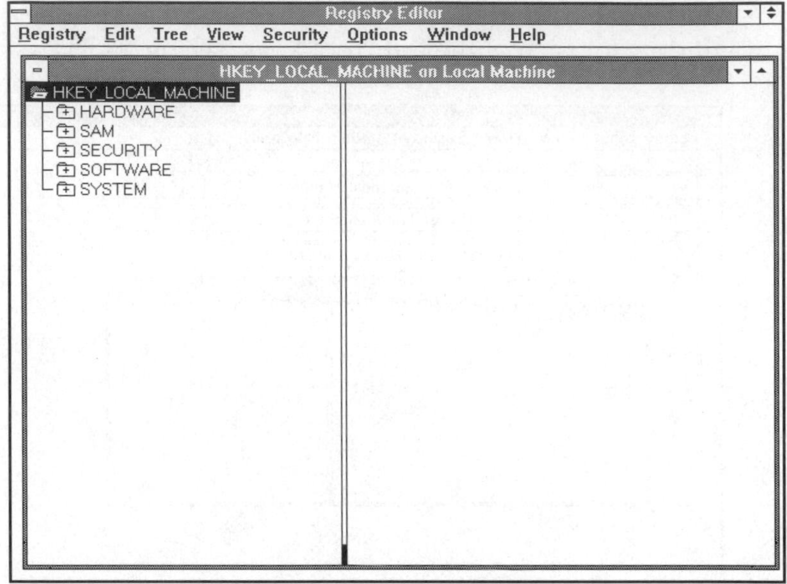

Figure 14.2: *File folders with subkeys are marked with +.*

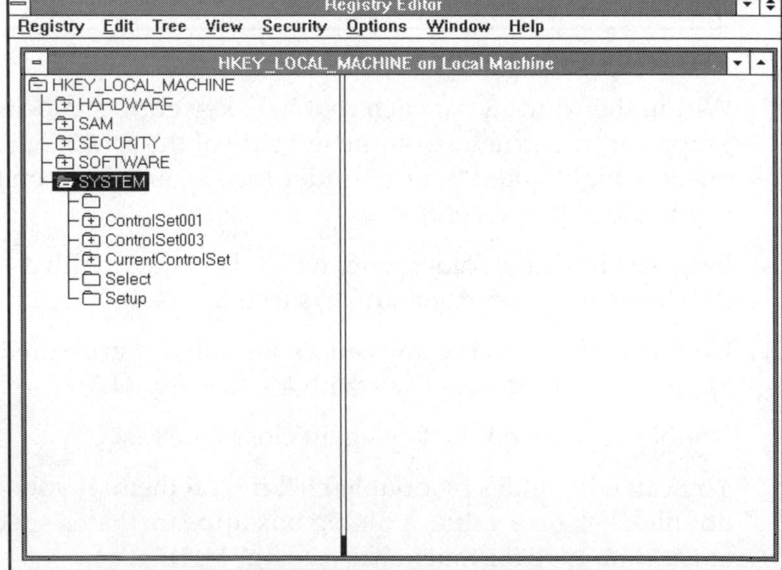

Figure 14.3: *Subkey structure for SYSTEM.*

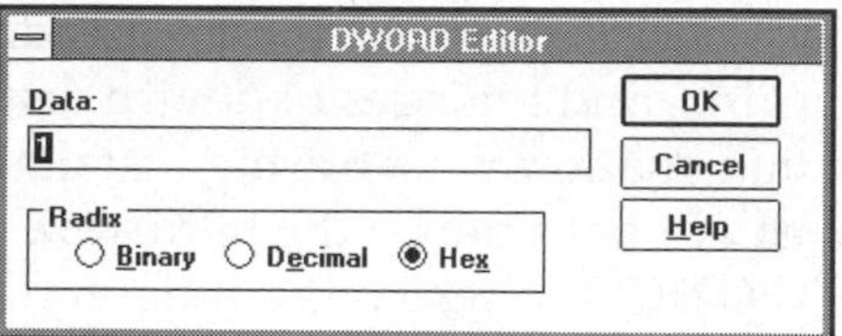

Figure 14.4:
DWORD Editor dialog box.

The Select Computer option under the Registry entry on the menu bar enables you to access the Registry on another Windows NT computer on the network.

You must have the appropriate security privileges to edit values.

Exploring the Four Root Keys

Windows NT's four root keys are discussed in the following sections.

The HKEY_LOCAL_MACHINE Key

The HKEY_LOCAL_MACHINE key has the most interesting information in the Registry. It includes the hardware and software configuration for the machine, as well as security information and the default boot configuration.

The HKEY_LOCAL_MACHINE key has five subkeys: HARDWARE, SAM, SECURITY, SOFTWARE, and SYSTEM. (Figure 14.2 shows this structure.) These subkeys are discussed in the following sections.

HARDWARE Subkey

The HARDWARE subkey has information about the hardware installed on the machine: the interrupt and I/O port used by a peripheral card, the video-adapter type present in the machine, and linkages to device drivers. Although some of this information is set during installation, many entries are refreshed at boot time by the hardware-detection program NTDETECT.COM, which is a hidden file in the root directory of the boot drive.

SAM and SECURITY Subkeys

The SAM and SECURITY subkeys have information that controls the security configuration for the computer, including user- and group-account information. You cannot directly change these keys; they can only be accessed in a limited and controlled way. Changes must be made by using the Windows NT security interfaces.

SOFTWARE Subkey

The SOFTWARE subkey has information about software installed on the computer. Applications are arranged under a subkey structure, using the vendor company's name and the name of the software package as its higher-level components.

The information under SOFTWARE is not specific to the individual user logged on; it is global to the machine and affects all users.

SYSTEM Subkey

The SYSTEM subkey is further subdivided into *control sets*. Each control set actually is a set of system parameters, which (with the other Registry entries) can control the operation of the computer. This structure is displayed in figure 14.5.

The CurrentControlSet subkey holds the information that was used when the computer was booted last. Previous versions of control sets are stored as *ControlSet001*, *ControlSet002*, and so on. If an incorrect entry is made in the Registry, you can restore and use a previous, correct System.

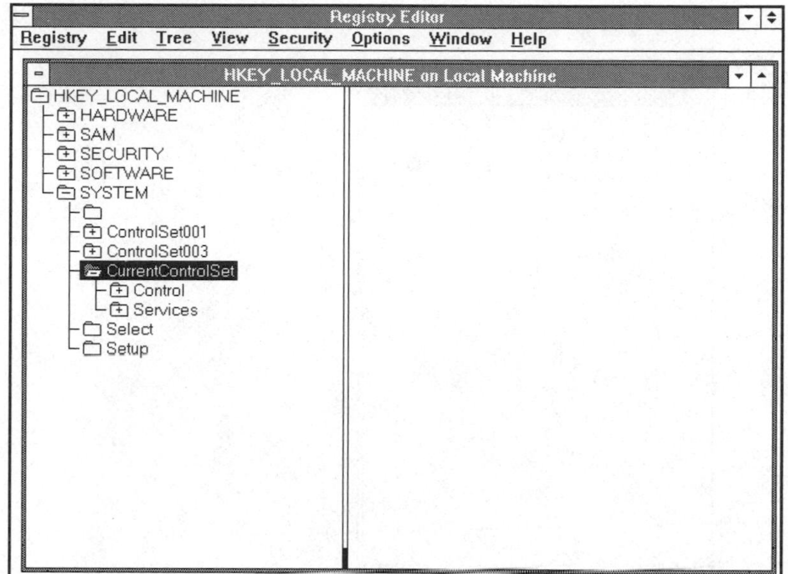

Figure 14.5: *The SYSTEM subkey.*

Under CurrentControlSet is the subkey *Services*. In Services, you find a list of the Windows NT services available on the computer. You can configure these special system programs, for instance, to start at boot time. Services are discussed further elsewhere in this book.

The HKEY_USERS Key

The HKEY_USERS key contains the actual user account information. Under this key are two subkeys: DEFAULT and another key that is encrypted—the encrypted identifier for the user currently logged on.

Information about Personal Program Groups, desktop preferences that are set by Control Panel, and other user-specific information is kept in this key. The DEFAULT branch holds default information for new users. The HKEY_USERS key is illustrated in figure 14.6.

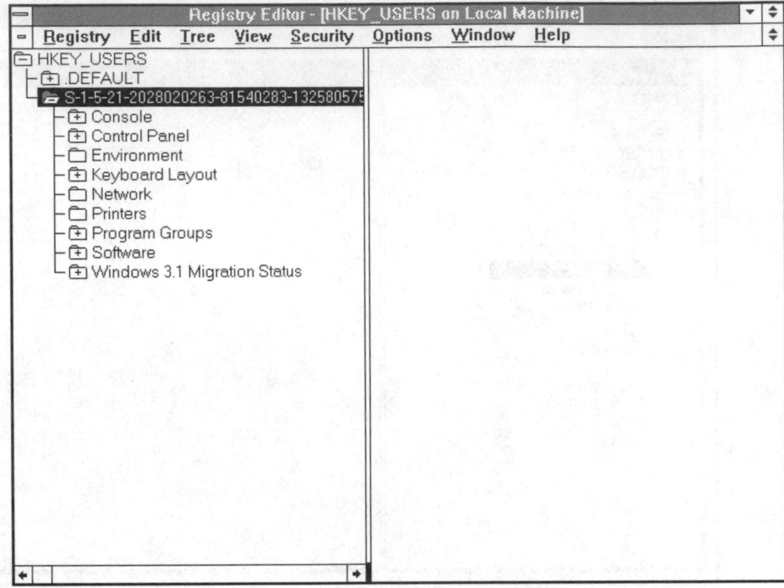

Figure 14.6: *The HKEY_USERS tree.*

The HKEY_CURRENT_USER Key

The HKEY_CURRENT_USER key is a duplicate of the branch of the HKEY_USERS key that refers to the currently logged-on user—the encrypted key described previously (see fig. 14.7).

Figure 14.7: *The HKEY_CURRENT_USER key.*

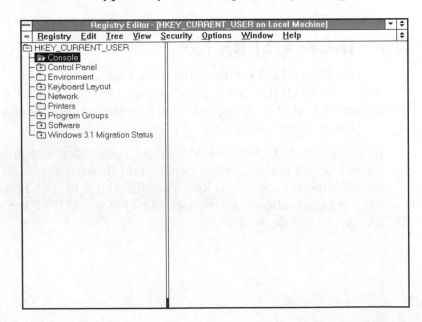

The HKEY_CLASSES_ROOT Key

The HKEY_CLASSES_ROOT key controls the association of certain file extensions with specific applications (for instance, the DOC extension that is used for Microsoft Word documents or the TXT extension for Notepad files).

This key also controls certain OLE information, and has information used to provide compatibility with Windows 3.1 applications. The HKEY_CLASSES_ROOT key structure is illustrated in figure 14.8.

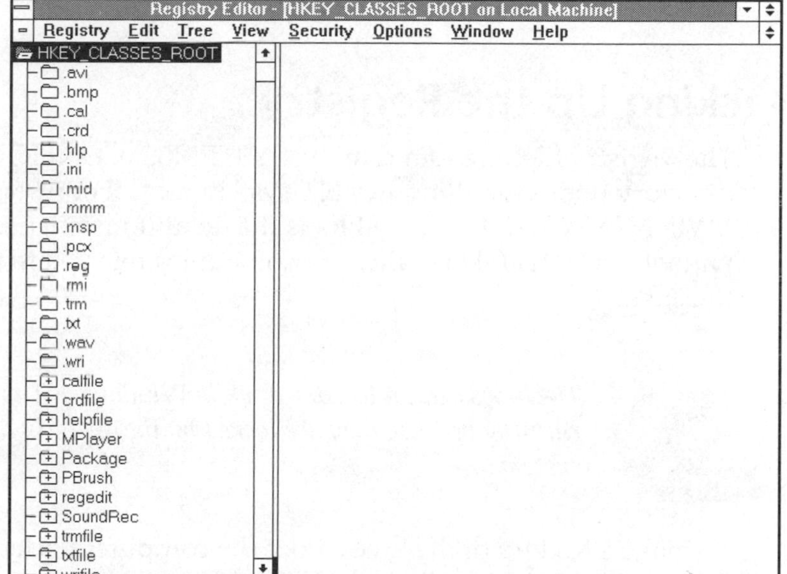

Figure 14.8: *The HKEY_CLASSES_ROOT key.*

Recovering the System with System Backups

One key use of the Registry is to back up a computer's configuration. During the installation of Windows NT, you are prompted for a blank disk. Windows NT changes it to an emergency repair disk, which you can use later to restore the machine's configuration to its state just after the original installation.

A copy of the contents of the Registry is on the emergency repair disk, which can be restored by Windows NT system services in case of corruption.

It also is wise to back up the Registry at other times (for instance, before you install a major new software or hardware package). If the installation fails, a working configuration can be restored. After the new component is installed and working correctly, another Registry backup saves the new System.

Backing Up the Registry

The Registry files are found in the SYSTEM32\CONFIG directory under the Windows NT system root. (For instance, \WINNT\SYSTEM32\CONFIG is the default installation path of \WINNT). These files are sometimes referred to as the *hives*.

The hives cannot be copied while Windows NT is running because they are locked by the operating system.

To make a backup of the hives, boot the computer under DOS, either from the Windows NT dual-boot manager or from a floppy disk. All files in the CONFIG directory should be copied, which can take several disks, depending on the complexity of the hardware configuration and the number of users defined.

If a previous configuration has to be restored, again boot the computer under another operating system to unlock the files. You then can delete the contents of the CONFIG directory and replace them with the contents of the backup disks.

The **R**egistry menu has an option that restores the Registry, either from a Registry backup or from raw hives files. If the Registry is corrupted, you may not be able to use this facility. The file-copy method described previously was recommended by Microsoft developers.

If the hardware or software configuration has changed since the last backup, some information will be lost. In the worst case, the hardware or software configuration can change so much that the computer does not even run.

It is important to maintain a current copy of the Registry contents. Deleting and restoring the Registry is a last-resort procedure.

Summary

The Windows NT System Registry provides a single storage point for all system configuration data for a computer. The Registry also acts as a consistent and remotely accessible interface to that information.

The Registry contains all configuration data for the Windows NT operating system and its base hardware, and it is designed to hold configuration information for all other vendors' software and hardware installed on that computer.

You can—and should—back up the Registry regularly to capture a current image of a computer's full configuration set.

15

CHAPTER

Exploring the Windows NT Advanced Server

The NT Advanced Server had not been released from beta testing at the time this chapter was written. The information in this chapter is, to the best of our knowledge, accurate.

You are encouraged to consult the Microsoft NT Advanced Server documentation for up-to-date information about the Windows NT Advanced Server. If you encounter a discrepancy between what you read in this chapter and the performance or behavior of the Windows NT Advanced Server, please contact the New Riders reader support line at (317) 571-3248, and we will correct the error when this book is reprinted. We apologize for any inconvenience we may have caused.

Microsoft expects one of the first significant markets for Windows NT to be network servers and client-server application support. For this reason, the Windows NT Advanced Server was developed.

Several features were specifically designed to provide a powerful and reliable network server platform: a network-aware and extensible security system; enhanced administration capabilities; and advanced storage-management features, such as disk mirroring and support for disk arrays.

In this chapter, you examine the Windows NT Advanced Server and other topics related to using Windows NT as a network server. This chapter discusses the following:

- Understanding client-server computing
- Understanding the Windows NT Advanced Server
- Exploring Windows NT Advanced Server storage-device management
- Learning how NT implements disk mirroring and duplexing
- Understanding Windows NT Advanced Server security
- Exploring Windows NT "impersonation" and IPC management
- Understanding remote access service

Understanding Client-Server Computing

The concept of *downsizing*, or the movement of computing resources from centralized mainframes to distributed networks of PCs, is perhaps today's hottest topic in corporate computing.

The enabling software technology behind this downsizing movement is the *client-server application*, which is a software application that runs partly on a network server and partly on an end user's desktop PC. The separate pieces communicate and interact across the network.

Although this technology is in its early stages—and many an unpleasant surprise has met those on the leading edge of what is sometimes called the "client-server revolution" —it is clearly the future of enterprise computing. The cost-effectiveness of client-server versus mainframe-based solutions is undeniable. To better understand the client-server technology, consider the following example of a departmental database.

Enterprise computing *can be loosely defined as computing technologies that are applied to handling the information management needs of large and small companies and organizations. The requirements of enterprise computing systems are very different than those of individual, stand-alone computers. Network security, reliability, and throughput are much larger concerns in a business environment than in a single-user situation. As the size of the enterprise system increases (often to several thousand users), these issues grow proportionally.*

Under the *centralized model*, a single large computer runs a number of terminal screens, from which the database can be accessed. Not only does the central computer store and retrieve data, it performs all calculations based on the data. It also manages the video screens, keyboards, and other attached devices. The terminals have no processing power, and all users are presented with the same interface and software tools by the central computer.

Under the *distributed model*, a central computer (the *server*) holds the database, storing and retrieving data for end users. In this case, however, a computer on the receiving end (the *client*) can perform calculations on the data received, and it manages the display and attached input devices.

The distributed model enables the server to concentrate on only those tasks needed to run the database, so the same performance presented by the centralized model is possible (with a much smaller and less expensive computer acting as the server).

If the system is properly designed to adhere to standardized access protocols, you can use a variety of different client-based applications to access the database, and you can choose the one best suited for your needs.

This quality of adhering to standards and the consequent capability to mix applications is referred to as an open-systems design, *which is another important aspect of client-server computing.*

To successfully deploy a reliable client-server application, the following components are necessary:

- A reliable network
- A powerful and secure server platform
- A simple means of administering these systems
- Extensive client-connectivity possibilities

The rest of this chapter examines the ways that Windows NT provides each of these components for a successful client-server environment.

Examining the Windows NT Advanced Server

A number of added features are available under the Windows NT Advanced Server that are not available under regular Windows NT. Some of these features are network-aware extensions to utilities that are found in Windows NT.

The network-aware extensions *enable these utilities to access certain of the network services provided by NT. For instance, it might be useful for a printer-server process to send a message via network IPC (interprocess communication) to the application requesting a print job if the printer is off-line or out of paper.*

The Print Manager utility is enhanced to provide for the administration of remote printers. Sometimes entirely new utilities are provided, such as the Server Manager and User Profile Editor in the Administrator Tools program group of the Windows NT Advanced Server. You can explore a few of these added capabilities in the following sections.

NT Advanced Server Storage-Device Management

A number of advanced storage-device management features are available through the Disk Manager utility, which is found under the Administrator Tools program group of the Windows NT Advanced Server.

Normal single-disk access proceeds in a linear fashion. The disk's read/write heads are initially positioned over the first track to be read (see fig. 15.1). As the data is read from the disk, the read/write head is moved incrementally across the disk to succeeding tracks containing data.

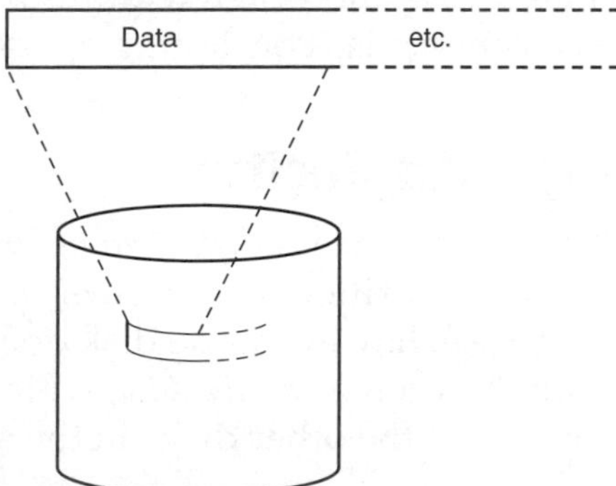

Figure 15.1: *Normal single-disk access.*

Windows NT provides very high-performance disk access through *disk striping*, in which data is broken up and written to several physical disks simultaneously, then recombined when the data is read (see fig. 15.2).

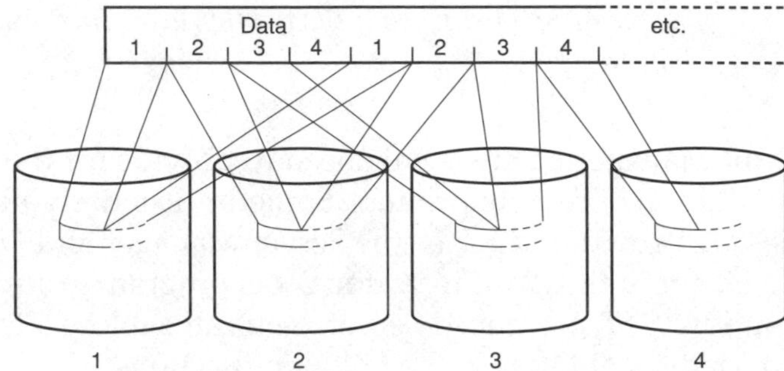

Figure 15.2: *Disk striping (four-disk example).*

All the data under all the read/write heads is read at one time. Because the read/write head on each disk needs to move only one-fourth as often, the speed with which data is moved to or from the disk is multiplied by a factor of four. You can use the Disk Manager to link as many as 32 disks together.

Fault Tolerance

A major concern in enterprise computing is *fault tolerance*, defined as the capability of the computer to tolerate errors in data transmission, power failures, and other conditions that can lead to data loss. Windows NT Advanced Server utilizes a number of fault-tolerant design features that enhance its suitability as an enterprise computing operating system.

Disk Striping with Parity

One form of fault tolerance is *disk striping with parity*. As in disk striping, data is written to a number of disks simultaneously. In this case, however, one disk does not receive actual user data; it receives *parity data*, which is information about the contents of the other disks in the array. Thus, if any one of the data disks fail, the missing information can be reconstructed.

You can specify Automatic File Replication of important files to other servers, to be carried out upon notification of a change to one of the files.

Because Windows NT is reading the parity disk at the same time as the other disks in the array, error correction can occur in real time. As Windows NT encounters a disk-parity error, the correction is applied before the data is passed on to the process that requested it.

Disk Mirroring and Duplexing

With *disk mirroring*, a complete duplication of all disk contents is maintained on two disk drives. In the event of a disk failure, one copy of the data is still available.

Disk mirroring is activated by choosing Establish Mirror from the Fault Tolerance menu in the Disk Administrator utility (see figure 15.3).

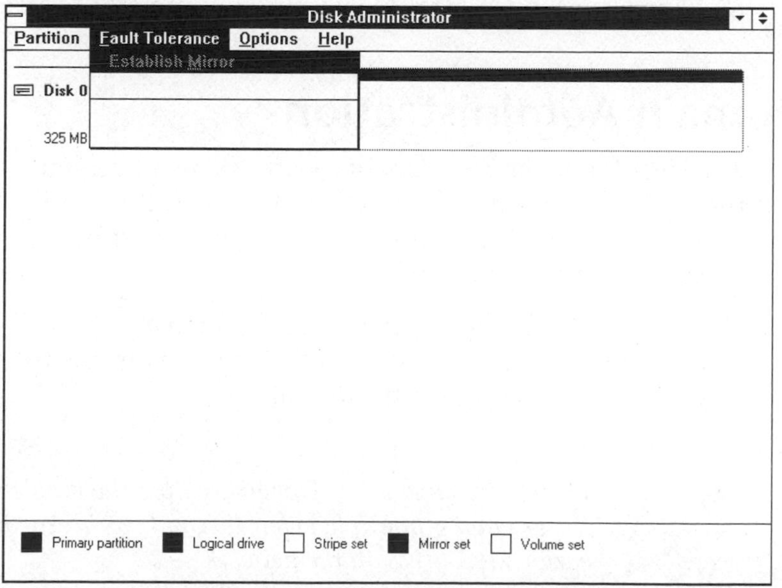

Figure 15.3: *Activating Windows NT disk mirroring.*

A similar feature, *disk duplexing*, adds the capability to use separate disk controllers to provide fault tolerance for controller or disk failure.

As in regular Windows NT, the Windows NT Advanced Server supplies fault-tolerance features, such as an Uninterruptable Power Supply (UPS) service under the Control Panel, and a full-featured Tape Backup utility under Administration Tools.

Understanding Security Features

If you move critical data to a networked PC server, the same high security standards should be available that were on the mainframe. (Windows NT has U.S. Department of Defense C2-level security and password encryption to the DES standard used in the banking industry, so it provides such a platform.)

The Windows NT Advanced Server provides an enhanced tool, the User Manager for Domains, to administer security.

Domain Administration

The User Manager for Domains is an enhanced version of the User Manager provided in Windows NT. It is a fully network-aware utility for managing users and groups across multiple Windows NT servers.

This utility enables you to define both global and local groups. A single network logon thus provides access to resources on all servers in the domain.

The User Manager for Domains solves the problem of a user having multiple logon IDs and passwords for various resources on the network.

Among the added features of the User Manager for Domains are a number of predefined groups, such as Account Operators, Backup Operators, and Domain Admins, which facilitate the management of large networks.

The User Manager, a utility for managing individual user accounts, enables easier management of such accounts across the network. It enables a system administrator to make changes to an individual's account from anywhere on the network. The system administrator does not have to log on to the system from the user's workstation or even copy files from the user's computer. All user-account management can be done remotely.

Figure 15.4 shows the User Manager utility screen. All common user-account management tasks (adding new users, assigning to user groups, and so on) are conducted through the User Manager utility.

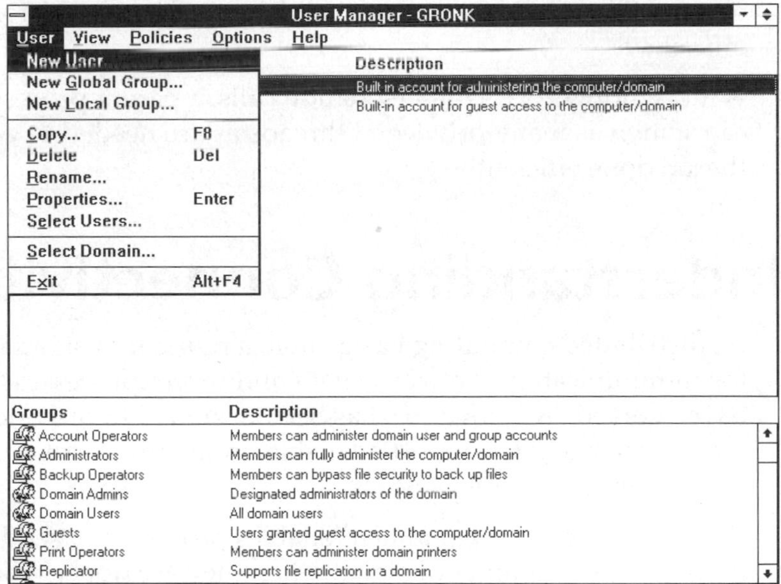

Figure 15.4: *The User Manager utility screen.*

Impersonation APIs

The Win32 API provides a set of impersonation calls that enable an individual thread of a client-server application to assume the security context of the client who is being served by that thread.

Impersonation *enables the control of access to server resources from attached clients. A process thread spawned by an ongoing process has the same security privileges as the parent process. The thread is able to open and modify files, send and receive messages, and behave in the same manner as the parent process.*

Impersonation properties can be applied to Named Pipe, RPC, and DDE transactions.

Impersonation side steps a lot of daunting security and performance issues. If a process thread had no privileges, the parent process would not be able to spawn independent threads. The parent process would have to perform each and every action requiring security privileges, affecting overall efficiency.

With Windows NT's impersonation calls, a parent process can spawn as many privileged threads as are needed to get the job done efficiently.

Understanding Connectivity

As distributed computing has grown, a number of standards for communications between client and server processes have evolved. Windows NT has been designed to provide the most extensive IPC support available under any current server-based operating system.

IPC (interprocess communication) enables processes to send messages to each other or signal when they are done. When properly managed, IPC greatly enhances the system's performance because processes can start and stop independent of each other.

The Microsoft LAN Manager standard of NETBEUI and Named Pipes is supported. Additionally, TCP/IP support for both Named Pipes and Sockets (the WinSockets API) and support for Novell's IPX/SPX standard are available. There is RPC support compatible with the OSF CE standard and DLC support for IBM SNA connectivity. Interfaces also are available to network-management protocols such as SNMP and SNA/NetView.

Understanding Remote Access Service

The Windows NT *remote access service (RAS)* provides remote access to Windows NT servers via modem for up to 64 simultaneous users.

A RAS user is integrated into the Windows NT network security system. After a RAS user is attached, you can access any server resources that are available to other network clients. You can implement callbacks for additional security, and passwords are encrypted and authenticated upon connection. RAS is optimized for client-server applications, with full IPC support available. A RAS administration utility is provided to control service, monitor usage, and manage access permissions.

Remote access service is intiated through the Remote Access Administration utility. After the **S**tart Remote Access Service option has been selected from the **S**erver menu, remote access to the target workstation is enabled (see fig. 15.5).

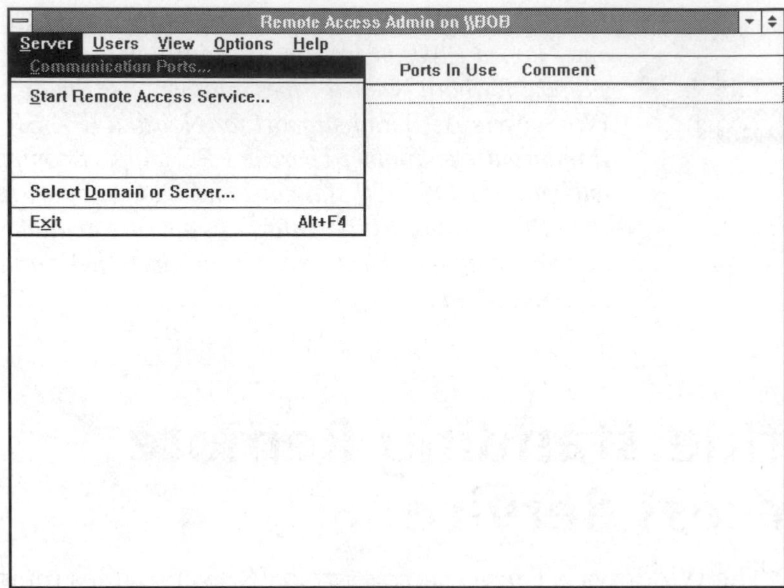

Figure 15.5: *Starting remote access service.*

Macintosh Services

As part of the Windows NT Advanced Server package, Macintosh Services provides for the sharing of printers, files, and applications on the Macintosh (with no new software needed).

This service maintains the Macintosh "look and feel" by presenting AppleTalk file-sharing features such as long file names and file/type associations. Full bidirectional sharing of PostScript printers on both AppleTalk networks and Windows NT servers is supported, as well as automatic conversion of Apple PostScript to other printer setups specified on Windows NT servers.

You can manage Macintosh computers as part of the network, and you can connect them to client-server applications, such as Microsoft SQL Server. Optional client software on the Macintosh enables DES password encryption.

Summary

This chapter has explored the principles of Windows NT client-server computing. Through its sophisticated security measures, fault-tolerant capabilities, disk striping, and interprocess-communications facilities, Windows NT is ideally suited for enterprise-computing environments.

Most user-account management can be mediated through the User Management utility from any workstation on the network. The remote access services (RAS) must be explicitly activated in the Remote Access Admistration utility before dial-up access to the Windows NT system is enabled.

Appendix

Windows NT Product Directory

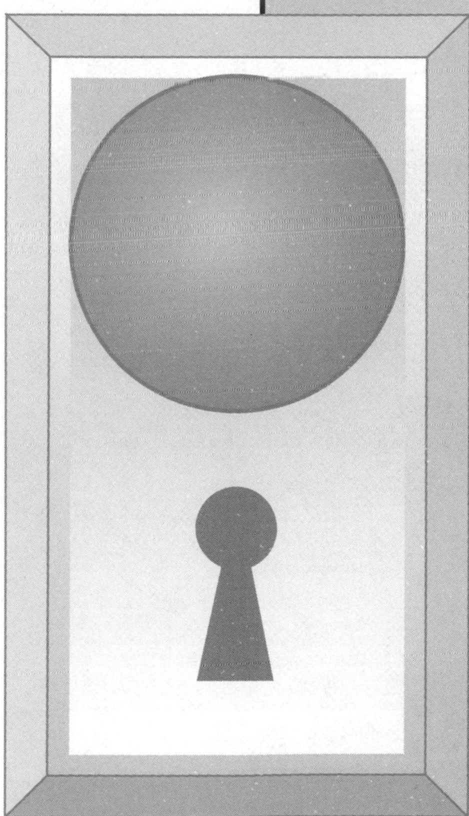

PART 5

Windows NT Product Directory

Although we believe the information in this appendix is accurate, New Riders Publishing cannot guarantee specific data and features of these NT products. The reader is encouraged to contact the providers of these products directly for additional information.

Productivity Applications

Academia

Professor Comp for Windows, Professional Version

Grade management, daily assignment preparation, and student information management.

Sigma NT Co.
770 West Las Lomitas
Tucson, AZ 85704

Retail Price: $105

Contact: Avery Moon
Phone: (602) 888-4626

Available: Third quarter, 1993

Accounting/ Financial

Accounting Vision/32

Completely modular design with unparalleled flexibility.

Intellisoft
2114 West Mayfield
Arlington, TX 76015

Retail Price: $995 and up

Phone: (817) 467-7243
FAX: (817) 467-7133

Available: Call

Accounts Payable with Check Writing

Accounts payable in any period, past or future.

Intellisoft
2114 West Mayfield
Arlington, TX 76015

Retail Price: $995 and up

Phone: (817) 467-7243
FAX: (817) 467-7133

Available: Call

Accounts Receivable with Invoicing

Accounts Receivable offers unlimited shipping to addresses and extensive freight and tax table calculations.

Intellisoft
2114 West Mayfield
Arlington, TX 76015

Retail Price: $995 and up

Phone: (817) 467-7243
FAX: (817) 467-7133

Available: Call

Data Manager

Import and export information from or to nearly any other source. Supported import formats include ASCII Comma Deliminted, ASCII Tab Delimited, and DDE with Microsoft Excel.

Intellisoft
2114 West Mayfield
Arlington, TX 76015

Retail Price: $995 and up

Phone: (817) 467-7243
FAX: (817) 467-7133

Available: Call

Fund Accounting

Fund Accounting offers fund restriction or budget verification for single or multiple entities.

Intellisoft
2114 West Mayfield
Arlington, TX 76015

Retail Price: $995 and up

Phone: (817) 467-7243
FAX: (817) 467-7133

Available: Call

General Ledger with Check Reconciliation

General ledger with 12 to 50 digits of alphanumeric account numbers. Complete control of account definitions.

Intellisoft
2114 West Mayfield
Arlington, TX 76015

Retail Price: $995 and up

Phone: (817) 467-7243
FAX: (817) 467-7133

Available: Call

Great Plains Dynamics

Accounting and business management software for Windows NT. Flexible interface and configurable for customized solutions.

Great Plains Software
1701 SW 38th Street
Fargo, ND 58103

Retail Price: Call

Contact: Sales
Phone: (701) 281-0550 or (800) 456-0025
FAX: (701) 281-3700

Available: Third quarter, 1993

Inventory Management with Bill of Materials

Full bill of materials tracking with serial numbers, lots, and bins. Photographic images of items can be stored with item records.

Intellisoft
2114 West Mayfield
Arlington, TX 76015

Retail Price: $995 and up

Phone: (817) 467-7243
FAX: (817) 467-7133

Available: Call

OptionTool 1.0

Option pricing calculator for bonds. Numerical partial differential equation (PDE) solver.

Financial Solutions, Inc.
3800 East 26th Street
Minneapolis, MN
55406-1886

Retail price: $4,995

Phone: (612) 729-2202
FAX: (612) 724-4698

Available: September 1993

Payroll

Flexible data entry and automatic pay or dedication calculations. Photo IDs can be stored in employee file.

Intellisoft
2114 West Mayfield
Arlington, TX 76015

Retail Price: $995 and up

Phone: (817) 467-7243
FAX: (817) 467-7133

Available: Call

Purchase Order

Complete purchasing and cost control measures. Controls receipt dates and required delivery dates.

Intellisoft
2114 West Mayfield
Arlington, TX 76015

Retail Price: $995 and up

Phone: (817) 467-7243
FAX: (817) 467-7133

Available: Call

RateTool 2.0

Nonlinear tool to estimate optimal parameters for interest and exchange-rate processes using daily sampling.

Financial Solutions, Inc.
3800 East 26th Street
Minneapolis, MN 55406-1866

Retail Price: $9,995

Phone: (612) 729-2202
FAX: (612) 724-4698

Available: September 1993

Sales Order

Full integration with all other modules and is designed for high-volume users. Support is provided for scheduled shipments or scheduled manufacturing per line item of the sales order.

Intellisoft
2114 West Mayfield
Arlington, TX 76015

Retail Price: $995 and up

Phone: (817) 467-7243
FAX: (817) 467-7133

Available: Call

StockMan Toolkit

Financial workstation toolkit for Windows NT. Integrates familiar objects into a sophisticated and fully extensible trading or research environment.

Dean Witter Reynolds
455 Capitol Mall,
Suite 115
Sacramento, CA 95814

Contact: Scott Collard

Phone: (916) 443-7413
FAX: (916) 443-3278

Available: 1993

System Manager with Vertical Market Tool Kit & Report Writer

Vertical market toolkit enables customization of all data entry, windows, and reports.

Intellisoft
2114 West Mayfield
Arlington, TX 76015

Retail Price: $995 and up

Phone: (817) 467-7243
FAX: (817) 467-7133

Available: Call

Timeline Financial Management Accounting

Develops client-server applications using Microsoft tools and database products to deliver accounting information.

Timeline, Inc.
3055 112th Avenue NE, Suite 106
Bellevue, WA 98004

Retail Price (the first number is per server, the second per client):

Financial Reporting: $7,500, $1,000
General Ledger: $5,000, $750
Accounts Payable: $5,000, $750
Accounts Receivable: $5,000, $750

Contact: Lawson Abinanti

Phone: (206) 822-3140
FAX: (206) 822-1120

Available: Fourth quarter, 1993

Communication

32Link

A Windows communications program, 32Link is a communications package that takes advantage of the Windows NT operating system.

Young Endeavors Software
240 West Nevada Street
Ashland, OR 97520

Retail Price: $50

Phone: (503) 488-4842
FAX: (503) 488-4842
Available: Fourth quarter, 1993

A-Talk

Comprehensive communications package for the Windows 3.*x*, Windows NT, and Windows for Workgroups operating systems.

Felsina Software
4440 Finley Avenue, #108
Los Angeles, CA 90027

Retail Price: Call

Phone: (213) 669-1497
FAX: (213) 669-1893

Available: Call

A-Talk

Communications package for the Windows 3.*x*, Windows NT, and Windows for Workgroups operating systems.

New Horizons Software, Inc.
206 Wild Basin Road, Suite 109
Austin, TX 78746

Retail Price: Call

Contact: Richard Unland
Phone: (512) 328-6650
FAX: (512) 328-1925

Available: December 1992

Alert Central for Windows NT

Wireless monitoring system. Monitor RS232 data for EVENTS.

Fourth Wave Technologies, Inc.
560 Kirts Blvd., Suite 105
Troy, MI 48084

Retail Price: Call

Phone: (313) 362-2288
FAX: (313) 362-2295

C Communications Toolkit/NT

Full-featured communications library and DLL for development in Windows NT. Protocols: ASCII, XMODEM/CRC/lk, Kermit, YMODEM, YMODEM-g, ZMODEM.

Magna Carta Software
P.O. Box 475594
Garland, TX 75047

Retail Price: $299.95

Phone: (214) 226-6909
FAX: (214) 226-0386

Available: April 1993

Chameleon32

TCP/IP for Windows. Chameleon32 is the first TCP/IP applications package running on Windows NT.

NetManage
20823 Stevens Creek Blvd.
Cupertino, CA 95014

Retail Price: $495

Phone: (408) 973-7171
FAX: (408) 257-6405

Available: Call

Combined 16 Trunk and 8 Station Interface (ATS 16/8)

A 24-channel analog interface to the MVIPTM bus that combines 16 loop-start trunk interfaces and 8 station-set interfaces.

Natural Micro Systems Corp.
8 Erie Drive
Natick, MA 01760

Retail Price: $4,500

Contact: Ron Bleakney
Phone: (508) 650-1300 or (800) 533-6120
FAX: (508) 650-1352

Available: Fourth quarter, 1993

DDE 6.2

APPC DDE extension. Enables users to connect data in their Windows applications to applications running on an IBM mainframe by using simple DDE macros.

Peakdesign
5825 Chelton Drive
Oakland CA 94611

Retail Price: Call

Phone: (510) 531-5331
FAX: (510) 531-5332

Available: Call

DECmessageQ for NT

Tools for building distributed software solutions for heterogeneous environments.

Digital Equipment Corp.
500 Enterprise Drive
Rocky Hill, CT 06067

Retail Price: $860

Phone: (203) 258-5235 or (800) 344-4825
FAX: (203) 258-5222

Available: June 1993

DECtp Desktop for ACMS

Programming interface for calling database application functions on VAX/VMS from desktop client systems.

Digital Equipment Corp.
151 Taylor Street
Littleton, MA 01460

Retail Price: $245

Contact: Jerry Hershey
Phone: (508) 952-4130
FAX: (508) 952-4197

Available: April 1993

Distinct TCP/IP - TCP - Tools

Multiple Telnet session, FTP drag-and-drop, TFTP client and server, and more. Integrated solution for corporations using both PCs with Microsoft Windows NT and other computers that run TCP/IP such as Sun, IBM, HP, and Digital systems.

Distinct Corp.
14395 Saratoga Avenue
P.O. Box 3410
Saratoga, CA 95070

Retail Price: $395

Phone: (408) 741-0781
FAX: (408) 741-0795

Available: Call

DynaComm

Communications software for Windows and Windows NT.

FutureSoft
1001 S. Dairy Ashford, Suite 101
Houston, TX 77077

Retail Price: Call

Contact: Blake McLANe
Phone: (713) 496-9400
FAX: (713) 496-1090

Available: Third quarter, 1993

DynaComm/Elite

Full-featured 3270 emulator for Windows and Windows NT.

FutureSoft
1001 S. Dairy Ashford, Suite 101
Houston, TX 77077

Retail Price: Call

Contact: Blake McLANe
Phone: (713) 496-9400
FAX: (713) 496-1090

Available: Third quarter, 1993

EXTRA! for Windows NT

3270 connectivity solution for Windows NT desktops.

Attachmate Corporation
3617 131st Ave. SE
Bellevue, WA 98006

Retail Price: $425

Phone: (800) 426-6283
FAX: (206) 747-9924

Available: Fourth quarter, 1993

FAXTalk Plus for Windows NT

Supports all popular Class 1, Class 2, and SendFAX modems.

Thought Communications, Inc.
275 Saratoga Avenue, Suite 200C
Santa Clara, CA 95050

Retail Price: $79

Contact: Pinnacle Sales
Phone: (800) 437-6324

Available: Third quarter, 1993

Golden ComPass/NT

Windows NT-based communications program designed to fully automate access to CompuServe forums, libraries, and mail.

Creative Systems Programming Corp.
P.O. Box 961
Mt. Laurel, NJ 08054-0961

Retail Price: $99

Contact: Donna Finkelstein
Phone: (609) 234-1500
FAX: (609) 234-1920

Available: Fourth quarter, 1993

HCL-eXceed for Windows NT

X-window system server and client support for PCs running Windows NT.

Hummingbird Communications, Ltd.
2900 John Street, Unit 4
Markham, Ontario, L3R 5G3
Canada
Contact: Ken Ristevski
Phone: (416) 470-1203
FAX: (416) 470-1207

HyperACCESS/NT

High-performance communications software.

Hilgraeve, Inc.
111 Conant Ave., Suite A
Monroe, MI 48161

Retail Price: Call

Phone: (313) 243-0567
FAX: (313) 243-0645

Available: Call

KEAterm 340

VT340 and VT420 Terminal Emulation under Windows NT. Provides access to VAX and UNIX host applications.

KEA Systems Ltd.
3738 North Fraser Way, Unit 101
Burnaby, BC V5J 5G1
Canada
Contact: Eric Alexandre
Phone (604) 431-0727 or (800) 663-8702
FAX: (604) 431-0818

LinkUP SNA Services for Windows NT Client-server 2.0

IBM Host and LAN SNA communications package for up to 256 LAN users.

Network Logics/ Computer Logics
14505 North Hayden Road, Suite 333
Scottsdale, AZ 85260

Retail Price: $2,995 and up

Contact: Ken Linker
Phone: (602) 998-1033 or (800) 431-3460
FAX: (602) 991-6713

Available: First quarter, 1993

LinkUp SNA Services for Windows NT Stand Alone 2.0

IBM Host and LAN SNA communications package for the desktop Windows NT user.

Network Logics/ Computer Logics
14505 North Hayden Road, Suite 333
Scottsdale, AZ 85260

Retail Price: $495

Contact: Ken Linker
Phone: (602) 998-1033 or (800) 431-3460
FAX: (602) 991-6713

Available: Second quarter, 1993

MicroPhone Pro for Windows NT

Full-featured interactive communications program with powerful scripting.

Software Ventures Corporation
2907 Claremont Ave.
Berkeley, CA 94705

Retail Price: $295

Phone: (510) 644-3232
FAX: (510) 848-0885

Available: Second quarter, 1993

MultiView DeskTop

Connects and integrates PC users with UNIX systems. Provides integration between a Microsoft Windows-based PC and a UNIX system.

JSB Corporation
108 Whispering Pines Drive, Suite 115
Scotts Valley, CA 95066

Retail Price: Call

Contact: Christine Harlan
Phone: (408) 438-8300 or (800) 359-3408
FAX: (408) 438-8360

Available: Second quarter, 1993

MX2000 Wireless Communications Processor

An open architecture software integration platform for wireless mobile data network applications.

Mobile Solutions, Inc.
P.O. Box 193
Mt. Airy, MD 21771

Retail Price: Call

Phone: (301) 831-7155
FAX: (301) 831-7155

Available: Fourth quarter, 1993

Netvisor

A window for monitoring the AISwitch network fabric, enabling easy management of data network operations.

Applied Innovation, Inc.
651 Lakeview Plaza Blvd.
Worthington, OH 43085

Retail Price: Call

Contact: Roger Nielsen
Phone: (614) 846-9000 or (800) 247-9482
FAX: (614) 846-7267

Available: February 1993

NetWorks!

Easily create client-server and peer-to-peer applications.

Symbiotics, Inc.
725 Concord Avenue
Cambridge, MA 02138
Contact: Duncan Mackay
Phone: (617) 876-3635 or (800) 989-9174
FAX: (617) 876-0157

OpenTOPS

Provides open, peer-to-peer networking solutions for connecting mixed computer platform environments.

Sitka Corporation
950 Marina Village Parkway
Alameda, CA 94501
Contact: Rick Brown
Phone: (510) 769-9669 or (800) 445-8677
FAX: (510) 769-8771

Available: First quarter, 1993

PATHWORKS for Windows NT

Digital's PATHWORKS family includes Windows NT systems integrated into corporate information environments.

Digital Equipment Corp.
500 Enterprise Drive
Rocky Hill, CT 06067

Retail Price: Call

Contact: DECdirect
Phone: (508) 635-8420
FAX: (508) 635-8724

Available: In Beta

PC-Translator

Translates documents between English and Spanish, French, Italian, German, Danish, Swedish, and Portuguese.

Linguistic Products
P.O. Box 8263
The Woodlands, TX 77387-8263

Retail Price $1,285

Contact: Evelyn Smith
Phone: (713) 298-2565
FAX: (713) 298-1911

Available: December 1992

PC-Xware for Windows NT

Transforms a PC into an X server, ready to run X applications residing anywhere on your TCP/IP network.

Network Computing Devices, Inc.
PC-Xdivision
9590 SW Gemini Drive
Beaverton, OR 97005

Retail Price: $545

Contact: Rob Warmack
Phone: (503) 641-2200 or (800) 800-9599

Available: First quarter, 1993

PIPES Platform

Provides a framework for the development and deployment of client-server and peer-to-peer applications.

Peerlogic
555 Deharo Street
San Francisco, CA 94107-2348

Retail Price: Call

Phone: (415) 626-4545 or (800) 873-7927
FAX: (415) 626-4710

Available: First quarter, 1993

RDCL/NT

Connectivity software for accessing remote VAX systems from Windows NT clients.

P.I. Technologies
9827 Independence Ave.
Chatsworth, CA 91311

Retail Price: $795

Phone: (818) 727-9035
FAX: (818) 727-9641

Available: January 1993

ROI/COM/400

AS/400-to-NT communication in real time without cards, protocol converters, emulations, or adapters, using the standard PC serial port.

ROI Company, Inc.
1117 Perimeter Center West, East Building
Atlanta, GA 30338

Retail Price: Call

Contact: Gerry Thurston
Phone: (404) 923-6105 or (800) 395-6105
FAX: (404) 923-0016

Available: Now

RUMBA

Desktop-to-IBM host connectivity with RUMBA software and Windows NT.

Wall Data Incorporated
17769 N.E. 78th Place
Redmond, WA 98052-4777
Phone: (206) 883-4777 or (800) 48-RUMBA
FAX: (206) 885-9250

RUMBA for the AS/400

Brings AS/400 applications to your PC.

Wall Data Incorporated
17769 N.E. 78th Place
Redmond, WA 98052-4777

Retail Price: $395 single user

Phone: (800) 48-RUMBA
FAX: (206) 885-9250

Available: Third quarter, 1993

RUMBA for the Mainframe

Brings IBM host 3270 or APPC applications to your PC or RISC workstation.

Wall Data Incorporated
17769 N.E. 78th Place
Redmond, WA 98052-4777

Retail Price: $495 single user

Phone: (800) 48-RUMBA
FAX: (206) 885-9250

Available: Third quarter, 1993

SecTalk

Easy-to-use, secure communications program.

Dagonet Software
2904 La Veta Drive N.E.
Albuquerque, NM 87710-3110

Retail Price: $195

Contact Louis Baker
Phone: (505) 883-0381
FAX: (505) 883-0381

Available: April 1993

SmarTerm 340 for Windows NT

Emulates Digital Equipment Corporation (Digital) VT series text terminals, providing complete PC-to-host communications.

Persoft, Inc.
P.O. Box 44953
Madison, WI 53744-4953

Retail Price: Call

Contact: Jackie Morgan
Phone: (608) 273-6000 or (800) 873-7927
FAX: (608) 273-8227

Available: Second quarter, 1993

SmartScreen/Open for PROFS

SmartScreen/Open for Office Vision/VM

Intelligent coprocessing client that enables access to IBM's PROFS or OfficeVision/VM.

Capella Systems, Inc.
1303 Hightower Trail
Atlanta, GA 30350

Retail Price: $395

Contact: Mark Thirman
Phone: (617) 961-3066 or (800) 542-2577
FAX: (404) 552-9912

Available: Now

SRSI->FORD

Multiprotocol, Windows NT-, WIN32-, WIN 3.1-to-Tandem connection facility loaded with features.

Salt River Systems International
5333 East Hearn Road
Scottsdale, AZ 85254-2922

Retail Price: Call

Contact: Ervin Mrotek
Phone: (602) 494-9609

Available: Second quarter, 1993

Super-TCP/NFS Apps

Suite of TCP/IP and NFS networking applications.

Frontier Technologies Corp.
10201 North Port Washington Road
Mequon, WI 53092

Retail Price: $495

Phone: (414) 241-4555 x217
FAX: (414) 241-7084

Available: Call

TalkThru for Windows

Communications software providing access to a wide variety of hosts through an extensive list of protocols for Windows NT.

Software Corp.
of America
100 Prospect Street
Stamford, CT 06901

Retail Price $150

Contact: Sales
Phone: (800) 966-7722
FAX: (203) 359-3198

Available: December 1993

Vista-eXceed

Comprehensive X Window Server for PCs running under Microsoft Windows NT.

Control Data Systems, Inc.
9315 Largo Drive, Suite 250
Landover, MD 20785

Retail Price: $500

Phone: (301) 808-4270
FAX: (301) 808-4288

Available: Second quarter, 1993

VistaCOM for Windows

Communications and terminal emulation.

Control Data Systems, Inc.
9315 Largo Drive West, Suite 250
Landover, MD 20785

Retail Price: $295

Phone: (301) 808-4281
FAX: (301) 808-4288

Available: Fourth quarter, 1993

Win 3770

Full-function 3770 RJE Workstation for Microsoft SNA Services.

Passport Communications
1101 South Capital of Texas Hwy, Suite 250-F
Austin, TX 78746

Retail Price: Call

Contact: Richard Pilgrim
Phone: (512) 328-9830
FAX: (512) 328-4773

Available: Second quarter, 1993

WinBEEP/NT

Enables users to send wireless messages (sentences and paragraphs of important information) to pocket-sized full-text pagers.

Fourth Wave Technologies, Inc.
560 Kirts Blvd., Suite 105
Troy, MI 48084

Retail Price: Call

Phone: (313) 362-2288
FAX: (313) 362-2295

Available: Third quarter, 1993

WinBEEP/NT SDK

Allows developers to "PAGE-ENABLE" their application using the WinBEEP paging transport engine and WAPI (Wireless Application Programming Interface).

Fourth Wave Technologies, Inc.
560 Kirts Blvd., Suite 105
Troy, MI 48084

Retail Price: Call

Phone: (313) 362-2288
FAX: (313) 362-2285

Available: Call

WinBEEp/NT Server

Wireless paging server for networks.

Fourth Wave Technologies, Inc.
560 Kirts Blvd., Suite 105
Troy, MI 48084

Retail price: Call

Phone: (313) 362-2288
FAX: (313) 362-2295

Available: Call

Zlink

Complete modem communications application for Windows NT.

Young Endeavors Software
240 West Nevada Street
Ashland, OR 97520

Retail Price: $50

Contact: Jim Young
Phone: (503) 488-1532

Available: Second quarter, 1993

Contact Management

ACT!

Organizer, scheduler, planner with activity follow-up.

Contact Software International
1840 Hutton Drive #200
Carrollton, TX 75006

Retail Price: Call

Phone: (800) 365-0606
FAX: (214) 919-9760

Available: Fourth quarter, 1993

Data Publishing

Atlantis Data Publisher for Windows

Incorporates text and graphics publishing around a full-bodied report writer engine.

Snow Software
2360 Congress Avenue
Clearwater, FL 34623

Retail Price: $1,295

Phone: (813) 784-8899
FAX: (813) 787-1904

Available: Second quarter, 1993

Database

4SITE

Maintenance and materials management system.

Fleming Systems Corporation
1118 Roland Street
Thunder Bay, ON P7B 5M4
Canada

Retail Price: $15,000 plus

Contact: George DenHaan
Phone: (416) 880-2473
FAX: (416) 880-4108

Available: Fourth quarter, 1993

APEX Query/EIS Facility for Windows NT

A comprehensive reporting tool designed to maximize the benefits of the Windows NT 32-bit operating system.

APEX Business Systems
15026 River Park Drive
Houston, TX 77070

Retail Price: Call

Phone: (713) 874-2208
FAX: (713) 251-3177

Available: Call

Document Manager

Document management for Windows NT. Provides document indexing, storage, and retrieval technology that enables the user to store paper documents electronically.

Tippecanoe Systems Inc.
5674 Stoneridge Drive, Suite 119
Pleasanton, CA 94588

Retail Price: Call

Phone: (510) 416-8512
FAX: (510) 416-8510

Available: Fourth quarter, 1993

EMERI Version 1.3

The Windows cardfile reader for MS-DOS.

Rhode Island Soft Systems, Inc.
P.O. Box 748
Woonsocket, RT 02895-0784

Retail Price: $19.95

Contact: Eric Robichaud
Phone: (800) 959-7477
FAX: (401) 658-4632

Available: Shipping

IDB Introductory Package

Object database tutorial and sample application.

Persistent Data Systems, Inc.
P.O. Box 38415
Pittsburgh, PA 15238

Retail Price: $99

Phone: (412) 963-1843
FAX: (412) 963-1846

Available: Call

IDB Object Database

High-performance distributed object database.

Persistent Data Systems, Inc.
P.O. Box 38415
Pittsburgh, PA 15238

Retail Price: $995

Phone: (412) 963-1843
FAX: (412) 963-1846

Available: Call

Idealist for Windows

The only full-text database manager for Windows, MS-DOS, and the Macintosh.

Blackwell Software
BSP Ltd.
Osney Mead
Oxford, OX2 OEL
UK
Contact: Peter Kibby
Phone: +44 (0)865791738
FAX: +44(0)865791738

Available: Third quarter, 1993

Personal Access

Database access and reporting tool that enables end users to create custom queries and reports quickly, simply, and independently.

Spinnaker Software
201 Broadway
Cambridge, MA 02139

Retail Price: $695

Contact: Jeff Boehm
Phone: (617) 494-1200 x555 or (800) 323-8088 x555
FAX: (617) 494-0173

X2c - The portable Xbase compiler

An Xbase compiler that creates executable 32-bit Windows programs for Windows, Win32, and Windows NT.

Desktop Ai
Fairfield, CT 06430

Retail Price: $700–$3,495

Phone: (203) 255-3400
FAX: (203) 259-8853

Available: Call

Desktop Publishing

APS-SoftPIP/NT

A high-performance PostScript Raster Image Processor (RIP) running under NT.

Autologic, Inc.
1050 Rancho Conejo Blvd.
Thousand Oaks, CA 91320-1794

Retail Price: $14,000

Phone: (805) 498-9611
FAX: (805) 498-1167

Available: In Beta

CheckMaster

Check printing software is designed to print checks on blank stock including the MICR line. Designed to take the place of the checks portion of your favorite forms supply catalog.

CheckMaster Corporation
2227 California Street
Oceanside, CA 92054

Retail Price: Call

Contact: Bud Aaron
Phone: (619) 757-6635
FAX: (619) 757-6635

Available: February 1993

eXcursion for Windows NT

Displays and controls X Windows applications on a PC. Receives X protocol requests over the network from remote applications, translating and executing them into Windows NT functions.

Digital Equipment Corp.
30 Proter Road
Littleton, MA 01460

Retail Price: Call

Phone: (800) DECINFO x NT
FAX: (508) 486-2311

Available: Second quarter, 1993

FotoMan

Digital Camera for computers. Add photos to your desktop publishing, multimedia, database, and other computer applications.

Logitech, Inc.
6505 Kaiser Drive
Fremont, CA 94555

Retail Price: $799

Phone: (510) 795-8100 or (800) 231-7717
FAX: (510) 792-8901

Available: Fourth quarter, 1993

FrameMaker 3.0 for Windows NT

Powerful document publishing. Combines powerful word processing and easy page layout in one easy-to-use application.

Frame Technology Corporation
1010 Rincon Circle
San Jose, CA 95131

Retail Price: $795

Phone: (800) U4-FRAME
FAX: (408) 433-1928

Available: Call

Free Form

A system that enables you to take the graphics image (BMP, GIF, PCX) of a printed form you have scanned in, and, using TrueType fonts, to fill in the form as if you were using a typewriter.

Paragon Consulting Group
4212 West Cactus, Suite 1110-229
Phoenix, AZ 85029

Retail Price: $195

Phone: (602) 437-9566
FAX: (602) 437-9566

Available: Fourth quarter, 1993

JUPITOR

32-bit object-oriented desktop publishing application that combines the power of graphics, word processing, versatile layout, and, with Windows NT Unicode, supports Far East languages.

Elite Technology
17407 Unit A, East Rice Circle
Aurora, CO 80015

Retail Price: $595

Phone: (310) 924-0028

Available: September 1993

JX-WIN32

Scanning software for Sharp's family of scanners, the JX-320, JX-450, and JX-610. Enables end users to take full advantage of the Windows NT OS and the high-resolution Sharp scanners.

Sharp Electronics Corporation
Sharp Plaza
Mahwah, NJ 07430

Retail Price: Free offer

Phone: (201) 529-0351
FAX: (201) 529-9117

Available: July 1993

MailAide 5.0

Office automation application utilizing the performance of Windows NT and user-desired off-the-shelf applications. Integrates with off-the-shelf word processing software.

Micro Research Industries
4900 Seminary Road, Suite 800
Alexandria, VA 22311

Retail Price: $1,995

Contact: John Kunkel
Phone: (703) 824-0161
FAX: (703) 824-8750

Available: January 1993

MediaViewer for NT

Utility to instantly view, present, and integrate multimedia files in a variety of formats. Plays audio, video, graphics, animation, and document files by dragging them over the MediaViewer window.

Lenel Systems International, Inc.
19 Tobey Village Office Park
Pittsford, NY 14534-1763

Retail Price: $195

Phone: (716) 248-9720
FAX: (716) 248-9185

Available: March 1993

PageMaker

Desktop publishing software, enabling you to integrate text and graphics from many sources into a wide variety of printed documents.

Aldus Corporation
411 1st Avenue, South
Seattle, WA 98104

Retail Price: $895

Phone: (206) 628-2320

Available: Fourth quarter, 1993

Poor Bill's Translator

Translator to convert SGML-tagged files into a format suitable for reading into word processing, desktop publishing, or database programs. Parses an SGML file according to a user-defined Document Type Definition (DTD) and creates output according to user-specified Translation Definition Table (TDT).

Zzytech
6360 S. Gibraltar Circle
Aurora, CO 80016

Retail Price: $35

Contact: Brian
Phone: (303) 680-0875
FAX: (303) 680-4906

Available: Now

ScanMan Family of Hand-Held Scanners

Hand-held scanners that offer high-quality image and text scanning at affordable prices. Scanners include the Logitech AutoStitch feature for automatic merging of multiple scans into one full-page or larger image.

Logitech, Inc.
6505 Kaiser Drive.
Fremont, CA 94555

Retail Price: $299–$699

Phone: (510) 795-8100 or (800) 231-7717

Available: Fourth quarter, 1993

XLabel

Print laser labels from file or screen, in single, multiple (single sheet), or multiple sheet modes.

Tenax Software Engineering
2103 Harrison Avenue NW, Suite 141
Olympia, WA 98502

Retail Price: $35–$75

Phone: (206) 866-1686

Available: October 1992

Desktop Utilities

Command View 2.0

Replaces the need for pull-down menus and toolbars with a series of iconic command pads that can be created for any Windows application.

ARTIST Graphics
2675 Patton Road
Saint Paul, MN 55113

Retail Price: $49.95

Contact: ARTIST Sales
Phone: (800) 627-8478
FAX: (612) 631-8424

Available: Shipping

Icon Manager

Provides a comprehensive feature set of icon management functions.

Impact Software
12140 Central Avenue, Suite 133
Chino, CA 91710

Retail Price: $24.95

Contact: Sales Contact
Phone: (909) 590-8522
FAX: (909) 590-2202

Available: Shipping

PANORAMIC!

View, print, and convert files.

Cimmetry Systems, Inc.
1430 Mass. Ave., Suite 306
Cambridge, MA 02138-3810

Retail Price: $129

Phone: (514) 735-3219
FAX: (514) 735-6440

Available: Call

Zip Manager NT

Archive file management program that works in conjunction with PKZIP and ARJ file compression programs.

Software Excellence By Design, Inc.
15414 North 7th Street, #8, Suite 292
Phoenix, AZ 85022

Retail Price: $69.95

Contact: Eric Anderson
Phone: (602) 375-9928
FAX: (602) 375-9928

Available: Shipping

Document Imaging

AxxiS

Information retrieval system. Incorporates scanning, indexing, and retrieval.

AxxiS Corporation
1255 Belle Ave #101
Winter Springs, FL 32708

Retail Price: Competitive

Contact: Steven Schwartz
Phone: (407) 696-4200
FAX: (407) 696-4201

Available: Fourth quarter, 1993

Document Management System

Interleaf 6 for Windows

An object-oriented document systems engine used for the creation, management, and distribution of electronic and paper documents.

Interleaf, Inc.
Prospect Place
9 Hillside Avenue
Waltham, MA 02154

Retail Price: Call

Phone: (800) 666-5323 x6623
FAX: (617) 290-4981

Available: Fourth quarter, 1993

PRONET For Windows

Document management system. Provides document management and control on a local area network (LAN).

NUS
2650 McCormick Drive, Suite 300
Clearwater, FL 34619

Retail Price: Call

Phone: (813) 797-7841
FAX: (813) 797-8341

Available: Call

Education

Astronomy Lab NT

Astronomy program for Microsoft Windows NT. Produces 7 movies that simulate a host of astronomical phenomena, 15 graphs that illustrate many fundamental concepts of astronomy, and 14 printed reports that contain predictions of the most important astronomical events.

Personal MicroCosms
8547 East Arapahoe
Road, Suite J-147
Greenwood Village, CO
80112

Retail Price: $17.50

Phone: (303) 753-3268

Available: Call

PC-FasType

A typing tutorial for Windows, based on the popular MS-DOS version for VGA monitors.

Trendtech Corporation
14 Ella Lane, Suite A
P.O. Box 3687
Wayne, NJ 07470

Retail Price: NA

Contact: W. Letendre
Phone: (201) 694-8622
FAX: (201) 694-2543

Available: 1994

Electronic Mail

cc:Mail

cc:Mail is the world's most popular LAN e-mail system.

Lotus Development Corporation
55 Cambridge Parkway
Cambridge, MA 02142

Contact: Kirty Davies
Phone: (617) 577-8500

PC Eudora

A clone of the popular Macintosh POP3/SMTP mail client of the same name.

QUALCOMM Incorporated
c/o John Noerenberg
10555 Sorrento Valley Road
San Diego, CA 92121

Retail Price: $20/Seat

Phone: (619) 597-5103
FAX: (619) 452-9096
Available: Third quarter, 1993

FAX Software

UltraFAX

Software for managing FAX communications on your Windows PC.

WordStar International, Inc.
450 Franklin Road, Suite 100
Marietta, GA 30067

Retail Price: $119

Phone: (404) 514-6387
FAX: (404) 428-0008

Available: Fourth quarter, 1993

Financial Reporting

Hyperion

Network-based software solution offering enterprise-wide business reporting capabilities.

IMRS
777 Long Ridge Road
Stamford, CT 06902

Retail Price: $125,000 HQ license

Contact: IMRS Department
Phone: (203) 321-3500
FAX: (203) 329-9730

Available: Call

Fonts

The Font Company Type Library

High-quality type library available as a value-added resource for application and hardware developers, systems integrators, and VARs.

The Font Company
7850 East Evans Road, Suite 111
Scottsdale, AZ 85260

Retail Price: Call

Phone: (602) 998-9711 or (800) 442-3668
FAX: (602) 998-7964

Available: Now

Forms Processing

JetForm Server

A client-server forms-processing product. The forms database library allows for the substituting or updating of forms on a network.

JetForm Corporation
Watermill Center
800 South Street, Suite 305
Waltham, MA 02154

Retail Price: Call

Phone: (800) 267-9976
FAX: (613) 594-8886

Available: Call

Paper Keyboard NT

Forms processing application for automated data entry with complete OCR, OMR, and hand print recognition capabilities.

Datacap Inc.
580 White Plains Road
Tarrytown, NY 10591

Retail Price: $6,995

Phone: (914) 332-7515
FAX: (914) 332-7516

Available: June 1993

TELEFORM

Turns any FAX machine or scanner into a data entry terminal. Automatically collects hand-printed, typed, or marked information from forms FAXed to a PC.

Cardiff Software, Inc.
531 Stevens Avenue,
Building B
Solana Beach, CA 92075
Phone: (619) 259-6430 or (800) 695-8755
FAX: (619) 259-6450

Available: October 1993

Graphics/ Graphic Arts

Acclerated Display Drivers for NT

Acclerated Display Drivers for Windows NT applications.

Binar Graphics, Inc.
30 Mitchell Boulevard
San Rafael, CA 94903-2034
Contact: Martin Ogawa
Phone: (415) 491-1565
FAX: (415) 491-1164

Available: Shipping

Altsys Virtuoso

PostScript language design and production program for Windows NT. Provides the tools today's artists need to create professional illustrations quickly and easily.

Altsys Corporation
269 West Renner Parkway
Richardson, TX 75080

Retail Price: $695

Phone: (800) 477-2131
FAX: (214) 680-0537

Available: Call

Arts & Letters Apprentice

Apprentice for home and office. An inexpensive package for home and business. Easy to learn and use.

Computer Support Corporation
15926 Midway Road
Dallas, TX 75244

Retail Price: $169

Phone: (214) 661-8960
FAX: (214) 661-5429

Available: June 1992

Arts & Letters Graphics Editor

Graphics editor for sophisticated graphics. Handles the most sophisticated drawing assignments.

Computer Support Corporation
15926 Midway Road
Dallas, TX 75244

Retail Price: $695

Phone: (214) 661-8960
FAX: (214) 661-5429

Available: June 1992

Arts & Letters Picture Wizard

Graphics program designed and written for kids and newcomers to computer graphics. Instructions are extremely easy to understand.

Computer Support Corporation
15926 Midway Road
Dallas, TX 75244

Retail Price: $89.95

Phone: (214) 661-8960
FAX: (214) 661-5429

Available: June 1992

Emma Jean

Performs off-line nonlinear editing and manipulation of image sequences. Captures video, perform nonlinear edits, then records the results back to video media.

Abaker
305 West Magnolia Street, #156
Fort Collins, CO 80521

Retail Price: $395

Contact: Jamison Gulden
Phone: (303) 493-2716

Available: September 1993

Fractal Design Painter

A 24-bit-color paint program that simulates the tools and textures of natural media.

Fractal Design Corporation
335 Spreckels Drive
Aptos, CA 95003
Contact: Stephen Thomas
Phone: (408) 688-5300
FAX: (408) 688-8836

HOOPS A.I.R

An add-on module for photorealistic rendering to HOOPS applications. Combines radiosity, ray tracing, and scan line rendering methods to produce interactive photorealistic rendering.

Ithaca Software
1301 Marina Village Parkway
Alameda, CA 94501
Contact: Amy Romanoff
Phone: (510) 523-5900
FAX:(510) 523-2880

Available: Now

HOOPS Graphics Development System

High-level graphics development system to simplify the creation of interactive and portable 2-D and 3-D graphics applications. A high-level graphics API.

Ithaca Software
1301 Marina Village Parkway
Alameda, CA 94501

Retail Price: $4,200 /DL

Contact: Amy Romanoff
Phone: (510) 523-5900
FAX: (510) 523-2880

Available: Now

HOOPS I.M.

An add-on module that extends user control by integrating display and immediate mode graphics techniques. Enables users to define and represent graphical objects and rendering methods. Primitives can be stored in the HOOPS database or directly rendered using portable HOOPS drawing routines.

Ithaca Software
1301 Marina Village Parkway
Alameda, CA 94501

Contact: Amy Romanoff
Phone: (510) 523-5900
FAX: (510) 523-2880

Available: January 1993

IMAGE Assist

Bit-mapped imaging software for AGFA and compatible film recorders.

McLain Imaging
1009 Tulipan Drive
San Jose, CA 95129

Retail Price: $1,495

Contact: Lisa McLain
Phone: (408) 252-6266 or (800) 826-2858
FAX: (408) 252-6267

Available: May 1993

IMAGE-IN COLOR PRO

24-bit photo image retouching.

CPI SA
50 Av. de la Praille
CH-1227 Geneva
Switzerland

Retail Price: $795

Phone: +41 22 343.68.00
FAX: +41 22 343.37.24

Available: Second quarter, 1993

IMAGE-IN-COLOR Professional

Image editing and photo retouching software for NT. Control size, shape and pressure, spacing, fadeout, paint mode, repeat rate, and tool edge with the right mouse button feature.

Image-In, Inc.
406 East 79th Avenue
Minneapolis, MN 55420

Retail Price: Call

Contact: Roy S. Ostenso
Phone: (612) 888-3633 or (800) 345-3540
FAX: (612) 888-3633

Available: First quarter, 1993

ImageTech

Image-processing system provides users with a single platform for capturing and editing live video images.

In-Tech
2412 Calico Street
P.O. Box 4673
Las Vegas, NV 89108

Retail Price: $150

Contact: Kevin Crawford
Phone: (702) 646-5523

Available: January 1993

IMSL/Graph for Windows NT

An interactive graphics library of application-level routines implemented as a Dynamic Link Library (DLL). Provides powerful capabilities for creating high-quality 2-D and 3-D technical graphs.

IMSL, Inc.
14141 Southwest Freeway, Suite 3000
Sugar Land, TX 77478-3498

Contact: Ken Beck
Phone: (713) 242-6776 or (713) 242 9799

Available: June 1993

LEAD Tools 32DLL for Windows

A 32-bit DDL for compressing, decompressing, converting, resizing, rotating, flipping, and viewing images.

LEAD Technologies
8701 Mallard Creek Road
Charlotte, NC 28262

Retail Price: $995

Contact: Mark Schaffner
Phone: (704) 549-5532 or (800) 637-4699
FAX: (704) 548-8161

Available: January 1993

MacroModel NT

Curved-surface 3-D modeling on Windows NT.

Macromedia
600 Townsend Street, Suite 310 West
San Francisco, CA 94103

Retail Price: Call

Phone: (415) 252-2184
FAX: (415) 626-0554

Available: In Beta

ModelView PC

A 32-bit rendering and animation application. Accepts Intergraph 3D MicroStation models and DXF files for rendering and animation.

Intergraph Corporation
Huntsville, AL 35894-0001

Retail Price: $2,500

Phone: (205) 730-2000 or (800) 345-4850
FAX: (205) 730-9550

Available: Now

MultiMedia Works

Universal multimedia application for Windows.

Lenel Systems International
19 Tobey Village Office Park
Pittsford, NY 14534-1763

Retail Price: $99

Phone (716) 248-9720
FAX: (716) 248-9185

Available: Call

Open Draw Professional

Data analysis tool for business, marketing, science, and technical fields.

Graphitti Software
1070 North Adler Avenue
Clovis, CA 93611

Retail Price: $249

Phone: (209) 299-7849 or (800) 484-111 x0419
FAX: (209) 299-1143

Available: August 1993

PhotoStyler

Color imaging processing program for creative professionals.

Aldus Corporation
411 1st Avenue, South
Seattle, WA 98104

Retail Price: $795

Phone: (206) 628-2320

Available: Fourth quarter, 1993

PowerShoW

Advanced imaging functions for Windows and Visual Basic. Retrieve, manipulate, display, and manage DIB, TIFF, and Targa bit maps. Palette manipulation, image colorization, zoom-in, zoom-out, and scrolling are supported.

ETN Corporation
Rural Route 4, Box 659
Montoursville, PA 17754

Retail Price: $495

Phone: (717) 435-2202
FAX: (717) 435-2802

Available: Call

Realtime VISION

Real-time database visualization. Provides graphical display objects such as trend charts, bar charts, gauges, and meters.

LABTECH
400 Research Drive
Wilmington, MA 01887

Retail Price: $395

Phone: (800) 879-5228 x234
FAX: (508) 658-9972

Available: Call

SeqWin 2.0

SeqWin-Multimedia sequencer for Windows.

Soft Zone Ltd.
23, Breakspear Road

Abbots Langley
Hertfordshire, WD5 0ER
UK

Retail Price: $150

Contact: Mike Patridge
Phone: +44-71-738-5444
FAX: +44-71-924-0950

Available: In Beta

Street Wizard

Low-cost desktop mapping for the entire county. Enter an address. Street Wizard will find it, highlight it, and display the surrounding area.

Adept Computer Solutions
1742 Garnet Avenue, #206
San Diego, CA 92109

Retail Price: $99

Contact: Nick Doran
Phone: (619) 270-4900 or (800) 578-MAPS

Available: December 1992

Surfer

Produces color contour and 3-D surface maps from irregularly spaced X,Y,Z data sets.

Golden Software, Inc.
809 14th Street
Golden, CO 80401

Retail Price: $499

Contact: Greg Johnson
Phone: (309) 279-1021 or (800) 972-1021
FAX: (303) 279-0909

Available: September 1993

TrapWise

Automatic trapping for EPS files.

Aldus Corporation
411 1st Avenue, South
Seattle, WA 98104

Retail Price: $4,995

Phone: (206) 628-2320

Available: Fourth quarter, 1993

WndSpeed Display Devices for NT

Accelerated display drivers. Custom display driver packages that utilize 32-bit processing for various Super VGA, 8514, and XGA chip sets.

Binar Graphics, Inc.
30 Mitchell Boulevard
San Rafael, CA 94903-2034
Contact: Martin Ogawa
Phone: (415) 491-1565
FAX: (415) 491-1164

Wren & Annie Get Personal

Three-dimensional computer graphics modeling, animation, and rendering package.

Abakar
305 West Magnolia Street, #156
Fort Collins, CO 80521

Retail Price: $395

Contact: Jamison Gulden
Phone: (303) 493-2716

Available: June 1993

Paint/Image Editing

Fractal Design Painter

Natural-media paint and image-editing application.

Fractal Design Corporation
335 Spreckels Drive, Suite F
Aptos, CA 95003
Retail Price: $399

Contact: Jennifer Andrew
Phone: (408) 688-8800
FAX: (408) 688-8836

Available: Call

Personal Information Managers

Ascend

Personal information manager and contact manager that helps you plan and prioritize your daily tasks, appointments, contacts, phone and address entries, calls, daily notes, etc.

Franklin Quest Co.
2550 S. Decker Lake Blvd., Suite #26
Salt Lake City, UT 84019

Retail Price: $199

Phone: (801) 975-9992
FAX: (801) 975-9995

Available: Fourth quarter, 1993

askSam for Windows NT

Information Manager that combines the functionality of text retrieval, a database, and a word processor.

askSam Systems
PO Box 1428
Perry, FL 32347

Contact: Phil Schnyder
Phone: (904) 584-6590 or (800) 800-1997
FAX: (904) 584-7481

Available: April 1993

KBS: People Management System

A people database package that enables you to keep track of people who interact with your organizations.

KBS Systems
1089 Ruppert Road
Marco Island, FL 33937

Retail Price: $129

Phone: (813) 394-9359
FAX: (813) 394-5965

Available: Call

Object Organizer

Personal object manager.

Object Productivity, Inc.
624 West University Dr.
Rochester, MI 48307

Retail Price: $79

Phone: (800) 446-2532
FAX: (313) 656-8960

Available: Call

Phonbook

A personal information management system for Windows 3.1 and Windows NT. Access to phone numbers, addresses, and other information you are keeping about friends and business contacts.

Doubleword
12976 Madrona Leaf Ct.
Grass Valley, CA 95945

Retail Price: $79

Contact: Dean McCoy
Phone: (916) 274-7218
FAX: (916) 274-7218

Available: January 1993

Presentation Graphics

CBIquick

Create interactive training for Windows applications. Authoring system that creates realistic stand-alone interactive tutorials to teach Windows applications.

AMT Corporation
183 Guggins Street
Boxboro, MA 01719

Retail Price: $2,995

Contact: Richard McMahon
Phone: (508) 263-3030
FAX: (508) 263-2265

Available: Second quarter, 1993

Cyclops

An interactive presentation pointer system for use with Proxima LCD projection panels. Provides interactive control over software during a presentation when used with a Proxima LCD projection panel.

Proxima Corporation
6610 Nancy Ridge Drive
San Diego, CA 92121-3297

Retail Price: $749

Contact: Customer Service
Phone: (619) 457-5500 or (800) 447-7694
FAX: (619) 457-9647

Available: December 1992

DEMOquick

Create realistic demos of Windows applications. Authoring system that creates an exact stand-alone simulation of a Windows application.

AMT Corporation
183 Guggins Street
Boxboro, MA 01719

Retail Price: $495

Contact: Richard McMahon
Phone: (508) 263-3030
FAX: (508) 263-2265

Available: Second quarter, 1993

GisPlus Geographic Information System

Geographic Information System.

Caliper Corp.
1172 Beacon St.
Newton, MA 02161

Retail Price: $2,995

Phone: (6127) 527-4700
FAX: (617) 527-5113

Available: September 1993

Harvard Graphics for Windows NT

Dynamic presentations for the business user.

Software Publishing Corp.
3165 Kifer Road
PO Box 54983
Santa Clara, CA 95056-0983

Retail Price: Call

Phone: (408) 988-7518

Available: Call

PowerPoint 3.0 for Windows

Presentation graphics package.

Microsoft Corporation
One Microsoft Way
Redmond, WA 98052

Retail Price: $495

Phone: (800) 426-9400
FAX: (206) 936-7329

Available: Shipping

Stanford Graphics-NT

Graphing and analysis software for Windows NT. Presentation graphics and data analysis for business, statistical, and technical users.

3-D Visions
2780 Skypark Drive, Suite 175
Torrance, CA 90505

Retail Price: $495

Contact: David Ulmer
Phone: (310) 325-1339
FAX: (310) 325-1505

Available: Fourth quarter, 1993

Windows Draw for Windows NT

Provides most of the functionality that entry-level Windows graphics users need.

Micrografx, Inc.
1303 Arapaho Road
Richardson, TX 75081

Retail Price: $149

Phone: (800) 733-DRAW
FAX: (214) 994-6475

Available: Preview Version

Project Management

Above &Beyond

Dynamic scheduler for Windows NT.

1Soft Corporation
PO Box 1320
Middletown, CA 95461

Retail Price: $149

Contact: Michael Westcott
Phone: (707) 987-0256 or (800) 326-4391
FAX: (707) 987-3150

Available: Call

Texim Project

Graphical project management software. Offers state-of-the-art project management capabilities that combine task, resource, and cost information.

Welcom Software Technology
15995 N. Barkers Landing, Suite 275
Houston, TX 77079-2494

Retail Price: $1,295

Phone: (713) 558-0514
FAX: (713) 584-7828

Available: Call

Report Writers

Snow Report Writer for Windows

Powerful report writer.

Snow Software
2360 Congress Ave.
Clearwater, FL 34623

Retail Price: $995

Phone: (813) 784-8899
FAX: (813) 787-1904

Available: Shipping

Simulation

Vensim

Modeling and simulation environment that enables you to represent complex business and social problems as straightforward cause-and-effect diagrams and, in turn, causal equations.

Ventana Systems, Inc.
Vensim Product Center
149 Waverley Street
Belmont, MA 02178

Retail Price: $2,001

Phone: (617) 489-5249
FAX: (617) 489-5316

Available: Call

Simulation/CAD

UfosNet

Transportation network editor and simulator.

HT Associates
13345 23rd Place NE
Seattle, WA 98125

Retail Price: NA

Contact: Robert Tung
Phone: (206) 365-2452
FAX: (206) 365-2452

Available: In Beta

Speech Recognition

Kurzweil Voice for Windows NT

Speaker-independent, voice-activated personal computing system for running Windows applications. Gives the ability to run popular Windows applications software by voice as well as by keyboard and mouse.

Kurzweil Applied Intelligence, Inc.
411 Waverly Oaks Road
Waltham, MA 02154

Retail Price: $8,000

Phone: (617) 893-5151
FAX: (617) 893-6525

Available: Fourth quarter, 1993

Spreadsheets

I-Bridge For Excel

I-Bridge-Excel to UNIX relational database middleware. Turns Excel into the ultimate client for Oracle and Sybase servers.

I-Kinetics
19 Bishop Allen Drive
Cambridge, MA 02139

Retail Price: $295

Phone: (800) 457-4555
FAX: (617) 661-8625

Available: Call

Microsoft Excel for Windows NT

Microsoft Excel for Windows, the award-winning spreadsheet for Windows, is currently under development for Windows NT.

Microsoft Corp.
One Microsoft Way
Redmond, WA
98052-6399

Available: 1993

VT Emulation

KEAterm 340 for NT

PC-to-host connectivity.

KEA Systems Ltd.
3738 North Fraser Way, Unit 101
Burnaby, BC V5J 5G1
Canada

Retail Price: Call

Contact: John Yuzdepski
Phone: (800) 663-8702
FAX: (604) 431-0818

Available: Third quarter, 1993

KEAterm 420 for NT

PC-to-host connectivity. Link to VAX and UNIX host applications.

KEA Systems Ltd.
3738 North Fraser Way, Unit 101
Burnaby, BC V5J 5G1
Canada

Retail Price: Call

Phone: (800) 663-8702
FAX: (604) 431-0818

Available: Third quarter, 1993

Word Processors

EXP For Windows

Graphical scientific word processing system for Windows NT.

Brooks/Cole Publishing Company
511 Forest Lodge Road
Pacific Grove, CA 93950

Retail Price: $295

Phone: (408) 373-0728

Available: December 1993

HyperWrite

Prepare hypermedia presentations in Windows NT.

Looking Glass Software, Inc.
11222 La Cienega Blvd., Suite 459
Inglewood, CA 90304

Retail Price: $149.95

Phone: (310) 348-8240
FAX: (310) 348-9786

Available: Second quarter, 1993

Microsoft Word for Windows NT

Word for Windows, the award-winning word processor for Windows, is currently under development for Windows NT.

Microsoft Corporation
One Microsoft Way
Redmond, WA 98052-6399
Phone: (206) 882-8080

Available: 1993

WOPR

Enhancement to Word for Windows, with dozens of indispensable aids for the office worker.

Pinecliffe International Advanced Support Group
11900 Grant Place
Des Peres, MO 63131

Retail Price: $49.95

Phone: (314) 965-5630
FAX: (314) 966-1833

Available: Call

WOPR Macro Library for Word for Windows

Add-on for serious WordBasic programming (16-bit or 32-bit). More than 100 commands that Microsoft forgot.

Pinecliffe International Advanced Support Group
11900 Grant Place
Des Peres, MO 63131

Retail Price: $49.95

Phone: (314) 965-5630 or (800) 659-4696
FAX: (314) 966-1833

Available: March 1992

WordPerfect for Windows NT

The 32-bit version of WordPerfect will take advantage of the improved performance, security and multitasking capabilities of Windows NT.

WordPerfect Corporation
1555 N. Technology Way
Orem, UT 84057

Retail Price: Call

Phone: (800) 451-5151
FAX: (801) 222-5077

Available: 1994

Workgroups

Cezanne

A Rapid Application Development Tool that optimizes the creation of complex mission critical business information solutions.

Netlogic, Inc.
915 Broadway, Suite 1708
New York, NY 10010

Retail Price: $1,495

Contact: Craig Christy
Phone: (800) 638-0048 or (212) 533-9090
FAX: (212) 533-9524

Available: February 1993

Cézanne

Workgroup-enabled rapid application development system: a rapid development toolkit for creating distributed applications.

Netlogic, Inc.
915 Broadway, Suite 1708
New York, NY 10010

Retail Price: $3,895

Contact: Michael de St. Hippolyte
Phone: (212) 533-9090 or (800) 638-0048
FAX: (212) 533-9524

Available: February 1993

Clock-IN!

Time management system.

Mission Critical Software
14536 Island Drive
Sterling Heights, MI 48313

Retail Price: $499

Phone: (313) 247-0394
FAX: (313) 247-8444

Available: Call

DocuPACT

Document imaging/information management.

InterTechImaging Corp.
115 Perimeter Center Place, Suite 299
Atlanta, GA 30346

Retail Price: $545–$895

Phone: (404) 671-1125
FAX: (404) 671-1460

Available: Call

Epoch

Calendar, scheduler, personal information manager.

Raindrop Software Corporation
833 Arapaho Rd., Suite 104
Richardson, TX 75081

Retail Price: $129.95

Phone: (214) 234-2611
FAX: (214) 234-2674

Available: Second quarter, 1993

eXcellent File Manager

Task-oriented, drag-and-drop file management system providing version control, automatic file compression/decompression, search, and access control features on files of any type.

XFM System Corp.
7-11 Legion Drive, Suite 15
Valhalla, NY 10595

Retail Price: $250

Phone: (914) 997-8023
FAX: (914) 997-8409

Available: First quarter, 1993

MediaOrganizer For NT

A multimedia "object management" application to manage, retrieve, play, and present multimedia data in a variety of formats from a range of storage media including videotapes and laser discs.

Lenel Systems International Inc.
19 Tobey Village Office Park
Pittsford, NY 14534-1763

Retail Price: $495

Phone: (716) 248-9720
FAX: (716) 248-9185

Available: March 1993

Notes

Notes is an environment for developing applications that enable groups of people to work together more effectively.

Lotus Development Corp.
55 Cambridge Parkway
Cambridge, MA 02142

Contact: Cliff Conneighton
Phone: (617) 577-8500

Object Publisher

Workgroup communications product. Provides tools for composing, organizing, and distributing document component objects. Supports the OLE and MAPI extensions for Windows.

Object Productivity, Inc.
PO Box 081118
Rochester, MI 48308-1118

Retail Price: Call

Contact: Robert Thompson
Phone: (313) 650-8716

Available: First quarter, 1993

PacerForum

Workgroup computing product for networks of Windows and Macintosh users. A collaborative computing product that provides bulletin board, broadcast, and conferencing functionality to Windows and Apple Macintosh clients on a network.

Pacer Software, Inc.
7911 Herschel Avenue, #402
La Jolla, CA 92037
Phone: (619) 454-0565
FAX: (619) 454-6267

Available: 1993

ProTEAM

A suite of customer information management tools. Information tracking and management systems specifically designed to help automate business operations.

Scopus Technology, Inc.
1900 Powell Street
Emeryville, CA 94608

Retail Price: $2,985/client

Phone: (510) 428-0500
FAX: (510) 428-1027

Available: Second quarter, 1993

WorkMAN

The e-mail–enabled workflow application platform.

Reach Software Corporation
872 Hermosa Avenue
Sunnyvale, CA 94086

Retail Price: $300 per desktop

Phone: (800) MAILFLO
FAX: (408) 733-9265

Available: Shipping

Miscellaneous

Address Plus BarCode for Windows

A Mail List/Labeling program that prints the address, ZIP+4, and USPS-approved bar code on envelopes or mailing labels.

Computer Systems Associates
422 GlenEagles W.
Statesville, NC 28677-7503

Retail Price: $75

Contact: James T. Madry
Phone: (704) 871-8367
FAX: (704) 871-8367

Available: July 1993

Almanac for Windows NT

Calendar/scheduler for Windows NT.

Impact Software
12140 Central Avenue, Suite 133
Chino, CA 91710

Retail Price: $79.95

Contact: Sales Contact
Phone: (909) 590-8522
FAX: (909) 590-2202

Available: Second quarter, 1993

Automated Data Center Security

Soza & Company, Ltd. (SOZA) provides productivity improvement services and products in the government and private sectors.

Soza & Company, Ltd.
Information Technology Division
2735 Hartland Road, Suite 300
Falls Church, VA 22043-3542

Retail Price: Call

Contact: Dwayne Conyers
Phone: (703) 560-9477
FAX: (703) 573-9026

Available: Third quarter, 1993

Ballistic Spectroanalyzer

This software package, the first of its kind in the industry, represents an attempt to fulfill a market need to allow members of the military, police, and recreational shooting communities to comprehensively examine the entire range of the performance characteristics of a gun-system and its ammunition.

Buckmore Enterprises
Alvah Buckmore, Jr., CEO & Chief Scientist
18 Tannery Road
Westfield, MA 01085-4822

Retail Price: $200–$300

Contact: Alvah Buckmore, Jr.
Phone: (800) 659-6355
FAX: (413) 568-4978

Available: Fourth quarter, 1993

DECtp Desktop for ACMS

Enables desktop system users to access ACMS-based transaction processing applications on the Open VMS VAX server.

Digital Equipment Corp.
151 Taylor Street
Littleton, MA 01460

Retail Price: Call

Phone: (508) 952-4130
FAX: (508) 952-4197

Available: Call

eXceed/NT X Development Kit

eXceed/NT X Development Kit for Microsoft Windows NT.

Hummingbird Communications Ltd.
2900 John Street, Unit 4
Markham, ON L3R 5G3
Canada

Retail Price: Call

Phone: (416) 470-1203
FAX: (416) 470-1207

Available: Call

NTBoundary

A 3-D boundary element analysis package. Provides real-time graphical display of stress analysis of given structures using the Boundary Element Method (BEM).

SewSoft
9807 Alexander Glen Drive
Charlotte, NC 28262

Retail Price: $1,095

Phone: (704) 547-1827
FAX: (704) 549-1293

Available: Call

The System Integrator

Provides sharing of dissimilar data over Windows NT platform environments. Implements sharing of dissimilar data from major packages, specifically accounting packages, word processors, spreadsheets, and databases.

Copley & Associates Software
4500 Campus Drive, Suite 117
Newport Beach, CA 92660

Retail Price: $195

Phone: (714) 474-5529

Available: Second quarter, 1993

Thinx Personal Application Developer

Enables the user to create a graphical interface to data without programming. Designed for the user who requires a custom application without programming.

Thinx Software, Inc.
9104 Guilford Road
Columbia, MD 21046-1803

Retail Price: $495

Phone: (301) 604-2588 or (800) 688-4469
FAX: (301) 608-2871

Available: June 1993

Development Tools

Business/Math/ Science Libraries

Brainstorm for Windows NT

Outliner and structured editor for Windows NT.

Bay to Bay Software
1630 N. Main Street, Suite 439
Walnut Creek, CA 94596

Retail Price: Call

Phone: (510) 945-1073

Available: February 1993

Calera OCR SDK for Win32/32s

The Windows 32-bit OCR development kit.

Calera Recognition Systems
475 Potrero Avenue
Sunnyvale, CA 94086

Retail Price: Call

Phone: (800) 4-CALERA
FAX: (408) 720-1330

Available: Fourth quarter, 1993

Clysmic Drag 'n' Drop Utilities for Windows NT

Drag 'n' Drop Utilities for Windows NT that provide easy-to-use functionality for the Windows NT desktop.

Clysmic Software
P.O. Box 2421, Empire State Plaza
Albany, NY 12220

Retail Price: $24.95

Phone: (518) 438-5548

Available: December 1993

Clysmic Icon Bar (Clysbar) for Windows NT

Windows NT program launcher.

Clysmic Software
P.O. Box 2421, Empire State Plaza
Albany, NY 12220

Retail Price: $39.95

Phone: (518) 438-5548

Available: May 1993

High Tech Basic (HTBasic)

Programming language for instrumentation, science, and engineering.

TransEra Corp.
3707 N Canyon Rd
Provo, UT 84604

Retail Price: call

Phone: (801) 224-6550
FAX: (801) 224-0355

Available: In Beta

HIPPX Programming Libraries

Library supporting over 95 percent of the functions of the POSIX 1003.1 API.

Hippo Software Inc.
448 East 400 South,
Suite 303
Salt Lake City, UT 84111

Retail Price: $239

Contact: P.K. Stoll
Phone: (801) 531-1004
FAX: (801) 531-1302

Available: Second quarter, 1993

IMSL/Math for Windows NT

A library of mathematical functions implemented as a Dynamic Link Library (DLL) for use in science and engineering.

IMSL, Inc.
14141 S.W. Freeway,
Suite 3000
Sugar Land, TX
Contact: Ken Beck
Phone: (800) 222-IMSL or (713) 242-6776
FAX: (713) 242-9799

Available: June 1993

IMSL/Stat for Windows NT

A library of statistical functions implemented as a DLL to solve a variety of statistical problems in areas such as quality control and financial analysis.

IMSL, Inc.
14141 S.W. Freeway,
Suite 3000
Sugar Land, TX

Contact: Ken Beck
Phone: (800) 222-IMSL or (713) 242-6776
FAX: (713) 242-9799

Available: June 1993

OPEN! Info Manager

Tools for application development, file control, and presentation.

Horizons Technology, Inc.
3990 Ruffin Road
San Diego, CA 92123

Retail Price: Call

Contact: Cynthia Mordaunt
Phone: (619) 292-8331

Available: January 1993

T.E.I.S.

System tool for the real-time presentation of true photographic images via phone lines.

INTELSoft Engineering
PO Box 95901
Atlanta, GA 30347-0901

Retail Price: $7,500

Contact: Angela Pimentel
Phone: (404) 498-4204

Available: Fourth quarter, 1993

White Lightning Toolkit

Software toolkit for the Windows NT power user. Includes file search utility, disk status reporting utility, file and directory manipulation utilities, and more.

White Lightning Software
PO Box 922
Mill Valley, CA 94942

Retail Price: $199

Contact: Timothy H. White
Phone: (415) 388-3664

Available: Summer 1993

Connectivity/ Networking

APPC Developer's Toolkit for Windows NT

APPC Developer's Toolkit for Windows NT that facilitates the development of communications applications based on the IBM LU 6.2 protocol.

Eicon Technology Corporation
2196 32nd Avenue (Lachine)
Montreal, Quebec
Canada H8T 3H7

Retail Price: $1,000 +

Contact: Wendy Shetler
Phone: (514) 631-2592
FAX: (514) 631-3092

Available: Third quarter, 1994

Cezanne

A Rapid Application Development Tool that optimizes the creation of complex mission critical business information solutions.

Netlogic, Inc.
915 Broadway, Suite 1708
New York, NY 10010

Retail Price: $1,495

Contact: Craig Christy
Phone: (800) 638-0048 or (212) 533-9090
FAX: (212) 533-9524

Available: February 1993

DEC ACA Services

Build and integrate applications across multiple platforms and network protocols to facilitate downsizing and develop distributed solutions.

Digital Equipment Corporation
30 Porter Road
Littleton, MA 01460

Retail Price: $350

Contact: Daniel Gilfix
Phone: (800) DIG-ITAL
FAX: (603) 881-0700

Nevisys NT

A suite of horizontal development tools for the creation of Win32 applications across an enterprise-wide network.

Nevis Technologies, Inc.
20797 Rockpoint Way
Malibu, CA 90265

Retail Price: $9,500

Contact: Richard Ghastin
Phone: (310) 338-0257
FAX: (310) 338-8563

Available: Fourth quarter, 1993

PATHWORKS for Windows NT Programmer's Kit

Incorporate DECnet support into Windows NT applications. Digital extends its Pathworks family to include both Windows NT-based clients and serves on Intel, MIPS, and Alpha AXP platforms.

Digital Equipment Corporation
30 Porter Road
Littleton, MA 01460

Retail Price: Call

Phone: (800) DEC PCPD or (800) 332-7237
FAX: (508) 486-2311

Available: Second quarter, 1993

Remote Execution Kit (REK)

Client-server API to UNIX. A programming interface that enables communications-independent client development to remote UNIX systems.

JSB Corporation
108 Whispering Pines Drive, Suite 115
Scotts Valley, CA 95066

Retail Price: Call

Contact: Dan Reis
Phone: (800) 359-3408 or (408) 438-8300

Available: Third quarter, 1993

SNA Function Mgmt Developer's Toolkit for Windows NT

High-level interface for the SNA protocol stack using a library of C function calls.

Eicon Technology Corporation
2196 32nd Avenue (Lachine)
Montreal, Quebec
Canada H8T 3H7

Retail Price: $1,000

Contact: Wendy Shetler
Phone: (514) 631-2592
FAX: (514) 631-3092

Available Third quarter, 1994

Standard Instrument Control Library for NT

Instrument control library that provides true portability of I/O code and applications.

Hewlett-Packard
3000 Hanover Street
Palo Alto, CA 94304

Retail Price: Call

Phone: (800) 752-0900

Available: Call

VBX 6.2

VBX 6.2 is a custom control that allows the user to directly exchange data in a Windows Visual Basic or Visual C++ application with an application running on an IBM mainframe.

Peakdesign
5825 Chelton Drive
Oakland, CA 94611

Retail Price: Call

Phone: (510) 531-5331
FAX: (510) 531-5332

Available: Call

X.25 Network-Level Developer's Toolkit for Windows NT

Communications tool that enables developers to design custom solutions with the aid of an extensive C function library.

Digital Equipment Corporation
30 Porter Road
Littleton, MA 01460

Retail Price: NA

Contact: Dina Gibbons
Phone: (514) 631-2592
FAX: (514) 631-3092

Available: Third quarter, 1993

OCR Development Tools

Calera OCR SDK for Win32/32s

The Windows 32-bit OCR development kit.

Calera Recognition Systems
475 Potrero Avenue
Sunnyvale, CA 94086

Retail Price: Call

Phone: (800) 4-CALERA
FAX: (408) 720-1330

Available: Fourth quarter, 1993

Tools/Libraries—Network/UI Abstraction

WAN Services for Windows NT, Version 3 Release 1

Eicon Technology Corporation
2196 32nd Avenue (Lachine)
Montreal, Quebec
Canada H8T 3H7

Retail Price: $495

Contact: Dina A. Gibbons
Phone: (514) 631-2592
FAX: (514) 631-3992

Available: Fourth quarter, 1993

X.25 Network-Level Developer's Toolkit for Windows NT

Communications tool that enables developers to design custom solutions with the aid of an extensive C function library. Contains a library of C functions that provide a high-level interface to the X.25 data stream.

Digital Equipment Corporation
30 Porter Road
Littleton, MA 01460

Retail Price: NA

Contact: Dina Gibbons
Phone: (514) 631-2592
FAX: (514) 631-3092

Available: Third quarter, 1993

Tools/Libraries—Other

Micro Focus Software Development Kit

Provides a powerful environment for creating new, industrial strength 32-bit COBOL applications and for migrating existing 16-bit applications to a 32-bit execution environment.

Micro Focus
2465 East Bayshore Road
Palo Alto, CA 94303

Retail Price: Call

Contact: Eveline Kowtko
Phone: (415) 856-4161

Available: Call

SmartHeap

Memory management library with exhaustive heap error detection.

MicroQuill Software Publishing, Inc.
4900 25th Avenue, #206
Seattle, WA 98105

Retail Price: $695

Contact: Tom Marvin
Phone: (206) 525-8218 or (800) 441-7822
FAX: (206) 525-8309

Available: Now

Utilities

4DOS for Windows NT

New version of the 4DOS command processor, tailored specifically for Windows NT. Substantially enhances usefulness and productivity of the command line. Replacement for the default Windows NT command processor (CMD.EXE). Enhances most Windows NT commands, and adds over 80 new commands, variables, and functions.

JP Software, Inc.
P.O. Box 1470
East Arlington, MA 02174

Retail Price: $69

Phone: (617) 646-3975 or (800) 368-8777
FAX: (617) 646-0904

Available: Second quarter, 1993

5215/5217 Emulator

Emulate the Aydin 5215/5217 display generators to create and display real-time pictures for process control or monitoring. 100 percent compatible with the Data Trend Channel Set (DTCS), Dot Addressable Channel Set (DACS), and Trend Charting features.

Aydin Controls
414 Commerce Drive
Ft. Washington, PA 19034

Retail Price: Call

Contact: Sales
Phone: (215) 542-7800

Available: First quarter, 1994

BACKUP EXEC for Windows NT

Full-featured 32-bit application for Microsoft Windows NT. A Win32 backup product for backing up and restoring data on Windows NT workstations and servers.

Conner Software
36 Skyline Drive
Lake Mary, FL 32746

Retail Price: Call

Contact: Kathleen Botz
Phone: (407) 262-8000
FAX: (407) 262-4239

Available: Call

CDi just BUTTONS NT

Management tool that combines functions including program launching, file conversion, system and file maintenance, text-data-voice-video e-mail, remote control, OLE 2.0 embedding, drag and drop, automation, and much more, all of which can be chained, scheduled, and dynamically linked.

Chrisalan Designs, Inc.
815 Lambert Street
P.O. Box 775
Wenatchee, WA 98807-0775

Retail Price: $199

Contact: Stuart Wyatt
Phone: (509) 663-7770 or (800) 472-7949
FAX: (509) 662-5948

Available: Fourth quarter, 1993

CT WayBack 1.0

3480, 3490, and 9-Track Tape Services for Microsoft Windows NT.

Cool Technologies
P.O. Box 158
Cool, CA 95614-0158

Retail Price: $399

Phone: (916) 889-1160
FAX: (916) 889-9409

DMS nt/QX

Batch Queue Manager System with easy-to-use setup and control windows for scheduling jobs across enterprise networks.

Data-Micro Systems
8147 SW 184th Street
Beaverton, OR 97007

Retail Price: $595

Phone: (503) 649-9376

Available: December 1992

HIBACK

Backup and archival product HIBACK and HIBARS which are designed to support multiplatform, network backup solutions supported by Optical and other mass storage media.

HICOMP America, Inc.
419 Canyon Avenue, Suite 215
Fort Collins, CO 80521-2670
Phone: (303) 224-9700 or (800) 323-8863
FAX: (303) 224-9702

Retail Price: $129 PC to $2,500 HP/700 Workstation

Available: December 1992

Noise for Windows NT

CD quality sound from your PC–sound effects.

Erudite Software
2408 Glenmary Avenue
Louisville, KY 40204-2103

Retail Price: $49.95

Phone: (800) 78-NOISE or (502) 451-7712
FAX: (502) 451-7681

Available: December 1992

Notebook For Windows NT

General-purpose Windows NT text editor with features to replace Notepad.

Mark Berlinger
1317 N San Fernando Blvd., #133
Burbank, CA 91504

Retail Price: $20

Contact: Public Software Library
Phone: (800) 2424-PsL or (713) 524-6394
FAX: (713) 524-6398

Available: Now

Open-REXX/NT

Language for scripting and automation designed for people.

IX
575 W. Madison, #3610
Chicago, IL 60661

Retail Price: $195

Phone: (312) 902-2149
FAX: (312) 902-2154

Available: Fourth quarter, 1992

Paragon Application Manager

Program launcher and application manager.

Paragon Consulting Group
4212 West Cactus, Suite 1110-229
Phoenix, AZ 85029

Retail Price: $49

Phone: (602) 437-9566
FAX: (602) 437-9566 x77

Available: First quarter, 1993

The Executor

Performs any action you choose when you click or double-click any mouse button.

MPSI, Ltd.
35 DiRubbo Drive
Peekskill, NY 10566

Retail Price: $49

Contact: Roger Grossman
Phone: (914) 739-4477
FAX: (914) 739-5545

Available: Now

Win SCSI-NT

System maintenance tool that interrogates and displays SCSI target information including mode page information, inquiry data, and defect data.

PDS Engineering
401 W Main, Suite 303
PO Box 458
Norman, OK 73070-0458

Retail Price: $125

Contact: Roger Ryan
Phone: (405) 329-2223
FAX: (405) 329-7373

Available: May 1993

Word for Word for Windows NT

Document conversion filters for over 90 file formats including word processing, spreadsheet, and database formats.

Mastersoft, Inc.
8737 Via de Commercio
Scottsdale, AZ 85258
Phone: (602) 948-4888
FAX: (602) 948-8261

Retail Price: $149

Contact: Lisa Lambert
Phone: (602) 948-4888
FAX: (602) 948-8261

Available: First quarter, 1994

Miscellaneous

WATCOM C/C++32

A professional, high-performance 32-bit C and C++ compiler and tools package for extended DOS, Novell NLM, OS/2 2.*x*, Windows NT, Win32s, 32-bit Windows 3.*x*, and AutoCAD ADS/ADI.

WATCOM
415 Phillip Street
Waterloo, ON
N2L 3X2

Retail Price: $599

Contact: Sales Department
Phone: (519) 886-3700 or (800) 265-4555
FAX: (519) 747-4971

WATCOM FORTRAN 77 32

A 32-bit FORTRAN compiler and tools package for extended DOS, Novell NLM, OS/2 2.*x*, Windows NT, 32-bit Windows 3.*x*, and AutoCAD ADS.

WATCOM
415 Phillip Street
Waterloo, ON
N2L 3X2

Retail Price: $599

Contact: Sales Department
Phone: (519) 886-3700 or (800) 265-4555
FAX: (519) 747-4971

Available: Now

Vertical Applications

Eis/Decision Support Systems

Natural Language

A data retrieval and decision support tool that enables end users to extract strategic information from relational databases.

Natural Language, Inc.
2910 Seventh Street
Berkeley, CA 94710

Retail Price: Call

Phone: (510) 841-3500 or (800) 654-5858
FAX: (510) 841-3628

Available: December 1993

Mathematical Analysis/Statistics

STATISTICA for Windows NT

Comprehensive statistical data analysis and graphics system offering advanced statistical procedures, graphics, and analytic database management facilities.

StatSoft, Inc.
2325 East 13th Street
Tulsa, OK 74104

Retail Price: $995

Contact: Thomas Peterson
Phone: (918) 583-4149
FAX: (918) 538-4376

Available: First quarter, 1994

Workstation Applications—CAD/CAM

ICAP Professional

Electronic circuit analysis system has schematic entry, SPICE 3 Features, mixed mode simulation, analog behavioral modeling, interactive graphical post processing, and Real-Time Waveform Display; all integrated under Windows NT.

Intusoft
222 West 6th Street, Suite 1070
San Pedro, CA 90731

Retail Price: $2,695

Contact: Charles Hymowitz
Phone: (310) 883-0710
FAX: (310) 883-9658

Available: September 1993

Pro/ENGINEER

Mechanical design automation tool that integrates the entire design-through-manufacturing process.

Parametric Technology Corporation
128 Technology Drive
Waltham, MA 02154

Retail Price: $9,500

Contact: John Hudson
Phone: (617) 894-7111
FAX: (617) 891-1069

Wide Area Networking

Access for Windows NT 3270, Release 3.21

A full-featured IBM 3270 display and printer emulator for the Windows NT operating system.

Eicon Technology Corporation
2196 32nd Avenue (Lachine)
Montreal, Quebec
Canada H8T 3H7

Retail Price: $495

Contact: Wendy Shetler
Phone: (514) 631-2592
FAX: (514) 631-3092

Available: Third quarter, 1993

Multimedia Authoring Tools

Cheetah 3D

3-D modeling and rendering package.

Looking Glass Software, Inc.
11222 La Cienega Blvd., Suite 459
Inglewood, CA 90304

Retail Price: $349.95

Contact: Sam Covington
Phone: (310) 348-8240
FAX: (310) 348-9786

Available: Second quarter, 1993

IconAuthor

Multimedia authoring software tool to create highly sophisticated, interactive multimedia applications.

Aimtech Corporation
20 Trafalgar Square
Nashua, NH 03063

Phone: (800) 289-2884 or (603) 883-0220
FAX: (603) 883-5582

MediaDB

Multimedia database application development environment, including C++ API, Schema Designer, and code generator.

Ravi Technologies, Inc.
3080 Olcott Street, Suite 220C
Santa Clara, CA 95054

Retail Price: $2,500

Contact: Chetan Saiya
Phone: (408) 748-7400
FAX: (408) 748-7402

Available: March 1993

MediaDeveloper For NT

Development tool to integrate multimedia into new or existing Windows NT-based applications.

Lenel Systems International, Inc.
19 Tobey Village Office Park
Pittsford, NY 14534-1763

Retail Price: Call

Phone: (716) 248-9720
FAX: (716) 248-9185

Available: Fourth quarter, 1993

POWER!Search Professional for Windows NT

Search text retrieval software with "Fuzzy Searching" ability.

Horizons Technology, Inc.
3990 Ruffin Road
San Diego, CA 92123

Retail Price: Call

Contact: Phil Morettini
Phone: (619) 292-8320

Available: February 1993

QuickAuthor

Authoring system for developing computer-based training (CBT) and multimedia applications.

Leading Way Technology, Inc.
15375 Barranca Pkwy., Suite A-207
Irvine, CA 92718

Retail Price: $700

Phone: (714) 453-1112
FAX: (714) 453-8115

Available: November 1992

Spinnaker PLUS

Object-oriented hypermedia development tool enabling users to create custom applications that run unmodified across Macintoshes and Windows.

Spinnaker Software
201 Broadway
Cambridge, MA 02139

Retail Price: $495

Contact: Jeff Boehm
Phone: (800) 323-8088 x 555 or
(617) 494-1200 x555
FAX: (617) 494-0173

Available: Now

SuperJAM!

Creates multimedia soundtracks with the click of a mouse. Create royalty-free music without copyright hassles.

The Blue Ribbon SoundWorks
PO Box 8689
North Highland Station
Atlanta, GA 30306

Retail Price: $129

Phone: (404) 315-0212
FAX: (404) 315-0213

Available: Now

Business Applications/ General Productivity

The System Integrator

Provides sharing of dissimilar data over Windows NT platform environments.

Copley & Associates Software
4500 Campus Drive, Suite 117
Newport Beach, CA 92660

Retail Price: $195

Phone: (714) 647-6325

Available: Second quarter, 1993

Index

Symbols

A

B

D

F

G

J

K

L

M

N

O

P

Q–R

S

T

U

V

W

X–Z

Inside Windows NT

REGISTRATION CARD

Fill out this card to receive information about future New Riders titles!

Name ______________________________ **Title** ____________________

Company ____

Address ____

City/State/ZIP ______________________________________

I bought this book because ________________________________

____

I purchased this book from:

☐ A bookstore (Name ______________________)

☐ A software or electronics store (Name ______________)

☐ A mail order (Name of Catalog ______________)

I purchase this many computer books each year:

☐ 1–4 ☐ 5 or more

I currently use these applications: ______________________

____

____

____

I found these chapters to be the most informative: __________

____

I found these chapters to be the least informative: __________

____

Additional comments: ________________________________

____

☐ I would like to see my name in print! You may use my name and quote me in future New Riders products and promotions. My daytime phone number is: ______________

New Riders Publishing 11711 North College Avenue • P.O. Box 90 • Carmel, Indiana 46032 USA

Fold Here

PLACE
STAMP
HERE

New Riders Publishing
11711 North College Avenue
P.O. Box 90
Carmel, Indiana 46032
USA

OPERATING SYSTEMS

INSIDE MS-DOS 6

MARK MINASI

A complete tutorial and reference!

MS-DOS 6

ISBN: 1-56205-132-6

$39.95 USA

DOS FOR NON-NERDS

MICHAEL GROH

Understanding this popular operating system is easy with this humorous, step-by-step tutorial.

Through DOS 6.0

ISBN: 1-56205-151-2

$18.95 USA

INSIDE SCO UNIX

STEVE GLINES, PETER SPICER, BEN HUNSBERGER, & KAREN WHITE

Everything users need to know to use the UNIX operating system for everyday tasks.

SCO Xenix 286, SCO Xenix 386, SCO UNIX/System V 386

ISBN: 1-56205-028-1

$29.95 USA

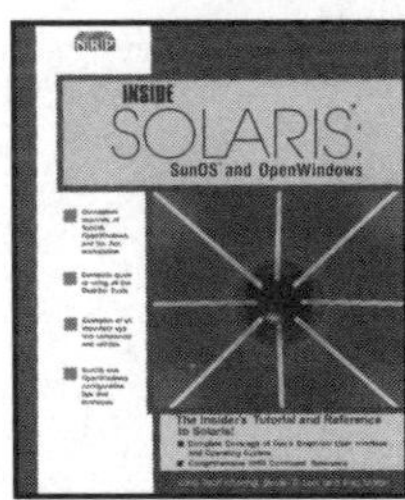

INSIDE SOLARIS SunOS

KARLA SAARI KITALONG, STEVEN R. LEE, & PAUL MARZIN

Comprehensive tutorial and reference to SunOS!

SunOS, Sun's version of UNIX for the SPARC workstation version 2.0

ISBN: 1-56205-032-X

$29.95 USA

To Order, Call 1-800-428-5331

NETWORKING TITLES

#1 Bestseller!

INSIDE NOVELL NETWARE, SPECIAL EDITION

DEBRA NIEDERMILLER-CHAFFINS &
BRIAN L. CHAFFINS

This best-selling tutorial and reference has been updated and made even better!

NetWare 2.2 & 3.11

ISBN: 1-56205-096-6

$34.95 USA

MAXIMIZING NOVELL NETWARE

JOHN JERNEY & ELNA TYMES

Complete coverage of Novell's flagship product...for NetWare system administrators!

NetWare 3.11

ISBN: 1-56205-095-8

$39.95 USA

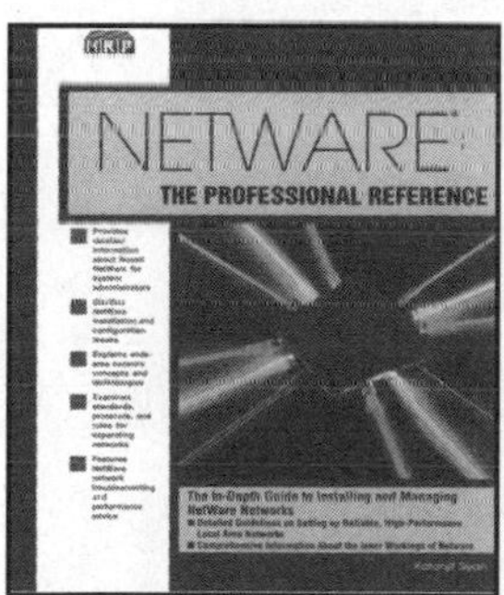

NETWARE: THE PROFESSIONAL REFERENCE, SECOND EDITION

KARANJITSIYAN

This updated version for professional NetWare administrators and technicians provides the most comprehensive reference available for this phenomenal network system.

NetWare 2.2 & 3.11

ISBN: 1-56205-158-X

$42.95 USA

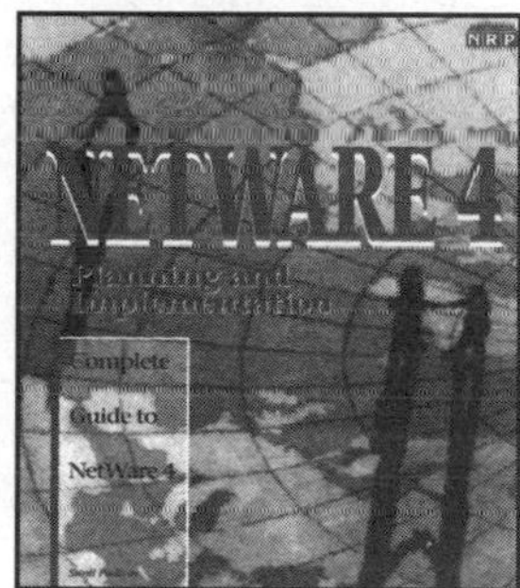

NETWARE 4: PLANNING AND IMPLEMENTATION

SUNIL PADIYAR

A guide to planning, installing, and managing a NetWare 4.0 network that serves the company's best objectives.

NetWare 4.0

ISBN: 1-56205-159-8

$27.95 USA

To Order, Call 1-800-428-5331

GRAPHICS TITLES

INSIDE CORELDRAW! 4.0, SPECIAL EDITION

DANIEL GRAY

An updated version of the #1 best-selling tutorial on CorelDRAW!

CorelDRAW! 4.0

ISBN: 1-56205-164-4

$34.95 USA

Coming Soon

CORELDRAW! SPECIAL EFFECTS

NEW RIDERS PUBLISHING

An inside look at award-winning techniques from professional CorelDRAW! designers!

CorelDRAW! 4.0

ISBN: 1-56205-123-7

$39.95 USA

CORELDRAW! NOW!

NEW RIDERS PUBLISHING

The graphics approach to using CorelDRAW!

CorelDRAW! 2.01 & 3.0

ISBN: 1-56205-131-8

$21.95 USA

INSIDE CORELDRAW! FOURTH EDITION

DANIEL GRAY

The popular tutorial approach to learning CorelDRAW!...with complete coverage of version 3.0!

CorelDRAW! 3.0

ISBN: 1-56205-106-7

$34.95 USA

To Order, Call 1-800-428-5331

HOT TOPICS

Get Your Coaching on

HOT TOPICS

from New Riders!

THE FONTS COACH
CHERI ROBINSON

A clear, concise explanation of how fonts work on different platforms!

Beginning-Intermediate

ISBN: 1-56205-130-X
$24.95 USA

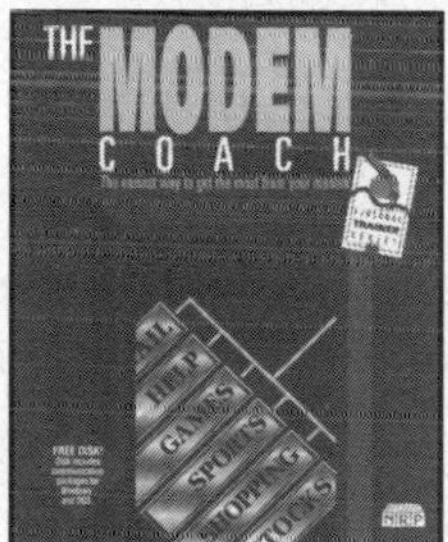

THE MODEM COACH
DANA BLANKENHORN, KIMBERLY MAXWELL & KEVIN STOLTZ WITH TOMMY BASS

Everything you need to know to get productive with your modem...fast!

Beginning-Intermediate

ISBN: 1-56205-119-9
$18.95 USA

CRANK IT UP!
KEITH ALESHIRE

Get the command reference that Microsoft didn't give you with DOS!

Beginning-Intermediate

ISBN: 1-56205-173-3
$16.95 USA

THE GRAPHICS COACH
KATHY MURRAY

The "what you need to know" book about video cards, color monitors, and the many graphics file formats!

Beginning-Intermediate

ISBN: 1-56205-129-6
$24.95 USA

To Order, Call: 1-800-428-5331

Become a CNE with Help from a Pro!

The NetWare Training Guides are specifically designed and authored to help you prepare for the **Certified NetWare Engineer** exam.

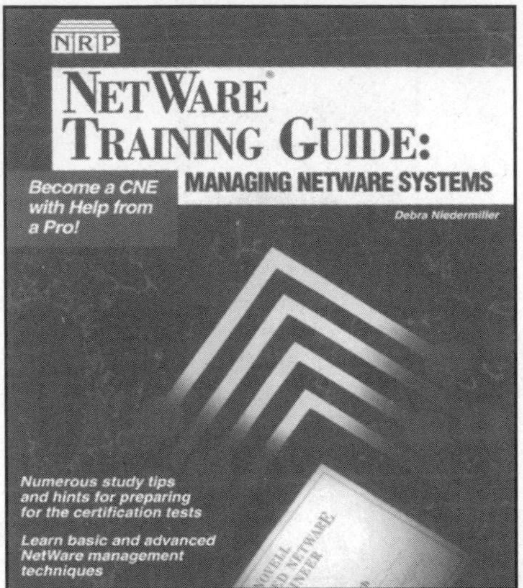

NetWare Training Guide: Managing NetWare Systems

This book clarifies the CNE testing process and provides hints on how best to prepare for the CNE examinations. *NetWare Training Guide: Managing NetWare Systems* covers the following sections of the CNE exams:

- NetWare v 2.2 System Manager
- NetWare v 2.2 Advanced System Manager
- NetWare v 3.X System Manager
- NetWare v 3.X Advanced System Manager

ISBN: 1-56205-069-9, **$59.95 USA**

NetWare Training Guide: Networking Technology

This book covers more advanced topics and prepares you for the tough hardware and service/support exams. The following course materials are covered:

- MS-DOS
- Microcomputer Concepts
- Service and Support
- Networking Technologies

ISBN: 1-56205-145-8, **$59.95 USA**

For more information or to place an order, call: 1-800-428-5331